Founding Friendships

Founding Friendships

Friendships between
Men and Women
in the Early American Republic

CASSANDRA A. GOOD

OXFORD
UNIVERSITY PRESS

OXFORD
UNIVERSITY PRESS

Oxford University Press is a department of the University of Oxford.
It furthers the University's objective of excellence in research, scholarship,
and education by publishing worldwide.

Oxford New York
Auckland Cape Town Dar es Salaam Hong Kong Karachi
Kuala Lumpur Madrid Melbourne Mexico City Nairobi
New Delhi Shanghai Taipei Toronto

With offices in
Argentina Austria Brazil Chile Czech Republic France Greece
Guatemala Hungary Italy Japan Poland Portugal Singapore
South Korea Switzerland Thailand Turkey Ukraine Vietnam

Oxford is a registered trade mark of Oxford University Press
in the UK and certain other countries.

Published in the United States of America by
Oxford University Press
198 Madison Avenue, New York, NY 10016

Cataloging-in-Publication data is on file with the Library of Congress

978–0–19–937617–9

3 5 7 9 8 6 4 2

Printed in the United States of America on acid-free paper

Contents

Acknowledgments

LIKE THE HISTORICAL men and women I write about, I am surrounded by a rich network of family, friends, and mentors. Writing about friendship is deeply personal for me: my friends, including many men, have played important emotional and intellectual roles in my life and the creation of this book. While I have tried as much as possible to distance my historical study of friendships from my own, my male friends have shown me that affectionate, fulfilling friendships between men and women are possible today. That experience surely made me open to seeing relationships in the historical record that have heretofore been missed or ignored. For this reason, I begin by thanking my male friends.

Of course, the people who shaped this book most profoundly are my advisors and editors. My graduate advisors have supported this project from its inception, and I offer them my immense respect and gratitude. Kathleen Brown has read and edited this manuscript more times than I can count, seeing the big picture in ways I could not and offering the encouragement I needed along the way. Her warmth, intellect, and astute advice shepherded me through graduate school, took this project from dissertation to book, and continue to inspire me. Michael Zuckerman's detailed, thought-provoking commentary and relentless push for a logical, well-supported argument sharpened my writing and thinking. I have learned so much from Mike's compassion and good-humored irreverence. Jan Ellen Lewis helped me think through big questions and my major arguments. As my many citations to her in this book show, her work on gender, politics, and emotion underpins much of my own. Daniel Richter provided me with the office space where I did much of the early writing for this project, as well as offering a thorough reading and helpful advice on this project. All four have been model academic mentors and I'm proud to have had the chance to work with them. At Oxford University Press, Susan Ferber has helped make this the book I envisioned, and her detailed, insightful editing improved the entire manuscript. The anonymous readers via Oxford University Press also offered extremely useful feedback and I'm grateful for their thorough comments.

This project developed while I was a graduate student at the University of Pennsylvania. At Penn, I found two intersecting, supportive communities: the history department and the McNeil Center for Early American Studies. Many thanks to my Penn history friends Gregory Ablavsky, William Kuby, Brian Rouleau, Justin Simard, and Beatrice Wayne, who have been with this project for many years and have offered feedback, copy editing, and great friendship. At the McNeil Center, Daniel Richter, Amy Baxter-Bellamy, and Barbara Natello have created an unparalleled community for early Americanists. The fellows and visiting scholars at the Center during my time there from 2010 to 2012 offered countless helpful suggestions and ideas; special thanks to Sari Altschuler, Paul Conrad, and Jessica Roney for their friendship and encouragement. Thanks also to several friends outside of these communities who read my work: Stephanie Corrigan, Katy Hardy, and Andrew Robichaud.

I have many intellectual debts beyond Penn as well. I began my career in early American studies at George Washington University, where my advisor Teresa Murphy helped me think through the questions that sparked this book. I had many fantastic professors at GW who motivated me to research and teach. During my time working at the Smithsonian Institution, a number of curators generously shared their time as mentors. Special thanks to Frank Goodyear and Ellen Miles, who opened their research files to me for this project. I completed substantial revisions for this book while working at the Papers of James Monroe at the University of Mary Washington. Editor Daniel Preston has been unfailingly supportive, and much that I learned from my work with him helped to improve this book.

I also offer thanks to a number of scholars of early America who have provided their time and knowledge. Zara Anishanslin, Andrew Cayton, Rachel Hope Cleves, Elaine Crane, Thomas Foster, Lorri Glover, C. Dallett Hemphill, Rodney Hessinger, Catherine Kelly, Mary Kelley, Charlene Boyer Lewis, Nenette Luara-Shoaf, Lucia McMahon, Jayne Ptolemy, Joseph Rezek, and Bryan Waterman have read and commented on my work. Konstantin Dierks, Katherine Gaudet, Clare Lyons, Peter Reed, and Anne Verplanck offered advice on tricky subjects. Brian Connolly, Thomas Foster, Sarah Horowitz, Catherine O'Donnell, and Bryan Waterman have shared articles pre-publication. Alea Henle, Whitney Martinko, John O'Keefe, and Beatrice Wayne have photographed very helpful letters in the archives for me. Thanks to the Society for Historians of the Early American Republic, the Colloquium on Early American Literature and Culture at New York University, the American

Historical Association, the Scholl Center at the Newberry Library, the Gender, Women's, and Sexuality Studies Graduate Student Colloquium at the University of Pennsylvania, the Omohundro Institute of Early American History and Culture, and the McNeil Center for Early American Studies for giving me the chance to present my work and receive feedback from great scholars.

I have, in addition, benefited from the advice and assistance of many archivists and librarians. At the University of Pennsylvania, history librarian Nick Okrent made sure I had all of the digital databases I needed. Thanks also to Interlibrary Loan coordinator Carla Bailey of the University of Mary Washington's Simpson Library for tracking down obscure books for me. I did a great deal of my research at the Library Company of Philadelphia and the Historical Society of Pennsylvania, and I am indebted to these institutions for an Andrew W. Mellon fellowship. I also did extensive research at the Maryland Historical Society, where I had a Lord Baltimore Fellowship. Special thanks to Sarah Heim and Steve Smith at the Historical Society of Pennsylvania; Rosemary Cullen at the John Hay Library at Brown University; James Green and Cornelia King at the Library Company of Philadelphia; Linda Hocking at the Litchfield Historical Society; Frances Pollard at the Virginia Historical Society; and Laura Johnson, Julia R. Hofer, and Katie Knowles at Winterthur. I also thank the archivists and librarians of the American Antiquarian Society, American Philosophical Society, Connecticut Historical Society, Friends Historical Collection at Swarthmore, Georgia Historical Society, Library of Congress Manuscript Reading Room, Maryland Historical Society, Massachusetts Historical Society, Mount Vernon Ladies Association, New York Historical Society, Rare Book and Manuscript Library at Columbia University, and the Southern Historical Collection.

This project is clearly a product of intellectual contributions from a vast network of people. But the hardest debts to fully express are those to my family. They knew long before I did that I would become an historian, and they have offered unfailing confidence and support. My extended family has taken an eager interest in this book and the long educational path that made it possible. My late grandparents Beatrice and Louis Ringol supported my education and would have been so pleased to see this book. I had the great luck of going to graduate school near my other grandparents, Frieda and Martin Good, who have shared their wisdom and love. Finally, my parents, Julie and Larry, and sister, Amanda, are my champions and best friends (along with our wonder dog Gracie). They have served as editors, readers, and sounding boards as I developed this book over the past ten years. They are everything to me, and I never could have written this book without them.

Founding Friendships

Introduction

FRIENDSHIP, NOT ROMANCE, came to mind as writer Margaret Bayard Smith crafted a scene between two lovers on the banks of the Potomac for her 1824 novel *Winter in Washington.* The lovers, Louisa and Sidney, listened to the sounds of the water, gazed at the view, and talked at leisure. For the forty-five-year-old Smith, the story of the young lovers brought to mind another pair: her younger self and her friend Anthony Bleecker, walking along the Raritan Bay in New Jersey. "I was as happy walking with my <u>Friend</u> on the shores of the Raritan, as Louisa was sitting with her <u>Lover</u>," she told Bleecker. Smith challenged the idea that romantic love was the supreme human pleasure, asking "has not friendship recollections as sweet & dear as those of love?" Her answer: "Yes, indeed it has—at least in my heart."[1]

Friendships between elite men and women like Bleecker and Smith were both common and highly valued in the early years of the new republic. Indeed, this period was ideally suited to such friendships. In spite of rhetoric that suggested these friendships were impossible, men and women formed friendships with one another that hewed more closely to the republican ideals of the era than any other relationship. Although much is known about same-sex friendships and marriages in this period, especially in the case of the founding fathers, these crucial relationships in the lives of elite Americans and the political system of the era have been overlooked. In a republican polity that relied on the virtuous bonds of its citizenry, male/female friendships gave women an entry point into the civic body and served as intimate ties building political, social, and religious networks. Thus, friendships between elite men and women helped create the social and political fabric of the new nation.[2]

Mixed-sex (or heterosocial) friendships were affectionate, reciprocal relationships that the historical actors themselves cast in terms of a friendship. Friends haphazardly built a common vocabulary to describe their relationships, taking cues from existing cultural forms and adapting them to their individual needs. They situated their friendships in relation to their families

and spouses, their church communities, and their social circles. They maintained their friendships through exchanges of letters, gifts, and services, establishing a dynamic of reciprocity that erased gender differences and built
on the strengths of each friend. The balanced exchange between cross-sex
friends created an even power dynamic for men and women in which to
define and conduct their relationships.

The language men and women used to express their affection often sounds
romantic to contemporary ears, but a careful consideration of how people expressed emotion and an openness to the notion that men and women could
be friends offers new, more nuanced readings. However, there was not a word
for a friendship between a man and a woman in this era. Although the term
"platonic" existed and was sometimes used to describe friendships between
men and women, its meaning at the time was most often associated with unconsummated romance.[3] Even the word "friend" was problematic because of
its multiple meanings. In the early republic, "friend" could refer to an acquaintance, a patron, a protector, a business partner, a diplomatic or political ally, a lover, a spouse, or a voluntary relationship based on affection and
common interest.[4] For men and women who became friends, the fact that the
term could apply to lovers and spouses complicated their efforts to define the
relationship as something apart from conjugal love.

Notably, sexual activity does not factor into this definition of friendship.
First and foremost, it is often impossible for historians to know whether or
not two people were sexually intimate. Friends who did not have a sexual
dimension to their relationship could still enjoy physical expressions of closeness such as a kiss in greeting, a hand clasp, or other physical articulations of
emotion. They might also express emotional intimacy in sensual language.
Modern interest in sexuality distracts from understanding what friendships
meant to historical individuals. The assumption of sexual attraction in cross-
sex relations forces anachronistic readings onto an era that understood emotion, sexuality, and friendship in ways quite different than our own.[5] In the
case of friendships between men and women, our contemporary assumption
of heterosexual attraction obscures the real intellectual and emotional value
in these friendships.

This definition of friendship between men and women, as well as its ca-
veats, could be applied to such friendships at any period in American history. These relationships are not a historically specific phenomenon; rather,
the ease with which men and women could form such friendships and the
meaning of such friendships within politics and society changes over time.
While certainly there are examples of friendships between men and women

in earlier and later eras, the evidence of such relationships proliferates in the early American republic.

The American Revolution not only ushered in a new political system but also spurred changes in the roles of and expectations for men and women.[6] The American and French revolutions inspired people on both sides of the Atlantic to experiment with new forms of relationships and even new ways of feeling. Intimate relationships were seen as key to the success of new political arrangements. The formation of a republic ruled by the people rather than a king meant that the bonds that held the polity together were vital; only through social ties would a body of people scattered across thirteen colonies connect as a political whole. Friendship, marriage, and family would knit together the body politic in the early decades of the young republic.[7]

Friendship in particular held an important place in ideas about creating a new, republican society in America. In the late eighteenth century, Americans believed that strong, virtuous friendships served as models for human interaction. These friendships would transform selves in order to improve society and build a new social order.[8] However, the form of friendship that Americans assumed was necessary to create a republican polity was fraternal. Friendly bonds between men, in the tradition of ancient Greek and Roman history and philosophy, were deemed fundamental to political life.[9] In the early republic, before established political parties and when only a nascent sense of national identity existed, personal relationships carried great weight.

Educated white women had a vital role to play in this new republic, although they were usually excluded from descriptions of civic friendship. Women were particularly valued as wives and mothers, helping to shape husbands and sons who would lead the country. Although they possessed innate virtue, women needed training to shape others: elite young women across the country were sent to newly formed female academies to learn both domestic skills and academic subjects including science, literature, and classics. While denied direct participation in the political system, elite women's roles as republican wives and mothers was understood by Americans at this time as a political necessity.[10]

Republican wives were by definition partners in companionate marriages with their republican husbands. Influenced by the ideals of voluntary allegiance that grew out of the American Revolution, in the late eighteenth century many Americans saw marriage as a social contract between mutually consenting, loving partners. The republican wife was an educated woman who could converse intelligently and connect emotionally with her husband. Historians refer to this conception of marriage as the "companionate ideal," arguing that elite Americans venerated it as the ultimate relationship for fulfillment, stability, and happiness.[11] By the logic that described the elite woman as an intellectual and emotional companion for her husband, surely women could play a similar role for male friends. Men and women who were taught to seek each other out for companionship as spouses found ready friends along with romantic partners.

In spite of the companionate ideal and the focus on marriage as the means to fulfillment, some men and women praised friendship as a more worthy relationship. Philosophers of love and friendship had long venerated friendship as superior to romantic love and marriage because it was more egalitarian and rational, calmer, and less passionate. British writer and women's rights proponent Mary Wollstonecraft wrote that friendship was "the most sublime of all affections," while love was a sort of "fever" that disturbed calm minds. She argued that women should prefer "the calm satisfaction of friendship, and the tender confidence of habitual esteem" to love.[12] Philadelphia salonniere Elizabeth Graeme Fergusson came to a similar conclusion. As a young woman in 1752, she had written a poem in her commonplace book praising love. Some thirty-five years later, having married and separated from her husband, she added another poem directly below it. "Let Girlish Nymph, and boyish Swains,/Their amorous Ditties Cherish!" she wrote. The "shady flame" of friendship "outshines that transient blaze" of passion as did the sun to a far-off star.[13] Friendship was, Fergusson learned from experience, preferable and longer lasting than romantic love.

Despite the conditions that fostered the possibility and even importance of men and women forming friendships, prevailing wisdom dictated that such friendships were impossible or at the very least quite risky. Etiquette books and letter writing manuals offered no instructions for conducting such relationships, and advice writers often cautioned men and women against forming friendships with the opposite sex. Many novels of the period also denied the possibility of friendships between men and women, depicting only two possible outcomes: romance or seduction. The popular novel *The Coquette*, for instance, depicted seduction as a result of the tragic heroine's trusting friendship with a man.

There were indeed real risks to these friendships. Men and women who had come of age in the previous generation often disapproved of heterosocial friendships. Margaret Bayard Smith discovered this as a young woman when an older woman admonished her for letting young men call on her. "Is it not ill natured," Smith complained to her fiancé in 1800, "that they should suppose, that like most of my sex, I delighted in the society of men, merely because they are men, & because their attentions have been considered as flattering?" Ill-natured or not, this was a common suspicion. Many could not believe, as Smith did, that often "in the intimate communion of mind with mind, there is not likewise communion of hearts."[14] Damaging rumors and gossip could emerge if people suspected that a friendship had turned illicitly romantic. Even if a woman was unlikely to be seduced by a male friend, she ran the risk, particularly if she was young and unmarried, of ruining her reputation.

Why, if the conditions of this period seemed to foster these relationships, did Americans at the same time so often condemn them? First, Americans distrusted relationships between men and women outside of the traditional bounds of family, courtship, and marriage. The existence of an alternative social space revealed the flexibility of the rules and expectations for successfully achieving manhood and womanhood, and challenged the societal work then invested in channeling men and women into marriage. At a time when the nation's leaders were concerned with rebuilding a stable social order after the American Revolution, the ascendancy of relationships that challenged such an order would have been threatening. Second, the notion of women as friends for men—and, likely, the knowledge that these friendships occurred with some frequency—may have led men to worry that women would have too easy an entry into the public sphere through friendships with men.[15] Many writers of this era foreclosed the possibility of long-term, emotionally fulfilling friendships between men and women, perhaps to exclude women from the polity.

That elite men and women formed friendships with one another despite these challenges demonstrates individuals' power to shape their relationships and gender roles. The frequency with which these relationships occurred suggests the limited ability of norms about gender and sexuality to impose an order on actual social relationships in the early republic. The warnings of advice writers did not determine the reality. Men and women could create new spaces for their friendships beyond accepted frameworks but without offering outright resistance. Friends carefully positioned their relationships with reference to marriage, family, and rules of propriety, both creating greater flexibility in these areas and supporting the very traditional relationships that friends eschewed. Friends never talked in terms of overturning the existing order; rather, they were seeking out a place for their relationships within it.[16]

Men and women must have felt it worthwhile to go outside the bounds in forming such friendships. Perhaps a sense of breaking the rules was in itself part of the reward. As one young man joked to a female friend, "these are revolutionary times; and any innovations tending to explode the errors of common fastidiousness, may be laudable!"[17] There was a certain thrill in testing limits and in experimenting with the rules. And of course, there were, as in any friendship, emotional benefits. Friendships expanded an individual's networks beyond marriage and family, offering new sources of affection, intellectual exchange, and practical assistance. Men and women could provide resources for one another in ways that often built upon gender differences. Most important, though, these friendships offered men and women entry into independent, egalitarian relationships that epitomized the values of the early republic.

Indeed, male/female friendships were paragons of central republican values: choice, freedom, equality, and virtue. These were not only political ideals but also personal ones in a nation where the virtue of the people would sustain the republican political system. In specifying the right to the pursuit of happiness in the Declaration of Independence, Jefferson laid out an American ideal that individuals should have the freedom to choose the path to happiness. American citizens were granted the right to choose a religion, to vote for candidates who represented their interests, and to select a spouse whom they loved. Freedom and choice were thus closely interlinked.[18]

Virtue and equality were at the heart of the republic. In its broadest sense, virtue was devotion to the public good: the good of the republic was an individual's first priority, above his family or himself. Proponents of virtue emphasized living a simple, austere life, a life compatible with the humble white agrarian farmers of early America. Many believed that the American experiment relied on the virtue of just such men. This public good was fostered through individual relationships and it depended upon equality among white men. Equality was, in one writer's words, the "life and soul" of the republic. Equality in this period meant an equality of opportunity that would allow the most talented citizens to rule the nation.[19] It did not mean social equality: indeed, women, blacks, and native people were increasingly marginalized over the first several decades of the new nation.[20] The ideals of this era, particularly equality, were to a large degree the purview—even privilege—of white males.

Friendships between men and women broke through many of the limitations on the founding ideals. These relationships were truer to the ideals of freedom, choice, virtue, and equality than any other relationships between men and women in this period, particularly the much idealized republican, companionate marriage. The choice of a spouse was still subject to parental approval and considerations of the wealth a partner could bring to a marriage. Women had the freedom to accept or reject marriage proposals, but once wed they were legally the property of their husbands. The marriage contract inherently granted power to a man, subsuming his wife's identity under his own through the legal concept of coverture; it essentially served as a labor contract for the wife to run the household. Whether or not a husband chose to exercise his patriarchal authority in a marriage, the relationship was inherently structured as hierarchical.[21] Despite its vaunted ideals of intimacy based upon emotional equality, companionate marriage could not truly be based in equality of condition when women were both legally and practically the subordinates of their husbands.[22] Nor could virtue, dependent on equality, thrive in such an institution. Similarly, family relationships between men and women were given, not voluntarily entered, and men maintained legal power and advantages over their female relatives.[23]

Friendships between elite white men and women offered correctives to all of these slippages between prescription and everyday experience. Men and women could choose to befriend each other without parental approval or financial considerations (although they generally befriended people of similar social stature). They were bound by no contract, and both man and woman were free to shape the terms of the relationship or break it off when it was no longer satisfactory. While society still privileged men over women, men held no legal or practical power over their female friends. Indeed, in forming friendships with one another, men and women entered a relationship in which their roles were not already scripted. Women were not consigned to the home by these relations, as they were (at least prescriptively) as wives and mothers. As friends, moreover, women were not limited to being empowered only in relation to husbands or male children. Men, in turn, had no legally sanctioned power over female friends, held no responsibility for providing for them, and derived no political legitimacy from friendships as they did from their roles as heads of household. As egalitarian, freely entered and freely chosen relationships, then, such friendships nurtured virtue.

It was these republican values that made friendships between men and women in America different from those in Europe. Like republicanism itself, male/female friendships were shaped in opposition to European norms. The two European countries Americans knew best—Britain and France—provided examples of what Americans did not want their friendships to become. In both countries, marriage was more often about exchange of property than pure affection, and extramarital sexual relationships were common.[24] In England, Adam Smith explained in his *Wealth of Nations*, "the breach of chastity" among elites was "treated with a good deal of indulgence."[25]

Friends and lovers were not clearly distinguished when it came to relationships between men and women. Perhaps most worrying to Americans, European women exerted great political influence over their male friends and
lovers, intertwining sex and politics in a political world Americans saw as
bereft of virtue.[26] The fears about women's sexual and political influence over
men made mixed-sex friendships in America more difficult and risky, but
also easier to define.

For American men and women to maintain friendships with one another,
they had to incorporate such friendships into their social circles and families in order to prove the relationships were virtuous, proper, and chaste—
in other words, suitable for a republic.[27] The assiduous positioning of these
friendships was not merely to guard against gossip, then, but also to demonstrate that these friendships were unlike European relationships between
men and women. Sex would not intrude on the virtue of these relationships
and challenge marital fidelity. In this way, then, mixed-sex friendships among
the elite took part in constituting the republican body politic in America,
giving them a more important and public role than in Europe.

The individuals who make up this story of friendships between men and
women include Americans abroad and at home, Northerners and Southerners, writers and artists, politicians and schoolmates. Many of the names are
familiar—Thomas Jefferson, Abigail Adams, William Ellery Channing, and
Gilbert Stuart among them—as the letters of prominent people are more
likely to be saved. But there are also lesser-known men and women, who leave
little trace besides a small cache of correspondence or may be known only to
historians of a particular time and place. Whether famous or unknown, however, these were white, educated, middling to upper class people who could
afford paper and the leisure time to write lengthy letters.[28]

If such friendships existed among lower class, black, or native people, evidence is difficult to find; these men and women did not have the means to
produce the letters, diaries, and gifts that would have demonstrated their relationships. The very notion of women as intellectual and emotional companions for men was restricted to those whites with education and a genteel
sensibility, making these friendships both a product of and a way of demonstrating elite status. Chastity, too, had become a sign of elite status,[29] making
a virtuous and nonsexual image of male/female friendship into a badge of
gentility.

Among elite men and women in the early republic, however, these friendships occurred in a wide variety of situations. Some were between men and
women of the same age, while other pairs had a wide age gap. Friendships

were often formed when men and women were young and sustained through adulthood, incorporating their spouses into the relationships. Since a majority of people married at some point in their lives, most friendships included at least one married person. The place of these relationships changed over the course of men and women's lives, at a young age supporting courtships, while later offering support in political or other careers, although they offered emotional and practical support continuously.[30]

These friendships were more likely to include Northerners than Southerners, for a number of reasons. Most simply, there are fewer letters from this period surviving in archives in the South. Even so, the archives offer ample enough evidence to show that it was rare for unrelated men and women in the South to write each other, whether in the form of love letters or friendly correspondence.[31] The convention that unrelated men and women should not write each other seems to have been more strictly observed in the South than the North. Northerners also had more opportunities for mixed-sex gatherings in the absence of their families, whereas Southern social events were often held in the home as family groups visited one another or at parties with many adults present.[32] Southerners who spent time in the North or abroad, however, were more likely to leave behind correspondence from their long-distance friendships.

Friendships between men and women were a national phenomenon whose story can be told from piecing together an array of sources. Letters, of course, offer the most direct access to the voices of friends communicating with one another. Diaries, too, are rich sources, particularly when writers recorded entire conversations with their friends. Friends also signed friendship albums, exchanged gifts, and commissioned portraits of one another. These material objects show the richness of such friendships. Finally, looking at what these men and women might have read is illuminating. Etiquette books, advice manuals, and even novels could both reflect what people at the time thought was proper behavior between friends as well as shape how people thought about friendships. Literary culture was transatlantic at this time, with British and even French works dominating the American market. Americans were more likely to read those works that fit their conceptions of proper roles and behavior, for instance eschewing the promiscuous *Dangerous Liaisons* for Rousseau's socially conservative works. If actual European friendships were not the model of choice for Americans' friendships, conservative literary examples certainly could be.

This book traces the foundations and consequences of heterosocial friendships through a series of seven chapters. The first chapter offers examples of three friendships to illustrate the lived experience of these relationships and how important they were in men's and women's lives. The second chapter establishes the literary discussions about friendship available to men and women in the early American republic, drawing on novels, advice literature, and poetry. These sources failed to provide adequate models for heterosocial friendships and in fact often implicitly argued that such relationships were not possible in the long term. Given the lack of a clear category for heterosocial friendships, chapter three explores how men and women distinguished between friendship and romantic love and what risks they incurred in crossing those boundaries. Chapter four demonstrates that men and women carefully positioned their relationships within larger social circles and institutions in order to mitigate those risks and clarify the amorphous categorization of their friendships.

Having established the challenges and strategies inherent in heterosocial friendships, the second half of the book explores how friendships operated and addressed issues of power and gender difference. Chapters five and six both look at the dynamics of exchanges between friends and the way friends framed exchanges to appear proper, with the former focusing on letters and the latter on gifts. The exchange of concrete objects left distinctive visual traces of the forms and rituals appropriate for conveying friendship between a man and a woman. Chapter seven shows how these friendships operated in the early republican political world, offering both men and women additional opportunities for access and influence.

This story is told thematically rather than chronologically. Heterosocial friendships did not change significantly over the course of this fifty-year period. Rather, the conditions surrounding them changed. By the late 1820s, there were two significant developments that affected friendships between men and women. First, the educated white woman's role in the home was increasingly emphasized. In theory and, to some extent, in practice, such women were removed from the public spaces that had once been mixed-sex venues. Second, as the two-party system solidified and universal white manhood suffrage triumphed with Andrew Jackson's election, the personal interactions that had fueled politics and provided a space for women's participation receded from the public sphere.[33] This would not be the end of friendships between men and women, but it would shift the meaning of such relationships and move them more squarely into the domestic arena.

This book illustrates what mixed-sex friendships meant for individuals and the nation in the early republic. These friendships highlight men and women as individuals, rather than in the roles dictated by their gender.

While Margaret Bayard Smith wrote her male friends with ease, she seemed less comfortable writing her fiancé. In a letter to him soon before her marriage, she admitted, "I have been sometimes mortified, that in your letters you have seem'd to have forgotten that I was a rational being, & have treated me as a mere girl." She begged of him: "Forget that I am a woman . . . remember only that I have a mind, which tho' now idle & contracted, nay, debased by ignorance, yet it is capable of activity & expansion." If not always with her husband, Smith could find "communion of mind with mind" with other men: friends like Anthony Bleecker, Charles Brockden Brown, and Thomas Jefferson.[34]

After saying goodbye to Thomas Jefferson in 1809, Margaret Bayard Smith wrote to her sister, "My heart is oppressed . . . with a weight of sadness, and my eyes are so blinded with tears that I can scarcely trace these lines."[35] Like Smith's lines obscured by tears, friendships like hers with Bleecker or Jefferson blurred the lines of the acceptable gender, social, and political order. Such orders were more flexible than we have imagined, and friendships between men and women both took advantage of that flexibility and reworked the very boundaries of their society. Men and women, including some of the most prominent people of the era, created an expansive form of social and political life in which gender was no barrier and in which the quest for emotional fulfillment defied the rules of convention.

I

Three Stories of Friendship

IT CAN BE hard to picture what a friendship looked like between a man and a woman some two hundred years ago. We cannot overhear snippets of conversation, sit at the dinner table, or take a leisurely walk with the men and women who formed friendships in the early republic. Fortunately, friends who lived apart from one another wrote letters, and in some rare cases both sides of the correspondence have been saved. That is the case with the three pairs of friends examined here: Thomas Jefferson and Abigail Adams; Eloise Payne and William Ellery Channing; and Charles Loring and Mary Pierce. All three pairs sustained friendships over many years, in some cases decades, allowing for the evolution of their friendships to be traced.

This chapter describes how these pairs met, what they discussed in their letters to one another, how they felt about one another, and how the friendship was a useful and important relationship in each of these lives. All of them had other friends of the opposite sex, but in each case this relationship was a particularly meaningful one. These wide-ranging pairs include people from North and South, urban and rural areas; young people and middle-aged adults; pairs of the same age and with a wide gap in ages; single and married. These friendships fit into the context of a wider circle of common friends as well as broader cultural trends of how such friends served one another. Each case shows how these friendships provided emotional support, substituted for family, and furthered courtships, with other pairs of friends with similar experiences introduced for comparison.

The three central relationships here all proved especially useful, whether in the case of Abigail Adams providing Jefferson political intelligence, William Ellergy Channing mentoring the young teacher Eloise Payne, or Mary Pierce furthering Charles Loring's courtship of her niece. While friendships could not be based purely on utility, friends often furthered each other's interests through mutual exchanges that cemented emotional bonds.[1] Friends supplemented the work of family members and spouses in providing support for one another, expanding webs of interdependence beyond the household.

They did not, however, follow the traditional pattern of gender roles in a marriage in which the man was the provider and the woman did the domestic work; these relationships provided venues for support between men and women outside of such conventional economic roles. The mutuality and reciprocity male/female friends built also crafted gender relations closer to equality and with greater freedom than any other relationship between men and women in American society.

It is especially notable that Thomas Jefferson, described by many historians as a misogynist, could enter into an egalitarian relationship with a woman. His relationship with Abigail speaks to the unique place of mixed-sex friendship in this era. The three pairs described here did not need to discuss women's role or notions of equality; they lived it in their relationships. These friendships were remarkably open, caring, and often messy relationships that suggest the ways people lived the values of the new republic.

Abigail and Thomas

Abigail Adams (Figure 1.1) and Thomas Jefferson (see Chapter 6, Figures 6.4 and 6.5) both arrived in Europe for the first time in 1784.[2] Both were around forty years old and had left behind their homes and young children to join John Adams in Paris. John and Thomas had been friends since 1776, and surely Abigail had heard her husband praise his Virginian friend, just as Thomas must have heard about John's intelligent wife. In Paris, they quickly bonded as parents missing their children, lovers of art and culture, and sharp intellectuals. They went to plays, concerts, and exhibitions together, and Thomas spent much of his time at the Adams home in Auteuil. Their friendship reveals the deep, affectionate connections that friends of the opposite sex could share.

Abigail's dynamic and loving relationship with her husband is well documented, but John was not the only man in her life.[3] Abigail admitted to her sister that she preferred socializing with "the gentlemen more than the Ladies" because she "found their conversation more to my taste."[4] She already corresponded with two of her husband's other friends in politics from Massachusetts, James Lovell and Elbridge Gerry. Keenly interested in politics herself, she valued the opportunity to converse with men at the center of the new nation's government. Thomas claimed a special place in her heart, however; she called him "one of the choice ones of the earth."[5] Like her other male friends, he was a safe and suitable companion for the married mother, as he was friends with her husband and John was often with them.

FIGURE 1.1 Unidentified artist, *Abigail Adams*, ca. 1795, oil on canvas. Fenimore Art Museum, Cooperstown, New York, N0150.1955 (Photograph by Richard Walker).

Thomas Jefferson had a unique ability to connect with women, and his relationship with Abigail was but one of a growing number of female friendships he formed after his wife's death in 1782. In 1800 he visited Margaret Bayard Smith at her new home in Washington. Although she did not know who he was and he did not introduce himself, he immediately put her at ease. He addressed her "with an expression of benevolence and with a manner and voice almost femininely soft and gentle," she recalled. "I know not how it was, but there was something in his manner, his countenance and voice that at once unlocked my heart."[6] Thomas unlocked several women's hearts during his time in Paris, including those of Alexander Hamilton's sister-in-law Angelica Schuyler Church, British artist Maria Cosway, and a number of aristocratic French women whose salons he frequented. While he was not in Paris for long, the friendships he formed there provided emotional sustenance to him for decades to come.

Abigail and Thomas's ten months in Paris is less documented than their years apart, because it was while separated that they corresponded. Soon after the Adams' arrival in London, Abigail sent Thomas a letter saying she regretted having to leave Paris particularly "on account of the increasing pleasure, and intimacy which a longer acquaintance with a respected Friend promised." At writing this first letter to her new friend, she expressed some diffidence, apologizing for "thus freely scribling to you" and hoping he would write her back. He replied by thanking her for starting "a correspondence which I so much desired," and thus began a continual flow of letters between the two.[7] John and Abigail often wrote Thomas separate letters on the same days, and he replied separately in turn. The letters between the two men focused almost exclusively on political business, while Thomas and Abigail mixed their political discussion with family news, shopping requests, and emotional support.

In Thomas, Abigail found both a sympathetic ear and a writer who could engage with her playfully. He wrote from Paris that, while selecting Roman busts to send to the Adams home, he passed over the figure of Venus because he "thought it out of taste to have two at table at the same time." He also joked with her about his dislike of the English, suggesting that "it must be the quantity of animal food eaten by the English which renders their character insusceptible of civilisation."[8] Playfulness aside, Thomas also reposed great trust in Abigail. When his youngest daughter Lucy died as a toddler back home in Virginia, Thomas became determined to have his middle daughter Polly sent to join him in Europe. She would arrive in England, escorted by an enslaved woman from Jefferson's estate, and go straight to the Adams home in London. Announcing these plans, Thomas told Abigail in 1786 that "I knew your goodness too well to scruple the giving this direction before I had asked your permission."[9]

In addition to an emotional connection and domestic concerns, Abigail and Thomas carried on intellectual and political conversations. While not formally educated, Abigail was quite well read. As a young woman, her sister Mary's suitor Richard Cranch supplied her with "proper Bookes" and helped cultivate her intellect. She also picked up a fair amount of French and was familiar with many classical texts as well as Enlightenment thought. After her marriage, John kept her well-informed of politics and she read newspapers regularly. She famously advocated for improved treatment of women (although her comment relates primarily to the law of marriage) when she implored her husband to "Remember the Ladies." For his part, John respected her political opinions throughout his career, referring to her while first lady as "Presidante."[10] Yet besides her sisters and Mercy Otis Warren, Abigail had few female friends with whom she could correspond about politics. Thus she frequently shared her ideas with her husband and male friends such as Thomas Jefferson.[11]

Their regard for each other gave Abigail the opening to discuss politics with Jefferson more openly than any other women could.[12] While to friends like Angelica Schuyler Church, the sister-in-law of Alexander Hamilton whom he befriended during her time in Paris, he wrote that "The tender breasts of young ladies were not formed for political convulsion,"[13] he made no such remarks to Abigail. In fact, after Abigail moved to London, he often relied on her for political news. Lamenting that he wasn't getting enough news from John, he told her that he hoped she would "be so good as to keep that office in your own hands." Eight months later, he jokingly complained that John's "head was full of whale oil" (John's last letter to Thomas had been on the market for this product) and he was relying on her for more news. "De tout mon coeur," he admitted, "I had rather receive it from you."[14]

She provided him with the latest information she and John had received from America, and she did not shy away from offering her opinions. After learning of Shays' Rebellion in her home state of Massachusetts, she wrote to Jefferson expressing disgust with the "ignorant, wrestless desperadoes, without conscience or principals" who had led the insurrection. She went on to say that she hoped the event would spur the state legislature to make positive changes. It was in response to this letter that Jefferson famously wrote "I like a little rebellion now and then."[15]

Jefferson also noted in one letter to her that he used the term "people" to refer to the French as it was "a noun of the masculine as well as feminine gender," presumably a choice in terminology to satisfy Abigail.[16] It was a playful remark, but it showed a deference to Abigail and recognition of her opinions on the equality of women long before most writers concerned themselves with gender-neutral pronouns. He shared his own opinions on politics with her, although he wrote more often in sweeping terms than in the close detail of his letters to John. It was politics, however, that ultimately came between Abigail and Thomas and ended their friendship.

Abigail maintained feelings of friendship for Thomas longer than her husband did, imploring her husband in 1796, after the fiercely contested election between Jefferson and Adams, and long after the end of the men's friendship, to resume their old comradery. Such a friendship "would tend to harmonize, and moderation, coolness and temperament would reconcile the present, faring interests to concord."[17] Two weeks later, she continued this thread in writing to her husband even more critically of Thomas that he was "wrong in politicks" and "frequently mistaken in Men and Measures." Yet he was not, she thought, "an insincere or coruptable Man." Political differences could not overpower the affection she continued to feel for him, and she told John that "My Friendship for him has ever been unshaken."[18] It was only when Thomas became president in 1800, when she felt that his political actions were direct, personal affronts to her family, that she stopped writing to him.

After Jefferson's daughter Polly's death in 1804, Abigail felt compelled to reopen the correspondence. Her letter started a remarkably frank exchange between the old friends through which they dissected the causes of the end of their friendship. Jefferson was pleased to have the opportunity to clear the air, writing to her that he had "opened myself to you without reserve, which I have long wished an opportunity of doing; and, without knowing how it will be received, I feel relief from being unbosomed." He declared his continued feelings of friendship for both John and Abigail, explaining that "one act of Mr. Adams's life, and one only, ever gave me a moment's personal displeasure." This act was Adams's appointment of judges who were Jefferson's "ardent political enemies" during the last hours he was in office before Jefferson became president.[19]

If Jefferson could look past these political affronts and still wish to remain friends, it was Abigail who could not. Abigail replied with her own description of Jefferson's offenses, which included freeing James Callender, a journalist who had slandered John Adams, and replacing her son John Quincy in a judicial appointment. She explained that her affection for him had remained despite their political differences, but she could no longer esteem him as a friend. Ultimately, while Jefferson still felt for Abigail the "highest consideration and esteem," Abigail's esteem for him had "taken its flight."[20] At this point, Jefferson sensed that "conciliation was desperate," and the correspondence ended.[21]

The old friends would not write again until 1813, two years after John and Thomas had resumed their friendship with the help of mutual friend (and indeed Abigail's friend as well) Benjamin Rush. In a postscript to a July 1813 letter from her husband to Thomas, Abigail wrote simply:

I have been looking for some time for a space in my good Husbands Letters to add the regards, of an old Friend, which are Still cherished and perserved [*sic*] through all the changes and vissitudes [*sic*] which have taken place since we first became acquainted, and will I trust remain as long as A Adams.

Jefferson, clearly delighted, wrote her back in August, expressing his interest in "whatever affects your happiness." She replied a month later that she was pleased that their friendship was "again renewed, purified from the dross" of political rancor.[22]

Like her husband, Abigail returned to a comfortable and affectionate correspondence with "the phylosopher of Monticello." Perhaps it was her daughter's impending death that had softened Abigail toward Thomas, for she wrote her postscript just over a month before Nabby's passing. Her first complete letter to Thomas was less than a month after Nabby died, and she wrote that "you sir, who have been called to Seperations of a Similar kind, can sympathize with your Bereaved Friend." Taking comfort in being able to share her anguish with her old friend, Abigail admitted that "the full Heart loves to pour out its Sorrows, into the Bosom of sympathizing Friendship." In his last surviving letter to Abigail, Thomas offered her "the homage of my constant respect and attachment." Soon after she died in October 1818, Thomas offered John his consolation and said that he would be "mingling sincerely my tears with yours."[23]

Emotional Support

The emotional support Thomas and Abigail provided for each other was common in friendships. Friends of either gender could serve as confidantes and sympathetic listeners. This was a role traditionally ascribed to same-sex friends or married couples. Why, then, would men and women need to turn to friends of the opposite sex? There are a number of answers to this question, the first being that mutual support is a key quality to maintaining a close friendship between any two people.[24] Second, for the many men (like Thomas) or women who were unmarried, a friendship with the opposite sex could be an important source of emotional sustenance. Even for married men and women, the ideal of companionate marriage in which husband and wife were best friends who could fulfill each other both physically and emotionally was not always realized. Abigail had a more egalitarian marriage than most women of that era, but even she could not expect her husband to meet all of her emotional needs. Finally, while both men and women could offer emotional support, their gendered experiences and perspectives likely offered a different perspective for their friends.

Increasingly, as the nineteenth century progressed, women were exalted for their role as comforters for each other and men. Friendships between women, who had similar struggles with bodies, pregnancies, child rearing, and domestic life, were important channels of emotional support.[25] But it was not merely their analogous life experiences that made them excel in this role; as sensibility and sympathy became feminized in the 1800s in America, women came to be seen as naturally better at offering comfort.[26] On the brink of this transition, one author claimed that he appreciated women's role as both comforters and advisors:

> In all the most serious and weighty matters of this life, I have trusted them [ladies] with my first and highest secrets; nay I have drawn such cordial comfort and such excellent advice from their sense of judgment, that I shall persevere in making them the oracles of my conduct, the friends of my bosom, and the confidents [sic] of my secrets.[27]

Here women excelled as comforters not just because of their greater sensibility, but because of their ability to keep secrets and provide sound advice.

When Philadelphian John Mifflin wrote his friend Elzina de la Roche about a disturbing injury to his daughter in 1801, he hoped she would write back with words of comfort. Despite the fact that she lived in France, de la Roche was "the only Person in the World who knows every Sentiment of my Heart and mind."[28] Mifflin was married and had other family in Philadelphia (although he claimed to have few friends), but evidently they did not understand Mifflin the way de la Roche did. It is unclear whether her comfort and sympathy would have been a supplement or a detriment to Mifflin's marriage; Elzina was a widow, so more easily able to befriend men, and lived thousands of miles away. As a young man, Mifflin had had very close friends, including female ones, and he had long relied on his friends for comfort.[29]

Mifflin held a special place in his life for friendships that his marriage apparently did not fulfill. "For one instant only to know such a woman and to feel all the happiness arising from her friendship and her too partial esteem—and then to lose her forever," Mifflin wrote Elzina in 1805, "leaves the deserted party the hopeless prospect of filling up her place." Indeed, he often complained to Elzina that he had not found an "intimate friend" in Philadelphia to replace her. Two years later, he explained that his feelings for her had changed "in proportion as I feel every year, every day, nay every hour, in increasing magnitude of the loss I have sustained in losing you and the impossibility of ever replacing it." Despite his efforts, Mifflin could find no one to "fill up the Chasm occasioned by [her] absence." His only choice was to rely on her support and advice through letters, and he admitted that "if it were not for the consolation & improvement I receive from your letters I should almost wish we had never met."[30]

Yet it was not only women who could be comforters; men, too, could play this role for their friends. Indeed, late-eighteenth- and early-nineteenth-century friendships between young men were expected to be emotionally rich relationships. Letters between male friends demonstrate that men valued the development of fellow feeling. Such men may have taken women as their model for sympathetic friendship, but they were often quite skilled at soothing female friends in need.[31] Abigail herself sometimes turned to a male friend for comfort. In 1777, with John Adams in Europe for years and rarely corresponding with her, Abigail relied on James Lovell as her emotional confidante. As she told Lovell, "it has been a relief to my mind to drop some of my sorrows through my pen, which had your Friend been present would have been poured only into his bosome."[32]

For ministers in particular, offering female friends and congregants emotional support came naturally. Indeed, for pairs of religious men and women whose friendships were alleged to be a connection of souls rather than gendered bodies, emotional sustenance was available from either sex. Indeed, ministers' close connection to God and role as comforters to their congregants made them common supporters for women. Even for a religious leader like Elizabeth Bayley Seton, male religious leaders were important sources of comfort. When her daughter passed away, her friend Father Bruté did "all that the kindest best invention of the most compassionate heart could do" and made her pain pass "as easily as if our high comforter had spread his soft wings over every fiber." It was as if this friend was the conduit of God's comforting presence for Seton.

Patty Rogers, a young woman in New England, turned to a male friend who was a local minister for support. While confined to her home to take care of her father during an illness in 1785, Patty Rogers appreciated her friend Dr. Tenney's visits. Patty admitted to Tenney that "I wished to have a Brother to write me every week, & encourage me—but now I have nobody." Tenney urged her to be patient, and she replied that she was trying, but "it is not often I have anyone to tell my grievances to." Tenney admitted that "I don't know who would be more patient." Patty seems to have taken solace in this and the rest of their conversation, ending her account of his visit by recalling "the comfort passed between us."[33]

Eloise and William

Eloise Richards Payne and William Ellery Channing (see Figures 1.2 and 1.3) were, in many ways, a perfect pair. The daughter of a man who made his career running academies for young men and women, Eloise was known to be a woman of considerable genius. She impressed a Harvard professor with her self-taught command of Latin at age fourteen, and by the age of twenty she had opened her own academy in Newport, Rhode Island. William, born in Newport in 1780 and seven years Eloise's senior, had shown himself to be a prodigy at Harvard. He, too, took a great interest in education and published writings on the topic throughout his career as a minister. They both studied theology and enjoyed philosophical discussions. Channing had a sensitive, caring manner and great respect for women that endeared them to him; Eloise's shining eyes and graceful conversation drew William to her.[34]

Although the two became very dear to one another, their relationship was one of friendship. Both were unmarried when they met, which was likely in Newport when William was on a visit home from Boston. Whether they ever entertained romantic feelings for one another is unknown, but by the time of their first extant letters in 1809, it is clear that William has taken on the role of a friend and mentor for Eloise. He addressed letters to her as "My dear Eloise," and she addressed him as "My dear friend." While this was in line with how lovers might write one another, the content and closings of their letters were not. None of the romantic language courting couples used at the time is evident in the pair's letters, and both had other friends of the opposite sex. William's nephew noted that many of his uncle's happiest times were spent with his female friends.[35] Eloise, too, had other male friends, but she seems to have had a special bond with William.

The two openly expressed how much their friendship meant. In Eloise, William wrote, "I have a sincere & affectionate friend, on whose attachment I may rely amidst all the vicissitudes of my life."[36] Eloise was particularly supportive of his engagement to his cousin Ruth in 1814, about which he must have expressed doubts to Eloise in a letter that has been lost. Her response reassured him that Ruth was well prepared to be a minister's wife and that the two were a good match for each other.[37] More often, however, William provided support for his younger friend. During the difficult times in her life, Eloise wrote, "had it not been for him, my spirit would long ago have yielded to the pressure of calamity." William had "supported & cheer'd me in scenes of the darkest sorrow & . . . spoken peace to me when all was anarchy." In their letters, Eloise "confided every action & every thought," and William, in return, "rebuk'd &

FIGURE 1.2 Unidentified artist, *Eloise R. Payne*, undated, ivory miniature. Collection of Anne Luquer Boswell. (Image courtesy of Frick Art Reference Library. Photograph by Ira W. Martin.)

counsell'd & encourag'd me." Because William was a minister, his support often had a religious tenor, and Eloise admitted that "should a single holy principle be ever developed in my heart to him next to heaven it will be owing."[38]

William and Eloise's correspondence was remarkably personal and emotional for friends of the opposite sex, who often had to write one another with some circumspection to avoid misunderstandings about the nature of their relationship. One of the only hints of the way the two exercised caution was in a letter William wrote to Eloise soon after she became engaged and he probably had started courting his future wife Ruth. He had apparently failed

FIGURE 1.3 Washington Allston, *William Ellery Channing*, 1811, oil on canvas. Museum of Fine Arts, Boston, Gift of William Francis Channing, 97.65 (Photograph © 2015 Museum of Fine Arts, Boston).

to respond to several of her letters, and she expressed her concern that he no longer cared for her. To the contrary, he explained, "You hold the same place in my heart as ever, & I can now say to you with more propriety than before, that few hold a higher."[39] Now that the two had romantic partners, William felt more comfortable expressing his affection for her. Eloise wrote him soon after, on the departure of her fiancé on some sort of dangerous trip, with heart-rending emotion. On a page smudged with tear drops, she told him that sometimes she felt "the bitterest & most hopeless anguish." Yet "the contemplation of your prospect of life," she continued, referencing his upcoming marriage, "has more than once check'd the tide of selfish sorrow & dried such tears as are now bedewing my page."[40]

But William was more than a source of emotional comfort for Eloise: he was a much-needed advisor and mentor. Her mother had passed away in 1807, she had no older brothers, and her father was ill (and unable to financially support the family). Burdened, along with her sister and fellow teacher Nancy, with the responsibility of providing for her family, Eloise asked William to serve as her advisor via correspondence when he returned to Boston. William described for Eloise "the office you have assigned me" as that "of watching over you, counselling & guiding you." He, in turn, expressed "an earnest desire to aid you in the ascent to wisdom, virtue, honor & immortality."[41] This became even more important to Eloise after she left Newport for New York at the end of 1810. When she was offered an opportunity to return to Newport, she leaned on William for advice. "My family are so far from me that I cannot consult them," she explained, and she wanted "judicious counsel" before she acted. The idea that he had had a positive influence on Eloise's character and mind was to William "one of my most pleasing thoughts," offering him an emotional return on the investment of his time and counsel.[42]

Their letters over the course of five years were often lengthy discussions of Eloise's career prospects, educational theory, and religious principles. Eloise took advantage of the attention of one of New England's leading theologians to discuss sermons she had heard and "express my thought with a freedom which you have always kindly encouraged."[43] She also discussed her challenges in finding work and in teaching itself, while he responded frankly and at times critically. He wanted her to do the same; in response to one letter when she praised him highly, he replied that he would prefer that she "had set before me the weaknesses, defects, disproportions, blemishes which must have forced themselves on so discerning an eye." Honest criticism, he continued, was the "highest & most disinterested office of friendship."[44] It was an office that he performed regularly with his female friends and that they in turn would perform for him.

Although William was Eloise's mentor, this did not necessarily make her a subservient figure in a hierarchical relationship.[45] Relationships like theirs were still friendships based on mutuality and reciprocity, premised on an egalitarian exchange between a man and a woman. Eloise and William were not related, and while he might take on the role of an elder brother or father, she was not beholden to him legally or emotionally. A female friend was not obligated to follow a male friend's advice, and often there were negotiations to come to an agreement on the best course to take. A friendship between a man and woman, even when the man served as a mentor, thus gave a woman the opportunity to engage as a man's equal, the freedom to shape the relationship to suit both of their needs, and the choice to leave the friendship if it no longer suited her.

Eloise made her relationship with William a partnership in which she relied upon him but also asserted her independence. She was careful to stipulate that while she wanted his advice and support, "I wish to avoid any thing like solicitation or patronage." She often tested out her ideas about religion and asked him for feedback and instruction. In response to one letter in which he criticized her views, she responded meekly, "I am a mere enquirer after religious truth & determin'd to listen to it in the spirit of docility & affection."[46] Yet letter after letter showed Eloise to be spirited and independent, chastening Channing when she felt he was unfairly judgmental. His mentorship and friendship with Eloise was a constant negotiation between her desire for his advice without his judgment, and his desire to guide without offending her.

An exchange between Channing and Payne in late 1810 or early 1811 illustrates this negotiation at its most intense. Eloise wrote Channing asking for advice about taking a teaching position in Newport. He first criticized her lack of initiative as a teacher, implying that she was too sensitive and vulnerable to be successful. Channing felt that Eloise should not "be confined to the drudgery of a common school" and that by taking his advice, she could "not only be one of the most *useful* women (I fear this encitement will be too faint) but you *may become* one of the most *distinguished* in the country." His next letter chided her for accepting the Newport job on the condition of better pay, for "I feared that you might be considered *too* desirous to make your establishment lucrative."[47] It was this last judgment that appears to have set Eloise off.

Angered by Channing's words and tone, Eloise wrote a lengthy reply to Channing defending her actions. She asked how he thought she could become such a great and active teacher when she was so often ill and confined to a sick room by her doctor. But it was the financial claim that most disturbed her.

> I did not look very sober at the passage in your letter which covertly accused me of being guided chiefly by mercenary views—a perfect conviction that I did not deserve it, preserv'd the composure of my features. . . . It is not an easy thing my dear Sir, for a young & solitary female to assert & maintain her own right, unsustained by friends, whose duty & inclination equally lead them to shield her from injustice & censure. . . .
>
> The rage of accumulation has never yet disturb'd my tranquility tho' the profession of competence is with me an object of desire—& the certainty that in a few months the dependence of my family will exclusively center in my exertions, may excuse a degree of anxiety.[48]

It is clear that Eloise could barely maintain her calm in refuting Channing's charges. Channing, in response, was apologetic. He admitted that "in the office you assigned me of watching over you," he had made some mistakes. "I cannot fear to think," he wrote, "that I have oppressed a mind languid with sickness, & fainting under many sorrows."[49]

Their negotiated friendship of mentor and mentee continued over a number of years, with Channing guiding and occasionally offending Eloise, but always offering his affection and support. Ultimately Channing changed in response to Eloise's criticisms, noting at the end of one polite letter, "You see how many fine things I have learned to say." He felt that the negotiations had not detracted from their friendship: "The kind regard which you have ever expressed tow[ar]ds me, notwithstanding my frequent admonitions has strengthened the friendship which I bear you, & has convinced me that you are worthy of reproof." Channing only wanted to mentor a woman he found worthy (of both caring about and criticizing), suggesting, if not equality, at least respect and appreciation.[50]

While Eloise died at a young age and never had a chance to realize great achievements as a writer and teacher, another of Channing's female protégées was the successful writer and reformer Elizabeth Palmer Peabody. Peabody, who grew up in a home where all the men were "failures, seducers, or tyrants," met Channing and began turning to him for guidance at only thirteen. Ten years later, when they were living near each other, she spent every evening at his home with him and his family.[51] He provided her spiritual and practical guidance, as he had for Eloise, and shaped her thinking about religion, teaching children, transcendentalism, and philosophy. Despite being old enough to be her father (and in many ways taking on the role of one), Channing's friendship with Peabody was characterized by "reciprocity and intensity."[52] She helped publish his work and wrote and published a book in tribute to him, *Reminiscences of William Ellery Channing*. Peabody went on to associate with leading minds such as Ralph Waldo Emerson, Bronson Alcott, Horace Mann, Margaret Fuller, and Nathaniel Hawthorne, but it was Channing who was "her first and most powerful mentor."[53]

Surrogate Family

Women without husbands, fathers, or brothers often valued male friends who could take on the role of surrogate brothers or husbands. Judith Sargent Stevens wrote to William Ellery Channing's precursor, the Unitarian minister John Murray, "with the freedom of a sister, conversing with a brother whom she entirely esteems."[54] She so relied upon him that when her brother Winthrop fell dangerously ill, she turned to him rather than to her husband or another relative to tell her mother. Judith knew that her mother was unwell and that her friend John Murray would deliver the news gently; "you will pity, you will sympathize with her," Judith explained. She knew this favor was a lot to ask from a friend, even as close a friend as Murray. She seemed frustrated in her note to him at having to ask such a favor, admitting, "I know it is a painful task which I impose." It was also a task that Judith felt went outside of the bounds of the usual exchanges between them, but it was not the first time. "What taxes have you not already paid," Judith wrote, suggesting that he had contributed more in the balance of their friendship than she had.[55]

An even more pronounced case of a man taking on a familial role for a female friend was that of the widow Delia Bryan and her friend John Randolph of Roanoke. When Bryan's husband died, Delia put her sons under Randolph's direction. Randolph, known more for his haughty, erratic, and vindictive behavior in Congress than for his capacity for tender friendship, was already a surrogate father to his sister-in-law Judith Randolph's fatherless sons. Randolph had a number of young men living under his guidance, allowing him to become a patriarchal figure despite being childless himself.[56] That women like Delia Bryan and Judith Randolph would turn their sons over to another man solved several issues for them as widows. First, women could have trouble controlling their sons without the help and male authority of a husband. Second, some worried that widows could "jeopardize the masculinity of a young son through overindulgence."[57] Delia thus chose to give her authority over her sons to her friend John. She and John discussed parenting of the boys throughout her letters, but John always had the final say; indeed, Delia had to ask him for permission for the boys to visit her.[58]

Many widows also looked to male friends for help with financial affairs after their husbands' deaths or became friends with those men who helped them.[59] It was not that widows did not know how to manage money; in fact, some wealthy widows may have been more business savvy than their husbands.[60] Elizabeth Powel, for example, had men purchase stocks for her or complete other business transactions. Her letters to men whom she saw only as business associates contain no language of friendship, but to those men who were both financial advisors and friends the letters differ. She called one such man, Edward Shippen Burd, "my amiable young friend," while she addressed a letter concerning investments to John Elliot Cresson as "my very good friend." While some letters between people who were merely business associates used this friendly terminology, Elizabeth Powel's did not.[61]

Charles and Mary

Charles Greely Loring (Figure 1.4) was anxious about leaving his fiancé Anna at home in Litchfield, Connecticut, while he ventured out to pursue his legal career. He had just completed his law degree at Litchfield Law School and was leaving Anna Pierce Brace to finish her degree at the Litchfield Female Academy. He knew that there was a constant influx of smart—and single—young gentlemen in the town who might steal Anna's affections. Fortunately,

FIGURE 1.4 William Page, *Charles Greely Loring*, c. 1840–1850, oil on canvas. Harvard Art Museums/Fogg Museum, Harvard University Portrait Collection, Gift of the children of Charles G. Loring to Harvard College, 1877, H2. (Photo: Imaging Department © President and Fellows of Harvard College).

FIGURE 1.5 *Mary Pierce*, ca. 1850, daguerrotype. Collection of the Litchfield Historical Society, Litchfield, Connecticut.

he had befriended Anna's aunt and guardian Mary Pierce (Figure 1.5). For the four long years of the engagement, from 1814 to 1818, Charles and Mary wrote each other regularly about their "dear Anna" and other mutual friends.[62]

Charles was one of many young people whom Mary Pierce befriended over the forty years she ran the Litchfield Female Academy founded by her elder half-sister Sarah Pierce in 1792. Mary was born in 1780 and, after the death of her father in 1783 and her eldest brother in 1788, it became clear that the five Pierce sisters would need to earn their own living. Mary ran the home in which she and Sarah lived and operated as a boarding home for their female students, as well as supervising their regular evening social gatherings. Young men from the law school often came to the house, and it was there that Charles likely met both Mary and Anna.

Charles was a nineteen-year-old Harvard graduate from Boston when he arrived in Litchfield to get his law degree in 1813. He, like many other Litchfield law students, met and fell in love with a student at the female academy. Anna Pierce Brace, the daughter of Mary and Sarah's sister Susan, studied there from 1811 to 1815. When her mother's health declined in 1814, she moved into her aunts' home. Around the same time, she and Charles were engaged. As a young woman, her brother John Pierce Brace recalled, Anna "was indolent and seldom roused to mental effort." With the training of her aunts and uncle (also a teacher at the school), however, Anna became "a good scholar, of uncommon strength of judgement and keeness [sic] of appreciation." Most notable, though, was her sense of humor, which made her "a capital comic actress."[63]

Some of Anna's vigor may have come from her aunt Mary, who was described by Anna and Charles's daughter Jane as having "a charming originality and force of expression." While her hair and eyes were dark, her face "lighted as she spoke, with animation and interest, so that no daguerrotype gives any idea of her." She was also known for her great kindness, having "boundless sympathy for all," and her caring manner attracted the young students of Litchfield to her.[64] Friendships between men and women in Litchfield were common, and Sarah Pierce counted among her friends the New York writer Elihu Hubbard Smith.[65] No other correspondence between Mary and male friends has been located, but the voluminous collection of her letters with Charles, filled with references to mutual friends of both sexes, suggests she had other male correspondents.

Charles was likely popular with women beyond the Pierce family, having a manner that his close friend and memoirist described as particularly suited to pleasing women. Despite having "all the elements of manliness," his friend recalled, Charles also had "the delicacy, the tenderness, the ready and affectionate sympathy which belong to women." While Charles became an eminent lawyer in Boston, arguing cases before the Supreme Court and becoming involved in social causes of the day, his greatest pleasure was in welcoming others into his home.[66] His chief difficulty throughout his life was eye problems, which is probably why he returned to his parents' home after law school and had to delay his marriage with Anna until 1818.[67]

Charles and Mary began a remarkably frank correspondence, both warm and warmly argumentative at times, when he moved to Boston in 1818. Despite frequent disagreements, it was clear that the two cared for each other. They addressed one another in their letters as "my dear friend" and signed their letters with closings such as "yours affectionately" or "your most affectionate friend." Mary declared to Charles that he had "a brother's place in my affections."[68] While he was fourteen years her junior, this was about the same age gap as between Mary and her late, eldest brother John. But unlike William and Eloise's relationship as fictive siblings, Charles did not serve in any sort of protective or advisory role to Mary. Rather, it was the reverse: Mary offered him the sort of advice and criticism that even an elder sister might be shy of giving. It was their lack of blood relation, the fact that Charles had chosen to maintain a friendship with Mary, that allowed her to take on such a forceful voice. Charles was all gratitude: in 1817 he wrote of obligations to her "which are infinitely great, and which I fear I shall never be able to repay." He could not remember having ever fully expressed his feelings for her, "yet I should feel miserable, if I did not think you knew them."[69]

Charles had largely accrued his obligations to Mary by relying on her for news of Anna during their four years apart. While he did write to Anna, as did his sisters, she was an unreliable correspondent. "I have been calling on Ann for some message to you," Mary reported to Charles in January 1816, "but can get nothing but simply 'Love'—which is not worth much to make a letter entertaining." In November of that year, she updated Charles on Anna's health and activities herself because "Ann has had a thousand excellent excuses for not writing today."[70] Even when Charles saw Anna or received letters from her, he felt that she sometimes showed "a reserve that pains me." She did not share her troubles with him, and he was concerned. Mary could reassure him that Anna still loved him and that his "efforts . . . to promote A's happiness, meet with a full and immediate reward."[71] Jane Loring Gray declared that long into her aunt's old age, Mary had a great "sympathy for young people and their romantic sentiment, to which she was always ready to listen, to understand, to help."[72] All of this she did for Charles.

She also assuaged his fears that another gentleman might usurp his place in Anna's heart during his absence. Given that many young men visited the Pierces' home, and Charles went for long periods without seeing Anna, it was a natural concern. Mary reported to Charles in the summer of 1816, in reply to a letter expressing his worries, that Charles needed to trust her. She appreciated his openness in sharing his fears and urged him "to continue it to me my dear friend I may perhaps often save your heart a bitter pang." Yet he must not write about this to Anna, as it would "greatly hurt" her. Mary then gave an example of Anna's fidelity, explaining that when one gentlemen tried to visit with Anna alone, Anna asked Mary to stay in the room, which Mary did.[73] As their marriage approached, Mary continued to remind Charles that "perfect confidence in each other" would be essential to a happy marriage. Yet in marriage, perhaps unlike courtship, happiness would also depend on "the most unreserved communication of unpleasant feelings as well as pleasant ones."[74]

Friends who wrote one another in the service of romance could also sometimes disagree over the best course, and this was certainly the case for

Charles and Mary. The two most often argued over what was best for Anna, among other subjects of dispute, for both seem to have been irritable. Jane Loring Gray recalled that "with all her kindness she [Mary] had a keen gift of criticism," perhaps bred over years of advising young people in Litchfield.[75] Charles, while not known to be critical, "was sensitive, and sometimes irritable," his friend reported. When Charles felt strongly about something, he displayed what the friend called "warmth of feeling."[76] Charles told Mary that "Never did I know one so fond of quarrelling as you seem to be," although he added "in a friendly way." Even Mary admitted to Charles that she realized "every winter since I have corresponded with you I have picked a quarrel with you."[77]

Their longest argument was over Anna's extended visit to the Loring family in Boston in 1817. To begin with, Mary disliked Charles's behavior on his visit to pick up Anna in Litchfield that June, and that was abundantly clear to him. "I was not in the least surprised," he wrote after receiving a letter from her on his return home, "that you 'did not like me' in my last visit to Litchfield." He pled that his apparent "heartless levity" was merely to raise Anna's spirits.[78] The next issue became the length of Anna's stay in Boston. It was acceptable and common practice for a young woman to visit her fiancé's family before they married to ease her transition into marriage and joining a new family. But "I fear you are making Ann appear guilty of impropriety in the opinion of the world, if not in that of your own family by making so long a visit," Mary told Charles in July.[79] He replied that there was nothing amiss and Mary was motivated by a selfish desire to have Anna at home. Mary replied with some anger and surprise: "I hardly know in what manner to reply to the letter I received from you." She held fast to her opinion and reminded him that Anna had her parents and aunts at home awaiting her return as well. But Mary often had a way of softening her strong words with teasing phrases, and she added to her list of arguments for Anna's return that "there is real danger that the world will suspect she likes you."[80]

Anna eventually returned home and Charles and Mary resumed their friendly correspondence. After Anna and Charles married in 1818, they shared what Charles's friend called a union "founded upon the sincerest mutual affection."[81] Anna bore three children before dying in 1836, but Charles remarried, was widowed again, and remarried a third time. Mary moved to Boston for some time to care for the Lorings' children after Anna's death. While there are fewer letters remaining after Anna's marriage, the latest surviving is likely from the 1850s, suggesting that the pair were friends for most of their lives.[82] In addition, letters survive from his and Anna's daughter Jane Loring

Gray until a month and a half before Mary's death in 1868.[83] This next generation of friendship was born of the long courtship that Mary had tended to and supported in the frank, open, and loving friendship she shared with Charles.

Courting Advice

Mixed-sex friendships were particularly conducive to supporting romantic relationships. Here was a case where a friend of the opposite sex could offer a perspective same-sex friends could not.[84] Friends turned to their opposite-sex companions when they were in search of both insider perspectives and in need of emotional support from somebody who might see the romantic entanglement more clearly from the other side. In some cases friends could serve as go-betweens because of rules of propriety that might separate lovers but allow space for a friendship.

Before Charles Loring became engaged to Anna Pierce, her brother John served as an intercessor for a female friend Charles had fallen for. Charles had flirted with a young Litchfield Female Academy teacher named Jane Shedden in the spring of 1813, and the two planned to continue the romance through letters when Jane went home for the summer. But Jane was concerned that Charles did not know what she called her "situation": she was the illegitimate child of a loyalist merchant whose fortune had been taken by her legal guardian. "I do not wish him to be deceived," Jane wrote to her friend John Pierce Brace that May. "I wish *you* John to tell Mr. Loring what I think & what I have written you—as much more of my former life as you please you may add."[85] Jane relied on Brace to share personal secrets with her lover, showing a great deal of confidence in her friend. Whether Brace carried out Jane Shedden's wishes is unknown; in any case, Loring shifted his attentions to Brace's sister Anna.

This role as go-between could also go on much longer; such was the role Eliza Slough played for her friend Fielding Lucas over the course of a lengthy correspondence. Lucas was in love with Eliza's best friend, Eliza Carrell. Carrell's father was against his daughter marrying Lucas, and Lucas's access to Carrell was limited. Eliza Slough had to assure Lucas that Carrell's "distant civility" toward him was the way she was forced to treat him in public, to convey updates on Carrell's health, and to advise him on how to proceed with the courtship. When Lucas worried that Carrell's father thought him "immoral and profligate," Eliza assured him that "he has respect for you" but wanted him to be more financially secure and to convert to Catholicism. Eliza demurred that "I do not presume to offer my advice upon the subject," but she made clear that she thought the conversion was the right thing to do.[86]

Lucas was not prepared to take that step, however, and it appears that Carrell's parents forbid her from seeing Lucas. During 1807 and 1808, Eliza Slough was Lucas's only channel of access to Eliza Carrell. He moved from Philadelphia to Baltimore, corresponding with Eliza in Pennsylvania. She continually advised him not to see Carrell, saying she and her friend would like to see him "were it possible to see you here without the *fear* of doing wrong." To see each other covertly for a few days and then have to separate again, Eliza argued, "would only add to your sufferings." The next month, when he again suggested meeting up in Philadelphia, Eliza reiterated her objection. Carrell was trying to remain obedient to her parents, Eliza explained, although "with a heart and affections all your own."[87] Eliza admitted that "when I disapprove of your visit to Phila I give up all selfish feelings," because she had a special friend she wanted to tell him about. Ultimately Eliza married in 1809, and Carrell wed Lucas by 1810, so if Eliza and Lucas's friendship continued it was no longer in the same form.

Ann Pinkney played a similar role as an intermediary for John Rodgers and Minerva Denison in 1803 and 1804 in Maryland. Rodgers and Pinkney were longtime friends who had grown up in Havre de Grace but were often separated by Rodgers's voyages as a commodore in the navy.[88] Rodgers first met Minerva Denison at a dinner in 1802 and fell in love with her immediately. She initially rejected Rodgers, saying she was still too young to marry, but he held out hope as he returned to sea. In 1803 he wrote his old friend Ann that, "through all the Storms of English, Italian and Spanish beauty which have alternatively threaten'd to Wreck my Constancy, my Heart has ever and without variation played me the Tune of" Minerva. He apologized for writing Ann only to inquire after Minerva, but advised her to "put only the right construction on my motives, and I am sure you will without hesitation pardon me."[89] Ann responded by explaining that there was little she could report: "I have seen your goddess but once since you left this country . . . , and as I am not her Confidant I cannot expect her to make a discovery of her heart to me." However, she comforted him by reporting that there were no other men vying for Minerva at the moment.[90]

When Rodgers returned to the United States in December 1803, he resumed his courtship of Minerva with visits from his posting at the Naval Yard in Washington, D.C. On January 11, 1804, Ann stayed up late into the cold winter night to report encouraging news about Minerva to Rodgers. After Rodgers's most recent visit to Minerva, she had revealed her true feelings for him to Ann. Minerva admitted that she had liked Rodgers from their first meeting, but since he was going to sea so soon after and might never return, she "consider'd it her duty, to at least, endeavour to supress any rising preposession while it might have been in her power." Now that Rodgers was home safely, however, she "with all honesty and candour confess'd her love and glorys in her choice." For her part, Ann concluded that she had "said enough" in her letter "to sate a man in love."[91] Indeed she had. Two days later, Rodgers wrote Minerva and signed the letter in romantic fashion "Eternally & incessantly yours." Within two months the pair was engaged.[92] Ann and John's correspondence, at least that which has been located, ends here as John's hopes come to fruition. As lifelong friends, however, it seems likely the two continued their relationship for years to come.

Single or married, young or old, men and women appreciated having friends of the opposite sex. As we have seen, mixed-sex friendships were important, meaningful, and useful relationships. Despite the many differences in place, time, and situation of these friendships, all three show the rocky but quite rewarding path to maintaining equilibrium in a relationship not bound by blood or law.

There are two important lessons to be learned from the roles men and women played for one another in friendships: one about the role of families and marriage, and another about power. To that first lesson, it is clear from the many tasks friends took on that spouses and family members could not fill all of an individual's emotional or practical needs. Historians often uncritically accept the early republic's companionate ideal and imagine marriage to be the central, all-fulfilling relationship in men's and women's lives. But married pairs could not be fulfilled only by each other, particularly when facing the legal realities of a relationship that erased women's identity and provided husbands with expansive powers if they chose to use them. Husbands and wives shared their lives with friends who could fulfill needs not met within marriage, forming bonds with other men and women in ways that linked marriages into larger webs of affiliation.

That friendships were removed from legally sanctioned power roles does not mean that issues of power were entirely absent, however. As one political philosopher notes, "there are always questions of power to settle between friends."[93] Particularly between men and women, it took careful work to create not equality of status but equality "of give and take." While these men and women cared deeply for each other, their friendships were all interrupted by disagreements. Nothing bound these friends to stay together; they could have left the relationship at any time, especially since they rarely if ever saw one another. But arguments seem to have become opportunities for adjusting the balance of power in the relationship. None of these women seems to have hesitated to fight back when she felt wronged, to express her feelings frankly and openly, and to clarify what she expected from her friend. In turn, their male friends learned from these experiences and adjusted their behavior.

What was it that made these close friendships with the opposite sex work? These pairs were not unique, because plenty of other men and women were friends in this period, as the rest of this book will demonstrate. But there are several common characteristics of these pairs that may apply in varying degrees to other pairs of friends. Perhaps most notably, Thomas, William, and Charles were all described by people who knew them as somewhat feminine. In the context of the time, this did not refer to sexual proclivities, but to a softness of demeanor, empathy, and an ability to connect with women. As Charles's biographer attested, Charles still retained qualities of "manliness": feminine qualities did not necessarily detract from manhood. The women, in turn, all had unusually sharp intellects that perhaps went beyond the intelligence thought becoming to a republican woman.[94]

These particular men and women, and perhaps others who became friends, pushed at the edges of standard manhood and womanhood in ways that were ultimately compatible. A woman with a "mannish" intellect and a man with a "feminine" demeanor could be a natural fit as friends. All three of these pairs of friends shared common interests, whether in children, politics, education, religion, or even the outcome of a romantic relationship. In some ways, these men and women were much more alike than different: intelligent, frank, strong-willed, and in need of friendship. Mutuality, reciprocity, and emotional connection overcame gender difference.

But being friends with someone of the opposite sex was not easy in an era in which people often suggested such relationships were dangerous or impossible. There were constant worries about propriety and appearances that all men and women who became friends had to overcome. The middle chapters of this book are aimed at unraveling just how so many pairs of friends managed to maintain relationships like Thomas and Abigail, Eloise and William, and Charles and Mary. Much of what they read and learned would have suggested to these men and women that such friendships were unwise, and there was no guide—no etiquette manual, no didactic novel, no universally accepted set of norms—to tell them how to be friends with the opposite sex.

2

Reading Friendship

FRIENDSHIPS BETWEEN MEN and women in this era must be understood in the context of larger discussions about behavior, expectations for men and women, and the meaning of relationships in the early republic. Those discussions occurred throughout printed literature. Etiquette books, magazine articles, novels, and poetry often addressed friendship, and literature could both reflect the norms of the time and shape the behavior of readers.[1] Of course, the interaction between literature and lived experience was always complex: how representative was a particular writer of the larger social milieu? How seriously did readers take the guidance offered by literature, and to what extent did it guide their actions? There are no easy answers. A broad look at the literature early American readers would have encountered, though, suggests a larger realm of concerns and ideas about heterosocial friendship that certainly influenced how men and women thought about and even learned to feel about these relationships.[2]

Both men and women read advice literature and novels as guides for their own behavior and how to properly express feeling, but they would have found little clarity in these sources on how to conduct a friendship between a man and a woman. Indeed, the discourse on male/female friendship was often contradictory, in some cases praising and in many others warning of the dangers of these friendships. Given that literature in this era saw both men and women as capable of friendship and as complementary parts who could join together for positive influence, it would seem that mixed-sex friendship would be depicted as a social good. However, two factors obscured the possibilities for friendship in much of the literature of the early republic. First was the preoccupation with romantic love and marriage as the pinnacle of relations between a man and a woman. Second, friendship between two men was seen as the ideal friendship, and men and women were thought to make different kinds of friends. The sole but widely read exception was in poetry.

Literature in the late eighteenth and early nineteenth centuries drew on the intertwining, transatlantic threads of sensibility and Scottish Enlightenment philosophy. Sensibility can be understood as a "mode of self" that proposed "a way of understanding and being in the world" that closely allied reason and emotion, mind and body, through perception and sympathy.[3] These linkages meant that exterior and interior worlds could influence each other and that an individual's feelings could shape surrounding individuals and even society. Sensibility thus operated between people, with particular focus on its use for creating social ties between people not bound by blood.[4] The best sources of virtuous feeling, the literature of the era argued, were elite, educated women. Men thus valued and sought out their influence. Similarly, Scottish Enlightenment philosophers saw women as a softening influence on men and socializing between men and women as good for society.[5] Prescriptive literature was often by these thinkers or influenced by them, while novelists were more often working within the culture of sensibility.

The reading material of Americans was dominated by British works, giving a transnational cast to the literary culture of this era. Americans did not read British and other European works indiscriminately, however; often, the books that were successful in America were those that more closely matched American ideals of virtue. Books that offered a different set of values—most famously, Lord Chesterfield's etiquette guide—were roundly condemned as improper reading for a republic. Novels in particular were screened or even altered for American audiences.[6] Since literature provided models of feeling, character, and virtue for Americans, reading materials had to be suitable for a republic. The content of the work, rather than the nationality of the author, served as the measure here. Thus, while actual friendships between men and women in Europe might not be models for American behavior, carefully chosen literary sources most certainly were.

In much of the literature on both sides of the Atlantic, ideas about women as proper companions emerged simultaneously with the valorization of romantic desire in the late eighteenth century. This vision of romantic companionship left little space for seeing women as friends for men; they were most often idealized as wives. Literature was a central force in the work of crafting marriage as the only acceptable relationship, helping to create the notion that men and women would always be attracted to one another. Thus, in the literature of sensibility, sex and desire too often get in the way of friendship. This was the predominant view in prescriptive literature and novels, although both offer some (qualified) examples of male/female friendship. However, these models positioned mixed-sex friendships in relation to lust and love in ways that reflected poorly on these friendships as lasting, fulfilling, and/or safe relationships. Male/female friendships that revolved around the heroine appeared to have two alternate endings: romantic love and marriage, or seduction and ruin. The only lasting, positive friendships are those that were on the sidelines of stories, either as relationships that were not central to the plot or as literary devices.

The literature in this vein provided the ideological context and backbone for valuing both friendship and the opposite sex but offered conflicting models and warnings for enacting male/female friendships. Advice gleaned through prescriptive literature and novels more often cautioned than encouraged men and women to enter cross-gender friendships. There were even exchanges of poetry published between pairs of friends, but there were no poems dedicated to describing and praising the relationship itself. In the end, the writers of this era could never reconcile the exaltation of friendship and equality with the valorization of romantic love and fears of sexual ruin when describing cross-sex relations. The same strength of feeling that was so prized was also a continual risk when at play between men and women.

Friendly Advice

Advice literature offered plentiful guidance on how men and women should act in each other's presence while rarely focusing on male/female friendships. Conduct books and periodical articles made concrete suggestions for how to judge men and women, where it was proper to meet in mixed company, and proper modes of expression and conversation. Reverend James Fordyce, whose published sermons were distributed widely in America, advised young men to "associate with a few of both sexes, who join good breeding, and liberal sentiments, to purity of mind and manners."[7] In a woman, part of this good breeding was conversing amiably, for Fordyce argued along with many of his fellow writers that conversation between the sexes was "a rich source of mutual improvement." Yet women had to avoid being witty or argumentative if they wanted to stay in a man's good graces.[8] Women also needed to remain circumspect about physical contact or flirtation with men to protect themselves from the dangers of seduction.[9] It was only in the proper display of feeling and polite conversation that women could safely benefit from and improve the men around them.

This is not to say that advice literature avoided the topic of friendship. To the contrary, in both advice literature and novels, the careful choice of friends, the benefits of friendly companionship, and the exalted love shared between friends were all topics of earnest discussion. Writers wrote paeans to pure, ideal friendship while lamenting how rare it was to find. Although many advice writers offered their own particular recipes for the ideal friendship, there was some consensus among writers in this era as to what made the ideal friendship. Drawing on Enlightenment and Christian ideals, as well as the classical ideal of the friend as a second self,[10] they identified the ideal friends as two equal, virtuous, pious individuals. Among the qualities writers frequently felt defined ideal friendships were reciprocity, mutuality, disinterestedness, esteem, affection, sincerity, and openness.[11] Hester Chapone listed the requirements as follows: "deep and sincere regard for religion," "due regard to reputation," "good sense," and "good temper."[12] Yet in her text and most others, friendship was either implicitly or explicitly defined as a relationship between two people of the same sex.

Articles on friendship as a general phenomenon universally referred to the friendship of two men and used male pronouns. "To be eminently distinguished as a friend," began a piece titled "On Friendship," "a man must, first of all be sincere." The model friendships the author went on to offer were two popular, ancient examples: Jonathan and David, and Damon and Pythias.[13] The former example emphasized the covenant between two strong male figures in the Bible who were described as "stronger than lions." David referred to Jonathan as his brother and declared that Jonathan's love for him was "passing the love of women."[14]

Another article's definition of friendship as "a warm benevolence to one or a few men" was a common one.[15] Even an article in a women's magazine in 1820 proclaimed that "A perfect friendship, as it is described by the ancients, can only be contracted between men of the greatest virtue, generosity, truth, and honour."[16] The "ancients," of course, thought women were unfit for friendship altogether.[17] There were more narrow articles on the genre of friendships between women, attempting to prove the strength of those relationships, but the literature overwhelmingly portrayed man as the ideal friend.

As late as the 1760s, the idea that women could be friends at all would have been viewed with suspicion. Classical philosophers like Cicero and Aristotle described friendship as a relationship central to individual and public life in which equals unite. But these two equals could only be men; this was a masculine ideal to be lived out in the (supposedly) all-male public sphere.[18] Scottish philosopher William Alexander pointed out in 1779 in his *History of Women* that "Montaigne, who is so much celebrated for his knowledge of human nature, has given it positively against the women; and his opinion has been generally embraced."[19] Indeed, as one of the male characters in Samuel Richardson's 1748 novel *Clarissa* explained, "Friendship, generally speaking . . . is too fervent a flame for female minds to manage: a light, that but in few of their hands burns steady, and often hurries the sex into flight and absurdity."[20]

While Americans continued to read *Clarissa* into the nineteenth century, many would not have agreed with this characterization of friendship by the 1780s. Changing visions of self and the sexes, particularly the increasing praise of women's emotional capabilities, opened the possibility that women could be friends. After acknowledging that Montaigne's views had been popular for some time, Alexander went on to say that "Friendship perhaps, in women, is more rare than among men; but, at the same time, it must be allowed that where it is found, it is more tender." Indeed, he continued, "it may be taken for granted that there is no young woman who has not, or wishes not to have, a companion of her own sex, to whom she may unbosom herself on every occasion."[21] Yet here even Alexander was cautious in his pronouncements, declaring female friendship less common than male friendship. Other writers, such as the author of a piece entitled "Female Friendship" published in 1804, argued that "it is a melancholy fact, that women of a certain age and character are incapable of sincere and lasting attachment to their own sex." "A young creature," the author continued, would provoke the jealousy of other single women around her.[22]

Writers agreed that men and women made different kinds of friends and thus that the dynamics of their friendships differed. The jealousy writers worried about between two young unmarried women was not echoed with corresponding worries about young unmarried men. Fordyce argued that, compared to young women, "young men have appeared more frequently susceptible of a generous and steady friendship for each other, than females as yet unconnected."[23] Men and women's friendships also differed because of their supposed differences in character and gender roles. Young men had their own interests to bind them together as friends, while female friends spent time together knitting, sewing, talking about clothes, and chatting during their "idle hours."[24] One writer suggested that women made better friends than men because of their greater capacity for feeling. Women's "especial manner" of "openness, sincerity, and artlessness" was "calculated to render them sincere and steadfast in friendship."[25] Indeed, women's reputation for close, emotional bonds with one another grew to the point that men modeled their own friendships on those they saw between women.[26]

This increasing value for women's friendship naturally led to the notion among some writers that men could benefit from women's companionship. Philosopher Lord Kames, Henry Home, wrote that while women were treated like animals in primitive societies, in civilized Britain "they are intended for the more elevated purposes, of being friends and companions, as well as affectionate mothers." Women were, for Kames, "delicious companions, and incorruptible friends."[27] Despite his repeated use of the terms "companion" and "friend," however, Kames wrote most often about women as wives. Only married women could serve as friends to their husband and maintain chaste social relationships with other men (although we know that he had female friends of his own).[28] For Kames and other Enlightenment philosophers, having an educated, mixed-sex society was a sign of historical progress and a tool for refining male citizens, and American writers who venerated republican womanhood agreed.[29] The woman was to be a casual companion or a wife, not a friend.

Mixed-sex society, writers agreed, would build relationships between men and women that took advantage of each other's differences for mutual improvement. A man and woman, paired together, completed each other through their complementary masculine and feminine qualities. As one woman wrote in a letter later published in an 1819 newspaper and her 1829 memoir,

> My opinion has been, that, by cultivating habits of rational intercourse between the sexes, the real good of both parties would be promoted; that the men would become more social and refined, without losing their strength, and the women more sound, without losing their gentleness.[30]

Similarly, another writer argued that women's companionship offered "patterns of delicacy" that would soften "the rough manners of man."[31]

These complementary differences led a small number of writers to advise not just spending time in company with the opposite sex but also befriending them. While such advice was quite rare, it did appear in one of the most popular advice books of the era, John Gregory's *A Father's Legacy to His Daughters*.[32] Gregory wrote "it should appear at first view more eligible for you to contract your friendships with the men." Unlike friendships between women, in which there might be the "jealousy or suspicion of rivalship," a man's friendship for women "is always blended with a tenderness, which he never feels for one of his own sex, even where love is in no degree concerned." Thus he premised his advice to befriend the opposite sex on natural gender differences. He also continued, "apply these observations with great caution." He then went on to write at even greater length about the dangers of men than he had of the pleasures of their friendship.

Another writer offered an unqualified endorsement of women's friendship for men. In a 1796 essay in *Massachusetts Magazine*, he advised his fellow male readers, "We ought therefore, perhaps, to desire the friendship of a man upon great occasions; but, for general happiness, we must prefer the friendship of a woman." While he believed that women made poor friends to each other, women had a "refined sensibility, which makes them see every thing. . . . Furnished with finer instruments, they treat more delicately a wounded heart. . . . They know, above all, how to give value to a thousand things, which have no value in themselves." In his experience, women were better for confiding in and offering comfort than male friends, and he would continue making them "the friends of [his] bosom."[33] Again, support for male/female friendship was based in difference.

There were several problems with this notion of complementarity.[34] First, an ideal friendship was based on sameness, equality, and mutuality. A complementary relationship between a man and a woman emphasized their differences rather than their similarities. James Fordyce, who published an entire sermon on the benefits men could receive from women's influence, believed that this influence grew from "that mental and moral difference of sex, which [Nature] has marked by characters no less distinguishable than those that diversify their outward forms."[35] This focus on inherent difference is unsurprising in this period, given the notion of differences leading to varied forms of friendship.[36] The other problem was a more practical one: for American writers even more so than for European ones, this complementary completion was achieved through marriage rather than friendship. Indeed, the ideology of the republican wife depended upon the woman's virtues softening the man's vices and his reason tempering her emotions.[37] This same logic should, it would seem, have applied to friendship; as historian Richard Godbeer argues, "an ideal friendship combined a woman's 'sensibility' with a man's 'judgment.' "[38] Yet the overwhelming focus on marriage largely obscured the possibility that this completion could occur through friendship alone.

In fact, it was far more common for writers to declare that friendships between men and women were unlikely or impossible rather than to present them as desirable. Those same complementary differences could, in some writers' eyes, make men and women too dissimilar to become friends:

> The distinctions which nature has established between the sexes, and the different occupations which they are led to pursue in this life, have all a tendency to dispose men and women to enter into habits of intimacy with persons of their own sex, in preference to those of the other.[39]

This writer argued for an indisposition to male/female friendship rather than its impossibility. It simply seemed illogical to him that the natural differences between men and women could be overcome to allow for friendship.

For most writers, though, it was romantic attraction or at least the suspicion of it that got in the way. The argument that romantic attraction prevented successful friendships between men and women was built on ideas about the natural emotions arising between men and women rather than issues of compatibility. As one author opined, "The sexes were not created only to gaze on each other." Inevitably, a man and woman who became friends would feel "such additional sensations of a softer kind, as the Omnipotent has destined the one sex to impart, the other to imbibe."[40] The author of an advice book for young women declared friendship "a passion too refined" to be held between people of the opposite sex. "In spite of every resolution to the contrary," he continued, "it must repine into love, or degenerate into lasciviousness."[41] A relationship might start as a friendship, but it could not remain in that state because of the forces of romantic attraction. It could become love, which could be a fine outcome if the feeling was mutual, or it could become lust and immoral sexuality. The idea that men and women would unavoidably be attracted to one another suggested a narrowed imagination of relations between the sexes. That narrowness led to summary judgments of relationships between men and women. As another author noted, "Such . . . is the natural suspiciousness of mankind, that we cannot concede to woman any feelings of regard for the other sex, independent of those of love."[42]

Thus for many writers, all friendships between men and women must be platonic attachments, meaning friendships with an element of unconsummated romantic love. Those were dangerous in themselves, for, as Mary Wollstonecraft argued, "Nothing can more tend to destroy peace of mind, than platonic attachments." While she was one of the few writers who did believe that men and women could be friends, she worried that, "if a woman's heart is disengaged, she should not give way to a pleasing delusion, and imagine she will be satisfied with the friendship of a man she admires, and prefers to the rest of the world."[43] A platonic friendship could easily turn into a case of unrequited love.

Richard Steele offered a similar argument in Paper 400 of *The Spectator*, which was first published on June 9, 1712. American audiences read *The Spectator* well into the nineteenth century, and the similarities between this 1712 piece on platonic love and those by later authors suggest a long history of skepticism of the notion of Platonism in friendships. He had, he wrote, "a low Opinion of *Platonick* love" and wanted to warn his readers against it.

Women "have no Manner of Approbation of Men," Steele wrote, "without some Degree of Love." Platonic friendships often ended in "Disasters" and had "fatal Effects."[44] Novels like *The New Heloise* and *The Sorrows of Young Werther* dramatically displayed the risks inherent in romantic friendships.

Another consideration against close friendships between men and women was that spending too much time with women could render men effeminate. This did not argue entirely against men's friendships with women, but certainly against close friendships in which a man and woman spent a good deal of time together. William Alexander warned in his *History of Women* that "Too much of their company will render us effeminate, and infallibly stamp upon us many signatures of the female nature." Some feminine influence was necessary to avoid falling into "rough and unpolished behaviour, as well as slovenliness of person," but that influence must be felt in moderation. "By spending a reasonable portion of our time in the company of women, and another in the company of our own sex," Alexander continued, "we shall imbibe a proper share of the softness of the female, and at the same time retain the firmness and constancy of the male."[45]

In an article offering advice on the "Art of Conversation" in a Philadelphia newspaper in 1801, the author similarly notes that men could pick up "elegant softness" from women but should be cautious:

> Lest to th'effeminate, *heedless, you decline:*
> *Be on your guard, the proper bounds to fix;*
> *Never their foibles, with their graces mix:*
> *Their friv'lous small-talk shun, and vanity,*
> *Passion for trifles bord'ring on insanity . . .*[46]

As another Philadelphia writer warned, "the mind receives an effeminate taint" when a man spends too much time with women.[47] Men who befriended women had to find a balance between the benefits and dangers of female influence.

The effects of female friendship could also be pernicious: the wrong sort of female friend could gravely endanger a man. In his sermon on the benefits of women's influence on men, Fordyce advised men to choose their female companions carefully, as "the company of artful women is always dangerous and often fatal." Men who became rakes and seducers often admitted, Fordyce said, "that they were first led astray by bad women." To avoid such "bad women," men had to be careful about where they spent their time; "gay resorts" and "genteel company" were not the best venues for finding good women. Men "should converse only with the daughters of Virtue."[48] But this sort of dire warning of men's downfall at the hands of women was unusual; most often, the concern was the reverse.

Seduced by Friendship

The risk most often portrayed in both advice literature and novels was the seduction of women by men who pretended to be their friends. The literature warned that men could use the term "friend" to seduce young women, drawing them into a seemingly innocuous relationship as a ruse for taking sexual advantage of them. This strategy made sense considering the varied meanings of the word "friend." Such was the ambiguity of the term, and thus the opportunity for its manipulation, that John Gregory warned female readers "Thousands of women of the best hearts and finest *parts* have been ruined by men who approached them under the specious name of friendship."[49]

Gregory's warning, coming immediately after his discussion of the benefits of friendships between men and women, spoke to the trepidation felt even by proponents of such friendships. Many authors of advice literature offered comparable warnings. In a book similar to Gregory's, a gentleman author offered advice to his young niece including cautions against male treachery in friendship: "Beware then, Susanna, of friendship from a man." A man might "assume the mask of friendship" in order to seduce her. So as to convince the young Susanna that these risks were real, he offered an example of an acquaintance giving him advice on dealing with a young woman: "If she is not to be gained by the common modes, make a pretension of being her friend." The author saw this as a prime example of friendship being "prostituted to screen the most infamous purposes."

The false appearances and words of men endangered girls who were not on their guard. Susanna Rowson's didactic novel *Mentoria* warned "the helpless fair":

> *In friendship with the other sex,*
> *Be cautious, they are apt to vex.*

Such friendships were "apt to vex" because men would use the screen of friendship and platonic love as "a phantom in the way/ To lead poor thoughtless girls astray."[50] Writers of both advice literature and novels were attempting to inculcate careful discernment in women who now had unprecedented freedoms in choosing their mates and spending time with men.

Even more than advice literature, the seduction novel was widely used for this didactic purpose.[51] These stories offered a bleak warning about the unintended consequences of friendships between men and women. This is the case in one of the most popular seduction stories in early national America, *The Coquette*. The tragic heroine Eliza falls in love with Major Sanford, who her friends worry (correctly) is a rake. Once he marries another woman for money rather than love, he attempts to retain his connection to Eliza by asking her to be friends with him. Eliza innocently believes Sanford to be sincere, writing to a friend:

> The substitution of friendship in the place of love for Major Sanford, I find productive of agreeable sensations. With him, he assures me, it is a far more calm, and rational pleasure. *He* treats me with the affection and tenderness of a brother; and his *wife*, who exceeds him in professions of regard, with all the consoling softness, and attention of a sister.[52]

Eliza not only calls the relationship a friendship but also invokes two of the strategies real men and women used to safely position male/female friendships. First, she compares him to a brother, using the language of family to suggest that the relationship is not sexual. Second, she refers to his wife, drawing the presence of a third party into the friendship. For a successful friendship, spouses were a necessary addition to the relationship to ensure its propriety.

However, Eliza's friends can see clearly through Sanford's positioning of the relationship as a friendship, remarking that Eliza "is flattered into the belief that his attention to her is purely the result of friendship and benevolence." Her friend Julia concludes "I have not so favorable an opinion of the man, as to suppose him capable of either."[53] Julia knows that Sanford is not a virtuous man and rightly suspects that he still has designs on Eliza. He is not the sort of man, Julia believes, who would spend time with a woman who was not going to go to bed with him. Eliza's friends are suspicious in part because of Sanford's inappropriate behavior: he makes long daily visits and spends time alone with Eliza. His wife does not accompany him, and there is no third-party chaperone. A man and woman who spent time alone were highly suspect.

Eliza's choice to reject a suitable offer of marriage in order to continue her dangerous friendship with Major Sanford and other men ultimately leads to her demise.[54] While literary scholar Ivy Schweitzer proposes that the novel "proffers a discourse of 'equalitarian friendship' as social alternative to unequal and privatizing Federalist marriage,"[35] this alternative model is shown to be quite risky. Sanford's friendship is not genuine because he is a rake and because he is in love with Eliza, and he uses the friendship as a pretense to seduce the vulnerable young woman and impregnate her. It is just as one of the advice writers had warned: friendship was "prostituted to screen the most infamous purposes." Eliza runs away from her family and Sanford in disgrace to give birth to her child and die alone and friendless, a result of her friendship with a man.

Similarly, Lady Caroline Lamb's novel *Glenarvon* depicts a heroine who is seduced by a man's claims of friendship. The rake Glenarvon tells the heroine, Calantha, that "there will be no danger in my friendship." Before long, Glenarvon is kissing her and singing her a love song. Calantha, a married woman and more aware than Eliza of the danger of the situation, tells Glenarvon to stop singing and admits that "I am lost irretrievably lost" if he should pursue an affair with her. Glenarvon responds by asking Calantha to trust him and "henceforward consider me only as your friend." Letting Glenarvon's expression contradict his words, the narrator adds, "He smiled in scorn as he said this."[36]

Calantha's friends, too, worry about her relationship with Glenarvon from its inception. The narrator reports that Calantha's friends reproached her for the time she was spending with Glenarvon. In response, she "boldly avowed her friendship for Glenarvon, and disclaimed the possibility of its exceeding the bounds which the strictest propriety had rendered necessary."[37] Calantha knows she is in love with Glenarvon, but she, too, adopts the word "friend" as a cover for a romantic and later sexual relationship. While "friend" could be a word for a lover, this is not how either Eliza or Calantha use it.

In *Glenarvon*, the lovers continue to use the term "friend" to refer to each other, confusing the categories of friend and lover. At one point the narrator reports that Calantha "saw her lover—her friend more than ever united to her." Soon after, Glenarvon asks Calantha to run away with him. He offers her a ring that he calls "a marriage bond" yet tells her to "Lean not upon a lover's bosom, but upon a friend, a guardian and protector."[38] It may be that Glenarvon is trying to cast the relationship as a companionate marriage, in which lust and strong passion had no place and the husband was indeed friend, guardian, and protector of his wife. These are precisely the roles that Calantha's own husband has not been fulfilling for her, roles that were perhaps even more important to her than that of a lover. Ultimately, Glenarvon leaves Calantha and writes to tell her that he is no longer her lover, but her friend. Even here the use of "friend" is specious, for in the next line, he writes "as a first proof of my regard, I offer you this advice, correct your vanity, which is ridiculous; exert your absurd caprices upon others; and leave me in peace."[59]

Even more pernicious than Glenarvon is the character of Belcour in *Charlotte Temple*, who unlike Sanford or Glenarvon never has feelings for the heroine. Charlotte has already been seduced by Montraville and left alone in a small cottage when his friend Belcour comes to visit her. He hopes to take advantage of Charlotte's fear and vulnerability, attempting to befriend her so that he, too, can seduce her. The narrator explains that Belcour "was determined, if possible, to make her his mistress," but when he visited Charlotte, "he assumed the look of tender, consolatory friendship."[60] Montraville, who truly loved Charlotte, never donned the mantle of friendship to seduce her. It is men like Belcour, Glenarvon, and Sanford, who seem more interested in sex than love, who are the real rakes. And one of their favorite tools of seduction is pretending to befriend their intended victims.

What would have been most chilling for readers of *The Coquette* and *Glenarvon* was the knowledge that both were based on real stories of friendship and seduction. The former was based on the story of Elizabeth Whitman. Elizabeth, like *The Coquette*'s Eliza, chose to remain unmarried but was eventually seduced and died. Elizabeth was friends with a number of men, including Joel Barlow, whom she playfully referred to as her husband.[61] It is unknown who ultimately seduced Elizabeth, but in *The Coquette* Hannah Foster suggests that it was just such a flirtatious friendship with a man that could be a woman's undoing. *Glenarvon*'s author, Caroline Lamb, wrote the book as a tell-all about her affair with the poet Lord Byron (he called it a "F— and publish").[62] Thus, readers would have taken these stories seriously as cautionary tales.[63] Mixed-sex friendship, in the world of the seduction novels, led not to virtue but to ruin and corruption.

Novel Models

There were more positive literary models for friendships between men and women, but these models were generally weak and not held up as exemplars of virtue. Sensibility novels used these friendships primarily as narrative devices or precursors to marriage rather than long-lasting, fulfilling relationships that could drive the plot of a story. The latter was reserved for same-sex friendships and romantic relationships. The new and growing focus on romantic love and the preoccupation with sexuality in this era, combined with sensibility's focus on reform through feeling, likely explains why male/female friendships were marginalized in these novels.

When male/female friendships were portrayed as lesser relationships taking place in the background of the story, they often served as devices to set the plot in motion or offer the reader access to the hero or heroine's feelings.[64] While on the surface this role for friendships diminishes their importance, what are we to make of the "enabling" part they play? If a friendship between a man and woman is necessary to telling the story, it has at the very least narrative importance. However, the overwhelming focus on the romantic relationships at the center of these stories obscures the male/female friendships and leaves them as instrumental rather than emotionally important. Thus, despite the implicit critique of these friendships as inconsequential, they prove to be necessary to holding together both the plot and the reader to the text in some novels.

The mixed-sex friendship as literary device appeared in novels in which the central narrative voice was telling a story that focused on a character of the opposite sex. The British novel *Ela: or, The Delusions of the Heart* (published in Boston in 1790) tells a typical tale of an innocent young woman who is seduced and abandoned. Unlike other seduction tales, the story is told through the voice of a young man named Mortimor in letters to his sister Caroline. Mortimor had befriended Ela and the man he presumed to be her husband, Henry Dormer. When Mortimor discovers that Dormer had never married Ela and has abandoned her, he offers her his aid. Ela calls Mortimor "My best, my only friend!" and "my inestimable friend, my more than brother."[65] Yet readers know very little about Mortimor, and even less about his friendship with Ela. The friendship is simply a device to allow Mortimor to tell Ela's sad tale, although without this friendship the story could not be told.

The narrator of Robert Bage's *Hermsprong*, Mr. Glen, is similarly elusive. His name rarely appears in the narrative; the story he has to tell is about his friend Caroline Campinet. He is also friends with the male lead, Hermsprong, allowing him to take the role of omniscient narrator with some semblance of credibility. Glen admits that his relationship with Caroline is a casual and admiring friendship; he was "admitted sometimes to her tea-table," played violin in accompaniment to her piano playing, and loaned her books and music. He suggests that he had "a spiritual affection" rather than romantic love for her, only because he felt she was too far above him to even think of romantically.[66] This is all we know about their relationship, although we can infer he was admitted into her confidence because of the information he has access to in telling the story. It is the story of Caroline's relationship with Hermsprong that Mr. Glen intends to tell, though, not his own.

Male/female friendships can also allow for a heroine's change of scene and thus set the story in motion. In Frances Burney's *Evelina*, Evelina's guardian, Reverend Villars, sends her to stay with his friend Lady Howard. This friendship is what initially removes Evelina from the seclusion of her home, sparking her transformation as she enters London society, but Villars and Howard's friendship is only demonstrated through half a dozen opening letters among the hundreds in the novel.[67] Similarly, in *Caroline of Lichtfield*, Caroline's father asks "his dear friend the Baroness and Canoness of Rindaw" to take care of his daughter. The Baroness was "pleased with the proposal" and "she promised eternal friendship, offered to take his daughter under her care, and educate her till the time of marriage . . ."[68] Thus Caroline, too, is sent to a new setting where her adventures and romance can begin.

In Maria Edgeworth's *Belinda*, Belinda's guardian Lady Delacour has a close friendship with a young gentleman named Clarence Hervey that also proves useful for the plot. She feels "the most sincere friendship" for him and he spends a great deal of time at her house. That relationship is what allows Belinda and Hervey to be in each other's presence frequently, without suspicion that Hervey is courting Belinda but nonethless providing the space for them to fall in love. While the story is told primarily from Belinda's perspective, the reader is often privy to Lady Delacour's conversations with Hervey. Thus both the hero and heroine express thoughts on their budding relationship in their conversations with Lady Delacour. The novel could work without Lady Delacour and Hervey's friendship, but the relationship makes the writer's work of plotting meetings and revealing feelings much simpler and more natural.

Belinda's relationship with Clarence Hervey demonstrates another model of male/female friendship in fiction, that of the romance that begins in friendship. Even female authors of the era who endowed their heroines with an unusual degree of autonomy took marriage to be the only possibility for a happy ending, woman's "natural and only destiny."[69] Companionate marriage in this era was the pinnacle of fulfillment, happiness, and gender identity. Marriage was, in one scholar's words, "the structure that maintains the Structure."[70] For a novel to suggest that friendship between a man and a woman could bring fulfillment and even love would have challenged this structure. It also would have subverted the typical narrative structure in which marriage—or its tragic counterpart, seduction—closes every story.

Thus, if the author wanted to wrap the novel up neatly and happily, a friendship between the heroine and a man was not enough; it must turn into romance and marriage. Novels like *Belinda*, *Evelina*, and *Emma* followed the narrative structure of the traditional novel ending in marriage, represented in the tragic form of the seduction story or the comic form of the courtship novel.[71] In courtship novels, women have some modicum of choice rather than playing the innocent victim, but the inevitable ending is in marriage.[72]

Even if the women in these novels are friends with the men they marry for the majority of the story, readers turned to such novels with a blueprint of the ending in mind. As a character in Susanna Rowson's *The Inquisitor* mused, it seemed curious that writers "could find no other subject to employ their pens, but love." He continued, "I wonder that the novel readers are not tired of reading one story so many times, with only the variation of its being told in different ways."[73] The predictable structure of these novels meant that readers would have known all along that romantic love rather than friendship was the inevitable—and desirable—outcome of the story. In these three particular novels, too, by the end it is revealed that these women were in love with their male friends all along, reinforcing the notion that a friendship between a man and a woman must result in attraction.

For example, in *Belinda*, there is an attraction between Belinda and Hervey early in the novel, but Hervey will not admit to any romantic feelings. When Lady Delacour asks him whether he is in love with Belinda, he laughs and tells her "it is not come to *that* with me yet, Lady Delacour, I promise you." He continues, "is not it possible to say that a young lady has dignity of mind and simplicity of character without having or suggesting any thoughts of marriage?"[74] Hervey challenges the assumption that any regard for the opposite sex is necessarily an attraction, but his love becomes clear as the novel progresses. Belinda, in turn, has feelings for Hervey that she attempts to suppress. She sees that he is "mortified and miserable if she treated him merely as a common acquaintance, yet she felt the danger of admitting him to the familiarity of friendship."[75] To show friendship could provide an opening to warmer feelings and put her at risk of falling in love with a man about whose character she is still unsure. In contrast, when she first meets Mr. Vincent, she feels more comfortable around him because "she considered him as a person who wished for her friendship, without having any design to engage her affections." The narrator goes on to say that Belinda was not a young woman "who sees in every man a lover, or nothing"; friendship with a man was a possibility in Belinda's mind.

However, Belinda cannot sustain a friendship with Hervey or Vincent. Both men fall in love with her, and she falls in love with Hervey (and tries earnestly to do the same with Vincent). The only man she can be friends with is the much older Dr. X, who is not a main character in the story. That Belinda's two most important friendships with men end in romantic feelings on at least one side suggests that a friendship between a man and woman of the same age is impossible. Edgeworth presents Belinda's belief that male/female friendships are possible as one of Belinda's virtues, yet then proves Belinda wrong. It was a virtue for a young woman to consider men as potential friends rather than objects of flirtation, but once a firm friendship was formed, love was inevitable on one or both sides.

The same stories of friendship ending in love characterize the romances of Emma and Evelina in their eponymous novels. Jane Austen's Emma is, until the final pages of the book, friends with her neighbor, Mr. Knightley.[76] As literary scholar Ruth Perry has pointed out, Emma suffers "the repeated frustration of women's friendships in a novel that emphasizes the importance of friendship."[77] She cannot bring herself to be friends with the elegant and intelligent Jane Fairfax, she loses her friend Mrs. Weston to marriage, and differences in class and intellect prevent a deep and lasting friendship from growing with Harriet Smith. The only friendship that ends well, then, is the friendship with Mr. Knightley—which ends in romance and marriage.

Unlike Belinda, Emma is unaware that she has long had feelings beyond friendship for Mr. Knightley until the final chapters of the book. It is not that Emma is missing the obvious; Knightley treats her with a fraternal sort of love.[78] Thus, when Mr. Knightley asks her to dance at a ball, she remarks that "we are not really so much brother and sister as to make it at all improper." The novel has numerous relationships between men and women that are described as friendships but suspected to be romantic relationships by those around them: Emma and Mr. Elton, Mr. Knightley and Jane Fairfax, Emma and Frank Churchill. When Emma's brother-in-law suggests that Mr. Elton might be attracted to her, she replies airily, "Mr. Elton and I are very good friends, and nothing more." That friendship, like all of the others in the book, does not last very long. Indeed, until the moment of his declaration, Emma calls Mr. Knightley her friend. Believing he is about to announce his affections for her friend Harriet Smith, Emma tells him, "If you have any wish to speak openly to me as a friend . . . as a friend, indeed, you may command me."[79]

Like Belinda and Emma, Evelina and her romantic interest, Lord Orville, are friends throughout most of the book. Orville is reluctant to succumb to his affections for Evelina, and Evelina is naively unaware that her feelings for Orville go beyond friendship. He positions himself as her friend, stepping in to protect her when another man is harassing her and entreating her to "allow *me* to be your friend." He goes on to tell her to "think of me as if I were indeed your brother" in order to demonstrate a lack of romantic attachment.[80] But

Evelina's guardian is worried from her letters home that Evelina already sees Orville as more than a friend. When Reverend Villars warns her of the danger of her attachment to him, she exclaims in response: "Oh Lord Orville! could I have believed that a friendship so grateful to my heart, so soothing to my distresses,—a friend which, in every respect, did me so much honour, would only embitter all my future moments!"[81] Villars is worried that Orville will seduce his young charge, but the story ends with Orville marrying Evelina. He declares his love for her in terms of a very different sort of friendship, telling her "you are the friend to whom my soul is attached as to its better half!"[82] Here the nonromantic friendship becomes a romantic one without even the need for a change in terminology, suggesting the easy and inevitable transition from friendship to romantic love and marriage.

Poetic Friendships

There was one narrow genre of literature, however, in which friendships between men and women took center stage: published poetic exchanges between men and women in magazines. Yet these poems, like the novels, offered only weak models of these relationships. That is because this poetry was more about displaying literary skill and emotion than about actual friendships between men and women; indeed, sometimes the writers did not know each other, and sometimes female pen names hid the identity of a male writer. Because of this, poetic exchanges between the figures of the male and female writer could revel in emotion without worrying about whether a friendship between a man and woman might lead to a woman's moral downfall. There was also less fear than with novels that the readers of such poetry would be negatively influenced; in fact, poetry was widely lauded as proper reading material for young women.[83] Thus it is quite likely these poetic, emotional models of male/female friendship were considered to be entirely socially acceptable. Reading poetry, like novels, could model behavior and feeling for men and women, but they might also write, transcribe, or receive poems. As hackneyed or saccharine as some of the poetry of this era might seem to readers today, poetry was a powerful force for men and women in early America.[84]

Poetic exchanges thus presented a sentimentalized but generic model of mixed-sex friendship. In 1787 the British poets Robert Merry and Hannah Crowley began a lyrical exchange in the newspaper *The World* under the pen names of Della Crusca and Anna Matilda that would later be reprinted widely in American papers. The two had never met, but their poems constructed a flirtatious friendship. Whereas women were previously the subjects of poetry for men, with this new genre of "Della Cruscan" poetry, women became "agents in the poetic exchanges."[85] Other men and women, including noted British poets Mary Robinson and Samuel Taylor Coleridge, also took up the form. Yet as much as these poetic exchanges were a give and take, they were also more focused on the writers' own feelings than on the exchange itself.[86] Indeed, when Merry and Crowley finally met after two years of printed poetic conversation, the meeting was a disappointment.[87]

Della Cruscan poetry was ultimately more interested in modeling a sentimental, even romantic relationship than in building an actual friendship. Literary critics have, understandably, focused on the uses of this poetry to build poetic careers and to engage another poet's work.[88] Writing such poetry was a way to get published, as was writing about male friends. One critic argues that this poetry uses "mental eroticism" and involves "sex in the head," because the flirtation is essentially between the expressions of imagination in verse.[89] Anna Matilda opens her first poem to Della Crusca: "Seize again thy golden quill/And with its point my bosom thrill;/With magic touch explore my heart/And bid the tear of passion start."[90] But whether these poems were about mental eroticism or publicity (or more likely, both), these lines of analysis only reveal what these poems meant to the two people who wrote them. For the many readers of this poetry, the exchanges displayed a sentimental, platonic relationship between a man and a woman as acceptable and even worthy of dedication to verse. If these poems were not exemplars of real relationships—and the fact that they were not led critics then and now to describe them as "false"—they did contain other truths about appropriate relationships between men and women.

Della Cruscan poetry had an immediate and long-standing resonance with American audiences. Reprints of exchanges between Della Crusca and Anna Matilda appeared in various magazines in America in the 1790s. Poems that declared themselves to be in the Della Cruscan style were printed in the following decades, and the originals were published as late as 1820 in a Philadelphia magazine. Even more widespread were poetic exchanges between men and women using romantic pen names that were unself-consciously in the same style. The forerunner of this poetry in America was Sarah Apthorp Morton, who published poems in the *Massachusetts Magazine* under the pen name "Philenia." Men replied to her poems, praising her poetry and character, and one poet in 1794 claimed both Philenia and Della Crusca as the two heirs of the classical poet Sappho.[91]

The timing was serendipitous: just as this genre of printed exchange between poetic "friends" developed, the American magazine industry expanded rapidly. With cheaper postage costs and more publications available, magazine reading spread to middling people. One study of the readership of magazines in post-Revolutionary New York finds that half of all subscribers were shop-keepers or artisans. While pieces were often geared toward women, both men and women read magazines.[92] As perhaps the most widespread form of printed literature in the era, magazines provided a broad, mixed-sex audience for Della Cruscan poetry.

The very fact that men and women both wrote and read these poetic exchanges fostered heterosociability if not close friendships. In most magazines that published poetry, there were scattered examples of poetic exchanges between men and women. But it is impossible to know, given the tradition in which these poets were writing, whether these poems were evidence of flesh and blood relationships or simply literary ones. In two special cases in Philadelphia, the *Philadelphia Minerva* in the 1790s and the *Intellectual Regale* in the 1810s, there were prolonged exchanges among a group of men and women.[93] In the case of the exchanges in the *Intellectual Regale* between 1815 and 1817, it appears that the writers may have been in the same social circle in Philadelphia and met at the editor's home.[94] As a literary model, however, the power of these poems came from their form rather than the actual relationships underpinning them.

The *Philadelphia Minerva* and *Intellectual Regale* offer two sustained examples of the way young people writing poetic exchanges took up Della Cruscan forms. Like their Della Cruscan forerunners, the American mixed-sex poetic exchanges used flowery language, ornate expressions of sentiment, and a dialogue with a poet of the opposite sex. The American examples are more friendly than erotic, eschewing the thrilled bosom of Anna Matilda for offers of supportive friendship. Indeed, many of the poets soothed their poetic friends' romantic woes by suggesting that friendship was preferable to romantic love. In one poem in 1815, "A" wrote "To Henry" that "I love thee no more" because "friendship, sweet friendship, has quite banish'd love." The friend who had accomplished this for her? Another man, Damon, "the friend I esteem and respect," whose "musical accents have power to cheer me."[95]

Some twenty years earlier in the *Philadelphia Minerva*, Albert offered to play this role for Stella, who had lost her lover Eugenius. He wrote:

> *Accept a* FRIEND; *let ALBERT share thy grief,*
> *Speak but the word, dear maid, to thy relief*
> *He flies; to soothe the anguish of your heart,*
> *With all the balm that* Friendship *can impart.*[96]

Albert's offer was infused with sensibility: grief, relief, and anguish would be softened by his friendship. As a friend, he sympathized with how she felt and offered her "the pathos of a feeling heart." The role of the feeling friend for the broken-hearted woman is one that many at the time, particularly novelists, imagined as naturally falling on another woman. But poems like Albert's show that within a culture of sensibility and sentiment, men could also play this role as men of feeling.

Poems like these offered readers a public example of acceptable expressions of friendship between men and women. But they were not concrete models that offered guidance for navigating the dynamics of a real friendship. Such guidance was notably lacking in the literature of this era, for all its praise of the complementarity between women and men. In an era when literature was such an important guide to social behavior and feeling, it was difficult for these men and women to know just how to behave in and describe these friendships. The difficulties that real men and women faced in figuring out how to maintain cross-sex friendships were due in part to the failure of contemporary literature to provide an adequate model for male/female friendships.

The literary representations of mixed-sex friendships were insufficient for imagining and describing these relationships, much less offering readers guidance.[97] Such limitations in the literature served the larger cultural project of channeling male/female relationships into marriages. The limits of the existing order must have been apparent to the many men and women who pushed its boundaries to befriend one another. To what extent did this stifle men and women's imaginations of what was possible? Certainly they found it possible to become friends, but were women on their guard against seduction (as many writers hoped they would be) with every man they befriended? Did single men and women secretly yearn or expect that their friendships would turn into love? The closure of the novel, the tragic or comic ending, was too narrow for real life, and the possible endings both more mundane and perhaps more satisfying.

3

Friends and Lovers

"FRIENDSHIP HAS NOTHING to do with sex," the naval hero John Paul Jones wrote a female friend in 1780.[1] Jones knew this was not the case, however; he was replying defensively to a friend with whom he had hoped to start an affair and who had turned him down. A well-known lothario, Jones would have been hard pressed to find a woman he had *not* flirted with or slept with. Jones was not like all men of his time, and plenty of men and women had friendships that were entirely chaste. But in a culture focused on romantic love and marriage, it was hard to escape the notion that relationships between men and women always included sexual attraction. The fact is that sex and sexual desire did often factor into male/female friendships, whether as public perception, unspoken possibility, or an acknowledged part of the relationship.[2]

Given that underlying sexual element, the line between a mixed-sex friendship and a romance was a complicated and unstable one. There was the dilemma, too, of the ideal of companionate marriage that extolled marriages based on friendship, thus collapsing the categories of romance and friendship.[3] This new cultural norm limited love between men and women to a narrow definition of romantic love. Men and women struggled over how to understand their own feelings for their friends and how to effectively negotiate the emotional status of a relationship. What constituted playful flirtation, and what signified actual attraction or even romantic love? It was an important line to distinguish, for the emotional stakes were high: men and women—and their reputations as virtuous citizens—could get hurt if feelings were not reciprocated or if passions spun out into seduction or an affair. While at a practical level emotional pain and sexual impropriety were the greatest risks of male/female friendship, at a more abstract level these friendships were risky because of the way they challenged established relationship categories like marriage and same-sex friendship as well as gender roles.

Mixed-sex friendships allowed men and women to collectively define the emotional and sexual character of a relationship. Unlike in a marriage, where a woman was relegated to a subordinate role, in a friendship a woman shared the power of defining the relationship with a man. Men and women both had the tools to control their own emotions, to signal those emotions to one another, and to decide whether to pursue a sexual dimension to the relationship. The contemporary literature that emphasized the impossibility of a safe, long-lasting male/female friendship attempted to close off this category and the space it offered for gender equality. But men and women in the early republic attended to the subtle signs they found in literature for distinguishing friendship from romance and adapted them into their own relationships, quietly reshaping the possibilities for relationships across the sexes.

Confused Feelings

It is difficult to pin down the line that divided a mixed-sex friendship from a romantic relationship, but three points are clear. First, romance and physical intimacy were not possibilities confined to friendships between opposite sexes. Evidence going back many centuries proves that same-sex friendships could also include a sexual element and, in extraordinary cases, turn into life-long romantic partnerships.[4] Second, there is a difference between emotional and physical intimacy. Many friends, whether of the same or opposite sex, used effusively sensual language in the tradition of sensibility literature to communicate emotion. The language used between friends must be read in its historical context; language that sounds romantic or even erotic to twenty-first-century readers might not have taken on these meanings to those several centuries ago. An emotionally intimate relationship between a man and a woman, even two young and unmarried people, was not necessarily romantic or physical, and the relationship could change over time. Finally, there is the issue of the elusiveness of defining sexual intimacy itself. What kind of physical intimacy is required for behavior to be classed as "sexual"?[5] For that matter, was sexual behavior always part of a romance? Thus discerning the line between a friendship and a romance is far more complex than merely documenting affectionate language.

The cultural focus on friendship in the context of romance and marriage contributed to the confusion for men and women about the status of their friendships with one another. As scholars of emotion have argued, there is a space in between a first inkling of feeling and the words used to describe the emotion.[6] With novels and advice literature depicting male/female friendship as inevitably leading to attraction, readers were conditioned to interpret their own feelings through a structure of romantic love. As the seventeenth-century writer La Rochefoucauld observed, "people would never fall in love if they had not heard of love talked about."[7] The structure of feeling[8] available constrained men and women to assume their emotions for each other must fall under the category of romance, and when that category did not fit neatly, they felt tension and confusion.[9]

Emotions are indelibly shaped by the language available to express them. Simply naming an emotion can change or clarify the feeling itself.[10] In the case of male/female friends, the words "love" and "friendship" were so broadly used, and had so many different meanings, that they were too imprecise to be of great use. Friends, lovers, and spouses had only one well of language to draw upon for describing relationships.[11] How were friends in mixed-sex pairs to understand and express their feelings without language to do so? While the French at this time used the term "amitié amoureuse," no such term to denote a loving friendship between a man and woman existed in America.[12] Historical letters and literature demonstrate the results of this language lacuna: confusion, emotional work, improvisation, miscommunication, and careful parsing of emotions. More so than other relationships with their own structures of feeling, then, men and women faced the challenge of a mutual understanding of the status of their relationships.[13]

Coming to a mutual agreement about the emotional character of a relationship was particularly difficult when men and women were unsure of how they felt or how to explain their feelings.[14] A woman's friendship with a man did not fit neatly in the structure of feeling established for relations between men and women, which emphasized romance. It is rare to find historical evidence of men and women discussing the character of their relationship, trying to pin down how each other felt. These were most likely conversations that happened in person rather than in letters, but one remarkable account of such a conversation survives in the writings of Elizabeth Peabody.

Elizabeth, born in 1804, was a New England writer and thinker who was friends with a number of men in transcendalist circles at the very start of that movement. Horace Mann, the Massachusetts politican and education reformer, moved into the boarding house where Elizabeth and her sister Mary resided in Boston in 1832. Horace, age thirty-five, had recently lost his wife and his hair had gone white with grief. In the Peabody sisters, he found intelligent friends and comforters. Elizabeth's sympathy for him went beyond words; she described how he "laid his head upon my bosom" shedding tears of grief, and at other times he sought comfort in her arms on the parlor couch. After he left the boarding house, he continued to visit the sisters, and sat with Elizabeth alone when Mary left for a lengthy trip to Cuba. Mary wrote

Elizabeth from Cuba with concerns about the propriety of Horace's visits (Mary was by now in love with Horace), but Elizabeth protested that there was nothing amiss. However, these concerns may have prompted her to the remarkably forthright discussion with Horace that she recorded for Mary.[15]

One evening in the fall of 1834, Elizabeth reported, Horace came to visit her "full of feeling and affection." They addressed the topic of "the difference between love and friendship," which Elizabeth acknowledged was "delicate." It was not an abstract question. "My friendship is a great comfort to him," she explained. "I only wanted to be sure that he would never feel that I felt more than friendship for him in order that he might have no sense of responsibleness in receiving many kind offices." Horace was apparently quite happy to hear this, and Elizabeth concluded from the discussion that "however affectionate we may be—It is a brothers & sisters love on both sides." They could continue their emotional and even physical intimacy without sexual desire intruding, Elizabeth implies.

But did Elizabeth truly see Horace as a brother? It seems that even she was unsure of how she felt, or at least could be made to feel. It could "be possible for Mr. M.- to make me love him exclusively. But I *could not* do it unless he *had* or *did* try for it," Elizabeth told her sister. Elizabeth had clearly considered the possibility of being in love with Horace, and that was not a sisterly structure of feeling. She went on to say that she knew "what the feeling of *love* is" from past experience. Having felt it before, she was confident that "deep as my interest is in Mr M—it is a totally different feeling."[16] Elizabeth's only way of understanding her feeling for Horace was in comparison to past experience. She had left the door open for Horace to change her feelings, although their discussion suggested that he did not intend to. The conversation had clarified intentions and refined the status of the relationship, but it may not have resolved how Horace or particularly Elizabeth actually felt.

More often, individuals, especially women, worked out their feelings for the opposite sex in private writings. The journal of a young woman in New Brunswick, New Jersey, named Rachel Van Dyke illustrates the confusions young women experienced as they entered the world of adult friendships and romance. There were three men with whom she was close friends throughout the diary; "Mr G—, John B[arker], and Henry Jackson—I may say—are all three, at least, my devoted *friends*" she recorded in July 1810. While she saw all three as friends, she wrote that Henry Jackson, who was then living in Europe, "loves—or thinks he loves me." Rachel felt that at their young age, Jackson "knows no more what real love is than—I do." In other words, it was entirely possible that this love was only the love of friendship or infatuation, rather than romance—but she was not confident that she or her male friends could decipher the difference.[17]

Rachel spent that summer and fall in an intense friendship with her former teacher Ebenezer Grosvenor, whom she calls "Mr. G—" in her journal. While in July she insisted to her diary that he and her other male friends "possess my warmest esteem—nothing more," by the time Mr. G—left New Brunswick in November Rachel was confused about her feelings toward him. In late November 1810, Rachel asked herself "why need I hesitate to own that I feel more than common sorrow to lose my good teacher, my Good Friend— nay I feel more than common sorrow—tho' I know not why." She attempted to answer herself by saying that she had become closer with him than any other "young gentleman" before. By February of 1811, she referred to Mr. G— as "my truest, my best, my ~ ~ ~ ~ friend." Rachel had no words to describe sufficiently her feelings. As the months passed, she frequently noted being in "the strangest of humours," alternating between liveliness and tears in the same day. Although her journal entries suggest that she did eventually fall in love with Mr. G—, there was a lengthy period during which she could not understand or articulate her feelings.[18]

The ambiguous nature of many male/female friendships gave individuals space to shape their own feelings and attempt to gain control over unwieldy affections. The 1785 diary of a young New England woman named Patty Rogers demonstrates the way one woman attempted to understand and even conscientiously mold her emotions in a friendship with a man. For Patty, an avid reader of novels, her diary was a space where she employed the language of sensibility drawn from her novel reading to process her own emotions.[19]

After splitting from a lover she referred to as Portius, Rogers formed a close friendship during the summer of 1785 with a man whom she called "Philammon." When she heard that Philammon was courting another woman, she insisted to her diary: "I only feel a friendship for him! I'll steel my heart to every sentiment of Love! & Bannish every idea of it from my mind!" Of course, had she felt secure that her only feeling for him was one of friendship, there would have been no need for her to "steel [her] heart." She seemed fearful that "*too great partiality*" would cause her to fall in love, and she insisted that her heart "knows too much to be *caught* again. *it never shall be*!" Several days later, she wrote of her concern that Philammon thought she was in love with him and protested, "I feel an ardent friendship for him, but not love!" By October of that year, she was pleased to report to her diary that with Philammon she could "now enjoy the pleasures of friendship exclusive of pain" and "look with indifference when he is *attentive* to others & yet *esteem* and *respect* him!" Yet in the very next line she warned her "*little fond foolish Heart*" not to fall in love and risk the pain she had suffered in her relationship with Portius.[20]

Patty Rogers did not merely record her feelings for Philammon in her diary. She used the act of inscribing her emotions to try to clarify these emotions for herself. She was not writing merely what she felt, but what she *wanted* to feel, using language found in novels of sensibility. This very act demonstrates the power of language to shape feelings and of the expression of emotion to affect the emotions themselves. Patty's almost obsessive writings in which she tried to shape her feelings for Philammon suggest that she feared losing control of her emotions. Without any models for a close friendship with a man, Patty was constantly worried that her feelings of friendship might be romantic. From her effusive writings about her love for Portius, it is clear that when she was in love she was fully capable of describing those feelings. In the case of Philammon, it appears that Patty wanted to reassure herself that whatever she felt for him must and should be only friendship.

The fictional stories after which Patty patterned her own emotional expressions demonstrate similar confusions. We cannot know precisely what Patty and other young men and women read, but stories of emotional confusion recur in novels during the period. One novel titled *Caroline of Lichtfield* was particularly preoccupied with the difficulties of understanding friendly and romantic feelings. The central conflicts of the novel revolved around Caroline's trouble in deciphering her own feelings for the two central male characters, Lindorf and Walstein. She initially believed she saw Lindorf as only a brotherly friend; "she supposed her love for Lindorf was the love of a sister, and her affection the affection of friendship." However, she came to realize that this affection is in fact romantic love. It is a struggle for Caroline, who has been promised to Walstein by her father, to overcome that romantic attachment to Lindorf. With Lindorf's help, she falls in love with Walstein, who in turn takes her expressions of affection as motivated by friendship rather than romance. He remarks that Caroline gives to friendship "all the appearance and expression of love." It takes some eighty pages for Walstein and Caroline to realize they both have romantic feelings for one another.[21]

Another female protagonist, Clara in Charles Brockden Brown's *Wieland*, suffered from similar confusions in her relationship with a man named Pleyel. For much of the novel, Clara was convinced that Pleyel was in love with her. She referred to him as her friend, but soon concluded that Pleyel loved her "but was hopeless that his love should be compensated." However, she could not reveal her love to him first; "He must not be assured that my heart is his, previous to the tender of his own." The rules of propriety in declaring affections—by a man only if he intended to marry the woman, by a woman only after a man had declared his own—further complicated the task of defining the emotional character of the relationship. Clara later found out that Pleyel had never loved her, and that in the help he offered her family earlier she had "mistaken the heroism of friendship for the phrenzy of love."[22]

The difficulties characters like Clara, Caroline, and Walstein faced in distinguishing romantic from friendly love highlight the lack of language for expressing the distinction. One of the fictional letters in the popular *Spectator* addressed this precise dilemma. The young woman, Mirtilla, "lately had a Gentleman that I thought made Pretensions to me, insomuch that most of my Friends took Notice of it and thought we were really married." One of Mirtilla's friends took it upon herself to ask the gentleman what his intentions toward Mirtilla were, and "he utterly deny'd all Pretensions to Courtship, but withal profess'd a sincere Friendship for me." Yet this did not help Mirtilla understand what the status of their relationship might be, for friendship was supposed to be the basis of marriage. Here the conflation of friendship and marriage within the notion of companionate marriage and the multivalence of the word "friend" caused considerable confusion. Mirtilla complained, "It is impossible to distinguish between Courtship and Conversation" and asked the editors "whether Marriages are proposed by way of Friendship or not." Until Mirtilla received an answer, she reported, she was acting "with so equal a Behaviour" that nobody would be able to see how she felt about the matter, either.[23]

Flirtation

Playful coquetry could exist in a friendship between a man and a woman without indicating any romantic intentions. This means that historians cannot assume, in looking at letters between men and women, that flirtatiousness translated into romance. There could be a note of romance or even sexuality in a relationship that neither friend intended to progress to a courtship or marriage. As sociologist Donald O'Meara explains, "the distinction between a romance and a cross-sex friendship is not the absence of sexual attraction or passion in the friendship, but the distinctively different function these elements perform in these two types of close relationships."[24] This distinction has led historians to assume a romance in many relationships between men and women when the situation may have been far more complicated.

Perhaps the most notable example of this was the relationship between Thomas Jefferson and Maria Cosway. The two met in Paris in the summer of 1786, when the twenty-six-year-old Maria was in town with her husband, the British artist Richard Cosway. Thomas, now without his friend and female confidante Abigail, immediately befriended Maria and spent the next two weeks touring Paris with her. Jefferson injured his wrist while out on a walk with Maria, and he stayed at home for two weeks to nurse the injury. Only a week after he recovered, the Cosways left Paris and returned to England. Less than a week later, Jefferson sent Maria a lengthy letter composed as a "Dialogue Between My Head and My Heart" to express the sadness he felt in parting with the Cosways.[25]

The motif of "head and heart," symbolizing reason and feeling, was a frequent one in this era. Jefferson's innovation in this letter is to write a conversation between the two, striving to achieve a balance in his emotions. His head warns him of "how imprudent it is to place your affections, without reserve, on objects you must so soon lose, and whose loss when it comes must cost you such severe pangs." The debate in the letter is (at least on its surface) not whether to be friends or lovers, but whether he should have entered friendships that would so soon end in separation. Notably, his head and heart are discussing friendship*s* in the plural, as he includes both Maria and her husband Richard as his friends.

Historians have argued over whether Jefferson and Cosway were friends or lovers, whether the relationship was chaste or sexual.[26] Yet this debate is misplaced.[27] One historian concludes that the relationship was "a flirtatious friendship . . . rather than a passionately erotic affair," while another sees their correspondence as "evidence of a deep and passionate love."[28] It is entirely possible, given how slippery terms were and the confusion over how individuals really felt, that the two never had a real consensus about the emotional character of the relationship. It is also important to keep in mind that Jefferson and Cosway were friends for forty years, and all but the first few weeks of the friendship was conducted through letters. The impossibility of a physical, sexual relationship for the majority of their friendship should color readings of their relationship.[29]

The thin line between friendship and romance, and the ability for flirtation to coexist with nonsexual friendship, may have even added what mixed-sex friends today find: an extra "zest and excitement and validation of physical attractiveness."[30] These friendships could include playful flirtations like Jefferson's as welcome spice in a relationship. That appears to have been the case for James Lovell in his friendship with Abigail Adams. Abigail often worried that Lovell's epistolary displays of affection were too flirtatious. For example, he wrote to her that upon receiving one of her letters, "it forced from me, almost audibly, in a grave Assembly where I broke the Seal, 'gin ye were mine ain Thing how dearly I would *love* thee'!" In another letter Lovell imitated Sterne in using the page break playfully: at the bottom of one page he wrote: "But really I doubt whether I shall be able to keep myself void of all Covetousness. I suspect I shall covet to be in the Arms of Portia" and continued onto the next page " 's Friend and Admirer-the Wife of my Bossom [*sic*]."[31] The letters are undeniably flirtatious, but this was a friendship that only occurred in letters—the relationship did not continue when Lovell came back to Boston from Philadelphia.[32]

Rosalie Stier Calvert, a prominent Maryland woman, described her friendship with Augustus Foster in similarly playful terms. Calvert wrote to her sister in 1806 that she was "*almost* in love with" Foster, the British minister Anthony Merry's secretary and "a very attractive and cultured Englishman." Having moved from a wealthy household in Belgium to a plantation in rural Maryland, Calvert clearly appreciated the entertainment and diversion of having a "cultured Englishman" visit.[33] She felt so isolated that in 1807 she wrote that besides one neighbor, "I don't have a single friend." Her husband was also a less than ideal companion: he fathered children with his slaves and seems to have disregarded his wife's wishes not to have any more children.[34]

One night while Calvert's husband was out of town, Foster spent the day with her, and Calvert asked her brother: "What do you say to your little sister passing the day tête-à-tête with one of the most charming young men she has ever seen?" After Foster returned to Europe, Calvert wrote to her sister "I am completely 'in love' with a man who is as few men are." The use of quotation marks around the term "in love" and her subsequent playful remark—"Now I can see you take on your severe expression, which I have always so loved to see, but never fear—the ocean separates us now!"—suggest that Calvert was joking. Calvert even could have been flirtatious with Foster, as long as everyone understood it was in jest.

Playfulness could turn into something more serious if women were not careful, however. Patty Rogers worried about this at times when writing about Philammon. One night in August, Philammon escorted her home and "he took some liberties that would not have been *strictly* decent had they come to light." When she protested that he "treated [her] ill," he put his hand on her breast. She tried to remove his hand "but found he was too strong for me." She begged him to stop, protesting "Its a great piece of immodesty Sir." He removed his hand, but replied "No, not between two friends!" Philammon was arguing (whether he truly believed this or not) that this sort of physicality was acceptable behavior between friends. It was certainly an allowable element of courtship in this period, but Patty's reluctance suggests that she found such physicality too intimate for friendship.[35]

While plenty of extramarital physical and even sexual intimacy occurred in this period, such physical intimacy was not publicly condoned.[36] Napoleon Bonaparte's brother Jerome discovered this the hard way when he took "some slight liberties" with a woman in a private carriage ride to a ball in Washington in 1804. According to some women, "his only fault was in not having proposed"; in other words, whatever petting or kissing might occur between a pair intending to marry was acceptable. The issue was not *pre*marital but *extra*marital intimacy. When word of his "slight liberties" spread, three men challenged Jerome to a duel. He escaped violence with a simple explanation: in Paris, when a woman would ride alone with a man in a carriage, she "will very rarely complain of the latter's attempting to embrace her, but in America it was otherwise he now saw." "The superiority of Atlantic virtue" meant that two young people of the opposite sex jostled together in a carriage could restrain their desire.[37] Chastity, in other words, was an American virtue.

Friendship Leading to Marriage

As the women who commented on Jerome's error suggested, flirtation could be a meaningful, deliberate step in moving the friendship into a romance and marriage. Some saw romantic love as simply an increase of the intensity of the feelings of friendship. Matthew Ridley asked his former friend-turned-fiancée Catherine Livingston "if there can exist" an "excess of Friendship," for "even between Men it would be called Love."[38] Yet the writer of a newspaper article simply titled "Love" argued that while love was "an increase of the friendship that subsists between man and man," it benefited from "the opposition of the sexes."[39] Another lover—none other than Benedict Arnold—begged his friend Margaret Shippen to "suffer that heavenly bosom . . . to expand with a sensation more soft, more tender than friendship."[40] Thus there is something more subtle than an increase in intensity along this spectrum; the character of the affection is, in Arnold's words, "more soft, more tender."

A successful romance, of course, led to marriage. Given that contemporary literature idealized companionate marriage, or marriage as a union of loving friends, beginning a romance as a friendship was in fact ideal.[41] While there are numerous examples of happy marriages growing out of friendships—including the Ridleys and the Arnolds—perhaps the person who best articulated this transition was Judith Sargent Murray.[42] In a lengthy letter to her sister-in-law in 1788, Murray explained that she had never felt passion for her first husband, expected that she would never fall in love, and intended to remain single. However, after getting over the shock of her husband's death, she began to have romantic feelings for her friend of more than a dozen years, John Murray. She realized that "my sentiments partook of rather too great a degree of tenderness" and she "carefully suppressed every rebellious thought." Yet when Murray left the country for an extended period, Judith realized, "I could no longer deceive myself." Without knowing how Murray felt, the passion was oppressive: "I had in fact become a slave," she wrote, "to the most petuous of all passions." In Judith's explanation of the transition, then, her romantic feelings for Murray arose despite her resolution to remain single (although it is impossible to know whether she was shaping a more publicly acceptable narrative of her feelings or if it was the reality). The long-lasting friendship yielded to passions beyond Judith's control.[43]

Fortunately for Judith, she received a letter from Murray declaring his love for her at the peak of her own frustrations. Unlike Judith, his feelings had undergone no change: "he acknowledged he had long loved me, even from the commencement of our acquaintance." For the first dozen years of their friendship, Judith was a married woman, and Murray never betrayed any feelings beyond friendship for her. While Judith told her sister-in-law she had not had romantic feelings for Murray until after her husband died, she hinted otherwise when she wrote to her brother, "My bosom hath long been actuated by the purest friendship—sentiments of a more tender nature, virtue forbad, and the most secret wish of my soul, was indignant at every improper idea."[44] Perhaps there were wisps of desire that arose for Judith that she banished from her thoughts so quickly that a fully formed romantic love for Murray still came as a surprise to her.

Sublimating Attraction

Either a man or woman could suffer from the pains of unrequited love, however. Two famous continental novels of this era that were popular in America portray the most tragic result of the inability to subdue passions in male/female friendships. Goethe's *The Sorrows of Young Werther* and Rousseau's *Eloisa* (also known as *Julie: or, The New Heloise*) share as a central theme the difficulty of transitioning from romantic love to friendship. In both novels, the only resolution is death for one of the lovers. As Eloisa explains in a letter to her lover St. Preux right before her death, their friendship after her marriage was "the fruit of an unparalleled conquest over a fatal passion—a passion which may sometimes be overcome, but is very rarely refined into friendship." Both had worked assiduously at this conquest; after her marriage he thinks it will be impossible for him to be in her presence, while she is convinced that "If you lose an affectionate mistress, you gain a faithful friend." Yet with the help of Eloisa's husband, they persevere and appear to have formed a tenuous friendship. It is not until after Eloisa's accidental death that we learn that she had never been able to conquer her "fatal passion" for St. Preux.[45]

A failed attempt to subdue romantic passion into friendship was also fatal for the hero of Goethe's novel. Werther falls in love with Lotte, who is already engaged to be married. Like Eloisa, her husband, and St. Preux, Werther spends time with Lotte and her fiancé as a mutual friend. He is unable to maintain a friendship with his former love, however, and is scared of his own feelings: "I am afraid of myself! Is not my love for her the most sacred, chaste, and brotherly love? Has my soul ever known a culpable desire?" He must ask himself this question precisely because his love is not that of a brother; he cannot conquer his desires. Lotte wants to be friends with him, suggesting he go travel and return after some time so that they could "enjoy the bliss of true friendship." By this time, Werther knows this is impossible for him and replies bitterly: "That would look well in a print and should be recommended to all tutors."[46] Werther feels that the only solution is for one of them to die, and so he takes his own life. It is a story, like Eloisa's, that on the surface is about disappointed love but at a deeper level is actually about the inability to shift romantic passion to the love shared in friendship.

Americans responded to this aspect of Werther's story with magazine pieces that lamented—and often criticized—the German hero's inability to subdue his feelings for Lotte into friendship. These responses complicated dominant literary representations about the difficulties of friendships between men and women. One poet, posing as Lotte visiting Werther's grave, asked him:

> *Why Werther, dost thou leave me so?*
> *Thy friends, thy kindred flee?*
> *Dost thou no longer Charlotte know?*
> *Have friends no charm for thee?*

Another poet also emphasized that Werther should have been content with friendship; the author addressed the hero as "Mistaken youth!" and noted that if he had waited longer, "virtuous friendship soon had set thee free."

Indeed, critical response to the novel in American magazines depicted Werther as a poor example for readers, a man who had been unable to control his emotions. One writer described visiting a friend who was crying over Werther and explained to her, "love is not blind . . . we can resist the impulse of feelings; our affections are in our own power." No reader of stories like those of Werther and Eloisa, another critic argued, "ever picked up rules of practical prudence, or gained more controul over his passions."[47] Werther, in particular, was treated as a real person rather than a fictional character, perhaps because people had witnessed the damaging psychological effects of uncontrollable passions. Indeed, there were newspaper stories claiming that the novel was in fact a true story.[48]

Clearly, it was difficult emotional work to maintain a friendship when romantic feelings entered the picture and a romantic relationship was impossible; imagine, perhaps, going backwards on the spectrum from romantic love to friendship.[49] Consider Patty Rogers's insistence in her diary that Philammon was only a friend and that she would "steel her heart" against developing stronger feelings for him. Patty was struggling during this same time with shifting her relationship with Portius from courtship to friendship. Portius did not help matters by continuing some of the rituals of courtship— including writing her letters and even kissing her—after marrying another woman. But Patty was determined to change her feelings toward him. In one entry she cut off her own rhapsodizing about him, writing "*but* be *silent* he is another's, and lest a wish should arise I drop the subject—*he is my friend*— and I'll be content."[50]

The difficulty was, as a character in *The Romance of the Forest* put it, "to reduce love within the limits of friendship."[51] Here again love is a spectrum on which the intensity must be lessened. This did not mean that expressions of effusive love were impossible in a friendship, but that they had to be worded differently. Elizabeth Bayley Seton, the Catholic leader of a religious sisterhood in Maryland, struggled to keep her love for the married friend who converted her to Catholicism, Antonio Filicchi, within proper bounds. Despite writing to him of her affection, she protested "dear dear Antonio why must I speak to you in a manner so little conformed to the feelings of my heart—but you know yourself drew the line, and the kindness and sweetness of affection must be veiled." They appear to have developed feelings for each other when Filicchi escorted Seton back to America after her husband's death in Italy, but Filicchi "drew the line" at a warm friendship. Seton was not alone in putting in emotional effort to maintain the chastity of the relationship; Seton wrote to him that she longed "to meet you in your state of perfection, where I shall receive the transfusion of your affections without your exertions."[32]

Sometimes, though, the emotional work of turning romantic love into friendship was simply too difficult. In some cases the pair were unable to maintain a relationship at all; Gouverneur Morris, for instance, told a former mistress that he could not be "only a friend."[33] It is likely that most men and women who were unable to become friends after a failed romance did not leave behind written evidence of their failure. Patty Rogers certainly demonstrated the difficulty of subduing her passions for Portius into friendship, but we do not know whether they ultimately remained friends in the long term. Certainly to make such a transition involved considerable labor and self-control to force a change in feelings.

A Subtle System of Signs

Friends also exercised a sort of emotional labor as they endeavoured to signal to a friend and in some cases the community whether a relationship was a romance or not. Men and women needed guidance on the discrete system of signs they deploy, as well as an understanding of how those around them might interpret behavior. From physical movements to carefully chosen words, men and women used a variety of tools to convey their feelings to one another. Both advice literature and novels offered guidance here, but given the tenuous line between friendship and romance, it was not a precise science. But for the larger community, there was one very simple sign that a relationship was a romance: an unmarried man and woman spending time together alone. Friends thus had to be carefully attuned to how they conveyed the emotional status of their relationship.

Advice literature instructed men and women that there were subtle signs that they could use to communicate friendly rather than romantic intentions. These signs were particularly important for women to learn in order to discern a flirtatious friend—or even rake—from a lover. To learn and practice this sort of discernment required careful study.[54] The advice book *A Father's Legacy to His Daughters* informed young women that "There is a kind of unmeaning gallantry much practiced by some men, which, if you have any discernment, you will find really harmless."[55] Acts of "unmeaning gallantry" included attending ladies in public, offering small services, and paying generic compliments. A newspaper piece in the *Hampden Patriot* in 1822 decried ladies' inability to distinguish harmless flirtation from evidence of love. Reporting on a story in which a man was fined $750 for breach of the marriage promise, the author noted, "If the daily and kind attention, and platonic assiduities of a gentleman, are to be construed by a lady into a marriage promise, and on these circumstantial and 'ambiguous giving out,' heavy damages are to be predicated, the age of gallantry will vanish."[36] A woman should not interpret "a little cream in a cup of tea; a touch of a toe under a table; a miscellaneous sigh or a languishing look" from a man as evidence of love and thus intent to marry her.

If a woman did perceive that a man was in love with her but she was not interested, she in turn could slightly alter her behavior to demonstrate her disinterest. *A Father's Legacy* explains that there are "a variety of ways" to accomplish this, including showing "a certain species of easy familiarity in your behavior, which may satisfy him, if he has any discernment left."[37] This appears to be precisely what the literary heroine Belinda did in Edgeworth's novel of that same name. When she wanted to show her disinterest in Clarence Hervey (despite her attraction to him, for she had learned he was already engaged to another woman), "she addressed her conversation to him with that easy, friendly familiarity, which a man of his discernment could not misunderstand."[38] A woman might also, the advice book advised, "shew that you want to avoid his company," but that was not an option "if he is a man whose friendship you wish to preserve." In that case, a woman might have to resort to having a friend explain her feelings to him. Just as a woman could not declare to a man her interest in him unless he had made the first declaration, so she could not declare her disinterest until that time either.

Women who felt friendship but not romantic love for a man seemed to rely particularly on the word "esteem" for signaling the emotional distinction. Esteem was, in the words of Thomas Cogan, author of *A Philosophical Treatise on the Passions*, "the value we place upon some degree of worth." It might be inspired by somebody "at a remote distance from our intimacy." Thus not only did esteem lack connotations of intimacy, it was only, in the author's words "the commencement of affection."[39] Mary Wollstonecraft echoed Cogan, arguing that passionate love could be "easily distinguished from esteem, the foundation of friendship."[60]

People readily employed this terminology in their own relationships as well, whether in life or fiction. Rachel Van Dyke insisted that her male friends had her "warmest esteem—nothing more." Patty Rogers reported of a possible suitor: "I feel indifferent as I ought — tho I *love* and *esteem* him as a *friend*."[61] Similarly, a character in *Caroline of Lichtfield* reported that the woman he was in love with "never testified any thing more than esteem for me."[62]

This use of the term "esteem" is illustrated most directly in Edgeworth's *Belinda*. Clarence Hervey denies to his friend Lady Delacour that he is in love with Belinda:

"In love!" exclaimed Clarence Hervey; "but when did I ever use the expression? In speaking of Miss Portman, I simply expressed esteem and ad—O, no and—"

"No additions," said Lady Delacour; "content yourself with esteem—simply,—and Miss Portman is safe, and you too, I presume."[63]

For Hervey, it was as if love were on a spectrum from casual friendship to romantic passion, and esteem was firmly at the friendship pole.[64] Esteem could escalate into higher passions, but in itself it was only a "commencement."

The female heroine in Ann Radcliffe's *The Romance of the Forest*, Adeline, turns down a proposal from her family friend Louis La Motte by emphasizing esteem. She begs him to "be assured of my esteem and friendship." When he protests, she returns again to the theme of esteem but explains that her feelings will not progress to romance. "Though your virtues will always command my esteem," she tells him, "you have nothing to hope from my love." These assurances do not comfort Louis, who protests that "I have long borne my passion in silence," apparently pretending friendship for her when he felt romantic love. Friendship is insufficient for him; he wants "a sentiment less cool than that of friendship."[65]

The decision of young women like Adeline to declare their passions untouched, their will intact, and only their esteem activated gave them considerable emotional power over men. This power was not confined to women alone; a 1790 poem entitled "Female love forsaken" is the story of the unrequited love of Lara for Colin. The two took meandering walks together during which Lara says, "friendship has oft been our theme." Yet while Colin "has own'd that I shar'd his esteem," he had "never confest that he lov'd." When Colin went on to court "a happier fair," Lara was distraught but not surprised.[66] She knew she had his esteem but not his romantic love. That sources do not depict men expressing this to women is a result of the fact that women could not declare themselves and give men the opportunity to reject them (unless they had been seduced). While men had the power to first declare their romantic love, women were not forced to accept; their choice of how to phrase their emotional responses to lovers gave them a negotiating power uniquely reserved for women.[67]

Men and women both understood that there were different types of love. Again, though, they were hampered by language: the word "love" was an umbrella term for the entire spectrum of friendship to romantic passion. As the titular character in Robert Bage's 1796 novel *Hermsprong* told his friend Miss Fluart, "I love you with every sort of love but one." That one sort that he does not name—romantic love—is reserved for the novel's heroine, Caroline. Hermsprong tells Miss Fluart "that one is at present, Caroline's exclusively. If I recover it—" Miss Fluart cuts him off to say "Don't trouble yourself, for though I love you with every sort of love but one, I love Caroline better; and if she is not amongst your collection, you may grub wood by yourselves."[68] Her joking reply is made in part to express her devotion to her best friend Caroline, as well as to disclaim any romantic feelings for Hermsprong. For both Miss Fluart and Hermsprong, it is entirely possible to feel the love of friendship but not romance for somebody of the opposite sex. Hermsprong creatively expresses this distinction in the idea of "every sort of love but one," creating his own linguistic solution where no good terminology exists.

In 1798 a male friend of Dolley Payne Todd (later Madison) came to his own creative solution. In writing to Dolley of a woman he had loved who had rejected him, he admitted "she still inspires a gentle flutter of spirits — a sensation of extraordinary pleasure and sometimes a Sentiment of delicious Tenderness when I am happy enough to be near her." His "Career of Passion," he concluded, was at an end, and henceforth he would feel only chaste but intimate friendship for her. Explaining his feelings, he continued: "I do not call this Love—nor can I call it Friendship." "It is," he concludes, "a golden mean—an union of Soul."[69] The term "golden mean" refers to "the avoidance of excess in either direction": here, not so casually friendly as to lose true intimacy, but not into the "ungovernable" realm of romantic passion.[70]

Language could not contain all of the cues needed to understand whether a relationship was a friendship or a romantic relationship. There were observable bodily manifestations of romantic passion: blushing, fainting, trembling, sighing, and even staring were involuntary displays of a passion that could not be governed by will. The French traveler Ferdinand Bayard observed physical displays as signs of attraction, including "amorous glances," "squeezing of hands," "a more expressive smile," or even simply "a gesture."[71] Mary Wollstonecraft similarly noted "a smothered sigh, downcast look, and the many other little arts which are played off."[72]

This link between passion and body was considered natural in a person of sensibility, particularly in women.[73] As Cogan observed in his *Treatise on the Passions*, passion was "communicated to the nervous system, and the commotions excited in that, indicate themselves both by attitudes and motions of the body, and particular expressions of countenance." Cogan pointed out that "it is alone by these visible effects, that the subject is discovered to be under the influence of any passion,"[74] which would be particularly true with romantic passions since men and women would not discuss romantic feelings until a man declared his love and proposed marriage to a woman.

Thus the language of sensibility emphasized romantic feelings through bodily signs. Novels described physical responses that come across as over-wrought to us today but seemed entirely natural to readers in the early republic.[75] In Rousseau's *Eloisa* (the American version of *Julie: or, The New Heloise*), Eloisa's lover St. Preux described his love for her through a physical reaction: "you make me shudder, my blood boils, my heart pants."[76] This was a passion that had completely consumed the lovers. Other characters, in novels and in life, offered subtler signs. Edgeworth's Belinda, for instance, believed that Clarence Hervey was in love with her because "she observed the extreme eagerness with which [he] watched all her motions, and followed her with his eye as if his fate depended upon her."[77]

Novel readers noted similar physical manifestations of romantic passions. A prime example is Patty Rogers, who often reported physical responses when seeing her former lover. On one visit from him, she reported, "I with trembling hand arose to meet him . . . my eyes eagerly met his and betrayed the *tenderness* I *felt* in seeing him."[78] These were discreet signs, but Patty was so overcome with emotion that after sitting down she "turned *pale* and *faint*," provoking her father's concern. A young woman in Philadelphia named Harriet Manigault was a careful observer of other people's physical signs of love, and the sigh seems to have been her key sign. A gentleman visitor named Mr. Craig seemed to Harriet to be in love: "he *sighs* too, poor young man! & they say that is a sign of love." She was particularly attentive to her sister's love interests. Another male visitor, she believed, had "a secret *penchant*" for her sister because of the way he said goodbye to the family. "He looked Mama and me full in the face when he bid us good bye," she explained, "& then bowed to Ch.[Charlotte] without looking at her, & at the same time sighed deeply." So clear was this sign that "as soon as the door was shut," Harriet broke out laughing at her sister.[79]

Criminal Lines

Evidence from adultery, divorce, and criminal conversation trials helps illu-minate the commonly agreed upon signs that a relationship had an illicit, sexual character. In many court cases, public perception of the status of a relationship was crucial to determining the sexual status of a relationship. What those around the presumptive couple offered as evidence were not emotional ties but physical ones, consistent with the notion that romantic attraction was conveyed between a couple through bodily signs. In stories of transgression, we can see the ambiguities of the line between friendship and romance, or at least sexuality, pinned down into moral and legal codes.

Titillating accounts of trials relating to illicit sexuality were pervasive in American print culture. Criminal conversation suits were a particularly popular genre. This was a legal claim similar to adultery, but rather than being brought between spouses, it was brought by a husband against the man who he believed has committed adultery with his wife. It depended upon the husband's ownership of his wife through coverture, and the husband sought property damages for the violation.[80] While these cases were not particularly common in America, there was an explosion of them in Britain between 1790 and 1830.[81] British and American readers alike devoured pamphlets and newspaper accounts, and even collected volumes describing cases of criminal conversation and adultery in lurid detail.

Criminal conversation tales in American publications were generally reprinted from British sources. As early as 1791, American newspapers published a critique from Benjamin Rush telling them to "Avoid filling your paper with anecdotes of British vice and follies, what have the citizens of the United States to do with the duels, the elopements, the crim cons, the kept mistress . . . of the people of Great-Britain."[82] American readers would have read these tales in a different context than those across the Atlantic. Precisely because these were stories of "*British* vice and follies," Americans would have seen them as negative examples to position themselves against. But they would also have recognized and internalized the tales' repeated, formulaic depictions of the signs distinguishing friendships from romances in cases where that line was a very serious matter.

A husband's success in a criminal conversation case depended on proving that his wife had been a sexual intimate rather than a chaste friend of another man. Criminal conversation stories often began with a happy friendship among the husband, wife, and another man.[83] What signs could husbands use to prove guilt? Of course, the most obvious sign that a friendship had crossed the line from chastity to sexuality was evidence of sexual intimacy. That intimacy could be described in vague terms or innuendo. A New York criminal conversation case included the testimony of a servant who provided evidence through a humorous innuendo. The man had asked the defendant why he was being brought to court, and the defendant said "he had been taking lessons on the Violin from the plaintiff, who charged him with a criminal connection with his wife; I then asked him jokingly, which fiddle made the best music, the husband's or the wife's; he answered that the wife's made the best music."[84] Another trial presented far more explicit evidence: the defendant "made particularly free with her, taking very great liberties; such as putting his hands in her bosom, and attempting to put them up her petticoats."[85] Unlike Philammon, the lawyer in this case saw such petting as evidence of inappropriate sexuality rather than an acceptable component of friendship.

For a man and woman to spend time with one another alone was also an important indicator to those around them that a relationship was suspect. In the Ure case, a servant testified "Dr. Pattison's calls for Mrs. Ure were frequent, and very often made at the hours when Dr. Ure was lecturing at the Institution."[86] Another cuckolded husband realized that his wife's adultery should have been obvious; when it occurred he thought the seducer's attentions to his wife were natural, but he later saw that "their long evening walks together! their frequent ridings out in his gig!" should have been an obvious sign of guilt."[87] In the case of *Massy v. Headfort*, the defendant's lawyer testified that Mrs. Massy "passed months at the houses of single gentlemen, unaccompanied or unattended." This suggested that Mrs. Massy might have had sexual relations with these gentlemen as well as demonstrating her husband's negligence in not supervising his wife.[88]

One particular criminal conversation case stands out as focused primarily on judging whether a relationship was a friendship or a sexual relationship. The case of *Lord Cadogan vs. Reverend Cooper* presented the jury with the explicit task of judging whether Lady Cadogan and Reverend Cooper had been friends or lovers. While Lord Cadogan initially thought his wife and Cooper shared only "the familiarities of friendship and conversation," he learned that more was going on from his servants. Cooper's lawyer, Mr. Law, protested that a friendship was indeed all that was going on. Cooper had Lord Cadogan's permission to visit Lady Cadogan on her sickbed and had spent time alone with her with her husband's knowledge. Mr. Law acknowledged that while "not an advocate for platonic love or friendship," he believed that "there may subsist between persons of different ages, with long habits of family intercourse, a great degree of tenderness, which may exhibit a number of appearances that may be misconstrued."

Mr. Law did not even ask the jury to accept the notion that men and women could be friends, but rather that there was a logical context here for affection devoid of physical intimacy. Reverend Cooper and Lady Cadogan may have been alone in her bedroom, but that did not prove illicit behavior. Law went on to argue that he could not see how one could assume a romance between an ill woman who was no longer beautiful and a young, happily married man. "The approach of a young man of 27, to the sick-bed of a lady who is mother of seven children, and at the age of 49," he continued, "is not a circumstance upon which you will bottom any well founded suspicions, much less will you draw from it, the ill-founded inference of criminality." Cooper's lawyer, however, was unable to convince the judge and jury that his client was a friend rather than lover to Mrs. Cadogan. In his charge to the jury, the judge contended that "strong, pregnant suspicions" rather than "positive proof" were enough to rule against Cooper. Apparently the jury agreed, granting Cadogan damages of two thousand pounds (a large sum, but far short of the twenty thousand Cadogan had requested).[89]

Risks

There were real risks, then, to befriending the opposite sex. The results could be as minor as having an unwanted lover, as tragic as death, as dangerous as seduction, as damaging to marriage as adultery, or as fatal to reputation as gossip over improprieties. These consequences each played out in popular literature as well as personal experiences. Men and women who formed friendships could not have missed these dramatic examples of friendship gone awry and would have had to keep the risks of the relationship in mind as they shaped their own friendships.

One category of risk was primarily emotional. Because the transition from friendship to romantic love could happen so easily, authors warned readers to be careful with friends of the opposite sex if they were not looking for a lover—or if they did not want to fall in love themselves. A man's "friendship for a woman is so near akin to love" that the writer of *A Father's Legacy to His Daughters* claimed that a young woman "will probably very soon find a lover, where she only wished to meet a friend."[90] Friendship might turn to romantic love before a man or woman realized what was happening; passion had the power to overtake the reasonable, measured feelings of friendship. As Mary Wollstonecraft argued when warning young women about forming friendships with men they very much admired:

> The heart is very treacherous, and if we do not guard its first emotions, we shall not be able to prevent its sighing for impossibilities. . . . To attempt to raise ourselves above human beings is ridiculous; we cannot

extirpate our passions, nor is it necessary that we should, though it may be wise sometimes not to stray too near a precipice, lest we fall over before we are aware.[91]

Writers doubted their readers' ability to walk along this "precipice" safely; as Maria Edgeworth explained of Belinda after her heroine realized that the man she was falling in love with was engaged, "she felt the danger of admitting him to the familiarity of friendship."[92]

It was a few short steps from "the familiarity of friendship" to seduction. A South Carolina woman named Eliza Wilkinson wondered in 1782 why "to commence a friendship with, or behave socially to a Gent. should put us under the dread & fear of some sad Catastrophe."[93] That "dread & fear" was just what the writers of seduction tales wanted. Women needed to be aware of and concerned about the possibility that the men they encountered might try to seduce them; they needed to show constant vigilance. The responsibility for preventing seduction was pinned on women, seen increasingly, as the nineteenth century began, as the more moral of the sexes. Men would be rakes, so women must be moral gatekeepers.[94] Beyond its implications for courtship, this arrangement meant that women would be more cautious about entering a friendship with a man than a man would be in befriending a woman.

As the legal examples demonstrate, friendships that strayed into adultery risked both the stability of a marriage and personal reputation—particularly for women. As William Thompson remarked in his 1825 *Appeal to One Half the Human Race*, "persecution desolation and death attend the footsteps of the wife if the husband only *suspects*" that there is a romantic relationship between his wife and a male friend.[95] While divorces were not common, adultery was sufficient grounds to legally end a marriage.[96] A spouse could also be brought to trial, in rare cases, for criminal conversation or adultery.[97] This could damage the reputation of a man, particularly in the sensational cases of ministers committing adultery with female congregants. A man seen as a cuckold suffered "a slur on both his virility and his capacity to rule his own household."[98]

But the greater risk was to a woman's reputation, whether charges were brought formally or circulated through gossip. A woman's reputation, unlike a man's, was in Mary Wollstonecraft's words "confined to a single virtue— chastity." Wollstonecraft deplored "the impossibility of [women's] regaining respectability by a return to virtue, though men preserve theirs during the indulgence of vice."[99] There were clear reasons for this double standard: the value on a woman's virginity before marriage contrasted to the irrelevance of a man's; the fact that a wife had no property rights over her husband, as he had over her; and the reality that a woman could get pregnant.[100] These practical concerns meant careful community policing of women's sexual behavior. This did not mean that all women showed restraint and never yielded to desire; indeed, the disciplining of women's bodies with the ideals of virginity and chastity was a response to increasing sexual license in the late eighteenth century.[101]

The ambiguity of the boundaries between friendship and romance or sexuality left friends particularly open to gossip and charges of impropriety. Relationships without their own clearly defined social categories were particularly susceptible to being seen as deviant. Thus gossip about these friendships was not mere chatter but a form of community regulation of what some saw as a subversive or unsettling category of relationship.[102] Gossip could permanently damage a reputation, and men and women both were anxious not to become fodder for it.[103] Gossip about sexual matters was particularly prevalent and often "blossomed into scandal," historian Cynthia Kierner explains, in a culture "which idealized companionate marriage and domestic tranquility."[104] This was also a time when men and women were always under the watchful gaze of their neighbors. Women had to be careful how they interacted with men at social gatherings, which men escorted them in public, and how they conducted correspondences with men.

Gossip was not only a matter of talk; it often found its way into newspapers in an era with a fluid boundary between talk and print.[105] Newspapers published stories about suspected liaisons between friends of the opposite sex when a story was either particularly salacious or involved a well-known figure. Even moral pillars of the community, like a Boston woman named Susan Huntington who was lauded in a religious memoir, could find her friendships with men becoming fodder for newspaper stories. In 1821 she recorded in her diary that she had recently visited "a young man, a former acquaintance of mine," with whom she chatted "with tenderness and affection." She was shocked to discover "that visit has been made the subject of a newspaper sarcasm, is much talked of, and much misrepresented."[106] While she does not say exactly what the gossip alleged, she goes on to attest that "If I have had any idol, it has been my good name" and to say that she feels no regret for the visit or what she said. It seems likely that the gossip pertained to an inappropriate relationship with the young man.

In other cases it is quite clear that the newspaper gossip was about romance between two friends. In 1797 Nelly Custis complained to a friend about newspaper reports that she and George Washington Lafayette, the Marquis's son who was staying with her family, were going to marry. "I wish they [newspaper reporters] would also allow her to *marry who* she *pleases*," Nelly wrote, protesting that Lafayette was more like a brother than a future husband to her.[107] This gossip, at least, was more of an annoyance than an attack on her reputation; other women were not so lucky. Perhaps the most notorious case came thirty years later in Washington with the story of Margaret (Peggy) Eaton. Between 1829 and 1831, there were hundreds of newspaper stories about the scandal surrounding her and her husband John Eaton, a member of Andrew Jackson's cabinet.[108] Gossip circulated that Peggy had had an affair with Eaton when she was married to her previous husband, while she protested that Eaton was only a family friend at that time.[109] These stories destroyed both Peggy's reputation and Jackson's first cabinet, as Jackson stood by the Eatons and Washington society snubbed them.[110]

Knowing the risks of male/female friendships caused men and women to exercise caution in their expressions of friendship, particularly in public. What men and women said or forbore from saying, how they acted, and in what context they spent time together could all potentially render them safe from the tongues of gossip. But shaping a public image for a friendship could be hard when privately men and women were confused about how to describe their feelings.

Thus, if the friends themselves sometimes had difficulty determining and explaining the status of their relationship, it is no surprise that those around them could be confused as well. The evidence in letters and diaries demonstrates that the risk of private or public confusion about male/female friendship did not prevent these relationships from occurring; on the contrary, they occurred more often than the literature at the time or the historical literature today suggest. Many men and women in these friendships raised the problem of the boundaries and public perception of their relationships; the topic comes up too often in letters and diaries to be an isolated fear.[111] The lack of a formal category for these relationships did not mean that they could not exist but rather that they faced particular difficulties in doing so. As Deborah Norris wrote of John Mifflin, he made "an agreeable friend" in spite of society's "poor opinion of platonic sentiments."[112]

Policing sexual boundaries in relationships between men and women, particularly friendships, was part of a larger American project of defining virtue among elite citizens in a republic. While casual relationships or friendships between elite men and women in England or France might have a sexual element, the intrusion of sexuality into friendly relations endangered the virtue of citizens. In America, chastity was a middle- to upper-class attribute, and thus presenting friendships as nonsexual had both class and civic valences.[113] Allowing sexual intimacy in a friendship between men and women would disrupt marriage, degrade individuals' genteel reputations, and tarnish their virtue. The public image of male/female friendship as proper, chaste relationships thus had both personal and political stakes, causing men and women to go to great lengths to present their friendships as safe, virtuous relationships that formed part of the larger republican community.

4

Propriety, Positioning, and the Public Face of Friendship

"YOU KNOW THE great circumspection required of young ladies who live alone," William Ellery Channing wrote to his young friend Eloise Payne in 1809. "You must select your acquaintance from the other sex with the greatest care," he continued, for "the world are ready to censure as a mark of inconsiderateness & levity" a woman's intimacy with men.[1] It was not just young single women who had to worry about being seen alone with men. The messiness of distinguishing between mixed-sex friendship and romance, the risks of public misunderstandings and gossip, and the American ideal of chaste virtue forced friends to shape public perceptions of their relationships and incorporate others into their friendships.

While the idealized picture of friendship in the early republic was one of a pair of isolated friends, usually two men, the reality was that friendships always involved other people and the larger community. The ideal of friendship as a dyad was impractical in a society where people lived their lives embedded in families, marriages, and networks of friends. That ideal might be practiced in moments of privacy, but the reality was that most pairs of friends had to consider how their friendship looked to those around them. Friends needed to position themselves in their families, social circles, and larger communities in such a way as to shape public perceptions of their relationships and prevent misconceptions and gossip.[2] The great deal of work required for men and women to be friends points to the strength of the new nation's cultural order prescribing that men and women would naturally be sexually attracted to one another, marry, and produce families. These friends had to build relationships in the face of a cultural order that suggested their friendships were unnatural, even deviant.

Friends shaped public perceptions of their dyad through improvised strategies and structures. The difficulty for men and women was that there were no clear models or guides for how to conduct a mixed-sex friendship.[3] The predominant roles played by elite men and women were child, spouse, family relation, or same-sex friend, and the culture's scripts for male/female interaction were those of family or romance. Thus the cross-gender friend had to, in effect, write her own script to follow. Friends found particular ways that they could structure their friendships to emphasize the propriety, safety, and asexual character of the relationship.[4] These were not always calculated moves, but sometimes maneuvers within and even beyond the rules and structures of their society.[5]

Most friendships triangulated through third parties; the difference for male/female pairs was that the concerns about sexual propriety rendered that triangulation more important and necessarily more visible. Whether that third party was a spouse, a family member, a religious community, or a social circle, drawing other parties into a friendship was a strategic move to ensure the propriety of the friendship. This chapter examines five different social structures and settings that provided language, context, and safety for friendships between men and women. The first and broadest of these were the mixed-sex social circles and salons that served as public settings for the formation of male/female friendships. The second was a very different sort of community, that of the church, which provided a comfortable home for spiritual, mixed-sex friendships. Third, friends used terms of kinship in reference to each other in a practice anthropologists describe as "fictive kinship." At the most intimate level, in the fourth structure, friends could position their friendships as appropriate by including their spouses. Perhaps the easiest setting for friendships between men and women, however, was the fifth and final one: that of adult, unmarried individuals who were mature enough to escape the imputation of sexual impropriety or free of the social bonds of marriage.

Such strategizing was not part of what Americans in this era pictured when they imagined an ideal friendship. Certainly, there was a considerable difference between the real and the ideal. But the same could be said to a lesser degree for homosocial friendships at the time: given that the family, companionate marriage, and polite sociability were all taking on greater importance, it is difficult to imagine friendship meaning a pair in isolation.[6] The notion of friendships embedded in larger schema is a better fit with the early republican ideal in which the affections fostered in friendships would spread to serve the good of the country. A friendship was not a hub radiating outward; it was one component of a web of friendships, religious and social groups, marriages, and families in which each relationship contributed to the unity of the community and thus the republic.

Mixed-Sex Circles

Convivial social circles fostered the growth of friendships that writers of the literature of sensibility hoped would transform selves in order to build a new social order.[7] Many social circles, beginning in the late eighteenth century, were spaces for both men and women. The intense and long-lasting friendships that formed within them buttressed broader ties of affection across a circle of men and women. To form a friendship within the matrix of a group of friends was also a way to position a friendship on socially acceptable grounds in the presence of a third party. Even for a married woman, such circles were acceptable places to form friendships with a third party present (here the group if not the husband). The same applied for single women who were in social circles without their brothers or fathers.

The challenges and opportunities for friendships between men and women varied depending on the age group of the social circle. For elite, young, single men and women, these circles were essential social settings for learning about romance and finding a spouse. Indeed, companionate marriage's focus on romance rooted in friendship meant that groups of young male and female friends were natural and proper places for budding romances.[8] Whether in the salons of Philadelphia, at the hot springs in Virginia, or at the student gatherings in Litchfield, Connecticut, young people came together in relatively free spaces to find both friends and mates.[9] For young people learning to socialize with the opposite sex in polite society, these circles gave them a chance to meet prospective mates in an atmosphere rooted in friendship and surrounded by supportive companions.[10] Splitting off as individual pairs of friends, however, could still hold risks for young people; keeping the friendship safely within the group or the presence of a protector was vital.[11] To be a young woman alone signaled lower class status, lesser morals, and greater sexual vulnerability.[12]

For adults, sometimes men and women who had been in the same circle as young people, mixed-sex gatherings were for sociability and friendship, not romance. Friendships formed in webs within these groups, making them communal rather than exclusive. These more formalized settings, sometimes in the form of the salon, offered a safe space for adults to socialize alone or, more frequently, in the company of their spouses. Salons in America, building off their European counterparts, were centered on witty and intellectual conversation.[13] Within the bounds of this particular institution, norms of communication and sociability differed from those of everyday life. A salon, then, was a more open environment for the formation of friendships between men and women.[14] From Martha Washington's gatherings in New York, to those of Elizabeth Powel and her niece Anne Willing Bingham in Philadelphia, to Dolley Madison's in Washington, these salons were at the center of networks of elite friendships.[15]

A more intimate and less formal version of salons sprouted up in small urban literary circles of young adults in the late eighteenth and early nineteenth centuries. Sometimes centered on a particular publication, for example Joseph Dennie's *Port Folio* in Philadelphia, historians have described these groups as comprising only men. Dennie, for instance, was said to have "created the *Port Folio* as a masculine community."[16] Similarly, New York's Friendly Club counted only men as official members. Yet these men spent much of their time in the company of women, who were not official members and might not have had their names show up in publications. For both men and women, these circles were about more than intellectual exchange: they were sites for the formation of "intense friendship."[17] The letters of Margaret Bayard (later Smith) show that her interactions with the Friendly Club drew her into close friendships with Anthony Bleecker, Charles Brockden Brown, and William Johnson. As she reported to her fiancé in May of 1800, these men each visited her weekly for private conversations, in addition to the time they spent together with other male club members and with Bayard's friends Maria Templeton and Maria Nicholson.[18]

Despite positioning these friendships in a larger circle and obtaining her fiancé's approval, Bayard found herself censured by an older woman for these private conversations. This critique likely stemmed both from generational differences and from Bayard's relatively bold step of spending time with male friends unsupervised by the group or by an adult protector. "A lady" chided Bayard for her habit of conversing with men and informed her that "few young persons of different sexes, meet frequently, to converse on serious & general topics; their intercourse consists of an interchange of frivolous attentions & unmeaning compliments."[19] "A lady" assumed that most gatherings of young people were places for light socializing and finding a mate, not for close friendships and intellectualism.

Some adults, like Bayard's critic, could not imagine or approve of a tight-knit circle of friends of both genders who fed on intellectual conversation. Young women, she and other doyens of manners assumed, did not participate in such conversations with young men. These gendered conventions of conversation were problematic for the formation of male/female friendships. If friendships like Bayard's were to be built on conversation, and conversation could take place only between people of the same gender (likely male), how were men and women to become friends?[20] The solution for many intellectual circles, beginning with the Friendly Club but evident in other circles that formed later, was to openly flount such norms and create an intellectual space open to both genders.[21] The standards and worries of women like the one who censured Bayard likely persisted, yet plenty of men and women did not let that dictate their behavior.

Perhaps the safest groups were the small circles, sometimes only a foursome, formed by married couples. The level of friendship between men and women varied and can be hard to judge from epistolary evidence. It would have been easier for reasons of propriety for wife to write wife, husband to write husband, and then for each couple to share the letters. Letters could switch between partners in each couple, one could write for both, or two letters could be enclosed in one packet. This did not mean that all of the players sent each other the same information, however, as there were unique friendships between individual pairs. Thomas Jefferson often sent separate letters to Abigail and John on the same day with entirely different content; his letters to John were all business, while with Abigail he revealed more emotion and affection, reported on shopping commissions carried out for her, and discussed his opinions on broad political issues. Yet, especially while in France, the three formed their own small circle of friends.

Mercy Otis and James Warren also were friends with the Adamses, and Mercy's biographer suggests "she may have cultivated Abigail in order to get greater access to John Adams." In any case, she wrote them separately and had different relationships with each one of them, although she discussed politics with both.[22] When Mercy requested a "token of love and friendship" in the form of a lock of hair from Abigail, Abigail sent back a lock of her hair along with one of John's, at John's request. Mercy replied graciously (despite a recent argument with John) that the locks of hair would be powerful reminders of "friends who have been entwined to my heart by years of endearment."[23]

Sacred Ties

While social circles provided congenial settings for friendships, religious communities and spiritual language were conducive to safe male/female friendships. For religious men and women, friendships rooted in spirituality were largely removed from worries of earthly sexuality.[24] Friendship, between people of whatever gender, was exalted in Christianity and formed the basis of voluntary religious communities, especially in evangelical churches. Mixed-sex friendships within church communities, then, were completely acceptable and even praiseworthy. A friendship with a fellow-believer, especially a minister, was situated within a religious community and implicitly included God as a third party in the relationship. Friendships were a means of bringing souls into closer connection with God, and the focus on soul over body also made friendships between men and women more natural than in secular settings. Souls, many faith communities emphasized, had no sex.

Christianity's focus on friendship had ancient roots. At its earliest, the biblical Jonathan and David's friendship was the model for Christian friendship, for as Catholic leader Elizabeth Bayley Seton wrote a male friend, "Jonathan loved David as his own Soul."[25] In early Christian communities of celibate men and women in ancient Rome, friendship between men and women replaced marriage.[26] This practice was not lost to history; later generations of men and women consciously attempted to emulate the reciprocal, equal, and affectionate male/female friendships of their religious ancestors.[27] Like the early Christian community, Christian communities in the early republic also used the terminology of fictive kinship to describe their friendships. Particularly in evangelical communities in which individuals rather than families might join a new church, the religious community became a surrogate family.[28]

Fellow believers, then, were not just spiritual friends but brothers and sisters. Unitarian minister William Ellery Channing beseeched his friend Catharine Maria Sedgwick "to talk to me with a friends or sisters freedom" on religious issues.[29] Elizabeth Bayley Seton called her friend Antonio Filicchi, who brought her into the Catholic church, "my most dear Brother" and signed letters to him as his sister. It was Catholic tradition to call nuns and priests "Mother" and "Father," and Seton was later addressed by many of her male friends as "Mother Seton."[30] In cases of a large age gap like that between a devout woman named Sarah Hawkes and her minister, the two referred to each other as father and daughter. Hawkes called Reverend Cecil "my revered minister, my father, and best friend," while he addressed her as "My dearest Daughter."[31]

Because relationships with God were centered on the soul rather than the body, a friendship positioned as being between two souls reduced the issue of gender difference in spiritual mixed-sex friendships. In an era when the body and soul were separated (and gender was increasingly tied only to the body), a friendship between souls could "be a mechanism for dissolving all alienating bodily differences."[32] As Judith Sargent Stevens (later Murray) wrote to her then-friend Reverend John Murray, "I am not much accustomed to writing letters, especially to your sex, but if there be neither male nor female in the Emmanuel [Jesus] you promulgate, we may surely, and with the strictest propriety, mingle souls upon paper."[33] The trope of "mingling souls" suggested an intertwining of selves that would be impossible between *bodies* of friends, giving spiritual friendship a special power. A poem that a male friend of Nancy Andrews recorded in her friendship album, titled "Friendship," attested to this power with the opening lines: "Blest be the power, that mingles soul with soul,/ Each joy to heighten, and each pang controul!"[34]

This notion of a connection among ungendered souls was particularly compatible with Quaker theology, and male/female friendships among the Society of Friends were common and well accepted. Quakers believed that the light of Christ entered bodies, whether male or female, of believers and supplied direct, personal experiences of God.[35] This belief meant that women's spiritual voices were taken just as seriously as men's, even if women could not be leaders in the church. Like men, women could be ministers and share their experiences of the inward light in meetings as well as serving as church elders.[36] Quaker theology went further than evangelical Protestantism in minimizing the body by arguing for the total abnegation of self. Giving up the self also meant giving up desire, allowing spirit rather than selfish human needs and impulses to guide behavior.[37] Presumably, then, a good Quaker who attended to the inward light would be untroubled by sexual attraction in friendships with the opposite sex. These theological underpinnings made the Quaker community a space in which men and women saw each other as religious fellows and potential friends.

Indeed, many Quaker men and women became close friends and wrote one another affectionate letters that intertwined faith and friendship. One Quaker man sent his "most cordial love" and hope that he would be "not only your truly affectionate friend, but according to my small measure, your faithful fellow-labourer in the kingdom and patience of Jesus Christ" to a female friend in 1787.[38] Another man told his friend Rebecca Jones that "thou hast been as an epistle written in my heart" and hoped "that if we keep our first love, we shall come to know an increase."[39] The word "love" was used unabashedly in Quaker friendships, unlike among other male/female pairs who had to be more circumspect. Many men and women addressed each other as "beloved friend." Esther Tuke, a prominent Quaker woman in England, wrote her friend George Churchman in Pennsylvania a letter with the opening, "My beloved friend" and continued, "For so I can call thee in the bond of gospel fellowship." The two had never actually met, but their religious connection made Esther convinced of their friendship: "though we are personally entire strangers, yet in this spiritual kindred we are far otherwise."[40]

Quaker friendships often crossed the Atlantic because of the active traveling ministry of men and women in the early republic.[41] While journeying to small, isolated communities, male and female Quaker ministers spent time on the road together. Women always traveled with a female friend for the sake of propriety, but male friends often escorted them.[42] The memoirs of traveling ministers (of which many survive because they all kept journals) frequently mention time spent with the opposite sex. Patience Brayton, a prominent female minister who traveled throughout America and Britain in the 1770s and 1780s, often recorded having male friends escort her or seeing them at meetings. In 1771 Robert Pleasants spent a week with her and her female companion, and in 1772 her "esteemed friend Ziba Harris" traveled with them for two weeks. She recorded seeing her close friend John Pemberton of Philadelphia multiple times during her visit to Britain in the 1780s.[43] The bonds formed during travels together were strong: as Elizabeth Foulke wrote to fellow Quaker minister William Jackson, there was a "oneness of Spirit in which we travelled together."[44]

The idea of a union of spirits that persisted across time and space extended the concept of a friendship of souls rather than bodies into an ethereal realm. While the term "union of spirits" was used in multiple denominations, it was Quakers who used it most commonly in describing their friendships. Philadelphia Friend George Dillwyn had such a union with Susanna Horne, and he drew upon it to tell the members of his meeting in 1813 that he knew she had landed safely in England before he could have received a letter from her. The author of an 1849 memoir who recounted this story said it offered an example of "the union of spirit which is sometimes permitted to disciples."[45] Usually such unions were called upon in less fantastical circumstances. For instance, Phoebe Prior wrote to William Jackson that she was "feeling a near sympathy & union of spirit with thee."[46] Such unions conquered the vast distances that separated friends who had met on their traveling ministries and maintained strong ties of friendship.

Christians of other denominations also expressed their friendships in terms of spiritual connections, explicitly tying God into their relationships. As a New Jersey woman named Anne Hart wrote to her former minister and friend John Stanford, she desired "a heart to love god supremely—to have communion with him—an entire confidence in his unchangeable love—as you kindly with me."[47] She saw earthly friendships as a model for love of God. Another pious woman, writing about several ministers she had as close friends, echoed this sentiment: "I would above all things desire, that my heart should be affected towards my Saviour, as it is towards a friend dearly beloved."[48] For men and women who were friends, the connection served the added purpose of positioning the relationship as incorporating God as an approving—if ethereal—third party. This is not to suggest that religious language was purely instrumental in these relationships but rather that it had implications that suggested the purity of the relationship.

Those implications were among the important factors that made friendships between women and ministers possible. But what made those friendships particularly desirable was the natural affinity between ministers and their female congregants. Like women, ministers were tasked with the role of caring for others and providing emotional support, while largely removed from the stereotypically male worlds of commerce and public life. Ministers were also sometimes seen as more feminine and sensitive than other men.[49] Whether those qualities were innate or cultivated, ministers took an interest in women's emotional and religious experiences. This was a matter of necessity, especially in evangelical churches, because of women's disproportionate involvement and influence in religious communities.[50] Such friendships may have been natural for many ministers. Two descriptions of ministers who befriended women suggest that people in this era believed that some ministers were simply more feminine than other men. Of the Unitarian minister William Ellery Channing, his biographer writes, "The feminine element, so strong in all men of genius, was dominant in his social nature. This attracted him . . . to women."[51] Feminine qualities were also attributed to a minister named Reverend Mason, whose virtues included affection as well as "meekness, prudence, and diligence."[52]

For women who were friends with ministers, there was nothing out of place about expressions of effusive affections for a minister because it signaled closeness to God. "Favoured with a call from my revered minister," wrote a Mrs. Hawkes of her beloved Reverend Cecil. "My heart burns within me when I hear the instruction and conversation of the godly."[53] Hawkes's burning heart came not from her friend, but from her connection to God through his friendship. The reflections in another pious woman's memoir at her minister's death suggest the depth of attachment the two had shared. "Oh, I feel alone," she wrote. "I should need large communications from his Master to fill up the blank. I cannot write for weeping."[54] Women could also express their love directly to their ministers, without the sort of maneuvering for propriety that men and women performed in other circumstances. Anne Hart finished one letter to her friend Reverend Stanford, "If you chide me, I will bear reproof—and yet love you,—My love and best wishes await your whole self."[55] The late eighteenth-century poet Sarah Apthorp Morton publicly declared her affection for her minister in a poem "to a beloved and revered minister of the Christian Church."[56]

Of course, it was possible for those expressions to raise concerns when accompanied by some evidence of impropriety. The friendship of Sarah Jones and her minister Jeremiah Minter offers one clear example. Jones wrote affective letters imbued with religious passion bordering on the erotic to a number of Methodist preachers. In a 1790 letter to Minter, she wrote: "I love your soul my precious brother!—I am forced to stop, while my lap is wet with tears . . . yes, you should be welcome to my gasping breath, and dying groans, rather than you should fall into sin."[57] Their relationship only became problematic when Minter took the remarkable step of having himself castrated, and the Methodist community suspected he had done so to prevent an affair between himself and Jones. A local Methodist leader interrogated Sarah for five days and Minter fled to the West Indies for a year. Both denied the charges of impropriety and Sarah's husband urged her to write to Minter again when he returned to the community. It is impossible to know the precise character of the relationship, but Sarah had followed the common practices of positioning the relationship safely by placing Jesus at the center of their friendship and referring to Minter and other ministers as "brother."[58]

Perhaps Minter and Jones's story says more about fears of the conflicts between spiritual and actual families than about the realities of one particular relationship. Minter's castration confined him solely to the church family and prevented him from creating his own private family. Indeed, the Christian priority on friendship with God and fellow congregants, expressed through terms of fictive kinship, could threaten sanguinal family ties. This was a central challenge in the southern United States for the evangelical church, where men and women were more deeply entrenched in family and patriarchy than the north.[59] That challenge was also so strong as to stretch beyond earthly families. Evangelicals in this era looked forward to an eternal place in heaven in which they would be united with their friends, not necessarily their families.[60]

Fictive Families

Friendships outside of the spiritual realm also drew on the salience of the sentimental family and the notion of elective families. Describing friendships through the vein of family language made sense in an era when the sentimental family carried increasing importance. No longer a purely patriarchal and instrumental body, the family became a site for building deep emotional bonds as well as the basic unit of the republican polity.[61] Despite this shift, fathers and brothers still took on the roles of guardians for women. Equality between a male and female family member was a gloss over the practical and legal realities, especially for fathers, or brothers acting in a deceased father's stead. Given these patriarchal holdovers, it is not surprising that voluntary bonds built on affinity were the basis of the ideal relationship. Such relationships were, like the nation, "voluntary union[s] based on consent."[62] Friendship stood above other relationships entered into by choice—more business-like contractual relationships, or the clearly hierarchical marriage contract—because it was described as an egalitarian relationship in which both parties contributed to defining the terms in a relationship centered on sympathy.[63] These notions of chosen friends and sentimental families came together when friends referred to each other as family members.

This was not merely a rhetorical gesture, however; these friends treated one another as actual relations and imagined family as "something chosen, rather than a given set of biological or legal relations."[64] This made logical sense for men and women separated from their own families by distance or death.[65] A friend could step in for an absent family member and take on the roles of protector, comforter, and/or confidante. Elevating friends to fictive family members raised these friendships to a greater level of permanence, loyalty, and affection.[66] In the public dimension, the language of fictive kinship signaled the propriety of the relationship to those around a pair and allowed each friend's family to serve as a third party.

Calling a friend "brother" or "sister" was particularly common in this era, an appellation that emphasized an egalitarian rather than hierarchical relationship.[67] Brother-sister ties were strong and highly affectionate in the early republic. These relationships offered spaces for siblings to interact outside of mainstream gender norms and patriarchy by sharing intimacy and interests.[68] Cross-sex sibling relationships, then, were quite similar to cross-sex friendships in this regard. Siblings often expressed their feelings for each other in sentimental, loving language that verged on the romantic.

Referring to friends as siblings allowed men and women to express their affections while shielding them from charges of impropriety. Writers of nineteenth-century advice books held up the brother-sister bond as chaste and pure in a world where sexuality was spiraling out of control.[69] Calling a friend a brother or sister signaled the purity of the friendship to others and pushed back against the assumption that men and women would naturally be sexually attracted. This was a particularly useful tool for single young adults. For example, when a young woman named Elizabeth Slough sought to reassure her friend Fielding Lucas that she enjoyed his lengthy letters, she wrote that "the interest I feel towards you is the same which a Favorite Brother . . . would excite." As the best friend of Lucas's love interest Eliza Carrell, Elizabeth Slough needed to position her affection for him within nonsexual bounds—particularly since she seems to have been sharing her correspondence with Eliza Carrell.[70] Brothers and sisters often offered advice and channels of communication to the opposite sex during courtship, which Elizabeth did for Fielding.[71]

A single woman who professed love for a man in the capacity of a brother shifted the meaning of that love from romantic to sisterly with a single phrase. Eloise Payne recounted the story of what a difference that phrase could make to her friend Catharine Maria Sedgwick. She prefaced the story by explaining that Catharine's brother Robert was "a prime favorite" with her. She then explained that in a crowd of friends in New York, perhaps including Catharine's brothers, Eloise had "expos'd [her]self to a laugh . . . via a very ingenuous expression viz that I lov'd Robert as a brother." However, just after she said "I love Robert," Eloise was "seiz'd with a fit of coughing & before I could gain breath to finish my sentence," and her friends broke out laughing. To have made a declaration of romantic love for Robert was so brazen as to be humorous, but to say she loved him as a brother was perfectly acceptable.[72]

Others evoked the language of kinship when questions about romance between friends of the opposite sex arose. When a newspaper reported that Nelly Custis was going to marry George Washington Lafayette, Nelly protested this claim by asserting that she saw him only as a brother. Nelly insisted that she would "ever feel an interest & sincere regard for my *young adopted Brother*" but that "as to being *in love with him* it is entirely out of the question."[73] Nelly's emphasis aligned the young Lafayette's status as her brother with the impossibility of sharing a romance with him. Similarly, Elizabeth Ann Bayley Seton, a deeply religious wife and mother, referred to two different men as her brothers. Before her conversion to Catholicism, she had a close friendship with her Episcopalian minister, Rev. John Henry Hobart, whom she imagined as her Brother—a term she employed when begging him not to cut her off when she converted.[74] She felt even greater affection for the man who became her guide in her conversion, Antonio Filicchi. She wrote him frequently and called him "my most dear Brother," signing her letters as "your sister." By the time of this friendship she had lost her husband, but Filicchi was married. The inclusion of the word "sister" in the subscription "Most truely, really, sincerely, simply without exaggeration, I am yours, all that is mine to give Your Sister Friend Servant EAS" perhaps dampened the romantic overtones of the letter.[75]

It was also possible to reposition an unrequited or failed romance with the language of kinship in order to maintain emotional intimacy but disclaim any sexual dimension. A 1785 poem published in the *Boston Gazette* provided this repositioning as a solution to unrequited love. When the woman the poet addressed failed to return his feelings, the man asked, "What alternative then can we substitute here?" He quickly concluded:

> *[HE:] The Statutes and Canons effectually parrying,*
> *We will Love, in spite of them all, without Marrying.*
> *This substitute settled, let us keep it in view—*
> *Be you then,* My dear Sister.—*SHE. And* My dear Brother, *you.*[76]

This is the same "substitute" that Dolley Payne Todd's failed suitor William W. Wilkins seems to have settled upon in the 1790s. Wilkins confided to Dolley in a 1794 letter that, "Time Absence and Reason have destroyed that Violence of Attachment which made me appear so unamiable in thy Eyes and must have injured me in thy Esteem." Now, he felt "a mild and gentle Affection" and wished to assure her "that I was now indeed thy Brother and worthy a portion of thy Regard." Dolley seems to have treated him in this way, writing him to ask his opinion on her marriage to James Madison. He replied that he approved of the match: "To such a Man therefore I do most freely consent that my beloved Sister be united and happy."[77]

For men and women with limited or strained family ties, fictive friends filled an important gap. Nelly Custis's sister Eliza had a large family, but her erratic personality led to her alienation from her kin.[78] She turned to David Bailie Warden as a surrogate brother. When Warden moved to Europe for a diplomatic post, Eliza was eager to maintain the relationship. She began writing him regularly with lengthy and often melodramatic prose. Particularly when seeking favors from him, she employed the terms of fictive kinship. In an 1814 letter asking him to help out her intended husband, she framed her repeated requests for his service as a way to show his brotherly affection for her. "At parting with me," she reminded him, "when tears attested to your sorrow you solemnly promised ever to be my faithful friend—ever to feel a Brother's affn for me, & do me service if in your power." She assured him that she felt "a Sister's affn" for him.

Both Nelly and Eliza, who lost their father at a very young age, saw their step-grandfather George Washington's friend the Marquis de Lafayette as a close friend and surrogate father. Lafayette addressed both women as their "paternal tender friend." The closings to his letters always offered some reminder of this familial affiliation, even if the rest of the letter did not: they ranged from reminding Eliza of "my affectionate sympathy and paternal love," to providing "the sympathies and love of your old paternal friend," to sending his "love and blessing" "most truly, tenderly, and paternally."[79]

But Lafayette went beyond labeling the relationship as paternal; he tried to fill the role of the father whom Eliza had lost at such a young age. When she wrote him worrying about her personal and family troubles in 1828, he replied in a lengthy epistle sympathizing with his "dear daughter" and saying "I . . . wish I was near you, trusting that my presence and tenderness could some what contribute to alleviate your affliction." He then offered his "paternal feelings" "in one point only," reminding her that while she was worried that her son-in-law would cause her daughter and grandchildren to stop loving her, this was truly impossible.[80] These were not Lafayette's "feelings," then, but more precisely paternal wisdom—if not subtle chastisement for her overwrought fears. Lafayette likely positioned this point as his "feelings" because he was not her true father, and he did not have the patriarchal authority to criticize her.

For Nelly, Lafayette served as a father, and his son, born the same year as Nelly, as her brother. When the two men visited with Nelly in Washington in 1825, Lafayette gave her an honor bestowed only once upon his own children: he "shewed me the picture of his wife, which he wears in his bosom, & permitted me to kiss it." George Washington Lafayette told Nelly that "I am happy to think that you have received from my Father, the most tender proof of affection in his power to bestow." After the men departed, Nelly wrote of the incident to her friend Elizabeth Bordley and shared her sadness at saying goodbye to "my Beloved *Father* & *Brother*."[81]

The American who created what was perhaps the most expansive fictive family, however, was Benjamin Franklin. While many Americans today think of Franklin as a philanderer, several scholars have insisted that Franklin saw his younger female friends as daughters rather than lovers. An array of women Franklin spent time with at French salons in the 1780s referred to him as "Mon cher papa"—all but one, his contemporary Madame Helvetius, the one woman with whom Franklin biographer Claude-Anne Lopez argues Franklin was in love.[82] For Franklin, young women like Madame Brillon in Paris, Margaret Stevenson Hewson in London, and Catharine Ray Greene in Rhode Island, provided him with surrogate daughters to meet needs his own family could not. As historian Jan Lewis writes, Franklin's own patriarchal family was unable to provide him "the companionship of equals or the communion of teacher and student, the ideals of the republican family." Thus

Franklin created a republican family that in many ways he treated better than his own, knowing no other way for describing his close friendships with women than as family members.[83]

Yet Franklin's fictive kin relations, more than most others, retained a sexual edge. He clearly flirted with his female friends, "hovering between the risqué and the avuncular."[84] It appears, however, that his female friends preferred to keep their relationships with Franklin nonsexual.[85] Madame Brillon presumably declined his advances when she wrote to him that "Perhaps there is no great harm in a man having desires and yielding to them; a woman may have desires, but she must not yield."[86] That Franklin had sexual desires for some of his female friends seems clear, but he conscientiously described the relationships in familial terms.

The notion that Franklin could occupy the role of both an uncle and a flirtatious friend hints at the fact that the precise definitions of family and incest were still in flux in this era.[87] This rendered the use of the terminology of fictive kinship—whether the language of siblings or parent and child—less of a safeguard than we might imagine. Given the societal investment in the notion that men and women must be sexually attracted to one another, what would happen between men and women from the same family? Novels in this period voiced anxieties about these unclear boundaries, particularly between siblings. Brothers and sisters who had been separated met and fell in love, only to discover their true relationship; and others who saw each other as brother and sister but were so by choice only could fall in love and marry happily.[88] Even young men and women who were raised together as siblings, such as cousins Edmund and Fanny Bartrum in Jane Austen's *Mansfield Park*, were presented as ideal mates. There was a substantive difference when it came to sexual relations, if not overt emotional expressions, between real and fictive kin.

Thus, to say that friends could be imagined as family was not the simple solution to the problem of positioning cross-gender friendships. The complicated boundaries of family and sexuality created problems for both real and fictive kin. Could the love of fictive families surpass that of sanguinal ones? In novels of the nineteenth century, those fears were repeatedly explored in stories in which relationships formed out of choice superseded blood relationships.[89] Finally, the shift away from patriarchal power had not erased the power of fathers and even brothers over women in the family. A chosen family was entirely outside of the strictures of patriarchy and provided a more egalitarian model of family than sanguinal families could. However, the priority for men and women was always first and foremost their sanguinal family; leaving that family for an elective one was precisely the accusation critics leveled against evangelicals. The prerogatives of the sanguinal family limited the revolutionary potential of the chosen family of friends.

Marriage

Nowhere was the dominance of the family over friendships more important than in the case of spouses. Indeed, the most important third party to include in a friendship between a man and woman married to others was the spouse. In marriages, as in other social settings, there could be extended lines of mutual friendships. But a marriage changed the status and role of a man or woman to a husband or wife, a figure whose identity was defined through the spouse. It was nearly impossible, then, to leave the spouse out of the equation. This was the case whether the friendship formed between already married people or had to adapt after a marriage.

Friends recognized that for either of them to marry would change the dynamic of their relationship by stretching their dyad to include a spouse. Shortly before her marriage to John P. Van Ness in 1802, twenty-year-old Marcia Burns received a letter from her friend Richard Claiborne bidding goodbye to Miss Burns and hello to Mrs. Van Ness. "Adieu sweet Girl," Claiborne, twenty-five years Burns's senior, wrote; "adieu that juvenile tete a tete, that delightful harmony, with which I was used to pass my evening with her, and which will ever dwell on my mind." It was not the end of their relationship, but it was a shift: "Come real friendship, and let me recognize my Marcia in the character of Mrs. Van Ness. I pray heaven to grant you mutual happiness."[90] Just as Claiborne shifted to using Marcia's married name, he addressed both her and her husband. Claiborne and Marcia could no longer have a private tete-a-tete; the friendship would be a circle of three. Claiborne remained friends with Mrs. Van Ness, passing along his affection to her through her husband in a letter the next year in which he told Mr. Van Ness: "Kiss [Mrs. Van Ness] as hard as you can."[91]

A British diplomat writing from Washington, D.C., in 1805 was less sanguine about the possibilities for continuing friendship with a woman after she married. Calling marriage "the first death of a woman," Augustus Foster lamented that when women marry, "I am sure all their friends, their male ones at least, receive a pang when they change Charactors so completely."[92] Foster's pang was over his friend Lady Caroline Ponsonby, who had married William Lamb a few months earlier. Foster had lived in Devonshire House with Lady Caroline for a year when both were teenagers and later corresponded with her occasionally. Now that she was married, he believed, the friendship would be at an end. This was probably in large part because Foster, away from home for many years, did not know Caroline's husband.

In some cases, however, friendships between a man and a woman were easier once one of them was engaged or married. The addition of the spouse as a third person in the friendship could have its benefits for propriety. A young woman named Jane Minot made precisely this point in a letter to her fiancé Harry Sedgwick, who had long been friends with Jane's group of female friends in Boston (the "friendlies"). Their friend Mary, Jane reported in an 1817 letter to Harry, had told Jane about a dream in which Harry appeared. Mary "has a most enthusiastick fondness for you," Jane continued. She then explained that: "The friendlies all seem to enjoy the privilege of speaking as highly of you as they wish: since there is now no danger of a wrong construction to their language."[93] While already ensconced in the safety of a mixed-sex group, Mary evidently felt that Harry's marriage made it safer to express her friendship with him.

Once a man or woman was engaged or married, it seems, both the friends and those around them were less likely to interpret friendship as possible romance. A married man or woman was no longer available for courtship, and for people who took the bonds of marriage quite seriously, this meant that a friendship across sexes would not be likely to be misinterpreted as a romance. A male friend of a recently married woman pointed out to her husband that it would be fine for her to write her old friend; "*now* she will incur no risque, she being yours *bona fide*."[94] Similarly, a single Savannah woman named Mary Telfair offered her married brother up as a companion to her friend Mary Few. "If your taste is similar to mine," Telfair told Few, "you prefer married Men to single." The reason, Telfair hypothesized, is that they could "entertain no apprehension of being pleased or pleasing too much."[95]

This presumed either that propriety would overcome true feeling or that it was impossible to develop romantic feelings for somebody already attached—both dubious propositions, but apparently liberating to those who worried about friendships between single men and women. There was less worry of a friendship being destroyed by misunderstood feelings, which was a real danger. It could also be that having a spouse provided an automatic third party for friendships, and one more secure than a social circle. This made the friendship more appropriate and less likely to be misinterpreted.

Yet the spouse had to be a willing third, and husbands in particular could place obstacles to friendships. For a married woman to befriend another man required at the least her husband's knowledge and at most his explicit approval. Writer William Thompson testified to this when he asked in 1825, "Is there a wife of civilized society who can dream to advance beyond acquaintances, to the formation of friendships with other women or with men, without the express approbation of her husband?"[96] Despite the rhetoric of companionate marriage, women remained legally subjugated to their husbands in the late eighteenth and early nineteenth century.[97] A husband and wife might negotiate power relations, but for legal purposes a married woman counted as a wife rather than an individual. A husband's control over his wife had both public and private importance, as demonstrating domestic authority served as a basis for a man's political rights.[98] One of the husband's prerogatives in the household, whether he chose to exercise it or not, was control over his wife's socializing and relationships.

It seems hard to imagine a situation more antithetical to the era's preoccupation with the formation of voluntary, sentimental bonds. As William Thompson (whose book was based on conversations with his friend Anna Wheeler and may often have used her own words) dramatically stated, even female slaves of the West Indies did not have to obtain approval from men in their choice of friends.[99] Granted, female slaves had no need for chastity and reputation as social capital. Surely Thompson realized this, and he drew on a thread of feminist discourse in Britain that compared wives to slaves as a rhetorical tool to demonstrate the oppression of women.[100] The lack of freedom in choice of friends, whether male or female, was only one instance of such oppression. Thompson's claims were not new, either; thirty years earlier, William Godwin had argued that marriage was "the most odious of all monopolies." For Godwin, like Thompson, husbands were jealous property owners who restricted access to their wives.[101]

In the case of a friendship between a married woman and a man, the friendship was subject to a husband's scrutiny, permission, and involvement, if he chose to exercise this power. The bachelor John Farmer, in a letter to his recently married friend Lucy Spalding, suggested that husbands' reason for restricting women's friendships with men was largely jealousy. Lucy was fortunate, John wrote to her, that her husband "does not regard me as an object of dread or as likely to estrange the affections of his wife."[102] Other women were not so lucky. Nancy Shippen complained that she "was not at liberty to indulge that friendship" with her former suitor "Leander" (Louis Otto) "because it would displease my husband."[103] Nancy lived separately from her husband in a different city, but she probably had concerns beyond angering her husband; she was likely worried that those around her would consider her friendship with Otto inappropriate in the absence of her husband as a third party. The longer the two were separated, however, the less force these fears had; Nancy ultimately saw Otto often. Over the years, Otto urged Nancy to reconcile with her husband, reinforcing his status as a friend rather than a suitor.[104]

The sheer frequency of friendships between men and married women suggests that husbands often permitted their wives to enter such relationships or simply did not exercise their authority by interfering. The existence of the protocol here did not prevent friendships between married women and men, suggesting the constant tension between rule and reality. Yet the very power to grant permission displayed the husband's authority. This element of authority over entry into the egalitarian realm of friendship pushed friendships between men and married women away from the sentimental ideal. Indeed, how could any married woman be in an ideal friendship if she did not retain the right to freely enter the relationship and define its terms without outside influence? This left men's friendships with each other as the central realm of ideal friendship and supported the notion that the model sentimental, republican friendship was a fraternal one.[105]

Husbands had greater freedom than their wives to determine their acquaintances and retain privacy in their friendships after marriage. A man's movements in society were shared with his wife only by "peculiar courtesy and condescension," Thompson claimed, and a husband might befriend any man or woman he chose without consulting his wife. This is not to say that men's friendships were unchanged by marriage. For both men and women, marriage involved new roles, obligations, and a lessening of personal space.[106] Thus, while husbands did not need to ask their wives for permission, some men referenced a wife's approval of their friendship. In the mid-eighteenth century, before Franklin's stay in Europe where he made numerous female friends, he befriended Catharine Ray with claims of his wife's blessing. He expressed his (perhaps sarcastic) appreciation for his wife's approval when he told Ray that "since she [his wife] is willing I should love you as much as you are willing to be lov'd by me; let us join in wishing the old Lady a long Life and a happy."[107]

Adult Women on Their Own

For married women who lived apart from their husbands, fears about sexuality were less acute than in the case of other women, and thus the social positioning was far easier. This is not to suggest that such women could befriend any man they wanted without fear of censure or that they had broad sexual license, but the fears were significantly diminished in their situation.

For divorced or widowed women, there was greater social tolerance as well as freedom from a male protector if they chose to form friendships with men. While they did not have a male protector to enter their relationships as a third party, their status as mature women seems to have loosened the societal concerns about propriety. After all, these women were considered safe escorts and moral police for younger women, so they were presumably experienced enough to behave properly.[108]

The way an independent woman positioned her friendships with men, however, could either circumvent or feed scandal. Bostonian socialite Hepzibah Swan, whose husband abandoned her and moved to London, was close friends with Henry Knox and General Henry Jackson.[109] Her relationship with Knox seems to have incurred no censure; although married himself, he escorted her in public and had a presence as a public figure in Swan's home in the form of a full-length portrait. Swan's relationship with Jackson, however, prompted whispering in Boston society because while he nominally lived at a boarding house, he spent most of his time at the Swan home. One of Swan's acquaintances wrote to another, "This the world would call scandal, but to you I know it be *sweet incense*."[110] Among her circle of friends, Swan's liaison seemed to be more a topic of gossip than condemnation. He took care of Swan's finances and even served as a father figure for Swan's children; Swan's daughter Kitty called him "le général" because of his firm authority. When Jackson died in 1809, Swan buried him in her garden with a tombstone reading "Christian, Soldier, Patriot and Friend."[111] While Knox and Swan were friends, Jackson was certainly a surrogate husband and perhaps a lover. Nonetheless, Swan presented both men as her friends; it was their position inside her household that ultimately shaped public opinion.

An ocean also divided Baltimore socialite Elizabeth Patterson Bonaparte from her husband, Jerome Bonaparte, before their eventual divorce in 1815.[112] Fashioning herself as "Mrs. Patterson" and enjoying financial independence, she was free to travel where she wished and socialize with whichever men she liked. Patterson never remarried, but she maintained numerous friendships with men in the European salons she visited and corresponded with Baltimore friends James McElhiney, Robert Gilmor, and David Bailie Warden. She also inspired poetry by male admirers at social gatherings in Washington.[113] Patterson likely knew another woman on her own in Washington society, Eliza Parke Custis, who kept a voluminous correspondence with their mutual friend David Bailie Warden.[114]

Perhaps the most successful of all independent women was Elizabeth Graeme Fergusson, who built an elite intellectual circle of men and women around her after she and her husband separated. Fergusson counted a number of prominent men as friends, including John Dickinson, Francis Hopkinson, Bishop William White, University of Pennsylvania president William Smith, and Benjamin Rush.[115] Fergusson wrote enough letters to Rush to fill a thick volume in Rush's collection of papers, addressing him as "dear friend" and discussing both her own writings and his interest in medicine. She expressed her deep care for him (and, perfunctorily, his wife) in many of these letters. She so feared for her friend's health during Philadelphia's 1793 yellow fever outbreak that she wrote to him, "I think of you every hour, and ask every Creature after you: I have rejoic'd every time I have seen your name in the paper because it is a proof you are alive." She could scarcely imagine how his wife must have felt "when I am tremblingly [alive] all over for you."[116] A feme sole like Fergusson, having passed her age of sexual vulnerability, enjoyed much broader scope for affectionate friendships with men than did other women.

Annis Boudinot Stockton was a widowed member of Fergusson's circle who, like her friend, hosted a number of male companions at her home. Her biographer argues that after the death of Stockton's husband, she "could more acceptably—in both the social and legal sense of 'acceptable' behavior—engage in political action." Such action was dependent upon fostering friendships with men, which was also easier without a husband present. Stockton's home at Morven, near Princeton, New Jersey, became the gathering place of statesmen while Congress was at Princeton in 1783. George Washington had already befriended Stockton during the war, and he continued to visit her while in the area.[117] Her widowhood allowed her to freely enter the domains of male/female friendship, politics, and even print culture as she wrote poetic tributes to male friends like Washington.

Social and legal practices bent by necessity for widowed women like Stockton. The survival of the family was more important than female propriety, and this meant that widows acted in ways and arenas that were closed off to married women.[118] In the South, while "white women's vulnerability beyond their own homes" was a common worry, "prosperous slaveholding widows traveled with comparative impunity, with or without chaperones." But widows were still ladies, and historian Kirsten Wood argues that the idea of "dependent ladyhood" drew men to come to a widow's aid to further "their own financial interests, familial honor, or personal reputation for chivalry."[119] This rather instrumental interpretation may not capture the entire picture; perhaps men recognized that a widowed woman offered an opportunity for friendship across gender lines. In the South, where social life was more circumscribed by distance and gender conventions, a widow offered a man a rare chance at a close friendship with a woman.[120]

Often the men who came to a widow's aid and befriended her had been her deceased husband's friends. That friendship had likely extended to the wife, but after the loss of her husband, epistolary evidence suggests that the friendships between the widow and the husband's friend blossomed. This was the situation for Delia Forman Bryan, whose husband Joseph had studied law in Philadelphia with John Randolph of Roanoke. That friendship continued even after Joseph returned home to his plantation in Georgia and John to his in Virginia. Their friendship was so close that Joseph and Delia named their first son not after a relative, but after John Randolph. No correspondence survives between John and Delia before her husband's death in 1812, but after that time the two shared a close friendship through letters. As John explained in 1816, he felt an "ardent attachment" to Joseph but had an equal attachment to Delia.[121] On Delia's part, she told John in 1819 that "I have _ever_ view'd you as my first and best friend."[122]

Their deep attachment to each other was rendered safe not just by Delia's widowhood but also by the fact that neither was inclined to marry or even, in John's case, able to be sexually active. John had suffered an illness in 1792 that "left him without palpable signs of manhood" and with a high-pitched voice and thin frame.[123] He was briefly engaged in 1799 but never married. As for Delia Bryan, she was only thirty when her husband died and she could have remarried. But John remarked after her death at forty-three that "her remaining a widow 13 years at her time of life & with her attractions & impulses to matrimony is her highest eulogium."[124] It would seem that Delia chose to remain single, a choice that John admired. The two formed their friendship around another entirely proper object: the education of the Bryans' sons. Whether at her husband's wishes or by her own choice, Delia had determined that John would raise her sons.

Some widowed women had male friends within their households who took on the duties of a surrogate husband, just as Swan had taken in Henry Jackson. Here, again, a friend was integrated into an imagined family. This occurred in the case of Margaret Stevenson. To sustain herself financially as a widow, Stevenson took on boarders at her house in London. That house became Benjamin Franklin's home for twenty years, and those who knew the pair treated them as husband and wife—despite the fact that Franklin's own wife was alive in America during much of that time. Franklin referred to their relationship as "our long continu'd Friendship" and continued to correspond with Stevenson occasionally after he left England.[125] He treated

Stevenson's daughter, Polly, as if she were his own daughter (and likely better than his actual daughter), as he had other young women during his time in Europe. He even convinced Polly to move with her young children to America to spend his last years with him. Franklin valued Polly's mother as a surrogate family member as well, but in this case as his wife.[126] A wife clearly differed from a daughter when it came to sexual relationships, and it is certainly possible that Franklin's relationship with Stevenson, like Swan and Jackson's, included the sexual intimacy of a marriage.

The value widows placed on men who could stand in for their husbands often trumped any worries about gossip about their relationships. As the narrator explained approvingly of the widowed mother Horatia in the novel *Antoinette Percival*:

> She had, however, one friend yet left, doctor Schomberg, who had for more than two years been a constant inmate in the house, and whom she desired to continue as such; wisely setting at defiance any censures, which a babbling, ill-natured world might pass on her, for acting thus contrary to its arbitrary laws, which she considered as trifles, when put in comparison with the solid advantages, which she hoped would result to herself and the children, from having such a man constantly with them.[127]

Had Horatia had a more public friendship with Schomberg as Swan did with Knox, she would likely have escaped criticism. But like Swan's choice to have a male friend live in her home, Horatia's decision to have Schomberg "a constant inmate in the house" raised concerns. As with other women in situations of social delicacy, Horatia weighed boundaries and benefits and ultimately decided the risk was worthwhile.

Horatia's decision in the face of her fears of the "babbling, ill-natured world" with its "arbitrary laws" points to a complicated and sometimes contradictory mess of rules of propriety. Loosely defined conventions singled out numerous instances in which friendships between men and women were improper. Women, in particular, faced risks at any stage of life if they befriended a man: as single women they risked seduction if they spent time alone with male friends; as married women, they supposedly needed the protection of their husbands; as divorcées or widows they could become fodder for the gossip mill if they brought a male friend into their households. Ideals even could be at odds with each other, at once prioritizing both friends and family as model relationships. Yet the exaltation of friendship in both religious and secular life, as well as the possible openings for safe positioning, seems to have left plenty of room for men and women to become friends. The relationship simply could not be an idealized private, self-absorbed dyad; society insisted that it display public evidence of its propriety.

To address public perceptions, friends created haphazard patterns working around the rules. It was these behaviors, as much as the fears and ill-defined rules, which actually constructed the norms of propriety for a new social order. For all the prescriptive writings on ideal friendships, it was the behavior of actual men and women that began to build the norms for the real, messy friendships of everyday life.[128] Their actions did not move toward radical change or toward confronting norms about how men and women would relate. Rather, men and women had to work so hard at positioning their friendships because they were invested in that very order: they, too, wanted to find sexual and marital partners and form families. These pairs of friends placed their friendships squarely within the nation's social institutions through subtle forms of resistance that would be as little disruptive as possible.

Friendships between men and women modeled the ways that friendships could and must remain part of larger social networks. Conversely, these friendships also demonstrate the way that families and marriages were themselves tied into communities. No relationship was an island, and by interlacing friends, family members, and spouses, men and women built a web of virtuous ties. All of these ties, Americans believed, were vital to sustaining the newly formed nation. Friendships between men and women could, with careful work, become part of the social glue that held the new republic together.

5

Friendly Letters

"ILLIBERAL CUSTOM PREVENTS a correspondence between the sexes," Nancy Shippen wrote in 1784.[1] Yet in letter writing as with personal interactions, friends broke from such "illiberal custom" and maintained their friendships with people of the opposite sex with careful positioning and hewing to virtuous, egalitarian ideals. Given how often friends were separated from one another, and sometimes for the majority of their friendships, letters were a vital means to keep up friendships and substitute for absent friends. Indeed, letters were more than means of conveying information. As Elihu Hubbard Smith wrote to his friend Idea Strong, "Correspondencies, like partnerships & marriages, may produce important consequences, & ought to be engaged in with some caution, & much meditation."[2] That caution and mediation was amply recorded in letters between male/female friends, and it was necessary in part because letters were much less private than we might imagine.

Examining the process of letter exchange and the ways friends framed their letters to one another illustrates how the boundaries and practices of mixed-sex friendships operated in everyday life. With no published models to turn to, the practice of writing letters also helped create the appropriate bounds for proper letterwriting between male/female friends as well as shaping the boundaries of the friendships themselves.[3] This was a practice not merely of writing, but of the exchange of material substitutes for absent friends through the written word, paper, and even personal seals.[4] These letters could model the proper forms for male/female friendship and how to carry on those relationships. In letters between male/female friends, then, there was an accretion of practices that gave men and women a sense for the acceptable forms for letters and expression in these relationships.

Many of these writers acknowledged that they were subverting an "illiberal custom"—or, in other writers' words, "foolish prejudice," "an established rule," "what prudes may call the rules of propriety," "errors of common fastidiousness," or "fictitious regulations." In other words, these writers were aware of a prohibition on writing between unmarried men and women.

Such a prohibition played an important part in crafting model heterosexual interactions that would lead to virtuous marriages. It is difficult to tell precisely how much of a hold this rule had on men and women because we cannot know how many friends were willing to forgo writing each other because of it, but there are many examples of the rule being broken and derided. The fact that men and women felt the need to apologize for or explain why they were breaking the rule, and to carefully position their letters within their social networks, suggests that they recognized their quiet, careful transgressions. It is not that these friends thought they could overturn custom, but rather that they could manipulate it to serve their own ends. Here are tactics that refuse to conform to the established order, lending a subtle political valence of resistance and creating some space for freedom in the everyday practice of writing a friendly letter.[5]

Letters as Public Objects

Letters were not merely private communications but also semi-public objects that could convey messages to circles of people. They were often read aloud or passed among a circle of friends. Especially for women dependent on a husband or father, letters could be monitored for proper behavior.[6] Even in transit, letters were not private. Letter writers often noted who carried a letter for them, particularly if it crossed the Atlantic, in part to signify the level of privacy the writer expected as the letter made its way to the recipient.[7] The choices writers made in shaping both the appearance and physical aspects of the letter, as well as its content, were important in shaping community perceptions.

Even the outside of a letter, with its address and seal, could incite gossip. Elizabeth Slough, whose best friend Eliza was courting their mutual friend Fielding Lucas, knew that his letters would "pass through several hands before they are delivered into mine." Thus, she asked Lucas to stop using his seal on the letters he sent her because "the *good* People here have determined that you are *my* Beaux."[8] For cross-sex friends, the worry was about more than private information becoming public. Their concerns turned on expressions of sentiment and whether that sentiment would be misinterpreted as romantic love rather than friendship.

As Elizabeth Slough's case demonstrates, however, sentiment was conveyed not just through words but also through material signs. The carefully folded pages, inscribed in a friend's unique hand and sealed with melted wax, constituted an object of exchange, an artifact that substituted for a correspondent's physical presence. Letter writing guides often specified proper posture, the way to hold a pen, even appropriate facial expressions, imbuing handwriting with the sense of the body being translated into ink on the page.[9]

At a time when letters were often delivered by an acquaintance, even if sent through the postal service, prying eyes would look for fodder for gossip. As Benjamin Franklin wrote his friend Catharine Ray in 1755, "I know very well that the most innocent Expressions of warm Friendship, and even those of meer Civility and Complaisance, between Persons of different Sexes, are liable to be misinterpreted by suspicious Minds; and therefore though you say more, I say less than I think."[10] Franklin was writing before the great expansion in personal correspondence, and particularly before it became common for well-educated women to write personal letters in the British Atlantic.[11] Already he had sensed the risks inherent in a pair of men and women corresponding (particularly when one was a famous public figure) and suggested how he would choose his words carefully. While by the early republic plenty of pairs of men and women wrote one another, Franklin's concern about "suspicious Minds" was still a problem.

Abigail Adams's friend James Lovell was not as circumspect as Franklin, causing her great alarm. After two particularly flirtatious letters, she chastised Lovell on the grounds that his words could cause them both public embarrassment. She asked Lovell, "What a figure would some passages of a Letter Dated Janry. 6th and another of Janry. 13th have made in a publick Newspaper? For a Senator too?"[12] If their letters had been intercepted, it was possible they could enter print for widespread public distribution.

Model Correspondence

Published letters most often served as a means for modeling the standard forms and practices of correspondence. Letter-writing manuals were the most important source of models for the practice of writing to people of various circles. As historian Konstantin Dierks argues, these manuals guided an emergent middle class that was somewhat new to letter writing in the late eighteenth century. By publishing common templates (so common that identical letters appear in many of the books), the manuals aimed "to harmonize circles of family, kin and friends with sentimentalism."[13] As the author of one of these guides advised his readers: "When you write to a friend, your letter should be a true picture of your heart; the stile loose and irregular; the thoughts themselves should appear naked, and not dressed in the borrowed robes of rhetoric."[14] Yet the manuals themselves offered highly stylized examples, and letter writers had to find the right balance between following form and maintaining sincerity. The guides did not suggest differing standards for men and women (except in narrow examples of courtship disputes), but in practice men and women shaped their identities as writers in differing ways. The manuals may have been a starting point, but it was up to individual letter writers to observe the standards of those around them and improvise.[15]

The proliferation of letter-writing manuals offered little guidance for correspondence between friends of the opposite sex, although manuals never declared outright that men and women could not write each other. Generic letters between friends in manuals almost always included friends of the same sex and most often unnamed recipients in these templates were referred to as "Sir." A majority of the letters between men and women involved family members or courting couples. That models for letters of courtship rather than friendship existed shows the dominant understanding of male/female relations as sexual rather than purely social. But even the courtship letters were of limited scope, providing models for difficulties in love, but not for the pleasures of it.[16] Only one manual included a letter criticizing male/female friendship and declared it could not exist. "A Lady" wrote in reply to a note from a man (which was not included in the guide) that "Real friendship . . . does not I think, generally subsist between the sexes" and thus it would be "dangerous for me to trust to your friendship." Yet she conceded that, "As an acquaintance, I shall always be happy to see you," implying that while they can continue to have affable conversations in public, they cannot be friends and certainly not correspondents.[17]

The closest thing to a model for letters between mixed-sex friends were those of a woman and her minister, such as a letter from Lady Russell to her clergyman in which she referred to him as "one so much my friend."[18] Because friendships between women and clergymen were socially acceptable, such correspondence would not be subject to the same scrutiny as letters between other male/female pairs. Still, there was no generic template provided for such letters, only an example in the back of a volume amidst sample letters by notable figures. Indeed, the only examples in manuals of letters between mixed-sex friends were printed letters written by actual people, rather than the models the books most often provide. Religious friends might also look to the memoirs of pious women for similar examples, many of which relied on letters to tell the women's stories.

Novels, too, were often told through, or at least included, letters, but very rarely were those letters between a pair of male/female friends. Unlike the disjointed model letters in conduct manuals, epistolary novels offered similar conduct advice through an exchange of letters that formed a plot. This was a more relatable way of learning the skills and rules of letter writing.[19] But because novels rarely included long-term, safe male/female friendships, there was little chance for them to offer complete models for correspondence in such friendships.

Hannah Webster Foster's *The Coquette* offers a rare example of a letter exchange between mixed-sex friends, but the course of the story ultimately subverts the message of the letter. When the main character Eliza and Reverend Boyer decide early in the novel to become friends and see if it leads to love, they begin writing one another. In response to Boyer's first letter to her, Eliza extols the virtue of "a correspondence, tending to promote a friendship and social intercourse." Here she ignores the possibility for future romance between the two. She goes on to admit that "An epistolary communication between the sexes has been with some, a subject of satire and censure; but unjustly, in my opinion." Eliza then turns to the idea of complementarity to support the usefulness of correspondence between men and women: "The knowledge and masculine virtues of your sex may be softened, and rendered more diffusive by the inquisitiveness, vivacity, and docility of ours; drawn forth and exercised by each other."[20] Ultimately, however, Eliza and Boyer gain no benefit from their correspondence; Eliza persists in avoiding marriage and the two stop corresponding when Boyer decides there is no possibility of marriage resulting from this friendship.

Of course, men and women had extensive experience with writing same-sex friends and family, and these letters modeled the most basic forms for letter writing. Letters often began with a mention of the last letters sent and received and ended by sending messages of affection to the recipient and friends and family in the same circle. The content of letters often included quotidian updates on the health of the writer and his or her family, as well as the latest news in the community. But the emotional tenor and choice of words to convey degrees of affection clearly differed based on the relationship between the writers.

Studies of same-sex friendships often quote the effusive phrases used in letters friends wrote one another, but such language is unusual in letters between friends of the opposite sex. Same-sex friendships could adopt the romantic language of courtship without the risks that mixed-sex pairs would incur.[21] "I knew not how closely our feelings were interwoven; had no idea how hard it would be to live apart," Daniel Webster wrote his friend James Bingham in 1800.[22] Of particular interest to scholars has been the suggestions of eroticism in some of these letters, as when William Wirt wrote his friend

Dabney Carr, "I wish I had hold of your hand—you should be electrified with a vengeance."[23] Similarly, Sophie DuPont's friend Eliza Schlatter wrote her friend that she wished she could "turn your good husband out of bed—and snuggle into you and we would have a long talk like old times."[24] Particularly for a form so easily made public as a letter, friends of the opposite sex could not have written such sentiments with propriety. Even for men and women quite practiced at writing letters to same-sex friends, such letters could not serve as templates for writing friends of the opposite sex.

Fine Lines

If there was no model for correspondence between male/female friends, what differentiated the friendly letters from the romantic ones? In some cases, the differences are very slight. The sort of visual, bodily clues that friends might offer in person were impossible in letters. The use of the term "friend" is also not helpful, as both courting and married couples commonly referred to each other as friends. Most letters between two friends, family members, or spouses contained similar content: the latest news on friends and family, discussions of books read or talks attended, and inquiries into each other's health. Sometimes the character of the relationship can only be understood within a larger context. But it is also the case that most surviving letters between male/female friends did not involve young, unmarried people who might later become romantically involved, but between pairs in which at least one person was married.

Elihu Hubbard Smith suggested an explanation for this: "Young people live together. They do not, therefore, write to each other. When separated, they have no means of regular communication." Certainly, there would have been more risk involved in misunderstandings of the terms of the relationship if young, unmarried men and women wrote each other. Yet Smith went on to say that when people married, they were too busy to write. In his estimation, it was slightly older, single people who found the time and desire to write one another. This was indeed the case in the letter in which he offers this explanation: he was twenty-six and single, and he wrote to the thirty-year-old, single school matron Sarah Pierce.[25]

Letters between both lovers and friends must be carefully compared for fine differences in word choice, particularly in the opening and closing rituals of the letters. The most comprehensive study of courtship letters examines letters of a slightly later period, beginning in the 1830s. In this study, Karen Lystra writes of openings and closings as ways of binding the sender and receiver together through "a highly ritualized display of the level of relational intimacy and commitment." Courtship letters frequently used first names or even pet names as the couple became more intimate, and the closings of letters evolved from more formal to effusive and emotionally intense. These letters also used the terms "love," "emotion," "delicate," "heart," and "impression on my heart."[26]

In contrast, letters between mixed-sex friends used different salutations and closings, or superscriptions and subscriptions. Most frequently, letters began with "Dear Sir" or "Dear Madam." While the writer might sign his or her first name, he or she rarely used the recipient's first name. Letters usually closed with a few lines conveying affection and good wishes to the recipient's family, spouse, or friends before the formal subscription. Unlike the effusively emotional endings of courtship letters, friendly subscriptions were more measured. They occupied a middle ground between the romantic and the business letter; the latter commonly ended with "very respectfully" or "your obedient servant." The most commonly used words in subscriptions of male/female friendship, by contrast, were "friend," "sincere," "esteem," "respect," and "affection."[27] These were all terms associated with genteel friendships, with "esteem" carrying the particular weight of distinguishing a friendship from a romance.

Another popular closing for letters in this era was "your friend and humble servant." To modern eyes, this sounds like a subservient and rather business-like way to close a letter. But at the time, this was a subscription used between equals.[28] This signature recognized that friends were each other's "servants" in the sense of being obliged to one another for mutual affection, gifts, services done for one another, and the receipt of the letter itself. Friends could also add multiple layers of subscriptions, and often combined declarations of affection with the "servant" subscription. For instance, John Rodgers signed an 1803 letter to his friend Ann Pinkney:

> I shall wait with impatience for your answer and am Dear Miss with affectionate Respect & Esteem
> > Your Old Huml. Servant
> > Jn Rodgers[29]

While both men and women could use this subscription, it appears to have been employed more commonly by men. This could have been in part because women incurred more risk than men for writing letters to the opposite sex, and thus the men felt an additional sense of obligation to female friends. It may also have been a sort of courtly politeness that some men felt was due to their female friends.

Settling upon the proper superscription and subscription could cause anxiety for men and women. When the Reverend Horace Holley, president of Transylvania University in Kentucky, wrote to Elizabeth Patterson Bonaparte in 1818, he opened without a superscription and then explained his dilemma.

> As I am not sure that you will like it, and as I have not enough of the "usage du monde" to be certain of the point of etiquette, I shall not follow the feeling which directs me to break the abruptness of this envelope by beginning it with "My dear Madam," or, to soften it a little and still preserve the spirit, "Ma chère Madame," or, to be very respectful, "Madam," or, to mix respect, and sympathy, and courtesy, "My dear lady," or, to fortify myself behind the authority of a known friend and get out the sentiment of admiration that I feel, without venturing to originate the expression, say, "To lady Morgan's beautiful Mrs. Patterson."[30] I am quite at a loss to know how you would receive any one of these forms, and therefore I have rejected them all, and written none, and mean to have the discussion of this question confined to my own breast.[31]

Of course he has not kept the debate "confined to [his] own breast," but used it as a way to illustrate his desire to express himself properly and respectfully to this prominent woman.

Holley and Bonaparte had only recently become friends when he visited her home in Baltimore, and he was writing to send her the lyrics to a song she had requested.[32] He knew, then, that he had her approval to write to her (she was unmarried and independent, and thus needed no male approval), but he was unsure of the correct way to go about it. Given that Bonaparte's papers include a list of proper salutations and closing for writing prominent individuals in France, this may have been a topic she discussed with friends and Holley perhaps knew that such rules were important to her. It is unclear whether his worries were about appearing genteel or remaining within the bounds of friendly propriety, but he does seem to be fixated on how much emotion he can safely express to her in a subscription.

A proper superscription or subscription could cover for an illicit romance. In a published case from England alleging breach of promise, the plaintiff Joseph Foster used a letter from his intended wife and accused jilter Esther

Mellish as evidence. Esther insisted in her letter that "you know that women cannot pay too much attention to the word *propriety*" and went on to try to figure out how they could meet secretly. She then applied that attention to the subscription. At the close of the letter, she wrote that she "must be careful *how* I subscribe myself" and ultimately settled on "Dear Foster/Very sincerely your friend." This letter, Foster's attorney argued, was evidence of Mellish's affection for and intention to marry Foster. Certainly the subscription alone she chose was appropriate, but Mellish's very mention of the care necessary suggests that she recognized the importance of her choice of words there.[33]

Writers could shape the subscription, then, to convey the status of a relationship. There is perhaps no better symbol of the heavy meaning attached to the subscription than James Lovell's closing to a letter to Abigail Adams. Having recently argued with her about whether his letters were too "saucy," he was careful to sign one 1779 letter: "Very platonically to be sure but, very, very affectionately your humb Servt., JL."[34] To insert the word "platonically" here qualified that there was nothing sexual about their relationship, should anybody else see his letter—or that he signed it "very very affectionately." Yet "platonic" did not mean without romantic love, but rather a *chaste* love. This was quite obviously the case since Adams and Lovell were only friends through letters and lived hundreds of miles apart. But Adams, too, suggested a special intimacy in her subscriptions. She signed these letters, as she signed those to her husband and her close friend Mercy Otis Warren, with her pen name, Portia.

Overly affectionate openings to letters could be suggestive of an intimacy beyond friendship. Elizabeth Bayley Seton began her letters to Antonio Filicchi with "My most dear A," or "My dearest Antonio."[35] Using his first name and "dear" make these openings more reminiscent of letters of love than of friendship. Similarly, Eliza Whitman opened many letters to Joel Barlow (with whom she had an ambiguous, flirtatious relationship) with "Mon cher" or even "Mon cher ame."[36] It is quite possible that both Whitman and Seton felt more than friendship for their male correspondents. But the superscription and subscriptions here mean that these letters ritually conformed more closely to letters of courtship rather than friendship.

The line could, as in person, be hazy. Numerous friends expressed misgivings or sought to defend the propriety of writing one another within their letters. Without letter writing or etiquette guides to prescribe the terms under which male/female friends might write each other, the letters themselves both reveal and construct the social norms. These norms appear to have been built up through shared notions among men and women of what counted as appropriate. Here, then, it was practice rather than recorded rules that guided men's and women's epistolary conventions.[37]

Inclusive Conventions

The most important rule to emerge in practice was that a man needed the permission of his female friend's male protector—husband, father, or even brother—before the pair could write one another. When Samuel Ewing first wrote Mary Abigail Willing Coale, he said he had hesitated to correspond with her until he read a passage in her brother Edward's letter suggesting it would be acceptable for him to do so.[38] In other cases, married men indicated to their female friends that they wrote with the knowledge of their wives. When Matthew Ridley wrote to his friend Catherine Livingston, he explained "I make no scruple to write you with all Freedom & talk of you frequently, even before Mrs. Ridley." Matthew's reference to his wife is a reminder that while, as a man, he did not need his spouse's permission to write a friend of the opposite sex, he would be including her in the circle of correspondence.[39] Of course, a man who was single or a woman who did not have to answer to a male protector found it easiest to write one another.

The inclusion of a spouse in letters between mixed-sex friends was an important way of incorporating a third party into the relationship. That inclusion was often rather formulaic, with a greeting to or from a spouse in the last line or two of a letter. This practice became so commonly accepted that when Sarah Apthorp Morton had to add a postscript sending along her husband's good wishes to her friend Joseph Dennie, she wrote apologetically that, "You may be very certain Mr. Morton did not omit his Compliments, and good Wishes, tho I neglected to insert them in the proper Place."[40] The body of the letter itself carried more weight than the postscript, as the latter was for various afterthoughts rather than substantive information and conveyance of affections.

Another convention was that, in sending greetings to both husband and wife, the letter was to be addressed to the husband rather than the wife or else there should be separate letters. Thus even when the letter from a male friend was for the wife, the letter could be addressed to the husband. Richard Claiborne did this playfully in beginning a letter to Mr. Van Ness that was intended for Claiborne's old friend Marcia. The letter opened simply: "I wrote you a few days ago—this letter is not for you—it is for your dear Marcia—so give it to her without reading another word." As Franklin had, Claiborne told the husband not to read the rest of the letter. Such prohibition could only have created a fiction of privacy, as it seems unlikely that the husband would not at least glance at the remainder of the letter. Claiborne began his note to Marcia: "Love often produces dreams—and why should not friendship? So I had a dream, and I send it to you, confirmed by waking sentiment."[41] In the dream, Marcia appeared as a sort of angel guiding him through paradise. After his description of the dream, however, he continued to report news from his life and provided an assurance of her mother's health. Indeed, there was little in the letter besides the playful question at the beginning that would have troubled Marcia's husband.

One letter that breaks the rules of how to write to husband and wife nonetheless explains the custom itself. When Aaron Burr, a man hardly known for his observance of social delicacies, wrote to a woman named Mrs. Gordon in 1809, he explained why he was writing only to her despite having received letters from both husband and wife. "You perceive, madam, that, without apology, I have taken the liberty to charge you with my reply to Mr. Gordon," he wrote. He explained his transgression with a list of reasons, saying to write them both separately "would have been rather fastidious" and that Mrs. Gordon had been the first to start a correspondence with him. Mrs. Gordon's letter was "the pure emanation of courtesy," while her husband's was written only at the request of another friend. "I could give twenty other reasons for the preference," Burr continued, ". . . yet I acknowledge that neither is the true one."[42] Although this last statement is somewhat enigmatic, it seems fair to conclude that Burr was better friends with Mrs. Gordon and saw that closer relationship as reason enough to write her on behalf of the couple.

Others felt more compunction and anxiety in writing married friends. The correspondence between John Farmer and Lucy (Kendall) Spalding reveals the delicate footwork required for most friends to feel comfortable writing each other once one had married. John and Lucy had grown up together in Amherst, New Hampshire. They corresponded with each other before Lucy's marriage, perhaps beginning when Farmer moved to Concord, New Hampshire, in 1821. By that time Lucy was twenty-five and John thirty-two. As Lucy's wedding in 1828 to Isaac Spalding, a Nashua merchant and justice of the peace, approached, she stopped writing to John. John was unsure of whether this was because of Isaac's wishes or merely because she was busy. In any case, John wrote to Isaac in May 1828 asking him to "command her to write," since it would be perfectly safe now that she was married.[43] Despite the fact that John and Lucy had written before without

apparent harm, John suggested that there was no risk whatsoever now that
she was married.

The two friends could now write, but the correspondence was on Lucy's
husband's terms. It was, according to John, Isaac's "unbounded confidence in
the fidelity of the partner of his lot" that led Isaac to grant Lucy permission
"to correspond with an old friend without any restriction or limitation."[44]
Yet to say that the correspondence was unrestricted would be untrue; as John
hinted in the very same letter, he expected Isaac to read his letters to Lucy
and the continuation of the correspondence was subject to Isaac's permission.
Despite Isaac's granting permission freely, John seemed continually anxious.
As late at 1836, a letter to his "dear Mrs. S." began, "I write to you first knowing that your husband will make no objections to such a liberty, and knowing
too, as I shall direct to him, he will of course have an opportunity of first
scanning its contents."[45] In order to continue his friendship with Lucy, John
had to end the privacy of their former dyad by incorporating her husband
into their epistolary conversations.

The styling of the superscriptions and subscriptions in the letters from
John Farmer to Lucy Spalding indicate the care he took to incorporate her
husband. His letters to Lucy addressed them both, with superscriptions like
one in 1829 to "My Dear Mrs. S. and her beloved husband." The subscription
to this letter, too, was careful to include Lucy's husband. John signed this
letter: "Yours, Madam, with the greatest deference & friendship, (the Justice of
course included)."[46] In that letter, John explained why he addressed them both:

> I am so in the habit of associating the Justice with you in my thoughts
> and epistles and whatever goes from me to Nashua, that I can hardly
> address you without conjoining his name in the salutatory part, and
> this perhaps, is as it should be, for the wife has her interests combined
> with those of her husband. What is of importance to one generally
> is of consequence to the other; at least all those little matters which
> enter the domestic circle, and especially such a thing as an epistle from
> a common friend.[47]

John styled himself as a mutual friend of the couple, placing his friendship
with Lucy as part of a trio in which her husband played an equal part. Since
their friendship was carried on through writing, the way John wrote his letters was an important means of shaping the friendship in this manner.

Other correspondents were less cautious than John Farmer. Bushrod
Washington wrote three letters to Elizabeth Powel without obtaining her

husband's permission after meeting her in Philadelphia in 1785. Elizabeth finally wrote back to him with some frustration at his impropriety:

> To erase from your Mind any Suspicion that I am indifferent as to your Concerns I am induced to break through an established Rule of never writing to a Gentleman that does not correspond with Mr. Powel. I thought your knowledge of what is proper & your Attachment to him would have rendered it unnecessary for me to give you any [Intimations?] on such a Subject. I cannot ascribe your Silence to any other Cause than a misplaced Diffidence. Had you, attentively, read the note you received by [Robert] Morris this Explanation would have been altogether unnecessary.

Robert Morris, a friend of Powel's, seems to have written Washington to explain the proper protocol. Perhaps Washington had ignored this important rule because he had already been a friend and regular visitor to her house for two years; perhaps he thought that having received a short note from Powel with a gift at New Year's that year, the correspondence was already open.[48] Nonetheless, Powel still felt it was a necessary courtesy.[49]

The remainder of the letter Elizabeth wrote to Bushrod was long and friendly. She responded to points from his letter and offered him advice. She closed the letter by offering "Mr. Powel's & my Compliments affectionately to your Family" and signed the letter, "believe me unfeignedly/Your sincere Friend."[50] The two continued a long and affectionate friendship through the following decades as Bushrod returned to his native Virginia. Elizabeth passed along her greetings to Bushrod's family at Mount Vernon and purchased items in Philadelphia for him and his wife at Bushrod's request. The next letter in the archive that exists after the rocky start to their correspondence contains the friendly subscription: "I am ever your affectionate friend."[51] That did indeed seem to be the case.

Playful Subversions

Before Bushrod Washington's exchange with Powel, he had bemoaned "that illiberal Custom should in this Country alone discountenance a correspondence between the Sexes." If the term "illiberal custom" sounds familiar, it was the very same term used by Nancy Shippen—the woman to whom he wrote the letter with this line. The two friends had likely discussed the challenge of writing between men and women and heard one or the other use this phrase; Nancy recorded it in her diary only eleven days before Bushrod wrote the letter. She had also given Bushrod permission to write to her, although she had not promised she would write him back. This we know because Bushrod's letter thanked her for "allowing me the pleasure of writing to you, and of assuring you of my Friendship," and saying he did not demand a reply. Rather, he wrote, "I can only lament" that "illiberal custom."[52]

Thus, men like Bushrod Washington knew that they were subverting custom in writing to women, but went ahead nonetheless. This was in part because of the disdain with which they all held this particular custom, and it appears that they relied upon their own judgment rather than societal strictures. They had the liberty to do this because men were put less at risk than women in breaking such rules, and indeed the many letters that apologize for breaking this rule were all written by men. Such subversion was, it would seem, possible as long as the writer offered an explanation that acknowledged the accepted norms. The only way for individuals to reshape the unspoken rules was for them to recognize the rules and employ strategies that subtly altered them. In many of these cases, the men seem to take a certain pleasure in their transgression and write with a playfulness that suggested that they scorned societal norms.

How much power did such norms have if there are so many examples of men and women breaking free of them? This is a difficult question to answer, since we can never know how many men and women chose not to write one another out of fear of committing an impropriety. Samuel Ewing referred to these norms as "a foolish prejudice which the world has adopted" in a letter to his friend Mary Coale. In his opinion, that "foolish prejudice" might "effectually destroy all epistolary intercourse between the Sexes" (except husband and wife) if not for the "good sense" women occasionally showed in agreeing to oppose it.[53] Ultimately, the frequent and lengthy explanations of why writers were breaking convention suggests that these norms were widely known even if they were not widely followed.

One remarkable letter sent by a man to a young woman is entirely composed of a lighthearted explanation for why it would be permissible for the two to correspond despite custom. John Fanning Watson was an unmarried man of twenty-six living far away from friends and family to work in New Orleans. In 1805 he wrote to Miss Susan Ridley, who was then seventeen and living in Massachusetts. He began the letter with a joke in the very first line: "Your most amiable, and enlightened aunt has imposed on me a most novel task: the opening of a correspondence with an unknown spinster!" Watson and Ridley were not already friends, but his friend Susan Livingston

Symmes apparently thought her niece would make a good epistolary friend for Watson.

That he wrote at Ridley's aunt's request already lent the approval of an adult protector to the correspondence. Watson went on to say that Symmes had "pledged herself to make [his] correspondence acceptable." He also tried to render the correspondence safer by telling her to "[t]reat me with the frankness & freedom of a brother." Even so, Watson admitted that, "I am fully conscious of the informality and eccentricity of my presentation." He went on to offer a reason custom could and should be broken: "these are revolutionary times; and any innovations tending to explode the errors of common fastidiousness, may be laudable!" Breaking the rules, Watson argued, might have positive results. Further, were she too to break the rule by writing back to him, it would demonstrate "a soul so much above common prejudices, that I cannot over rate you, in assigning you the highest rank among your sex." By labeling this custom as "fastidiousness" and "prejudice," Watson made circumventing custom a virtue rather than a sin.

Watson went on to set unusual expectations for the correspondence. "With you Miss, I shall be chaste without restraint, & familiar without licentiousness," he wrote. If she were to continue the correspondence, she would have to accept being part of a "unique" venture, a "novelty." He directly addressed the issue of their both being young and unmarried, saying:

> I shall seldom reflect, as I do now, that you are a very coy maiden, & that I am an insidious Bachelor. I shall imagine you too remote to be beguiled by my art; & shall presume myself, equally distant from the Basilisk influence of your eyes; your [?] tongue; and Calypsonian person & understanding. I shall only dread the eloquence of your letters; & even there, I shall pass it through the crucible before reading.

She should not be worried about attraction, Watson argued, because they were interacting in writing and not in person.

"As we are not to be lovers," Watson continued, "we will profess the *platonizen*[54] of an harmless Philosophy; & from this time avow the indissoluble ties of real friends." Men and women who could not be lovers could still be friends. Watson also acknowledged the power of letters to form strong bonds of friendship. While not knowing each other in person would protect them from falling in love, it did not prevent them from coming to know each other well. Through their letters, Watson wrote, "I cannot be very far from the true knowledge of your heart, mind, manners, & even person." The idea that the two were communing in some way through writing was reinforced through Watson's saying at the end of the letter that "I reluctantly leave such good company" and that he looked forward to her "kind reception at the next visit."[35]

The idea that letters between friends could be imagined as social visits was another young man's justification for writing to a female friend. John E. Hall and Rebecca Gratz were part of a circle of friends in Philadelphia in the early 1800s that wrote for the *Port-folio*.[36] John's first letter to Rebecca contained no opening superscription, beginning directly with "You will no doubt be surprised when you open this letter and recognize the pen." However, he was emboldened to write her because of a message delivered from her via his sister—likely spoken rather than written—which was "a reiterated proof of [Rebecca's] regard," John explains. This proof had convinced John "to infringe what some prudes may call the rules of propriety, that I may have an opportunity of saying how grateful I am for your remembrance."

John lamented the "fictitious regulations" that impeded "the intercourse of the sexes" for the rest of the page. He went on to argue that "there appears to me no difference between conversation and letters, between friends."[37] His argument was in keeping with the advice of epistolary manuals, which urged writers to treat letters as "written conversation." Authors of guidebooks suggested that letter writers write as if they were conversing with the recipient, creating a sense of natural conversation. Yet how could one be natural in a genre so pinned down by conventions?[58] It is this contradiction that John E. Hall has captured in his letter to Rebecca Gratz.

John took advantage of this contradiction to tell Rebecca that she should receive his letter as a "familiar visit." He suggested that between cross-sex friends, such a visit was considered entirely within the bounds of what, he said, "some prudes may call the rules of propriety." Thus, to suggest that the letter was equivalent to a conversation in person took the epistolary culture's notion of "the familiar letter as intimate conversation" entirely literally.[59] The letter no longer merely pretended to represent the embodiment of the writer; John treated the letter as a physical substitute for the self in order to circumvent the rules governing cross-sex correspondence. At the same time, he realized that this imaginary trope could only be carried so far; he conceded: "That the visit will be returned I scarcely dare to expect." Yet John must have received a reply from Rebecca not long after; while her response does not survive, there is a slim folder of his affectionate letters to her between 1807 and 1808 in the archive. He continued to contend that "Letters are the representatives of conversations," and he beseeched her to continue writing, for letters from his friends were "the dearest ligament that binds me to society."[60]

Reciprocity to the Letter

For letters to stand in for conversation required a steady rhythm of exchange. As Elihu Hubbard Smith told his friend Idea Strong, "Letters are designed as substitutes for conversation; and that regular succession of them, which obtains the title of a Correspondence, may be considered as analogous to the intercourse of neighbours."[61] There was an expectation of reciprocity to create "a regular succession" of letters in which the timeliness of the response had symbolic weight. Etiquette required a prompt response, so delayed responses were interpreted as communications of "displeasure, indifference or contempt."[62] Alternatively, a lengthy delay might mean the friend was too ill to write. Either way, a delayed response could cause considerable anxiety.

These worries were particularly acute when the writer had sent multiple letters with no reply, upsetting the balance of the exchange. Samuel Ewing interpreted Mary Abigail Willing Coale's lack of responsiveness to his letters as indifference. "But why, my sweet young friend, why in this should you treat me with the distance of a Stranger?"[63] he asked. Similarly, Abigail Adams wondered how James Lovell could "suffer Letters repeatedly to reach him and not deign a line in reply?" She had not received a letter from him in six weeks, and she believed she was "inti[t]led to a return where I have not remitted a refusal."[64]

Maria Cosway was even more concerned at not receiving a reply from Thomas Jefferson in the summer of 1788. She wrote to express her worries, but said she would not write again until she received a letter from him because "a string of *punctellios* and *formalités* stand frowning before me waiting for the happy time, which brings me letters to answer." She had already written him twice with no response and asked how this could be so:

> What can be the reason? It is either obstinancy, or constancy in me: but what does your silence mean my dear friend! It seems that opportunities absolutely force themselves on you to recall me to your remembrances, should I have otherwise so much courage or should I be so bold as to *insist* in a correspondence![65]

Her worry clearly went beyond the "*punctellios* and *formalités*." Maria assumed that Jefferson's silence signified that he was not thinking of her.

If letters served as "halves of conversation," a reciprocal exchange of letters was necessary to denote that the recipient/listener recognized his friend's continuing existence and had a desire to keep the friendship alive.[66] A regular epistolary exchange maintained the distant friend's memory, sending textual traces of the self. A letter answered served as a concrete sign of the continuation of a friendship; a lengthy wait for a reply or no reply at all might mean the friend had been forgotten.[67] Having only spent time with Jefferson in person for two weeks, and with little prospect of seeing him again, Cosway knew that their relationship depended on exchanging letters. Without letters, memories of each other would fade and the relationship would end.

Elizabeth Graeme Fergusson made this point explicitly in a playful poem she sent to her friend Benjamin Rush. It is unclear how often he wrote to her, because the letters she received do not survive, but he saved enough letters from her to fill a heavy bound volume. A poem filed in 1793 suggests he had plead a lack of free time to write her as often as she wrote him; it is entitled "An Epistle from a Lady in the Country, to a Gentleman Who complained that he was much pinched from Time." Fergusson asserted her expectations for the exchange quite clearly: "One Letter a week she surely might claim,/ To keep alive Friendship; and fan its pure Flame."[68] The flame of friendship required careful, regular tending through letters.

The tempo of the exchange of letters was not merely a matter of demonstrating friendship, however. The space between receipt and response in an exchange was the space of power. By controlling the tempo of an exchange, here in the case of letters, a man or a woman had the power to shape a friendship. In a correspondence, women had an unusual right to demand responses, to decide how long to wait before sending a response, and to convey the intimacy of the relationship through the symbolic forms within letter writing. These elements were key to the production of friendly feeling, as letters sent regularly evoked a sense of gratitude and gratitude, in turn, became affection.[69]

Letters thus brought together power and subversion, affection and gratitude, as they fostered friendships between men and women who lived apart. While it was usually men who joked about subverting norms, letters provided a unique space of power for the women who chose to respond to those men as well. Writing a letter was an act of shaping both a relationship and a vision of the self, and within the conventions of correspondence women had a latitude lacking elsewhere in their lives to express themselves.[70] Letter writing was at its very core a reciprocal process in which men and women could expect and even demand equal returns—whether in content or the sheer number of letters sent.

An exchange of letters was the exchange of two objects of equal symbolic value, but did this mean that the exchange of letters rendered men and women equal? Both men and women could derive power from the quiet resistance of writing one another in the first place, and then of determining the timing of their responses. They could play with forms of subscription and superscription. But the correspondence still had to be positioned within larger social ties, and worries of propriety were an ever-present backdrop to correspondence. There was a seesawing balance of power, then, held on the terms with which each writer felt comfortable. The very practice of exchanging letters helped establish the contours of male/female friendships, pushing the possibilities and boundaries of freedom, equality, virtue, and choice every time a writer put pen to paper.

6

The Gifts of Friendship

AS WITH LETTERS, friends who gave gifts were offering a version of a virtuous self as well as conveying affection. The dynamics of gift exchange differed greatly, however. One letter prompted another with certain predictability, but a gift was about memorializing a relationship, cementing it with a material object. Whether that object was a portrait, a lock of hair, a household object, or even a poem scribbled on a piece of paper, the meaning came from the act of giving the object. For men and women who had to carefully craft their relationships in person and in letters for purposes of propriety, gift exchange took on added complications. Both the meanings of and constraints upon friendships between men and women are elucidated by examining the form, framing, and display of gifts they exchanged.

The reciprocity inherent in gift exchange set up a continuing and reciprocal dependence, putting the friends on equal ground. The recipient was always indebted to the giver, and from this dependence grew a particular power for the gift giver, one equally available to men and women. The indebted friend would be expected to make a return of equivalent emotional (not commercial) value, thus in some sense owing oneself to a friend.[1] These gifts, then, reminded the receiving friend not just of the giver but also of the giver's power in the relationship.[2] As Judith Sargent wrote to her friend John Murray in 1784 in a letter accompanying some locks of her hair, "I require you, and all my other friends, to consider them as so many proofs of my indubitable right, to that attention which I shall not fail to exact."[3] Women could assert this right even with men who had a great deal of political power.

A letter like Sargent's served to frame the gift of her hair to her friend. This constituted the performative aspect of gift giving, with a structured interaction between friends that set the meaning of the gift in motion.[4] Meaning was latent in the form of these objects until they were granted, received, and "read." The recipient had to interpolate the meaning through the way his or her friend had made choices in the object's form and presentation, and then decide the proper way to reciprocate. A gift needed its own narrative, many of which were conveyed in the form of letters. With mixed-sex friends, there had to be a particular attention to the propriety of the choice of object and its framing, for this performance had an audience. Given the networks of people involved in a friendship, opportunities abounded for the meaning of a gift to be interpreted—or misinterpreted—by those outside of the friendship.

The propriety of giving gifts between friends of the opposite sex could be problematic. As with other aspects of behavior within friendships between men and women, there was little guidance in the literature about gift exchange in these relationships. One letter writing manual does provide some guidance—but in the form of two completely opposite responses. The popular manual *The Complete American Letter-Writer* includes a model letter "from a Gentleman to a Lady, begging her acceptance of a present." He offered the lady a "trifle" as a "token of respect" that "will call to remembrance that undisguised friendship which I possess for the most worthy of her sex." The gentleman apparently recognized that there could be an issue of propriety here, because he told her to "let no delicate punctillio raise an objection to this humble offer." The only clue to what sort of gift this was was in the gentleman's order to "accept and wear it," suggesting it was a small piece of jewelry. There is no information as to whether this model gentleman and lady are young or old, single or married.

The manual then offers two possible responses from the woman, one of acceptance and another returning the present and protesting the impropriety of a man sending a woman a gift. While the first response is a very brief note accepting "the gift of friendship," the second contains a lengthy explanation declaring the impossibility of accepting a gift from a young man. "Prudence forbids my acceptance of any present from any gentleman, however kindly intended," the lady wrote in the model letter. She was merely "adhering to that decorum which should always be the rule of our sex." She risked the censure of "the penetrating eye of the world" that might judge her guilty (of what she does not say) "upon circumstantial evidence."⁵ The juxtaposition of these two opposite responses offers only one certain conclusion: there was no broadly agreed-upon propriety for the exchange of gifts between men and women. Friends would have to consider the context of the friendship and the exchange very carefully.

Given this, men and women improvised in the exchange of gifts as in other aspects of these ill-defined relationships. The particular advantage of looking at gifts is that they offer a visual record of the working of friendships between men and women. Among the objects exchanged were portraits, miniatures, silhouettes, hair, jewelry, poetry, and album entries. The choice of form, the manner in which it was given, and the way the friend displayed the gift were all factors in determining a gift's propriety. Thus, each genre of object provides a different angle on friendships. We cannot look in on friends at a salon or during a chat at a tea table, but examining the objects they commissioned, exchanged, and held brings us closer to envisioning these friendships.

Portraits

The best available views of men and women who befriended one another is in the portraits they exchanged. A portrait offered a view of the friend to a wide audience, mediated by the artist who created it. Once complete, a portrait was displayed in the home (usually in a fairly public room) and seen by others, unless it was so small, as were miniatures, that it was intended only for the eyes of the recipient. The visibility of this type of exchange opened the friendship to scrutiny, further necessitating care to delineate the relationship as a friendship rather than a romantic relationship.

Portraits served as the best visual substitutes for absent friends, viewed not as static images but as sparks for memories. As the eighteenth-century theorist Jonathan Richardson wrote,

> The picture of an absent relation, or friend, helps to keep up those sentiments which frequently languish by absence, and may be instrumental to maintain and sometimes to augment friendship, and paternal, filial, and conjugal love, and duty. Upon the sight of a portrait, the character, and master-strokes of the history of the person it represents, are apt to flow in upon the mind, and to be the subject of conversation.[6]

The idea of portraits as a spark for memory and conversation provides a deeper way of understanding the exchange of portraits between friends than traditional notions of women as merely the objects of the male viewer's gaze. In this period, too, women's appearances had symbolic weight in the transfer of a woman's legal place from her father's household to her husband's.[7] For the husband, frequently the commissioner of portraits of women, to own a portrait of his wife was to own a representation of the body he possessed.[8]

Because of the power of portraits to stand in for friends, portraits were sometimes commissioned by friends or given as gifts.[9] The portrait given as a gift is perhaps the most literal form of the gift as a way of "giving oneself."[10] Thus, when portraits were exchanged, there was a clear vision of the self embedded in the object. The very choice of giving an image of oneself to a friend, in an era when even public figures had substantial control over their image, indicated an important relationship.[11] Of course, only a small proportion of people could afford to give such an expensive gift. For those with sufficient wealth, it appears that a portrait was a socially acceptable gift between male/female friends—under most circumstances.

We can also understand the self a friend wished to portray within a friendship by examining the way he or she is represented, since in portraiture the sitter often had substantial control over the way he or she would be seen.[12] In other cases the person who commissioned the work had control over how she would like to see her friend. Either way, a finished portrait exchanged between friends created a particular image of the sitter that embodied the relationship between sitter and recipient. The form of the portrait, the framing of the exchange, and the way the art was displayed were all important parts of presentingthe relationship—and showing it was proper.

Perhaps the most prolific purveyor of his own portraits as gifts was Benjamin Franklin. His likeness was on souvenir goods in Paris during the height of his popularity there. However, for his close friends he had special portraits made. According to Charles Sellers, author of a lengthy catalogue describing the hundreds of portraits of Franklin, Franklin saw giving his portrait to friends as "a way of visiting distant friends 'in person.'" Moreover, Sellers argues, Franklin "knew also how the personal image gave strength to feelings and ideas."[13]

This was precisely the case for his young female friend Georgiana Shipley, who received a small portrait of Franklin on a snuffbox as a special gift from him in 1780 (Figure 6.1). The obvious expense of the gift signaled the depth of his friendship for Georgiana. Indeed, when Georgiana requested a portrait from him, she noted that "numberless are the prints & medals we have seen of you, but none that I quite approve." Upon receiving the snuffbox, she reported that she had kissed it "1000 times" and that the resemblance was so strong, "it is my very own dear Doctor Franklin himself, I can almost fancy you are present." In Franklin's absence, Shipley continued, the image "will ever be my constant & favorite companion."[14] Her kisses allowed her to make physical her connection to her absent friend, an act that would certainly have been perceived as romantic had this been a miniature. But Franklin's choice of a snuffbox meant that he had given her a more public object than a miniature, an object that Georgiana might carry with her and use at social events. To keep Franklin company, Shipley later sent him a self-portrait.

George Washington also gave small copies of his portrait to female friends. Washington had his portrait commissioned rather sparingly, only paying to

FIGURE 6.1 Benjamin Franklin gave his friend Georgiana Shipley this snuff box as a gift. Snuff box with portrait of Benjamin Franklin, 1780. The Library Company of Philadelphia, Gift of Stuart Karu, 2007.

have portraits done of himself in the form of miniatures for his wife and granddaughters.[15] When Madame de Brehan, the sister-in-law of the French minister the Comte de Moustier and an acquaintance of the Washingtons, volunteered to paint him, he perhaps took the opportunity because it would be an inexpensive and unobtrusive way to get a small portrait of himself that he could give to friends. She painted it at his home in New York the following fall, creating a grisaille (a style of painting in shades of gray) profile image of him (Figure 6.2). It is a classical rendering of the president, painted as a cameo with a laurel wreath around his head to symbolize victory. Brehan made a medallion with the original, mounted with another image she created in the same style of his step-granddaughter on the reverse side, for Martha. After Madame de Brehan returned to France, the Comte de Moustier sent him engraver's proof impressions of the portrait, which Washington gave to his friends Mary Morris and Deborah Stewart. He also gave a later, watercolor version to Anne Willing Bingham.[16] While the portrait bears a resemblance to Washington, it shows Washington as a classical, distant figure rather than Washington the man. As a gift for female friends, this portrayal meant there would be no worries about propriety.

In the same year, Washington also gave quite a different portrait of himself to his wife. The 1789 miniature by John Ramage of Washington is a delicately painted, full-color rendering of Washington in his military uniform (Figure 6.3). His gaze is soft and his eyes a gentle blue, making this portrait for Martha more intimate than the grisaille profile he provided his female friends. The addition of George's hair to the back of the miniature, visible in a criss-cross pattern behind glass, also added to the function of the portrait as a substitute for himself and increased its intimacy. It is unclear whether George or Martha commissioned the portrait, but either way it was done to her tastes.[17] Granted, the difference in the portraits is attributable in part to what Washington paid for them, but it is apparent that he was only willing to buy intimate paintings of himself for family members. The decision was likely motivated by both cost and choices about what image of himself he wanted to convey to his friends.

Giving copies of a portrait to multiple friends could provide a common image of the absent friend to tie together a social circle. The women to whom Washington gave his portrait were in the same elite Philadelphia circles. An even clearer example is that of John Trumbull's miniature portrait of Thomas Jefferson that Trumbull gave to Angelica Schuyler Church and Maria Cosway.[18] Church and Cosway were close friends with each other and with Trumbull and Jefferson. It appears that Jefferson did not commission the portraits; Trumbull wrote Jefferson in March 1788 reporting that Cosway "teases me every day for a copy of your little portrait." The same day Cosway wrote Jefferson asking for permission to have Trumbull make a miniature based on the artist's portrait of Jefferson in the history painting *Declaration of Independence*. By July, Church wrote Jefferson to report, "Mr. Trumbull has given us each a picture of you."[19]

Both of these women, then, had small (4.5 x 3 inch) square portraits of Jefferson rendered by their friend Trumbull (Figures 6.4 and 6.5). The portraits are very similar. While both copy Jefferson's pose, clothing, and far right gaze from the *Declaration* painting, Church's is a porthole-style image with a gilt frame. Church reported that Cosway's version was "a better likeness," and it was painted with a finer hand and a more careful attention to Jefferson's facial features. Perhaps this was because Cosway had been the one to request the portrait and Trumbull put more effort into her copy. In creating the image

FIGURE 6.2 Washington gave engraved copies of this image to Deborah Stewart and Anne Willing Bingham. Those copies have not been located. The above image shows the original set in a locket, with an image of Washington's step-granddaughter Eleanor Parke Custis Lewis on the opposite side. The locket was made for Martha Washington. Marquise Jean-Francoise-Rene-Almaire de Bréhan (Anne Flore Millet), *George Washington*, 1789, watercolor (grisaille) on ivory. Yale University Art Gallery, New Haven Connecticut, Mabel Brady Garvan Collection, 1947.220.

of their mutual friend, Trumbull made a gift representing both himself and Jefferson for Church and Cosway.

The way Cosway displayed her copy of Jefferson's portrait gives clues as to how she saw their relationship. First, it is important to note that this miniature was too big to wear on the body, and it was made in a square shape so it could be framed and hung on the wall. While it is unknown how Cosway initially displayed the portrait, she hung it among a gallery of miniatures on her wall in her room at the Italian convent where she moved in the 1790s.

FIGURE 6.3 This miniature was created for Martha Washington. The reverse has George Washington's hair and the monogram "GW," as well as a later engraved inscription tracing ownership of the piece. John Ramage, *George Washington*, 1789, watercolor on ivory, gold frame. Private collection (Image © Christie's Images Limited 2001).

The room also included a large portrait of her estranged husband Richard Cosway.[20] All of this suggests that while her friendship with Jefferson remained important throughout her life—indeed, they wrote each other for decades—she wisely portrayed him as one among many social ties.

In the case of the portraits of Mrs. Perez Morton, or Sarah Apthorp Wentworth Morton, the visual representations themselves offer insight into her relationships with male friends. Gilbert Stuart painted three different portraits of his friend Morton between 1798 and 1820; the order and dates are uncertain. One of these portraits is typical of Stuart's portraiture, showing Morton against a dark background and with a faint image of books to her right (Figure 6.6). It is unclear who commissioned or received this portrait, although it came into the hands of Morton's granddaughter.[21]

FIGURE 6.4 This small portrait of Jefferson was made for Angelica Schuyler Church. John Trumbull, *Thomas Jefferson*, 1788, oil on mahogany. The Metropolitan Museum of Art, New York, Bequest of Cornelia Cruger, 1923 (Image © The Metropolitan Museum of Art).

A variation on this image appears in the portrait of Morton commissioned by Stuart and Morton's mutual friend John Dunn (Figure 6.7). Dunn, an Irish lawyer, was visiting the United States when he met Morton, probably in Philadelphia. They may have shared a common interest in native peoples. After receiving Morton's portrait, Dunn sent her his own portrait, also painted by Stuart.[22] No documentation of this friendship exists outside of the portrait exchange, so our only clues to the relationship come from the portraits themselves.

The rendering of Morton that Dunn owned portrayed Morton as a patriotic author, in contrast to the more traditional portrait of her. While she

FIGURE 6.5 Maria Cosway's copy of Trumbull's portrait of Jefferson, considered to be a better likeness than her friend Angelica Schuyler Church's copy. John Trumbull, *Thomas Jefferson*, 1788, oil on panel. The White House Historical Association (White House Collection), Washington, D.C., Gift of the Italian Republic.

wears a similar dress and expression in both images, in Dunn's version she is at a writing desk with paper and quill before her and a bust of George Washington in the back left. Washington's presence in the portrait is so large that his sculpted head is bigger than Morton's. His presence is tied to the writing utensils, referencing Morton's published poem "Beacon Hill," which praised

FIGURE 6.6 This portrait of Sarah Apthorp Wentworth Morton is typical of Stuart's portraiture. It is unclear for whom the portrait was created, but it came into the hands of her granddaughter. Gilbert Stuart, *Mrs. Perez Morton (Sarah Wentworth Apthorp)*, about 1802, oil on canvas. Museum of Fine Arts, Boston, Juliana Chency Edwards Collection (Photograph © 2015 Museum of Fine Arts, Boston).

FIGURE 6.7 This version of the portrait, showing Morton as a patriotic author, was owned by her friend John Dunn. Gilbert Stuart, *Mrs. Perez Morton (Sarah Wentworth Apthorp)*, about 1802, oil on panel. Winterthur Museum, Winterthur, Delaware.

Revolutionary soldiers and particularly George Washington. Morton was well known as a gentlewoman poet in Boston, and perhaps it was this that Dunn most admired about her. Whether it was Dunn, Morton, or Stuart who made the choices for this portrait, we know that it was the image of Morton as authoress that Dunn took home to Europe with him. It is possible that this portrayal of Morton as an author rather than merely as a woman legitimated having a portrait of an unrelated woman in his home.

The portrait Dunn sent to Morton, however, is a typical Stuart rendering of a figure turned partially toward the viewer with a soft gaze. He is set against a dark background and the only movement in the portrait is his thin fingers clasping the lapel of his jacket. Dunn thus gave Morton a much less dynamic image of himself than he owned of her. Interestingly, Morton sold this image of Dunn soon after his death in 1827. This, in addition to the fact that it was Dunn who commissioned both the portrait of Morton and of himself, suggests that Dunn may have valued this friendship more than Morton did. Here the gift lost its emotional meaning and became a commodity.

FIGURE 6.8 Stuart kept this portrait of his friend for his own collection. Gilbert Stuart, *Sarah Wentworth Apthorp, Mrs. Perez Morton*, about 1802, oil on canvas. Worcester Art Museum, Worcester, Massachusetts, gift of the grandchildren of Joseph Tuckerman.

The third portrait of Morton is the most unusual (Figure 6.8). This portrait was the only one of the three images of Morton that Stuart kept for himself. It is even more active than Dunn's version, as in this one she is either lowering or raising a sheer veil over her head. The portrait likely began as a traditional image of Morton (the pentimento[23] of her arms crossing her waist is still visible) and has been described as unfinished because of the blurriness of the face and looseness of the brushstrokes. However, the painting is more complete than Stuart's other unfinished works. The soft colors and depiction of a private moment suggest a quiet intimacy that, one scholar suggests, shows Morton as "the artist's muse."[24]

Morton and Stuart developed a friendship centered on each of their arts. Morton wrote several poems about Stuart's work, and most notably the two shared a poetic exchange about Stuart's portrait of Morton (likely the simplest version) that was published in *The Port-Folio* in 1803. The poems were similar in form to the published poetic exchanges between other men and women. While Stuart was already a well-regarded painter, a well-known poetess's praise of the artist's work would have been good publicity for her friend. Her poems were a sort of gift in return for Stuart's having painted her. Morton wrote of the communicative power of Stuart's portraits, saying his works "speak with skill divine." His portraits were not merely images, but "expression in its finest utterance" that had "character that breathes" and "soul that twines" around the canvas. In exchange for her portrait, then, Morton created a poetic vision of Stuart's work as a public gift to him. He replied in her own art of poetry, writing of the superiority of poetry to painting but also the weight Morton's praise carried. He also rather extravagantly praised Morton's own beauty, saying that his portrait of her was merely "the copyist's humbler art."[25] By publishing a conversation in poetry, Morton and Stuart framed their friendship as relationship of creative kindred spirits. This was not just a relationship of convenience, however; it was important enough to Stuart that he kept his unusual portrait of Morton until his death.

Another set of works by Stuart offers insight into cross-sex friendships. He painted Generals Henry Knox and Henry Jackson for Hepzibah Swan, who traveled in the same social circles in elite Boston as Morton and leveraged her independent fortune and connections for Stuart's benefit.[26] But the two most important men in her life, after her husband left her and moved to France, were Knox and Jackson. She met them as a young woman in 1776, when they were quartered at her father's Boston home. The generals were friends with each other and with James Swan before he left the country, with Jackson serving as a business agent to both men. The unmarried Jackson acted as a surrogate husband intermittently for Lucy Knox when Henry Knox was in Washington, and for Hepzibah Swan for many years.

The portraits of Knox and Jackson that Hepzibah commissioned and hung in her home represented the roles of each man in her life. As Stuart expert Carrie Rebora Barratt explains, the depiction of Knox in his military garb signaled his more public role. Knox escorted Swan in public and thus his portrait is "as large as its subject and rich with iconographic references to his achievements."[27] It was indisputably a portrait of a public figure, the kind that could have as easily been hung in a public building. Swan's friendship with Knox had the marks of propriety and distance, as she shared her friendship with his wife Lucy and was seen with him at public functions.

Jackson's portrait, on the other hand, does not depict his public role as soldier or businessman. While Knox's portrait is full-length, Jackson's is bust-length and smaller than any of the other portraits Stuart painted for the Swan family. Barrett concludes that "Jackson's head radiates the affability and care the man brought to the Swan household." Unlike the other, public portraits Swan commissioned of Knox and her own family—even that of her estranged husband—the portrait of Jackson is "a devotional image."[28] Its size, intimacy, and content support the public suspicion that the relationship between Swan and Jackson was perhaps that of lovers.

Men and women who wanted to express intimacy rather than friendship often chose the form of the miniature. Here were portraits not to be hung on a wall, but to be held in the hand or pressed against the breast. Only one person at a time can properly view a miniature. The mode of holding and viewing a miniature formed a bond between sitter and owner that was too private to be safely shared between cross-sex friends.[29] The important exception, of course, was images of whatever size of prominent individuals. As Franklin wrote his sister in 1779, there were "so many Paintings, Bust's, Medals & Prints to be made of me, and distributed throughout the Kingdom, that my Face is now almost as well known as that of the Moon."[30] Surely a face so well known would not carry the same intimacy as a typical miniature would when held by a female friend.

The popular novel *Eloisa (La Nouvelle Heloise)* by Jean-Jacques Rousseau demonstrates the intimate handling of miniatures that made them ideal for exchange between lovers. The title character sends her lover, St. Preux, a package with a miniature of herself and explains that he should open the package in the privacy of his own room. She never refers to it as a miniature as such, but as "a small trinket" or "a kind of charm which lovers gladly wear." Eloisa instructs him to gaze at it daily, and "it is then applied to the eyes, the mouth, and next to the heart." This went far beyond a close gaze to connect the viewer's body closely to the image. So strong was the tie between the miniature and the person it represented, Eloisa told him, that the miniature "communicates the impression of kisses from one to the other, though at the distance of an hundred leagues."[31] For Eloisa and St. Preux, the miniature reinforced their romantic bonds at a distance.

Indeed, miniatures were most often exchanged between openly courting or else married couples. When a young Rosalba Peale attempted to give her aunt's husband a miniature portrait of herself painted by her cousin Anna, her disapproving grandfather Charles Wilson Peale asked Rosalba's father, "Why [would she] give her picture to any married gentleman?"[32] The elder Peale was not against mixed-sex friendships, as he had female friends, but he saw this exchange as overstepping boundaries. The popular perception of miniatures as an item of exchange between lovers could lead to misunderstanding if Rosalba gave her miniature to a male acquaintance, even a man within her family circle. At the murky border between friendship and romance, a miniature was a publicly accepted sign of a romantic relationship.

That a gift of a miniature intimated a romantic relationship, whether intended or not, is illustrated by the Countess of Lowendahl's relationship with the naval hero John Paul Jones. Jones met the young, ambitious comtesse in the salons of Paris in 1780. Jones's friend Caroline Edes wrote home to London that Jones "is greatly admired here especially by the ladies, who are wild with love for him, but he adores Lady [Lowendahl] who has honored him with every mark of politeness and attention."[33] One such mark was a miniature of Jones backed with hair, likely his, which Lowendahl sent to him after he left Paris (Figure 6.9). Lowendahl was studying with the artist Van der Huyt, and her painting of Jones's miniature was more likely intended to serve her artistic interests than to flatter him. She was looking for help getting a commission for her husband and capping her flirtation with Jones with such a handsome gift could cement an alliance.[34] This was only a flirtation in the French mode of the *amitié amoreuse*—a loving, flirtatious, nonsexual friendship.

FIGURE 6.9 The Comtesse de Lowendahl, a friend of John Paul Jones and an amateur artist, sent Jones this miniature as a gift. Charlotte-Marguerite de Bourbon, Comtesse de Lowendahl, *John Paul Jones*, 1780, watercolor on ivory. National Portrait Gallery, Smithsonian Institution.

Jones, less schooled in the modes of friendship in French salon culture, took the gift of his portrait from the comtesse as a sign of romantic attachment rather than a bargaining tool. When he received the portrait, he wrote back to her in the effusive language typical of his letters to his amours: "You have made me in Love with my own Picture because you have condescended to Draw it." He then proceeded to try to move their friendship into the romantic register by sending her a cipher for writing each other "very freely and without risque" and by requesting that she send him a miniature of herself to wear around his neck.[35] While the comtesse apparently saw the gift of a miniature of Jones himself as an act of friendship, she shared his belief that bestowing upon him a miniature of herself would signal a romantic relationship. Sending Jones a miniature of himself showed her artistry, while one of herself would give him intimate access to her image.

She refused his overtures, choosing not to send him a miniature, and Jones demurred by pretending to mistake the symbolism of such a gift. He asked "But, as you are a Philosopher, and as Friendship has nothing to do with Sex, pray what harm is there in wishing to have the picture of a Friend?"[36] A picture—perhaps a paper sketch, an engraving, even a large portrait—might have been a harmless token of friendship. But the intimacy of the miniature of a person of the opposite sex signaled to men and women on both sides of the Atlantic an attachment deeper than friendship.

Perhaps the most titillating exchange of a miniature between a man and woman supposed to be friends is the miniature that artist Sarah Goodridge sent to Daniel Webster (Figure 6.10). The two were known to be friends during their lifetimes, but it was only after Webster's death and the discovery of a 2 ⅝ x 3 ⅛ inch rectangle of ivory that Webster's family realized there was likely a sexual aspect to the relationship. On this small ivory was a lifelike rendition of the artist's breasts, identified as her own with a small birthmark and with the title on the back "Beauty Revealed." No other miniature like this has ever been found from the period, making this miniature a unique form of self-expression. One scholar calls it "a kind of visual synecdoche" that said far more about her than her more conventional self-portraits.[37] Another scholar suggests that the miniature was a private display of a perhaps complex relationship in which he might have her bosom, but not her whole.[38] Webster was not her husband and thus did not own her body, so for him to have an image of only part of her body signaled Goodridge's independence.[39]

Piecing together the portrait, the very act of its exchange, and the documentary record allows for the recovery of something of the texture of Webster and Goodridge's relationship. Letters exchanged between Goodridge

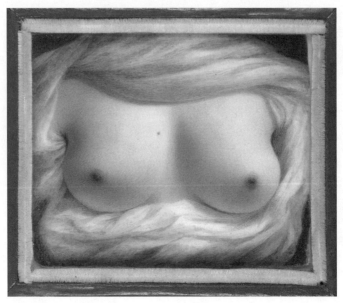

FIGURE 6.10 Goodridge sent this miniature, only 2 ⅝ x 3 ⅛ inches and set in a small box with a hinged lid, to Daniel Webster. Sarah Goodridge, *Beauty Revealed*, 1828, watercolor on ivory. Metropolitan Museum of Art, New York, New York. (Image © The Metropolitan Museum of Art)

and Webster show that the two became friends in the early 1820s in Boston. Goodridge was a successful miniaturist who had trained with Gilbert Stuart, and she painted Webster five times. One of Webster's biographers remarks that most portraits of Webster "make one think of a bullfrog immersed in the gloom of thought" while hers "suggest a faun in sunlight." A close relationship between artist and sitter might have influenced this more tender portrayal of such a prominent public figure. Webster also commissioned Goodridge to paint many other members of his family and aided her as she grew her business by finding her a studio and rooms. Goodridge became so commercially successful that she was later able to lend him five hundred dollars, which he apologetically failed to ever fully repay.[40]

Soon after Webster's first wife passed away, Goodridge gave him the "Beauty Revealed" miniature during a visit to Washington in 1828. None of their letters previous to—or even after—this date offer evidence of a sexual liaison. Goodridge's letters no longer exist, but Webster's letters to her are mostly about visits or apologies for failing to visit her while in the Boston area. The progression of salutations in the letters transitioning from "Madam" to "Dear

FIGURE 6.11 This Vanderlyn nude may have been the artistic inspiration for Goodridge's *Beauty Revealed*. Note the similarity in the shape, size, coloration, and surrounding of white gauzy cloth. John Vanderlyn, *Ariadne Asleep on the Island of Naxos*, 1809–14, oil on canvas, 1878.1.11. Pennsylvania Academy of the Fine Arts, Philadelphia, Pennsylvania, gift of Mrs. Sarah Harrison (The Joseph Harrison, Jr. Collection).

Madam" to "Dear Miss G." and finally "My dear, good friend" demonstrate a deepening friendship.[41] But the image is the sole evidence of a friendship that was sexually intimate. Goodridge could have easily painted a conventional self-portrait miniature to give to Webster on that 1828 visit, knowing that even such a gift would signify a romantic relationship. But it seems that Goodridge had decided that if she was going to overstep boundaries, she might just as well go further. There was an enormous boldness in even painting such an image in an era when women were not supposed to paint nudes.

It seems, too, that there is playfulness in this defiance of conventions of art and exchange. Despite the photographic rendering and the mark on the right breast suggesting that these are a specific woman's breasts, they are not the breasts of a forty-year-old woman (which Goodridge was by this time). The shape, size, coloration, and surrounding of white gauzy cloth are in fact quite similar to John Vanderlyn's image of bare breasts in his controversial nude *Ariadne Asleep on the Island of Naxos* (Figure 6.11). That painting was displayed in Boston in 1826, two years before Goodridge sent Webster this miniature, and the public exhibitionof a nude woman brought crowds of viewers. Goodridge likely saw the painting in person or in one of the many prints made of it, and perhaps Webster even knew she was referencing the famous image. Goodridge's innovative miniature was not the sort of portrait a woman seeking to be Webster's wife would give him, despite the fact that by this time both were unmarried.[42] It is a portrait that acknowledged a sexual aspect of the relationship but in such a private form that the two could maintain a public image of propriety as friends.

Other Representations

There is one final genre of visual representation that was cheaper, easier to acquire, and more widespread than oil portraits or miniatures: the silhouette. The opacity of these outlined forms mirrors the difficulty in finding and analyzing traces of them. The exchange of silhouettes was rarely mentioned in letters and diaries, and they were much less likely to be preserved than costly works on canvas or ivory. Residents of Philadelphia and Baltimore could have silhouettes done at the Peale Museums in either city, and by folding the black paper over twice, the sitter could get four copies of his or her profile. Elsewhere itinerant silhouette makers or even prominent silhouette artists like Saint Memin could create the images in multiple copies. These could then be given to friends, family, or acquaintances in the community.[43]

Peale advertised his machine for creating silhouettes, the physiognotrace, as a tool for creating gifts for friends because "friendship esteems as valuable even the most distant likeness of a friend." Within "less than a minute," museum visitors could get "the truest outlines of any heretofore invented" to keep for themselves and give as gifts.[44] Ann Ridgely, a Delaware woman visiting Philadelphia, probably had her silhouette done at the Peale Museum there, as had her circle of friends. She wrote her mother in 1803 to report that "I had my profile taken, 'tis the image of me, consequently too ugly to shew. All my friends here want one, but I will not leave one behind." She had received profiles from "a number of my acquaintance," which she lists as including both men and women. While an accurate representation of the outlines of a face, the lack of detail and the cheapness of these images made them appropriate gifts between male/female friends.

One of the rare surviving examples of a silhouette relating to a friendship is that of Mary Roberdeau in the collection of John Quincy Adams (Figure 6.12). Adams recorded in his diary on March 4, 1829, that silhouette

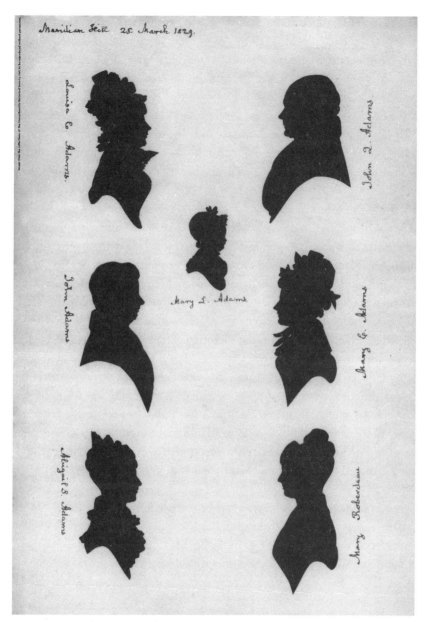

FIGURE 6.12 John Quincy Adams mounted the silhouette of his friend Mary Roberdeau on the same 10 by 6.5 inch piece of paper with those of himself and his family. They are labeled in Quincy Adams's hand. Jarvis Hanks, *Family of John Quincy Adams*, 1829, silhouettes. From the Silhouette Collection, Adams Family Silhouette, Massachusetts Historical Society (Gift of Richard Ames).

maker Jarvis Hanks came to his home and "cut me out and all the family in paper."[45] Included in this family group of silhouettes, all mounted on one page and labeled in Adams's hand, is one of his friend Mary Roberdeau. Mary must have been at the Adams' home frequently, as John Quincy Adams recorded in a poem to her around this time that "many a pleasing day/Cheer'd by thy conversation I have past."[46] Her inclusion with the carefully lined-up silhouettes of Adams family members depicted her as both a friend of the family rather than just Adams, as well as showing the intimacy of that friendship. By agreeing to sit for her silhouette that day, Roberdeau gave Adams the chance to have an image to remember her by shortly before he left Washington.

Like silhouettes, hair could provide a cheap visual representation of an absent friend. Of course, giving a lock of hair involved neither the costs nor the necessity for an artist as intermediary. There were few choices for presentation; the lock could be given unadorned and straight from the head of its owner, it could be twined onto the page of an album, or it could become part of a piece of jewelry. The latter two presentations are called "hairwork," a genre that expanded greatly in the Victorian era. In the early republic, presentations of hair were usually quite simple. Hair was already a common addition to the backings of miniature in this period, however, directly associating hair with representations of people. A single lock of hair was a synecdoche for both the absent friend and the emotions shared between the giver and receiver of the hair.[47] Hair was immortal: unlike the head from which it came, it never faded or decayed. For this reason, hair was often used to memorialize deceased family members and friends in jewelry pieces or friendship albums.[48]

Here, perhaps, was the perfect gift between a male and female friend: intimate and evocative of emotion, but because of its cheapness and inexhaustibility, without connotations of romance. One individual could give many clippings of his or her hair without much effort or any cost. It was the context in which the hair was given and how it was stored or presented that determined its meaning. Certainly hair given as part of a miniature was a romantic gesture, but even jewelry made of hair could safely signify a friendship. Sometimes the recipient could shape the presentation of the hair by commissioning the jewelry piece him or herself, choosing to fashionably display the lock as a sign of friendship.

Two jewelry pieces made of George and Martha Washington's hair were given to General Lafayette and his son George on their visit to America in 1824. Lafayette received a ring with the Washingtons' hair from their grandson George Washington Parke Custis on a visit to Washington's tomb.[49] Since Lafayette was also friends with Custis's sisters Eliza and Eleanor, this was probably a gift on behalf of the family. A circle of the hair of two deceased members of this group of close friends cemented the ties of the living, and the act of giving the ring while at Washington's tomb further emphasized keeping the memory of him alive as part of this friendship. Eleanor also arranged for George Washington Lafayette to receive a "handsome breast pin" with George and Martha's hair. Eleanor wrote of the pin to a friend that George "will value it more than anything I can give him."[50] Both men and women, then, could wear hair jewelry pieces.

Elizabeth Stoughton Wolcott, whose husband Oliver Wolcott was secretary of the treasury and a friend of George Washington, also owned pieces with George and Martha Washington's hair. In 1797, at the end of Washington's term, Washington gave his cabinet members small gifts. Mrs. Wolcott supposedly asked Martha Washington for a lock of George Washington's hair. This was not to be merely a token of Oliver Wolcott's service, but a memorial of the couples' friendship; the couples saw each other socially and George and Oliver wrote each other frequently.

According to one account, "Mrs. Washington instantly took her scissors, and with a happy smile, cut a large lock from her husband's head, added to it one from her own, and presented them to her friend."[51] Martha must have cut one very long lock or several short ones, because three pieces featuring Washington's hair and an inscription about the occasion survive. It is unclear whether the Wolcotts or the Washingtons had the pieces made. There is one locket with a small strand of brown hair curled in a loose circle against a white background (Figure 6.13). This was apparently only George's hair, and the inscription (probably added later) on the locket records this as a gift from Martha to Mrs. Wolcott. There is also a framed piece with both George's and Martha's hair. Finally, an oval medallion to be worn as a necklace or pin has both the Washingtons hair entwined (one brown lock and one white) under beveled glass and with the word "WASHINGTON" at the top of the medallion. Engraved on the back is the same story of the hair's origins: "Hair of George and Martha Washington cut by Martha Washington for Elizabeth Wolcott in March 1797."[52]

Using hair from both husband and wife visually captured and memorialized a friendship of a triad in which friends brought spouses into a male/female friendship. One such gift was that of a hair ring with John and Abigail Adams' hair. While John Adams and Mercy Otis Warren were the closest of the Warren/Adams pair of friendships, after an 1807 rift broke up their

FIGURE 6.13 Martha Washington gave this locket with George Washington's hair to their mutual friend Elizabeth Wolcott. The back of this piece has a later inscription reading "Hair of George Washington cut by Martha Washington for Mrs. Oliver Wolcott great grandmother of George Gibbs V." Locket, 1797, gold, copper, glass, ivory, paper, human hair, W-1150. Mount Vernon Ladies Association, Bequest of George Gibbs V.

friendship it was Abigail's hair that Mercy requested in 1812. Mercy sent Abigail a lock of her own hair, and in reply Abigail sent both her own and John's hair entwined in a ring. Abigail wrote Mercy that she included John's hair at his request, a symbolic gesture bringing him back into the friendly circle. Mercy saw it this way, telling Abigail that "it is an assurance that he can never forget former amities." This was not a single gesture, but one that would carry forward with a visual reminder of friendship. Mercy wrote that the hair ring would cause her to "be daily reminded from whose head the locks were shorn."[53] Like a miniature, then, a piece of jewelry featuring hair could provide a close and constant reminder of a friend. Unlike miniatures, however, hair jewelry was less intimate and could be worn publicly without concern.

Framing Gifts

Gifts that did not suggest visual representations of the friend needed to be framed in such a way as to explain the significance of the gift and fit it into the contours of the friendship. The choice of a gift, however mundane, might form part of an ongoing conversation between friends. In cases of the exchange of mundane objects, even more so than with portraits, manuscript evidence explains the context of the gift. A gift as simple as a rose bud sent by Philadelphia congressman and poet John Swanwick to Sophia Chew in 1787 was given added significance by the poem that accompanied it. The poem recounts that Swanwick found the rose bud on the floor after a party and "So sweet its appearance, so blooming its hue,/I could not suppose but its owner was you."[54] As Swanwick was nearly thirty years Chew's senior, it was unlikely such a gift would be interpreted as romantic. Indeed, Swanwick published this poem in his poetry book, making the exchange public and thus suggesting its propriety.

The recipient might also reinforce the meaning of the gift in explaining how he or she would use and value it. Mary Roberdeau sewed a purse for John Quincy Adams in 1832, and Adams's letter of thanks survives. The sort of purse she made was similar in usage to a wallet today, although worn like a purse. It was thus a rather practical item, although Adams described it as both "elegant and useful." "Be assured," he wrote, "that your gift shall be as perpetual an appendage to my person as the Red Ribband of the Bath was to that of Sir William Draper." He reported that he had thrown out his old linen bag, which perhaps Roberdeau had noticed and intended this gift to replace, making the new bag a sign of her attention to him. He certainly saw the purse as a mark of friendship, telling her "so long as the purse itself shall endure I shall have that in my pocket, which is better than money—a token of your friendly regard."[55]

Other small pieces of jewelry or accessories were also safe gifts between friends of the opposite sex. Martha Washington received a gold chain, perhaps for a watch or necklace, from her husband's aide and younger friend David Humphreys in 1797. In separate letters on the same day in February 1797, Humphreys sent this gift to Martha and a pair of specially made topaz buckles to George. Martha thanked Humphreys for the "token of your remembrance" but told him "I wanted nothing to remind me of the pleasure we have had in your company at this place [Mount Vernon]." She needed no object to substitute for Humphreys in his absence, then, but she would keep the chain "as an emblem of your friendship."[56] The plain gold chain became a symbol not of the giver but of the relationship itself.

To memorialize a friendship rather than a friend was perhaps the aim of Litchfield Female Academy student Martha Ann Bartlett, who gave her teacher and friend John Pierce Brace several hand-painted watchpapers. Brace was a popular teacher and befriended many of the young women he taught. The gift Martha created for him was an inexpensive but personal one: watchpapers are small, thin paper backings to be placed under the glass on watch faces to customize the design. The papers Bartlett made for Brace are perhaps one inch across and so thin that their preservation is rather remarkable; Brace must have valued them and put them away for safekeeping. None of the watchpapers depict Bartlett, but one is decorated with the word "l'amitié" (Figure 6.14). Worn as part of an object Brace would have looked at frequently, Bartlett offered a token of their friendship. Their size, content, and usage on a publicly displayed piece of jewelry suggest that these were appropriate gifts from a woman to her male friend.

FIGURE 6.14 Bartlett, a student at Litchfield Female Academy, gave her teacher and friend John Pierce Brace a set of watch papers, including the one shown above. Martha Ann Bartlett, watchpaper, 1818, watercolor and ink on paper. Collection of the Litchfield Historical Society, Litchfield, Connecticut.

Besides serving as reminders of absent friends and special friendships, some gifts were given in order to stimulate and support conversation at a distance through letters. One quite practical example of this was a lap desk that the Marquis de Lafayette sent to Eliza Parke Custis. The desk is a square mahogany piece with a gold border that opened to provide storage for writing implements and letters. Perhaps Lafayette gave the desk to Eliza as encouragement to write to him, and she might have stored the letters she received from him within it. It would certainly have made an elegant writing surface and served as a tangible reminder of the very friend to whom she wrote.[57]

Poetry

To bolster conversation and ties of friendship in person, men and women with literary inclinations offered poems to their friends. Such poems presented a ritualized representation of what friendship should be. The exchange of original poetry was particularly important for mixed-sex friends, who could with total propriety trade poems overflowing with sentiment. In poems to each other, friends of the opposite sex could and often did say more than they felt. Certainly Della Crusca and Matilda could have an overblown romantic friendship in print, but poems exchanged in person could still be effusive if not overtly romantic.

These personal poetic exchanges grew out of the mid-eighteenth-century culture of belles lettres, in which men and women exchanged playful poems in an ongoing conversation that mixed print and in-person sociability. These texts were part of a gift rather than a market economy, circulating in handwritten volumes or even on stray sheets of paper. While some of these texts were eventually printed in newspapers, they were generated within the polite circles meeting at tea tables and in coffeehouses.[58] Not all of these texts circulated in mixed-sex coteries and in fact, some of the poems exchanged between men and women were centered on that pair rather than the group. The poems did not demand a direct, reciprocal exchange; rather, they were tokens of friendship that built relationships and communities of friends.[59]

This was the case for Annis Boudinot Stockton, who met Washington after publishing her first poetic tribute to him. The poem had attracted his attention, and he visited Stockton's home in-between nearby battles in 1781. The two became friends and Stockton's poems began to expand from public tribute to expressions of private friendship. Soon after dining

together in September 1783, Stockton wrote a poem about him that ended
with these lines:

> *Some tuneful Homer shall in future days*
> *Sing thy exploits, in celebrated lays,*
> *While my ambition has no other aim,*
> *Then as thy friend to set my humble name.*
> *Emelia*[60]

Earlier that month, Stockton had written Washington to apologize for com-
posing such effusive—and numerous—poems about him. Washington had
replied by suggesting that she have dinner with him and "go thro' the proper
course of penitence which shall be prescribed." In an unusually playful letter
for him, Washington told Stockton that he would attempt to "assist you in ex-
piating these poetical trespasses on this side of purgatory—nay more, if it rests
with me to direct your future locubrations, I shall certainly urge you to a rep-
etition of the same conduct, on purpose to shew what an admirable knack you
have at confession & reformation."[61] By the late 1780s, Stockton was referring
to the way his friendship "stole on my soul exquisitely sweet" to inspire her
poetry, and Washington admitted, "we can never be cloyed with the pleasing
compositions of our female friends."[62] Poetry seems to have opened a forum
for banter and playfulness for the normally serious and stoic Washington.

A friend of Stockton's, Elizabeth Graeme Fergusson, also wrote poems and
circulated albums among her coterie of friends. These might be poems on particular friends who came to Fergusson's salons, or they might be on friendship
at large or nature. Some of these poems were later published (which Fergusson
recorded with annotations in the albums), while others were copies of those
given directly to friends. Many of the poems were in memory of deceased
friends, and their circulation would perpetuate the deceased's memory and
reinforce bonds of the rest of the circle. There are also several poems written
to Elizabeth Powel, another female friend of George Washington's. One of
these was commissioned by Washington as a birthday gift for Powel, and thus
it was a gift from two of Powel's friends. It also conveyed Washington's respect
for Fergusson's poetic talents, making the gift also a tribute to Fergusson.[63]

Fergusson sent many of her poems to Benjamin Rush along with her letters to him, and one even became an exchange about an exchange. In 1793 she
sent him a poem titled "An Epistle from a Lady in the *Country*, to a Gentleman Who complained that he was much pinched for *Time*." She suggested
that he should take time away from his work to relax with his wife, Julia, or
else come visit Fergusson in the country. If that failed, "One *Letter* a week she

surely might claim,/To keep alive Friendship; and fan its pure Flame."[64] Her small gift of a poem not only gave advice, but also addressed the tempo of the exchange of letters between them. Rush did not need to send poetry, or even his own original writings (which he sometimes did) back to her—he merely needed to keep up their correspondence, that outer exchange that enclosed the more sporadic exchanges of writings.

Poetry exchanged between men and women could also be in the form of impromptu pieces rather than carefully crafted gifts, suggesting a spontaneous effusion of feeling in the moment of interacting with a friend. It did not take an accomplished writer to produce such poems. Take, for example, Philadelphia businessman and congressman John Swanwick. While he later published the poems he had written to friends, he described them "as trifles by which the cares of a busy life were diverted or assuaged." Thus, whether he put time into writing them or not, he wanted his readers to imagine the poems as objects of pleasure rather than literature. The titles of the poems themselves suggest that he wrote them on the spur of the moment: "TO ELIZA, On seeing her abroad early in the morning"; "To a young Lady, on seeing her at Church Sunday March 26, 1786"; "To Mrs. Livingston, On hearing that Lady play on the Guitar."[65] These were not poems that offered any evidence of deep feeling or knowledge of the women he wrote to, but he appears to have felt they were worth giving to his acquaintances. He seems to have made a rather ridiculous figure: one historian describes him as a "pompous, vain little man" who "wore big cravats," and there was a poetic pamphlet published in 1796 satirizing his "consummate vanity" even before he published his poetry. Swanwick may have been trying to insinuate himself in circles of genteel society in which he was not entirely welcome as a self-made man, but it appears his poetry made him more fodder for gossip than valued friend.[66]

The materiality of the poem written on paper could also be part of the exchange of the poem as a gift. A poem to the seventeen-year-old Elizabeth Patterson (later Bonaparte) titled "To Miss Patterson on her birthday the 6 February 1802" from family friend Robert Gilmor was written on a piece of peach paper with gold embossing. This was no impromptu scrawl on a scrap of paper, but a gift of both literary and visual merit. The poem imagined Elizabeth as "a little tender flower" that was blooming into a "blushing Rose." The poem closed:

> *And Venus now will give the pow'r*
> *To him whose heart disdains disguise,*
> *To pluck this tender, blooming flow'r,*
> *and in his bosom fix the prize.*

Here Gilmor expressed his hope that Elizabeth would soon find romantic love. As a family friend eleven years Elizabeth's senior, this wish for her was likely an appropriate way of expressing his care and friendship. Indeed, the two continued to be friends into Elizabeth's adulthood.[67]

Friendship Albums

The tradition of poetic exchange among friends of either sex found a new genre for expression beginning in the 1820s in the form of the friendship album. This genre started in fifteenth-century Germany as the "album amicorum," books with signatures of friends and acquaintances to serve as introductions for traveling students.[68] The albums that became popular centuries later in America shared this semi-public nature, but the entries were quite different. Friendship albums, sometimes erroneously referred to as autograph albums or commonplace books, began in America as small notebooks with cardboard covers in which friends copied short poems and aphorisms.[69] During the 1820s, bookmakers began to create sturdy, thick, leather-bound books, some with lithographs scattered throughout, expressly for use as friendship albums. Around this time, too, entries became increasingly elaborate and included drawings, locks of hair, lengthy poems by famous authors, pressed flowers, and clippings from other sources.

Friendship albums, generally considered to be a feminine genre, were in fact mixed-sex spaces for the performance of friendship.[70] Most contemporary commentators on albums saw them as the province of young women, and one male writer described them as "almost indispensable in a lady's education."[71] Yet some men kept albums themselves, and many more signed the albums of their female friends. While commentators assumed albums would be owned by women, they published articles advising men on what to write or complaining about the difficulty of finding the right thing to say. One short piece wryly defined the album as "an instrument of *torture* invented by some cruel fair one to *rack the brains* of her male acquaintance."[72] Albums were a narrowly tailored genre in which friendly expressions required particular knowledge and careful thought.

Nearly all of the poems in friendship albums were copied from books or magazines, with works by British poets of sensibility such as Felicia Hemans, Lord Byron, and Mary Balfour appearing widely. One writer complained that people wasted their time "looking over a volume of old newspapers" to find appropriate entries for albums rather than reading more serious material.[73] The goal of the album writer was not to display originality, but to select the appropriate expression of sentiment. While the poetry appears hackneyed and unimaginative to a contemporary reader, the choice of a proper poem was about expressing proper sentiments, analogous to the choice of a store-bought greeting card today.[74]

Friendship albums served as material venues for structured interaction between friends of both genders. The albums fostered interaction and conversation when the entries were written or read. They later served as collections documenting friendship, feeling, and memories for the owner of the album when taking up the book for private contemplation or for friends and relatives of the owner when the album was passed among them. These albums compiled social ties that varied in strength, and because of the tendency for overly sentimentalized language, it is difficult to decipher the intensity of friendship between the album owner and signers. As one critic of albums complained, "They abound in the most palpable flattery and extravagant professions of esteem and friendship."[75]

However, what mattered to album owners was not the level of friendship of the signer, but the album as a compendium of his or her social relationships. Entries could be from people of the owner's age, relatives, clergymen, family friends, school acquaintances, and even visiting celebrities (Lafayette was a favorite during his 1824–1825 visit). Another male writer described albums as a resource for understanding a woman's social circle, suggesting "were I in pursuit of a wife, I would in the first place go to a young lady's Album, to find out the taste and judgment of the society with which she associated."[76] Unlike other gifts between friends, leaving an entry in an album tied friends into larger social networks so that others could literally read the records of a person's relationships.

Here was an appropriate space for friends of any level of intimacy to declare their ties to the album owner. There were multiple layers to any album entry, as it served as a sign of both self and the relationship to the album owner, and it could be read textually and visually. The choice of an entry reflected on both the signer and his or her feelings for the owner, particularly if the entry was an original piece. The entry would, as the aforementioned writer suggested, show "the taste and judgment" of the signers. The textual content stood for the self in this sense but could also, if the author chose a poem on feeling rather than nature or religion, convey something about the character of the signer and owner's relationship. The latter was particularly tricky because of the effusive sentimentality of the poetry, although as the poetry exchanges published in magazines showed, poets could sometimes say more than what they felt. The difficulty in choosing the proper way to express friendly feelings was likely behind the plethora of articles advising people on what to write in albums and the frequent anonymous publishing of poems from albums as models for readers.

An entry would also serve as a visual sign of self in the same way an object given as a gift could. Simply seeing the handwriting or signature of an absent friend would bring to mind that person.[77] The careful penmanship of many entries suggested the importance of this visual signification. Indeed, the most popular poem copied into albums was an early nineteenth-century poem by Mary Balfour that began, "Oft as thine eye shall fondly trace,/Each simple wreath, I twin'd for thee;/What e'er the time, what ever the place,/Oh! think of me."[78] The "wreath" was a popular metaphor for album poetry, suggesting a visual display that the eye would "trace" rather than read. A male friend could thus cheaply and without risk leave a trace of himself for a female friend in an album.

The way men expressed friendship for women through poetry in friendship albums differed markedly from the earlier poetic exchanges in magazines— and from the entries of other women. In all of these cases, the poems were about expressions of sentiment. But while women's entries were often about love and the immortality of friendship, most men's poems were notably less intimate.[79] Men left sentimental poems about religious devotion, women's proper role, or nature; poems about friendship were phrased in a religious rather than personal language. Unlike women, who often incorporated the woman's name into the poem, men's poems were generally unaltered, generic copies.

Many men chose poems for women's albums about women's proper roles and behavior. These poems praised women's sensibility and admonished their vanity—both characteristics that albums might foster. In the album of a woman named Elizabeth Dodge, a poem from Rugus Gilman recorded in 1825 equates the characteristics of a woman's album with those of the woman herself:

> See to your book, young lady; let it be
> An index to your life—each page be pure.
> By vanity uncoloured, and by vice
> unspotted. Cheerful be each modest leaf,
> Not rude; and pious be each written page.
> ... Spare many leaves for charity—that flower
> That better than the rose's first white bud
> Becomes a woman's bosom. There we seek
> And there we find it first. Such be your book
> And such, young lady, always may you be.[80]

Gilman likely found this poem in the Wilmington *Circular*, where it was published earlier that year, and his choice suggests that he believes both women and albums should be modest, virtuous, polite, pious, serious, and charitable. Here is a vision of woman at her antebellum best.[81]

Men who chose to express more than they felt with what one author called a verse from "the love sick effusions, or impieties, of Moore and Byron" were criticized in periodical articles.[82] An 1827 magazine article titled "Confessions of an Album Writer" parodied those who did not understand the overblown nature of the sentiments in album poetry. The confessing writer claimed to have written in 246 albums, and in 195 of them, he "made love outright to the charming proprietors, though two-thirds of them excited no feelings in my naturally cold and passionless heart." In one woman's album he praised blue eyes, and in another black. Writing with false sentiment had its consequences, as the confessor admitted: "all my flights of fancy have been construed into serious declarations of passion." So seriously did women take him that he claimed to "have narrowly escaped ten suits for breach of promise, in which the only witnesses against me would have been Albums, and an unpoetical jury would have infallibly convicted me."[83] While this is parody, the article points to real (although certainly lesser than portrayed) risks in how men expressed their friendship in albums.

The confessor's mention of the "unpoetical jury" here is key; he signals that people who understood the genre of poetry should have known that sometimes poets said more than they felt. Just as the poetic exchanges between men and women in magazines were seen as literary exercises, so should his poems be understood. Yet clearly exaggerating women's misreading of his entries, he says he was deemed "a perjured swain, a breaker of vows, a hypocritical pretender, an unfeeling wretch, and (horresco referns!) a male flirt!" For a man to express more than he felt perhaps carried some risk. An 1826 magazine article suggested that "the loving swain will sometimes select this mode [writing in an album] to discover his affection" and that albums gave young women "the best and most delicate opportunity to become acquainted with any *favorite* they may wish without the risk of being charged with too much curiosity or fondness." Here appeared to be one of the few arenas for interaction between men and women where the greater risk was to the man—although likely in terms of misunderstanding, rather than anything as extreme as breach of promise—than to the woman. This hearkens to a much older notion of men needing to be as good as their word, and women as good as their chastity or reputation.

Octavia Walton LeVert's male friends seemed more inclined than most to write poems suggestive of love. Octavia was seventeen when she began keeping her album during a visit to Baltimore with her father, the governor of Florida. It is likely that these men were friends of her father's and befriended his young daughter, who was apparently well-educated and comfortable in the adult world from a young age.[84] Henry Clay was one such friend, a man thirty-three years her senior who became a lifelong friend and the namesake for her third daughter, Henrietta Caroline. On August 15, 1827, Clay copied a published poem into her album that praised women's love:

> Oh! not when hearts are lightest,
> Is fond woman's fervour shown;
> But when life's cloud or'take us,
> And the Cold world is clothed in gloom,
> When summer friends forsake us,
> Then true love is but in bloom.

This poem, while on the topic of love, never specifically addresses Octavia. Her friend Edward Coots Pinkney, however, began his poem to her "Love lurks upon Octavia's lip" and went on to describe the beauty of her face. Pinkney, a married poet eight years Octavia's senior, closed his poem with the lines:

> Say from what far and sunny shore
> Fair wonder does thou rove
> Lest what I only should _adore_
> I fondly think to Love—[85]

This was likely just the sort of poem that the critic of men's "love sick effusions" was thinking of, but it also demonstrates the propriety of conveying perhaps even more than one felt in an album.

Most often, however, men's strongest sentiments were displayed in farewell entries. Albums were often signed just before a woman left her home or school or during an extended trip, so such entries were common. Poems begging friends to "Remember me" reflected the same anxiety as portraits and letters: without physical friendship, a relationship would wilt away. These poetic farewells were final bursts of emotion and visual traces that kept the friend in the mind and heart of the album keeper.[86] There are numerous emotional farewell poems in Le Vert's album, including one original poem signed simply "Juan" that closed in this way:

While none of the sorrows of this life distress thee,
Such is the prayer that Friendship now offers for thee,
Dear girl then remember him who'll remember thee
While the throb of his heart is unfetter'd and free.

The physical throb of the heart was often a sign of romantic love, and here its appearance in a semi-public space suggests it was an appropriate expression of emotion.

Another example of the intensity of emotions at parting is evident in John Quincy Adams's original poem for Mary Roberdeau in 1829:

We part—but wheresoever thy lot
Shall lead thee, over this world of care—
Friendship shall consecrate the spot—
My Heart, in Memory, shall be there.
... Take the thought burning from the Soul;
Tis feeling too intense for Rhyme.[87]

Parting could be a wellspring for a "burning from the Soul" that was friendly rather than romantic; these friends might never see or even write one another again. A Colombian man named Alberto who was parting with his friend Nancy Andrews in New York left a farewell knowing that they might correspond again: "It may be that I am now leaving my last testimony of friendship."[88]

One published poem signed "Malcolm" from a woman's album closed with the thought that "some frail leaf" like the page of the album in which the poem was written might be "The sole remaining trace of me—/To tell I lived and died."[89] Malcolm was right: the poems and signatures left in friendship albums are sometimes the historian's only "remaining trace" of a person from this time period. But the entries can also be the only trace left of a friendship, as relationships from the past are even harder to pin down than people. This makes album entries a window into myriad relationships that would otherwise be invisible, but relationships with so little contextual information they are difficult to read.

There is one rare album in which the identity of the album owner and signers are well enough documented to make more detailed conclusions about the friendships recorded within it. This album, given to Mary Wallace Peck by her future husband Edward D. Mansfield in 1825, was kept while Mary was in Litchfield, Connecticut. Litchfield was home to both Sarah Pierce's female academy and Tapping Reeve's law school, and its residents are so well documented that it is possible to piece together Mary's friendships from the entries in her album.[90] The album offers a record of the community in which Mary and her future husband were embedded and the ways Mary and Edward's friendships were woven together. Of fifty-seven identifiable signers, twenty-nine were men, an usually high number for a woman's album, and twenty-eight were women. Most were either Mary or Edward's contemporaries or Mary's students, as she was an art teacher at Litchfield Female Academy. It seems likely that Edward and Mary were already planning to marry at this time, because Edward left for Cincinnati later in 1825 and Mary had joined him there by 1826.[91]

Almost all of the signers of Mary's album were residents of Litchfield. There is an entry on aging from the local doctor, in his seventies at the time of its writing. There are several original poems from the writer and educator Catherine Beecher, who was the same age as Mary and had attended Litchfield Female Academy with her. One particularly beautiful entry is from the artist George Catlin, whose uncle had adopted Mary (Figure 6.15). Catlin was four years Mary's senior and was an unmarried man beginning his career as a portrait artist when he left a drawing and poem in Mary's album signed simply "G.C." The left-hand page shows cupid struggling with the world on his back and below the poem "Lay down the world! you little arrant thief:/What! think you thus on worlds we wish to ride?/We know thou'rt sovereign, universal thief,/Of power, to tyrants and to gods denied." On the facing page, cupid has fallen and the globe lies cracked on the ground. The poem continues,

> But hold, Love! die not__I did not chide thee,
> The world is all thy own, I know not whether
> Such evil fate would e'er betide thee:
> I own 'twas thee that held the world together.

The playful piece on the power of love appears to be a way to showcase his drawing talent rather than his own feelings, as the drawings are done with far more care than the penmanship and take up the majority of the space. Clearly, as a fellow artist, Mary would have appreciated the artfulness of Catlin's entry.

Many of the male signers of Mary's album were classmates of Edward's at Litchfield Law School and likely mutual friends. The men and women of Litchfield socialized together frequently, and Mary already might have befriended these men before she courted Edward. One particularly interesting entry comes from John P. Jackson, a law school student who in 1826 married Mary's friend Elizabeth Wolcott. Edward described Jackson as "my intimate

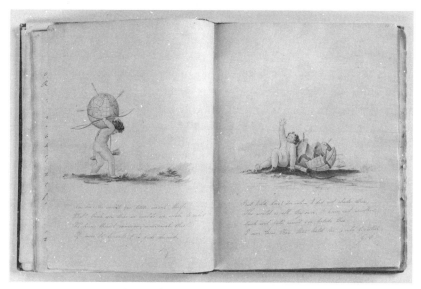

FIGURE 6.15 Artist and Litchfield Law School graduate George Catlin created this entry for Mary Peck Mansfield's friendship album. Mary Peck Mansfield Album, 1825–1826, pages 58 and 59. Collection of the Litchfield Historical Society, Litchfield, Connecticut.

friend," and it seems likely from Jackson's three pages of prose and poetry entries that he was also Mary's good friend.[92] His careful penmanship suggests he put time into copying his chosen items into Mary's album. While most of the items he chose were generic pieces on religion, he made one rather extraordinary choice.

Jackson copied an abridged version of a poem by Lord Byron titled "To Florence," first published in *Childe Harolde* in 1812 as "To ***." This particular poem was written to a woman Byron met in Malta and fell in love with, and he wrote to or about her under the pen name "Florence." She was Constance Spencer Smith, a married woman, and Byron had planned to elope with her.[93] It is unclear if American readers knew this back-story, but Byron's illicit love for a married woman would explain why Byron apologized for saying that all who saw Florence must love her. Byron, in Mary's album co-opted by Jackson, continued:

> *Forgive the word, in one who ne'er*
> *With such a word can more offend;*
> *And since thy heart I cannot share,*
> *Believe me, what I am, thy friend.*

Whether aware of the story of Byron and Smith's affair or not, on its face the poem suggests that the writer loves the person he is writing to, but barred from receiving her love in return, he will be her friend. Given how public Mary's album would have been—it has many more signatures than most albums and must have circulated widely—and the fact that Edward would have seen this, this poem is probably another example of a writer saying more than he feels. This was likely intended as a declaration of close friendship, not romantic feeling.

Another entry by a classmate of Edward Mansfield's suggests collaboration between Mary and the writer. Mary's album is beautifully illustrated, and given that she was a drawing teacher and the similarity in style of some of the images, it appears likely that Mary added images to her friends' entries. Frederick Bronson's entry, a prose selection about prayer from a sermon by a seventeenth-century British minister, corresponds with the image just above it. The poem uses the image of a bird struggling to fly upward but finally gliding through the air as a metaphor for "the prayer of a good man," and the drawing shows a man reclining under an arch of vines and watching a bird soar into the sky. While small, the ink drawing is skillfully rendered. Mary and Bronson likely collaborated on this entry, offering evidence of a dynamic exchange of ideas and skills in memorializing their friendship.

It can be difficult to see evidence of precisely how an exchange between a pair of friends like Mary and Frederick worked in a friendship album, given that men usually did not own albums. It was not a literal exchange like that of letters, or even a roughly equivalent trade of gifts. For a man to be asked to make an entry in a woman's album may have been a compliment, and his entry took the form of a compliment offered in return. As one periodical piece noted, "It is considered a compliment by the gentlemen to be asked to write in an album. It argues a favorable opinion, and a desire to become more acquainted."[94] But surely for people who were good friends the entry was part of the continuous exchanges of services that characterize any friendship. That exchange, which leaves less of a material trace, can be harder to see.

The giving of gifts between friends, while constrained by propriety, ultimately reinforced the ability of friendships between men and women to exemplify the values of the early republic. Giving a gift was a visible display of virtue, on its face a selfless granting of the time or money of one person for the good of another. A gift that conformed to the bounds of propriety demonstrated the virtue of a man or woman who could give to a friend of the opposite sex in a way that signaled only chaste intentions. This was a skill in itself that required perceptiveness, caution, and care. It also depended on choice in several ways: first, the choice to give or return a gift, and second, of the proper gift to present. Most crucially, however, the exchange of gifts fostered equality. Men and women were equally able to offer gifts to one another, and the unspoken rules of reciprocity in exchanges made gift-giving a concrete expression of equality between friends.

However, reciprocity in the course of a friendship was not one equal exchange after another, but a tapestry of material, emotional, and practical offerings that accreted over time to maintain equilibrium. Friendships went on for many years, leaving men and women plenty of time to balance accounts in the course of their relationships. The equality established through exchange of advice and love, letters, and gifts built strong friendships in which women were empowered to speak and act as in no other relationship. It was that empowerment that proved crucial to the way these friendships bolstered the construction of an early republican polity and politics.

7

The Power of Friendship

THE ONGOING EXCHANGES between friends are most visible in the form of letters and gifts, but friends with political connections also exchanged political access, information, and influence. In the lifetime of a friendship, the exchange of political power was one of many. To take an interest in the success and well-being of a friend and his or her family meant offering emotional support, comradery, gifts, and, in cases of the politically connected, political power and favors. A large number of elite men in this era served in local or national political office for at least a short period in their careers, meaning that many friendships included opportunities for politicking.[1]

In an era before a true two-party system, personal interactions were central to the workings of political life.[2] There was no true division between public and private, political and social. Thus, personal interactions between male and female politicians—for women, though unelected, were political actors—formed important nodes in the networks of power of the early republic. Women, even those married to men in power, accessed power through their male friends. Male leaders benefited in particular from female friends married to politicians; this was especially true in the case of men who befriended first ladies.

Friends helped one another politically in a number of ways. Perhaps most easily discerned in surviving letters are requests for patronage, which often passed through a chain of friends. Friends also took advantage of their connections to pass along political intelligence, eminently useful in an era before congressional proceedings were published fully and when so much political action happened via personal interactions. Men and women alike also capitalized on the closeness of their relationships to influence political outcomes and to offer candid opinions. Whether via patronage, political information, or influence, women in particular gained political power via their friendships with the opposite sex. Through the efforts of men and women within friendships, power and emotion became closely linked in relationships that modeled how mutuality and reciprocity could overcome difference even in the political world.

Women on the Political Stage

The political spaces of the new nation were conducive to the flow of power between male/female friends. This was particularly true in the nation's capital of Washington City (as it was then called), although state capitals shared this characteristic to a lesser degree. Both the overwhelming ratio of men to women and the nature of social life and space in Washington were favorable for such friendships. Because many politicians left their wives at home, Washington City had a predominantly male elite. Many men lived in boarding houses, and the few private homes clustered around the White House were too small for large, gender-segregated parties.[3] Much of daily, even working, life for politicians took place in homes with mixed-sex company rather than in Congress, as sessions usually lasted only four hours.[4] In Washington as in state capitals, when the legislature was in session, there was no clean divide between public and private. In many cities in the early republic, and certainly in Washington, men and women mingled together in both homes and the halls of Congress.[5]

The frequent mixing of men and women and lack of large homes in which men and women could socialize separately relaxed the rules of propriety for interactions between men and women in Washington. Margaret Bayard Smith observed:

> I think the manners here different from those in other places. At the drawing room, at our parties, few ladies ever sit. Our rooms are always so crowded, that few more could find a place in the rooms, the consequence is, the ladies and gentlemen stand and walk about the rooms, in mingled groups, which certainly produces more ease, freedom and equality than in these rooms where the ladies sit and wait for gentlemen to approach to converse.[6]

Visitor Frances Trollope also noticed a difference in manners during her travels in America, observing that "it was not very unusual at Washington for a lady to take the arm of a gentleman, who was neither her husband, her father, nor her brother."[7] Indeed, women's writings show that male friends often escorted them on outings. In 1829 Judith Page Rives recorded that she and a female friend went to a party at the White House "escorted by two of the leaders of the administration, Mr. Everett and Gen. Van Rensselaer."[8] The closeness of men and women fostered interactions that led to friendships.

Women also mixed with men in official political spaces. Attending congressional debates or arguments at the Supreme Court was a favorite activity for Washington women as well as visiting ladies. Margaret Bayard Smith wrote of a few days in January 1820 when the vice president allowed women to sit in the seats intended for foreign ministers on the Senate floor and, when those filled, any other empty seats on the floor.[9] The debate over the Missouri Compromise drew an especially large number of visitors. Louisa Catherine Adams also attended the Senate frequently during this period, reporting on one day that "The room was so thronged with Ladies, the Senators could scarcely keep their proper seats."[10]Allowing women to sit among the senators not only acknowledged the importance of female approval and an appreciation for their intellects, but also provided women a chance to converse with senators (who were sometimes their friends) during important political debates.

Women clearly enjoyed being friends with men involved in politics because it gave them the opportunity to talk about public affairs and learn from men they highly respected. Abigail Adams admitted to her sister in 1796 that she preferred socializing with "the gentlemen more than the Ladies" because she "found their conversation more to my taste."[11] Her daughter-in-law, too, enjoyed socializing with the nation's top minds. Louisa remarked: "It has ever been my desire to obtain the esteem and good will of men whose respectable characters, shining qualities, or superior merit make them objects of public praise or of publick noteriety."[12] As Philadelphia salonierre Elizabeth Powel told her younger friend (and later Supreme Court Justice) Bushrod Washington, "to cultivate the Friendship & Affection of a sensible virtuous Man is a Pursuit worthy of a truly great Mind."[13] Women like the Adamses and Powel befriended men who shared their interest in politics and engaged with them as political beings.

Male leaders often recognized their female friends as political beings who sought the best interest of the new nation. George Washington told Annis Boudinot Stockton in 1788 that women had helped America win the Revolution and that "you Ladies are in the number of the best Patriots America can boast."[14] In 1775 John Adams wrote that "I have ever been convinced that Politicks and War, have in every age, been influenced, and in many, guided and controuled" by women. The next year, Adams wrote to James's wife Mercy Otis Warren of his hopes for a new republican government. At the beginning of the letter, he declared that "the Ladies I think are the greatest Politicians," but tempered his language by stating that his letter was "a very grave and solemn Discourse to a Lady. True," he continued, "and I thank God, that his Providence has made me Acquainted with two Ladies at least, who can bear it."[15] Perhaps not all women could engage in politics, but many men certainly believed their wives and friends could.

Indeed, this was the era of the "female politician," meaning women who were invested in politics and, while they did not run for office, were recognized as political actors.[16] Women, however, often admitted their political role with some circumspection.[17] Louisa Catherine Adams prefaced an expression of her political opinion to Joseph Hopkinson in 1823 by demurring that he would "think her romantic" and that she was "unused to write to Gentlemen and particularly on any serious subjects." Yet she then went beyond expressing her opinion; she also made an argument for women's superior political acumen. "We women have no rule by which to form our opinions but daily experience," she explained, "and if this fact admitted of close observations nine times out of ten our practical knowledge would be found to be correct."[18] Even first lady Dolley Madison prefaced political news to a male friend by denying her political role, saying "If I was a politician I would collect for you a great deal of news."[19]

Women made such disclaimers in part because they were aware that some Americans were wary of women's involvement in politics. One writer opined that female politicians were "disgusting and unnatural." Another writer similarly remarked that women who showed an interest in politics would "excite contempt and disgust." The concern was that women's delicate feelings would be perverted by political passion, making them agitated and "ruin[ing] their disposition."[20] It was not that women lacked the intellect to participate in political debate, some writers argued, but that they were temperamentally unfit for it.

While she later became quite politically engaged, as a young woman Margaret Bayard Smith shared some of these concerns. She told her fiancé in 1800 that "I am in danger of becoming a politician." She explained that she had recently "felt a strong interest in all political concerns," then reported on a conversation she had had with her friend Charles Brockden Brown. He asked her what party she identified with, and she "laughed, & assured him I was too ignorant to have formed any." Brown then guided her through the positions of each party and helped draw out her own opinions, concluding that "your sentiments are just, & indicate reflection on this subject." Why then, he pushed her, did she hide her interest in politics? "I am afraid," she replied, "of becoming a partisan. . . . I have strong feelings, & when I allow them to fix on any subject, they become exclusive & partial. . . . The warmth, I should be too apt to discover, would be unbecoming my sex." It was a male friend, one who had written extensively and sympathetically on the topic of women's political involvement himself, who helped her learn to become a female politician.[21]

Yet even men who shared these concerns might at the same time discuss politics with some of their female friends. Thomas Jefferson is perhaps the clearest example of this.[22] He was worried about the negative effects of political passion, on men and women alike. In a famous letter to American salonniere Anne Willing Bingham, Jefferson criticized French women for their involvement in politics.[23] America was superior, he argued, because women there could "soothe & calm the minds of their husbands being ruffled from political debate." As a widower, he relied on his female friends and daughters to take on this task.[24] He continued on that American women "have been too wise to wrinkle their foreheads with politics." And yet, as always with Jefferson, his behavior with female friends shows he did not live by this rule. Perhaps he felt that some women were smart, virtuous, and committed enough to their home and family to wrinkle their delicate foreheads. Chances are, he did not think Bingham was one of these women; there are only a couple of letters between them, and it appears that they were acquaintances and not friends. In the same period he wrote this letter to Bingham, he kept up a regular correspondence with Abigail Adams that was full of political discussion on both sides.

As Jefferson's critique acknowledges, the female politician was not an American creation; she had a long history of operating in British and French politics, where she also depended on male friends. In Great Britain, where House of Lords seats descended through families, elite women were involved in politics out of familial duty. Wealthy widows even had some electoral privileges and controlled the votes of the freeholders on their properties.[25] In France, elite women's political role was less overt but perhaps even more powerful.[26] American politicians who spent time in Paris— and there were many, including Jefferson, Adams, Franklin, Gouverneur Morris, Aaron Burr, John Quincy Adams, and Albert Gallatin—realized that befriending women was of great help in achieving their political goals. "The purest and most useful friend a man could possibly procure, was a Frenchwoman of a certain age who had no designs on his person," Franklin reputedly opined while living in France. "They are so ready to do you service, and from their knowledge of the world know well how to serve you wisely."[27] Americans thus formed the political structures of the new nation with an awareness of women's role as political actors who could make quite useful friends—but kept in mind fears about how these friends might corrupt politics.[28]

Political Opinion, Persuasion, and Influence

Indeed, another female politician explained that private conversation between friends was precisely how women could share political opinions and influence. In 1774 Mercy Otis Warren explained:

> I disregard the opinion that women make but indifferent politicians.... When the observations are just and do honor to the heart and character, I think it very immaterial whether they flow from a female lip in the soft whispers of private friendship or whether thundered in the senate in the bolder language of the other sex.[29]

Women shared their observations in the only way society allowed at the time: in quiet conversation rather than public speeches. The ability to do so required a level of access to male leaders only available to personal friends. Friendship rather than an open public forum was a space for politics. Implicit, too, in Warren's statement is that observations were not mere chatter; they could influence broader political opinion and effect change.

Warren certainly spoke from experience. Her friend John Adams valued her political insights. Indeed, he wrote James Warren in June 1774 before leaving for the First Continental Congress in Philadelphia to request "the Favour of your Sentiments and Mrs. Warrens what is proper, praticable expedient, wise, just, good necessary to be done at Phyladelphia." Adams again praised the political judgment of Abigail and Mercy, admitting that "I suspect they understand it [politics] better than we do." The Warrens wrote back separately but on the same sheet, with James providing specific advice and Mercy suggesting "that a preparatory Conference should be held" for her to share her opinions.[30] It is unsurprising, then, that Mercy would comment on the political value of "the soft whispers of private friendship" later that same year.

Elizabeth House Trist, a longtime friend of Thomas Jefferson, explained the importance of women sharing political observations in a letter to Jefferson days before his inauguration.[31] She opened the letter with an expression of her "exultation on the Triumph of Republicanism." Trist then shared with him that "it has mortified many of your friends that you have express'd such favorable sentiments of Mr. Adams" and said that "I hope you will not Compliment him in your Inaugeration address." For this unsolicited advice, she explained that she "need not apologize" because:

> The only privilege our sex injoy is that of freely communicating our sentiments. We are generally thought of little consiquence in the Political World. but if we are incompetent to decide properly on these subjects, we certainly can revibrate the opinion of others—and I have often thought that those placed at the head of the Nation have been led to do unpopular things for want of a Friend that wou'd candidly inform them of the real sentiments of the people.[32]

This was certainly not an expansive statement of women's political power; indeed, it illuminates the limits of the political power even of women with close ties to the president. But under the limiting conditions of her society, Trist carved out what she presented as quite an important role: providing an honest gauge of popular opinion to an elected official, which as a female private citizen she was well-qualified to do. It took a true friend, with an open and mutually respectful relationship, to offer this valuable information.

Trist continued to write Jefferson throughout his presidency, albeit more often with patronage requests than opinion, including a lengthy letter in October 1807 criticizing Commander General of the US Army General Wilkinson in the aftermath of the Burr conspiracy. Trist was well-placed to offer her opinions on this subject, since she lived in Louisiana and had seen Wilkinson in action. In retrospect, it is unclear exactly what Wilkinson's role was in the conspiracy; it was on his word that Burr was prosecuted for treason, but Wilkinson had clearly had plots of his own.[33] She was concerned that Louisianans might still try to leave the union and was appalled that Jefferson was leaving Wilkinson in office, "for do I sincerely and devoutly believe him to be as Traitorous a character as we have in America." Trist was not alone in this view, but she was able to report what Wilkinson had been saying about Jefferson in New Orleans. Wilkinson spoke well of Jefferson to his supporters, Trist explained, but "was quite abusive of" Jefferson when speaking to opponents. After expounding at length on Wilkinson's faults, Trist concluded by saying that "I have perform'd my duty at least it is what gratitude and friendship have urged."[34]

Thus it was not only her prerogative to share public opinion with Jefferson, but an obligation.

Women did not share their opinions idly; these were indirect efforts at persuasion and influence. The meanings and uses of women's influence were contested during this era, however. Many writers at the time viewed women's influence as a positive force, but construed that influence quite narrowly. Women's influence, one writer argued, should "reform" men and "awaken" their morals, religion, and virtue. This influence was necessary to "the very existence" of states and societies. Yet this was the same writer who also called female politicians "disgusting and unnatural."[35] Thus, to him, as to many proponents of female influence, that influence was to be essentially domestic and moral, not political.[36]

There were writers, albeit in the minority, who argued for women's use of persuasion and influence to guide political life. Hannah Mather Crocker, a New England writer, took a moderate approach in her 1818 text, *Observations on the Real Rights of Women*. While women should use "reason and persuasion" to "sooth the turbulent passions of men," she ventured that "perhaps even on the subject of law, politics, or religion, they [women] may form good judgement."[37] It was only when borrowing the words of French writer Pierre-Joseph Boudier de Villemert that Crocker argued more forcefully for women's political role. Villemert's book was published in America in 1803 as *The Friend of Women*, and he argued that women's "government is that of persuasion." Women should advise men because "they are endowed with a vivacity that makes them catch objects which escape us." Further, he explained, women could understand the workings of men's minds and feelings, and thus play on these to achieve women's own ends. "It is by this art that they make us do whatever they wish," he explained, "and that the strongest is in fact governed by the weakest."[38]

Much of the criticism of female influence suggested that, even if the results were positive, women manipulated men. But manipulation and persuasion are not the same: manipulation is the use of another person to further personal goals, while persuasion is a process that promotes the mutual goals of the persuader and persuadee.[39] The conflation of these two forms of power lent negative connotations to persuasion and influence in general, and women's use of political influence in particular, although this was certainly not a tool only of women. It was simply the only tool available to women, and it allowed them to maintain claims of gender difference while simultaneously claiming real power. Thus the poem "Woman's Empire" by Horace

Twiss, a British poet and admirer of Wollstonecraft, copied into an American woman's friendship album:

> *Dear Girl, in my simple opinion,*
> *Your sex are to blame when they pant*
> *To possess, as a right, the dominion.*
> *Which is not denied as a grant.—*
> *Prerogative seems not the basis,*
> *Best suited to Woman's command;*
> *Whilst influence keeps them their places,*
> *And gives them the rule of the land.*
> *The proudest is far from a Goddess,*
> *The brightest less bright than a star,*
> *And as you are not heavenly bodies,*
> *I think you are best as you are.*
> *In your sweet simple nature of woman,*
> *You gain the ascendance you seek,*
> *You are worshipped, because you are human,*
> *And potent, because you are weak.*[40]

Here difference, even weakness, is what enables and underwrites female power. Even Abigail Adams adapted a line from Alexander Pope and told her husband that women "charm by accepting, by submitting sway."[41] When women expressed their power in this way, it may have been more as a ruse to cloak their power than an actual recognition of weakness.

Indeed, Abigail Adams was quite forward in her use of political influence. In 1781 she wrote her friend Elbridge Gerry to request that he take action against the appointment of Benjamin Franklin to a peace commission to which John Adams had already been assigned. She praised Gerry, then a member of the Continental Congress, for his devotion to his country and noted that "I will not deny Sir, that personally I feel myself much Interested in your attendance" in Congress. A letter from Franklin critical of "our friend," as Abigail described John, had been presented to Congress and she thought it was unjust to "clog" Adams "with a Man, who has shewn himself so Enimical to him, who has discovered the marks of a little and narrow Spirit by his malicious aspersions, and ungenerous insinuations." She foresaw "nothing but dishonour, and disgrace attending his most faithfull, and zealous exertions for the welfare of his Country" were Franklin to join Adams.

Abigail was aware of the boldness of her request. "Will you suffer Female influence so far to operate upon you," she asked, "as to step forth and lend your aid to rescue your Country and your Friend?" In a republic in which leaders were to serve country first, she was wise to appeal to the national rather than merely the personal good. Their friendship had made her feel secure in writing such a letter, and to emphasize that close relationship, she signed the letter with her pen name, Portia. Gerry did not seem disturbed by the request. He wrote a detailed letter in response explaining that instructions for a joint commission had already been ordered, but he had some hope of revoking these and making Adams the sole negotiator.[42] That never happened, but his responsiveness alone was a small victory.

Elizabeth Powel was similarly forthright when she issued George Washington a strongly worded appeal after he confided that he did not intend to run for reelection. She emphasized to him "the Impracticality of carrying your Intentions into Effect" and argued that his resignation would "elate the Enemies of good Government and cause lasting Regret to the Friends of humanity." As for the notion that there were others "equall to the Task," she argued that, "If there is not a Confidence in those Abilities and that Integrity they cannot be beneficially applied." Thus she "venture[d] to assert that, at this Time, you are the only Man in America that dares to do right on all public Occasions."[43] It is unclear how much weight her opinion carried with Washington; Washington shared his intention to resign with Jefferson a month later, but after another two months told Jefferson that he decided to stay on as a result of "strong solicitations" in Philadelphia. Curiously, Washington went on to tell Jefferson that he had "never ment[ione]d his purpose of going out but to the heads of dep[artme]nts & Mr. Madison."[44] Was it a chorus of voices that had convinced Washington, or did he not want to admit to a man he knew distrusted female influence that Mrs. Powel had been persuasive?

Patronage

Perhaps the best known, as well as most disparaged, political role for women was as patrons. Men and women were called on by strangers and friends alike for help obtaining offices, but patronage operated most often through friendships rather than casual ties. The competition for government offices was fierce in an era when such careers were both prestigious and profitable, and the prospects in business uncertain. The best way to get an application for a post taken seriously was through the patronage of a friend or family member, quite often a woman.[45] At the same time, Americans were uncomfortable with a system of assigning government posts that was more associated with the cronyism of aristocracy than with a meritocracy. Americans were well aware of the way offices were traded as the property of the elite, often at the behest of women, in Europe.[46] Yet even there, patronage was never purely instrumental; it was a system that helped build mutual dependence within extended networks of friends and families.[47]

The ambivalence about patronage is illustrated in James Lovell's simultaneous critique of and request for patronage of his friends John and Abigail Adams. Lovell wrote Abigail in 1789, concerned that John Adams might replace Lovell as the naval officer for the port of New York with somebody who requested that office as a favor. He wrote a more formal letter to John Adams, and on the same date, wrote Abigail in a playful style, admitting that, "I could say twenty Things to you which I would not dare to trouble your Husband with." At times, petitioners felt more comfortable addressing women, particularly since for politicians to offer preferred treatment in direct response to friends and family was associated with aristocratic corruption.[48] Writing a female friend was a way of defusing that concern, because the requester was addressing someone who was not in public office. Particularly when the person making the request was friends with a politician as well as his wife, he might write separate letters to both of them, making the more emotional appeal to his female friend. Lovell went on in his letter to Abigail to criticize the "Insurgents" and "Tools" who would write the Adamses with patronage requests. Yet he asked to retain his position in part based on personal connections. Abigail replied that she had written her husband in support of Lovell and explained that she assumed that decisions on replacing government officers would be made on the basis of merit.[49]

Even frequent requesters of patronage expressed their discomfort (although surely this was sometimes a more formulaic than heartfelt reticence) in making such requests. Elizabeth House Trist pressed the causes of numerous male friends and family members with Thomas Jefferson, whom she had befriended when he stayed at her mother's Philadelphia boarding house from 1782 to 1784. In one such letter she explained why she felt patronage requests were justified. "A man diffident of him self has little chance of being notice'd," Trist argued, "unless his talants are transcendently conspicuous or his friends of importance in the Political World." Despite her recognition that political appointments worked through patronage, Trist still felt "repugnance to solicitation in behalf of my friends."[50] Similarly, Catharine Greene asked her friend Alexander Hamilton's pardon for requesting an appointment for her brother, saying she felt "like a culprit" for making the request. "Why blush and condemn myself," she continued, "and at the same time I am Justified by my reason, and prompted by my affection to commit it." Such diffidence, often accompanied by flattering declarations of affection, on the part of supplicants like Lovell, Trist, and Greene was part of the script for making patronage requests.[51]

Friends recognized that because of the American distaste for patronage, it was necessary to invoke ties of friendship, affection, and the importance of family when asking for help obtaining offices. Dolley Madison's friend Anthony Morris took this approach when asking for an appointment for himself. He reminded Dolley that his obtaining an appointment "involves in its consequences ... so much the fate of our darling Phoebe," invoking the good of his daughter (who referred to Dolley in correspondence as "Mother") to play on Dolley's affections.[52] He wrote James on the same date, but it was Dolley who was his longtime friend and to whom he offered an emotional appeal. Dolley apologized that James was unable to get Morris's appointment approved in Congress, but soon after, James made Morris a secret envoy to Spain. Phoebe wrote Dolley in 1814 to report that her father's time in Spain had greatly improved his health, "for which I shall never cease to be thankful to you & my dear President."[53] Indeed, when friends made and fulfilled patronage requests, the favor became more than political; it was entangled with emotions and the dynamic of exchange of favors and feelings already at work in a friendship.

Thus, a refusal of patronage services could be a personal affront and had to be couched in terms of republican principles rather than a breach of friendship. When Alexander Hamilton refused his sister-in-law and close friend Angelica Schuyler Church's request for an office for her father, he opened his letter by stating, "There is no proof of my affection which I would not willingly give you." Yet it was not "practicable" to help her father, because "Our republican ideas stand much in the way of accumulating offices in one family."[54] John Adams responded to Mercy Otis Warren's request for offices for her husband and son with even more vehemence. "I should belie the whole course of my public and private conduct and all the maxims of my life," Adams wrote, if he helped friends and family get offices. "The Constitution has wisely made the President the Judge in the first instance of the pretensions of all." Nor could he grant offices even if he wanted to, he declared: "I have no patronage."[55]

Qualms about the virtue of patronage aside, patronage requests by friends to fill vacant offices were often successful in this period. John Adams was not being truthful with Warren; he gave others patronage appointments, but apparently he felt uncomfortable giving the Warren men appointments when they had a history of controversial views.[56] Jefferson also gave political offices to friends and political allies, shoring up Republican support across the government.[57] Indeed, John Randolph complained in 1806 that "There is a proneness to seek office & favor amongst us which is truely mortifying & distressing to the true republicans, the number of whom it is to be feared, diminishes every day."[58] Patronage was not just a prerogative of the president, however. Heads of departments, particularly the Post Office, Treasury, and War Departments, had considerable power to choose men for offices across the country and often granted patronage requests. Patronage also figured prominently in the workings of some state governments, particularly in New York. To be clear, though, patronage at this time was largely exercised only to get family and friends into office. It was not until after Andrew Jackson's election in 1828 that patronage was transformed through the spoils system and into a form of exchange for votes from legislators.[59]

The limited form of patronage in this era persisted because of the ways it cemented personal and political ties. Establishing a friend's family member or chosen friend in a post, whether in the new Louisiana Territory or a French port, built loyalty across vast geographic distances.[60] Since a government office supplied a salary that supported a family, patronage appointments created political ties and obligations beyond just the man granted the office. Those ties and obligations were more political, such as voting for the person or party from whom the office was received, and less emotional the farther removed the appointee was from the appointer. But for the intermediate friends working on the man's behalf, the act generated friendly feelings that strengthened social neworks.

Patronage requests thus worked their way through networks of friends that provided a structure for governing in the nation's capital during the early decades of the nineteenth century.[61] When Eleanor Custis Lewis was trying to get a military appointment for her friend's nephew Mr. Bordley in 1824, she "employ'd two or three friends to plead" Bordley's case. These friends, she explained, would go to General Andrew Jackson for the young man, creating a chain of intercessors between Bordley and the official who could then "use his influence." The favor and obligation were thus transferred along a line of people, distancing the emotional and personal claims for Mr. Bordley from the trading of offices. That the request originated in sympathetic feeling was the important element: as Lewis conceded, she might not be able to accomplish anything but "at least my friends will give me credit for a sincere desire to serve them."[62]

Elizabeth House Trist's desire to serve a friend, Alexandria merchant David Easton, resulted in a series of letters that exemplify the way the patronage process operated. Easton had lost a ship and its cargo from the Carribbean when it was taken by a French privateer in 1793. Trist made her first request on Easton's behalf several months after Jefferson took office, opening her letter by admitting that she knew he must be receiving "numerous recommendations" every day. Trist concisely presented Easton's situation, family history, the consular office he sought, a mutual friend who could recommend him, and a short disclaimer about her affectionate motives for making the request. When she did not receive a response, she raised the request again two months later, reminding Jefferson that she was "greatly interested" in Easton's appointment. She assured him she would never ask for his preference for an unworthy man, and thus "I am therefore confidant that you will not forget him."[63]

Trist persisted, writing the next spring with a reminder of Easton's request. Multiple friends had written on his behalf but as there had been no progress, Trist reported, "he seems almost in dispair." His last letter to her "excited my Sympathy in so great a degree as to make me miserable," she explained, and gave him "a claim at least to my commiseration." Trist here traded the currency of her sympathy for Easton to evoke a feeling of obligation in Jefferson, serving as a conduit of feeling and power. Jefferson finally replied to the request, explaining that Easton's bankruptcy was a mark against him for a consular appointment. However, Jefferson thought he had a vacancy he could give him, and two months later he nominated Easton as consul to Martinique.[64]

Trist's long friendship with Jefferson was likely the key factor in Jefferson's responsiveness to her requests, but she also showed considerable political astuteness. She leveraged one friendship with a powerful man for the good of another male friend. A woman like Trist never had the opportunity to obtain political office herself, but the friend she served was not the only beneficiary of the exchange. Patronage was one of many elements offered in a reciprocal exchange of feeling and services over the duration of a friendship, and Trist could presumably call on Easton for a favor at some point in the future, particularly since he would now have some political power. At the very least her support strengthened her ties with him. Women's patronage requests gave them a stake in politics and established them as useful ties in the larger political and social network.

Political Access and Information

The system of patronage functioned because of a network of personal relationships that provided various points of access and information. Political information traveled along the same networks. Men and women alike took advantage of having friends with intimate access to facilitate the formation of political consensus, shape opinion on recent events, and keep leaders fully informed on issues of debate. Women who lived in the capital city fit seamlessly into the flow of information since they socialized and befriended political leaders. This was a natural and important role for female politicians that was far less likely to provoke criticism than patronage or direct influence peddling.

For example, the women that Senator William Maclay encountered when the capital was in New York were quite eager to collect and share news on the first federal Congress' proceedings. He reported that on a walk with his friend Mrs. Bell, "the subject of the removal of Congress from this place was her constant theme." She reported to him on Robert Morris's opinions on the debate, presumably gleaned from private discussion with him: "Mr. Morris was not sincerely attached to the Pennsylvania interest on that subject; that his commercial arrangements were calculated for this place [New York]; that the [New] Yorkers depended on him, but were lately staggered by an oath which it was said he had sworn that he would have Congress away."[65] Mrs. Bell's information enabled Maclay insider access to the opinions of a powerful member of Congress. This was not idle gossip, but a political service offered to a friend.

Morris's wife, Mary White Morris, also served as a conduit of information for Maclay because of her close friendship with George and Martha Washington. George Washington visited her home frequently while the capital was in New York and Robert Morris served as a senator from Pennsylvania. During one of his visits, Washington had shared his opinion on salaries for government offices. As it turned out, Maclay had been trying to figure out what Washington's views were on this topic. He had thought that Washington's address to Congress had seemed "quite republican," but he wanted to know "General Washington's private opinions on the pompous part of government." When he dined at the Morris home on June 11, 1789, he got the information he sought. After dinner, Mrs. Morris "talked a great deal" and revealed that Washington supported "generous salaries" in order to attract "proper persons" to government service.[66] It was not information that pleased Maclay, but it could at least help him strategize for furthering his own positions. His friendship with Mrs. Morris, like that with Mrs. Bell, thus furthered his political goals.

In some cases, men depended on their wives to share political intelligence with mutual friends. When George Logan undertook an unofficial mission to France in 1798 to try to avoid war, he entrusted his wife Deborah Norris Logan with keeping their friends up to date on his progress. After a meeting with Lafayette in July, he reported that Lafayette was "very anxious that harmony may be preserved between America & France." Logan asked his wife "to inform our friends Dickinson Jefferson and other real Patriots of this circumstance, & that they should use every means in their power to promote the same friendly disposition on the part of the United States." Two days later, he sent her "a long political letter," which he asked her to copy and send to Dickinson and Jefferson. He left it to her discretion whether to send it to General Clinton as well.[67]

Logan in effect made Deborah a partner in his mission, his liaison on the ground back in America.[68] There was less risk that correspondence with his wife would be intercepted and opened than letters addressed to politicians, so he took advantage of Deborah's gender to cover what were largely political rather than domestic matters. He also apparently believed that Dickinson and Jefferson, as mutual friends of his and Deborah's, would be agreeable to having her act as their informant. Deborah's friendships with Dickinson and Jefferson facilitated her husband's mission as well as offering these politicians vitally important information on the status of his controversial negotiations. Affectionate ties smoothed the way for her to become a conduit of news from across the Atlantic.

Sometimes people preferred to send information indirectly via a friend rather than conveying it directly. Male friends took particular advantage of first ladies' access to the ear of the president, writing them in lieu of the president when they had delicate messages to impart. These men were relying on the influence of their friends as both wives and savvy political players. Joel Barlow, for instance, often wrote Dolley in lieu of James Madison on sensitive political topics. In 1811 he wrote to Dolley from his diplomatic mission in France explaining his difficulties there:

I have been here three months at work very hard for our blessed country yet I am afraid I shall have produced but little effect, & the president may think I have been idle. If he should approve my conduct I wish you would let me know it. For you cannot reallize how much I am attached to him & his administration. It is therefore natural that I should be anxious to merit his approbation.[69]

Dolley would pass along this message to James, then reply to Barlow with James's reassurances. Like Deborah Norris Logan, Dolley could serve as a domestic ally for Barlow's mission.

Joseph Hopkinson was even more explicit about using Louisa Catherine Adams as an intermediary to deliver a message to her husband. He wrote her a lengthy letter in January 1823 criticizing John Quincy Adams's lack of energy and action in his campaign for the presidency, couching his letter in friendly terms by asking her to imagine "that you and I are sitting, with or with out a bright moon, as you please, on the piazza looking into the garden, in familiar chat." At the end of the letter, he added a very important post-script: "P. S. You will understand I would not dare to say or write half of the above to Mr. A., but you may do what you please with it." Louisa did show it to her husband, who wrote a lengthy essay in response explaining his philosophy against campaigning.[70] Hopkinson might not have changed Adams's behavior, but with the help of Louisa, he found a comfortable and polite way to offer Adams his political advice.

Louisa's mother-in-law Abigail Adams, who clearly had access to the latest information on political developments, wrote letters full of news and opinion to her male friends.[71] When John Adams nominated a set of envoys to negotiate with France in 1797, Abigail wrote her friend Elbridge Gerry with an update on the Senate's nomination debates. Adams had tried to nominate Gerry, but his cabinet had requested Francis Dana instead as a person of greater Federalist credentials. She described the "attack" by the "Jacobins" on Adams's nominees, reporting on the vote tallies and the names of those who spoke out particularly strongly against the nominees—although she noted, "I tell you Names. you will however keep your informant out of Sight." When Dana declined to serve and Adams finally secured Gerry's appointment over some congressional opposition, Gerry wrote to Abigail to tell her that he was not hurt by the opposition and to assure her of his loyalty to the administration. He explained his vote against the Constitution and asked "is there not, madam, an intimate difference between voting on a <u>bill</u> for a constitution, & negotiating in behalf & under the instructions of a supreme executive?"[72] In other words, past differences would not affect Gerry's ability to follow the president's instructions. Gerry surely knew that Abigail would pass along his sentiments to the president. There seemed to be a level of comfort for many men in sharing sensitive information with a female friend rather than a male one, and allowing her to take advantage of her role as wife and confidante to convey the information.

Other female friends, too, were valuable sources of information for men who were abroad. Aaron Burr, in exile in London in 1809 after his failed conspiracy plot, wrote home to a female friend asking that she keep him informed of "something of the state of parties and politics as affecting me." He told her that he was being pushed out of England and decided it was not wise to return to America yet. He had gotten permission to go to Sweden, probably with the help of the Swedish consul in New York, Henry Gahn. Burr then requested that she thank Gahn for him.[73] For Burr, the intelligence his friends shared from home was not merely a matter of political manuevering, but of vital importance to when he might be able to return to his home and family.

Most men abroad sought information that had much lower stakes but would nonetheless influence their work. David Bailie Warden relied on his friend Eliza Custis for news during his years in Paris, where he struggled to hold on to government appointments between 1808 and 1814. News of the political climate and machinations in Washington, then, was necessary to him during this time. Eliza tried to figure out who had prejudiced the government against him after he was removed from his position as consul, reporting in an 1814 letter that "I never heard a word to your disadvantage from any of the Govt people." She then discussed the general political climate, reporting that "the govt is now unpopular" and that she would be pleased to see Madison leave office. She also reported that Congress was working on the budget, then supplied detailed news on the success of the manufacturing industry during the War of 1812.[74] Since many Americans serving in lesser diplomatic posts earned money through engaging in commerce, this, too, would be relevant information for him. Their letters combined affection and information, providing Warden with emotional sustenance and political intelligence while far from home.

Women also valued access to political news obtained through their male friends in political office. This was a central aspect of the friendship between Abigail Adams and James Lovell while John Adams was abroad during the American Revolution. Lovell, in his position in the Continental Congress, could supply inside information to Abigail on politics and the Congress' plans for her husband.[75] While in America John had "always indulged" her in sending along political news, but during his time in Europe, she needed Lovell to keep her up to date on "any important and interesting matters which may take place." "Am I entitled to the journals of Congress[?]," she asked Lovell; "if you think so I should be much obliged to you if you would convey them to me."[76] It appears that it was a special favor for women to receive such information, making friends who did supply it—like Lovell—particularly valuable.

Around the same time, Catherine Livingston learned the latest developments from the battlefield from her friend Alexander Hamilton. Hamilton, who had been friends with the Livingston family of New Jersey for many years, wrote Kitty a playfully flirtatious letter from the encampment of the Continental Army in Morristown in April 1777. He had heard from Kitty's sister Susanna that Kitty had "a relish for politics" and thus Susanna "wishes me to engage on the footing of a political correspondent." He would write her about politics, he said, but he would "make excursions in the flowery walks, and roseate bowers of Cupid." Whether this was a serious romantic gesture or not, Kitty appears to have rebuffed it while continuing to press Hamilton for updates on the war. Since she and her family had moved several times to avoid fighting, such updates were a matter of great importance to her and he was a useful friend to have. She was surely pleased to hear from him the next month that some believed the British would soon leave New Jersey.[77]

Nearly fifty years later, Margaret Bayard Smith relied on a male friend for political updates while she was in New Jersey visiting her sister. During her absence from Washington, her friend Samuel Southard wrote to share the latest news. As a senator from New Jersey, he was well placed to share information with her, unlike her husband, who had long since left his post as editor of Washington's first newspaper. Southard began the section of his letter with political news by saying that he assumed she was informed of what was happening in Congress from the newspapers, then proceeded to give her insider information on the upcoming presidential election. "The price of Presidential stock has varied in the market considerably since you left," he explained. "Crawford has fallen some. Clay & Adams risen some—Calhoun stationary." Southard knew that this was particularly valuable news for Smith, who was a close friend and supporter of William H. Crawford.[78]

Soon after, Smith gained a unique perspective on the presidential election because she spent every evening with Crawford the week of the election, making it "one of the most interesting weeks in my life." Smith's friendship with the candidate allowed her access to "some of the most distinguished actors in this interesting drama." Unlike others who had to rely on speculation and rumor, she "knew the causes of their circumstances and the motives of their actions." Smith's enjoyment of this insider information was not merely a political matter; she explained that her interest in public affairs was melded with "friendship and affection."[79] It seems hard to imagine that Smith merely sat on the sidelines of this drama; in the company of those making important campaign decisions, it is likely she would have shared her opinions.

Risks

Women's involvement in politics, even within the "soft whispers of private friendship," did carry some risks. There was a conflation of manipulation and persuasion that gave a negative edge to women's influence. Women's political activity was also coded as sexual promiscuousness in an era when a woman out in public—whether for political or other purposes—could be called a "public woman," meaning a prostitute. After the French Revolution, men on both sides of the Atlantic began to tie female influence and public visibility to unhealthy sexual desires and practices.[80] Regularly socializing with male friends could feed gossip of improprieties about politically prominent women. This was certainly the case with Dolley Madison. In 1804 rumors about Dolley and her sister's promiscuity almost led to a duel. During the 1808 election, newspapers published stories alluding to her involvement in adulterous affairs, and John Randolph hinted at her improprieties in a letter to Madison's opponent for the Republican nomination, James Monroe.[81] In 1814 Madison's postmaster general Gideon Granger revived those rumors by threatening to reveal (as a form of blackmail to save his own position) the sources for these old rumors.[82] While no evidence was ever brought forward on these charges, the rumors swirling about Dolley were clearly attempts to use charges of sexual deviance to push back both her and her husband's political power.

Deborah Norris Logan faced similar charges when serving as her husband's intermediary during Logan's unofficial mission to France. In response to Logan's actions, the House of Representatives passed a law banning private citizens from undertaking diplomatic negotiations on behalf of the country. During the debates on the bill, congressmen quoted from Connecticut poet Richard Alsop's satirical poem *The Political Green-House*, particularly the verse that accused Jefferson of a dalliance with Deborah during her husband's absence:

> *Send Deborah's husband off to France,*
> *To tell the Frenchmen, to this cost,*
> *They reckon'd here without their host;*
> *Whilst thou, to smooth the ills of life,*
> *Held sweet communion with the wife.*[83]

Jefferson had in fact visited Deborah alone during her husband's absence, according to her, in order to "inquire after my wellfare." Her cousins were visiting when Jefferson arrived but quickly departed, leaving the two to converse privately on the status of the mission.[84] The combination of a private tete-a-tete between the two and Deborah's publicly known role in furthering her husband's political work made allusions of sexual impropriety a natural joke for the Federalist press.

Philadelphia writer John Murdock made a similar connection in his fictional account of two women arguing about the Jay Treaty. In the opening scene of his 1798 play *The Politicians; or, A State of Things*, Mrs. Violent and Mrs. Turbulent take opposing positions. Mrs. Turbulent says she had advance intelligence from several men, including two senators, that the treaty would come out this way and anger the French. These were, perhaps, male friends who were sharing information with her, just as many friends did in reality. She also obtained information on the treaty from Mr. Lisp, whom she describes with clear sexual overtones: "Mr. Lisp is a man of penetration—Mr. Lisp is a man of parts—of most extraordinary parts."[85] The two women argue viciously, suggesting that an excess of political passion could also signify excessive sexual passion.

Perhaps the most infamous scandal to link women's influence and sexuality was the Eaton affair, also known as the "petticoat affair." Mrs. Eaton, née Margaret O'Neale, was the daughter of an innkeeper in Washington and had grown up surrounded by political figures who frequented the establishment. She married a navy purser named John Timberlake in 1816, and four months after his death, an interval too soon for public approbation, married the couple's longtime friend John Eaton. Public gossip and newspaper accounts accused the two of having an affair while Timberlake was at sea, explaining why they married so soon after Timberlake's death. When Andrew Jackson, who was close friends with the Eatons, named John to a cabinet position in 1829, Washington society erupted in censure of Eaton's wife. The incident eventually broke up Jackson's cabinet.[86]

While the scandal arose out of a variety of factors—animosity toward Jackson, discomfort with a working-class woman entering Washington society, concerns about women who did not conform to genteel, modest expectations—one that is often neglected is mixed-sex friendship. Margaret Eaton defended herself against the accusation by saying that she had been friends with John Eaton for ten years and that nothing romantic had taken place between them until after her husband's death. In her autobiography, she deliberately placed their friendship in a broader social context to demonstrate its propriety, explaining, "I had known him as a gentleman, as my father's friend, as my mother's friend, as my husband's friend." Indeed, one strand of the gossip about an inappropriate relationship between the two accused her of riding alone in a carriage with Eaton, going back to the notion that an unmarried man and woman should not be alone together. Jackson himself defended her against this charge, reporting that "Mr. Eaton never traveled in company with Mrs. Timberlake but once, & then her husband went along."[87] Jackson's friendship did not necessarily help Mrs. Eaton's case, since Jackson himself had faced charges of sexual impropriety.

The accusations against Margaret Eaton surely stemmed in part from the intersection of her friendships with politics. One newspaper, rising to her defense in March 1829, claimed that she had "probably made enemies from the free manner in which she has ever advocated the election of General Jackson at all times and on all occasions."[88] Other women campaigned for male friends, but perhaps it was Eaton's forward, "free manner" that attracted censure. Two years later, after Jackson had stood by his friend to the detriment of his cabinet, a New Hampshire paper declared that "like some of the corrupt monarchies of other days, our political system must be convulsed by female influence." The paper decried Jackson's "palming upon the community a woman of reputed profligacy of character."[89] While the papers attacked Mrs. Eaton, it was the wives of the cabinet secretaries who had refused to visit her and thus touched off the real political implications. While their snubbing surely had a class dimension, these women were also protecting their ability to retain their politically useful friendships with men without losing their virtue.

Although the linkage of sexuality and political power never gained the same currency in America as it did in France and Britain during the years after the French Revolution, it was a connection that could only add to the other concerns of a mixed-sex friendship. The operation of politics via networks of friends of both sexes fed worries about both moral and political improprieties. The danger here went beyond implications for pairs of friends: there was a larger political danger of women's passions being fed by male friends enabling women's power. Given the dominant type of influence being promoted for use by women—promoting virtue and morality in men in their households, which would ensure the virtue of the polity—it is clear how sexually corrupt women could pose a danger. Whether the limiting, domestic view of influence fed the fears of women lacking in virtue or whether the existence of such women led to the creation of a limited and domesticated place for women's influence is unclear. Either way, the result meant a heightened caution was required for women engaging in both politics and friendships with men. In this light, the disclaimers women often offered when discussing politics seem unsurprising. As in the broader concerns about the risks of mixed-sex friend-ships, however, many women were not scared off from exercising whatever power they could carve out.

Friendships between men and women became important nodes in net-works of power transfers in the early republic. Both genders could benefit from the political dimensions of friendship, as the more access points to power, the more opportunities to exercise power and influence. These friend-ships were a particular boon to women, however, whose role as female poli-ticians was limited to operating through personal interactions rather than on the public stage. Precluded from voting, serving in office, or testifying in Congress, women could not dominate or coerce people into action through the threat of sanction (e.g., voting for another candidate or against a particu-lar bill). Their use of persuasion and influence drew on other ways of making things happen.[90]

Examining power as it operates through relationships thus points to the existence of a different sort of power. This is not a coercive type of "power over," but rather a "power with" that operates through collaboration. One can study power from the side—as in friendships—rather than from above or below. This power works through persuasion and influence, collaboration and reciprocity, rather than dominance.[91] These proved particularly effective methods for exercising power in the early republic. In a political climate in which achieving consensus was nearly impossible due to complicated loyal-ties and a lack of institutionalized parties, persuasion could help to settle conflicts. This was also a form of power that could play into early republican notions of women's greater capacity for sympathy and emotion, as persuasion requires a mix of emotional and intellectual appeals.[92]

Political influence and access must be understood, however, as a prerog-ative of both friendship and class. Only elites could enter into the types of friendships and networks of political leaders that allowed them to exercise in-fluence and have access to the increasingly restrictive social world of the polit-ical upper classes. Power through collaboration, then, was premised on class distinctions that determined who the collaborators could be. Like domina-tion, persuasion and influence are forms of power exercised by small groups of the few rather than the many. While collaborative power created openings for women, it closed possibilities for those in the lower classes, as it cloaked operations of power from public view.

This behind-the-scenes form of politicking, the "soft whispers of pri-vate friendship" as a means of doing political business, points to the com-plicated ways in which friendships between elite men and women were part of ongoing exchanges of emotions, services, and powers. The mutuality and reciprocity that characterized these exchanges allowed men and women to build relationships on the basis of equality, at least of give and take if not of legal status. In trading political power, these pairs also built new models for the way power could work within relationships. The equilibrium between men and women in such friendships offered a form of gender relations closer to equality than any other relationship between men and women in American society. It was a model of what relations between men and women could be in the new republic.

Afterword

THOMAS JEFFERSON WAS correct when he told his friend Angelica Schuyler Church that any image of their friendship would depict "something out of the common line."[1] Indeed, friendships between men and women existed outside many common lines—of friendship, gender, power, and the narratives of history. Against much literature and popular wisdom denying the possibility of these relationships, men and women carved out a space for relationships that were meaningful and fulfilling. It is not that they were trying to rebel or create a new order; rather, they were making do within the restrictions of their society. Their actions did not leave broad historical imprints, but delicate images that require careful excavation to find.

It is perhaps easiest to see how these relationships shifted the meanings and workings of the category of friendship itself. The dominant notion of the ideal friendship was one between two men, or at least two people of the same sex. But ideal relationships existed more in language than in reality. The prominence of that ideal constrained the ability of men and women to describe their own friendships and forced them to strategize about positioning those relationships safely. Friendships between men and women were one viable relationship among many available in the Early Republic. There were surely many more of these friendships than those that survive in the archival record, particularly between friends who lived in the same place and had no need to write letters to one another.

Friendships between men and women escaped the bounds of gender roles inherent in family, marital, or same-sex relationships. The ability to meet on relatively equal ground in a relationship with the opposite sex was a unique and attractive characteristic of these friendships. That this possibility existed demonstrates flexibility in the gender order. Indeed, this study supplements the work of other gender historians who have challenged the categories that have traditionally defined this period, including the firm line between public and private spheres.[2] The work on companionate marriage and its inevitable failings in an era of legalized gender inequality also makes clear that marriage was not the pinnacle of fulfillment. It should not be surprising that men and women looked to each other as friends as well as romantic partners.

Those friendships, as *Founding Friendships* has shown, had particular salience for the political life of the new nation. The image of an exclusively male founding fraternity obscures the many friendships with women that this generation of men had. While women gained no legal power through these relationships, by befriending male citizens they entered the civic body more directly and equally than they ever could have done through marriage. An understanding of the broader forms of heterosocial networks and relationships in which men and women were involved can enrich studies of political history in this period and help explain the process of historical change.

The political salience of these friendships did not survive the transition to a more democratic political system, however. Elite women's influence through and upon their husbands and male friends may have been so effective that it had the unintended consequence of driving women out of the political process. When women demonstrated that they had the intellect and power to become political actors, they challenged the centuries-old assumption that women were unfit for political participation. It became impossible to for men to continue to argue that women could not participate in politics. By the 1820s, men seeking a rationale for women's exclusion increasingly took up newly popularized arguments about women's biological difference and inferiority. The same argument would be applied toward the exclusion of free blacks, not coincidentally at a time when the vote was expanded to all white men in the late 1820s. Indeed, universal male suffrage depended on naturalizing the exclusion of women and blacks.[3]

Another political shift in the 1820s also pushed friendships between men and women to the sidelines of the political process. Before the institutionalization of the two-party system, individual relationships were central to the political process. Without an institutional party structure, reaching consensus on issues happened through many individual discussions rather than through a party leader's influence and priorities. Many of these discussions included women and offered them a de facto place in the political process. However, by the late 1820s, a system of political parties had emerged, making the decision-making process less open to outside influence and more structured by party unity. Thus, women increasingly found themselves excluded from this process.[4] Friendships between men and women within the political elite no longer carried the weight of tying together a polity, nor did these friendships offer women the same latitude to exert influence.

Ideas about emotion also underwent change at the same period as this transition. The ideal of sensibility weakened gradually in the early decades of the nineteenth century, and reason and emotion were decoupled. New ideas about science, the body, and gender altered the emotional landscape. Reason became male, emotion female;[5] sensibility had shifted to sentimentalism.[6] The very language for expressing emotion shifted, as did the notion that men and women both could feel in similar modes. Friendships were idealized between those who were best able to feel deeply—women.[7] Neither men's emotional expression nor women's intellectual abilities retained the same value.

These developments provided new obstacles to both the meaning and practice of heterosocial friendships, further distancing the social places and roles of men and women. They also fundamentally displaced friendship as the glue of the republic and transformed the ways men and women could conduct and express their friendships. The period in which there appeared to be possibilities for reconfiguring social relations, even moderately, had passed. Friendships lost their public salience, although they retained great personal importance.

There have been no comprehensive studies of friendship between men and women for the remainder of the nineteenth century, but examples of friendships abound, especially in the case of women artists, writers, and reformers less bound to the home. Ralph Waldo Emerson and Margaret Fuller were part of a circle of friends who exchanged emotionally charged letters and fueled the transcendentalist movement. Emily Dickinson and Thomas Wentworth Higginson formed a friendship based around her poetry. Abraham Lincoln befriended society woman Eliza Caldwell Browning as a young man and remained close friends with her the rest of his life.[8] And of course, some of the friendships examined in this book extended past 1830. Charles Loring and Mary Pierce were friends into the 1850s, while William Ellery Channing continued his friendship with Elizabeth Peabody until his death in 1842 as well as befriending another generation of female intellectuals including Margaret Fuller and Catharine Maria Sedgwick. As in earlier years, men and women found a way to make their friendships work, and have continued to do so until the present day.

From the birth of the new nation, then, friendships between men and women have been a constant presence in American life. Certainly, the meaning of these friendships has changed over time, as has their prevalence. In the absence of longitudinal studies on the topic, it seems a fair hypothesis that these friendships rise in prominence at times and within communities in which men and women's intellectual and emotional capabilities are seen as relatively equal. Today, that egalitarian gender ethos in America transcends class boundaries to a much greater degree than it did two hundred years ago, making male/female friendships possible across the social spectrum. Still, as one critic laments, "I cannot think of another area of our lives in which there is so great a gap between what we do and what our culture says we do."[9]

Indeed, popular culture and opinion continue to deny the possibility of such relationships.[10] Particularly given the lower risks to reputation associated with premarital sexuality in the twenty-first century, it is puzzling that these friendships continue to be difficult to describe as well as carry on. One sociologist who outlined the challenges of mixed-sex friendships in 1989 could have been describing the situation in 1789, as he identified the difficulties in agreeing on the emotional character of the relationship and presenting the relationship as safe and nonsexual to others. Incidentally, the film *When Harry Met Sally* also appeared in 1989, and Harry's famous statement of the thesis of the movie that "men and women can't be friends because the sex part always gets in the way" became a much discussed and debated point in popular culture. His position is widely supported, even if it does not reflect the realities of many people's relationships.[11]

Why is it that so many Americans continue to believe that "the sex part always gets in the way"? Just as in the past, sex can enter into same-sex friendships as well. Particularly with the widespread understanding of multiple types of sexual desire, how sex comes into play in friendships has become more complicated. What has not changed about ideas of sexual desire is the assumption that people, particularly men, will automatically be attracted to anybody of the opposite sex with whom they have an emotional connection. The efforts of early Americans to make heterosexual attraction appear natural have left their mark on America today. Indeed, new studies seem to appear every few years coming to the same conclusion as Harry, stamping the idea with imprimatur of scientific fact.[12] Few ask why sexual attraction is considered inevitable or consider the possibility that friendship and attraction can coexist.

Americans today also share with their forebears a notion that the ideal outcome of sexual desire is companionate marriage. While certainly a more flexible institution than in early America, marriage continues to be depicted as the pinnacle of fulfillment for both men and women, whether homosexual or heterosexual. As a relationship already considered as under siege by many, heterosexual marriage is still challenged by the existence of friendships between men and women. A married man or woman who befriends someone of the opposite sex has his or her sexual fidelity doubted and raises questions about why he or she is not completely fulfilled by a spouse. As Harry explains to Sally, a partner often "can't understand why you need to be friends with the person you're just friends with. Like it means something is missing from their relationship and 'why do you have to go outside to get it?' "[13]

Companionate marriage was and is freighted with more expectations than it can bear. As the happy ending of books and movies, it represents the achievement of adulthood, the single outlet for sexual fulfillment, and the primary relationship for meeting emotional needs. Marriage is also the avenue to a package of rights from the state, granting it official political recognition. But is it wise to vest one relationship with so much importance? Given the high rate of divorce and the many configurations of families, friends, and communities that support and enrich our lives, bestowing state and social preferment solely on marital relationships may no longer reflect more complex realities.[14] Friendships, whether same-sex or mixed-sex, are only likely to gain more importance in Americans' lives as marriage fails to meet individual and societal needs.

Yet the term "friendship" encompasses a wide array of relationships, as it did in the past, and it lacks the specificity needed to adequately capture the centrality it holds in many people's lives. There is still no appropriate language to describe friendships between men and women. Granted, the term "platonic" has lost its connotations of romantic desire and is now widely used to describe male/female friendships. But the word still maintains its association with an ideal that is impossible to realize. Mixed-sex friends with a physical or sexual component to their relationship do at least have the terms "f—k buddies" or "friends with benefits." While these terms are helpful for some men and women, they contribute to the assumption that relationships between men and women will inevitably be sexual. That the only three terms available for describing male/female friendship reference romance or sexuality contributes to the difficulty many mixed-sex friends have in describing nonsexual friendships.

Given that language and concepts help shape what we imagine to be possible, this is more than a linguistic issue. As the female protagonist Frances Wingate of Margaret Drabble's 1975 novel *The Realms of Gold* muses:

> She'd often argued . . . that there was no sex at all in her feelings for Derek and John and Bruce . . . it's friendship, or comradeliness, she would say lamely, but she'd never been able to make it sound very convincing, there weren't any good words for what she was trying to describe . . . she recognized the existence of things that lacked good words to describe them.[15]

For Frances, as for many others, friendships with the opposite sex are very real, but she has trouble proving this to her partner in the absence of the right words. She cannot nail down just what these friendships are or what they mean.[16]

Prejudice and imprecise language aside, friendships between men and women are meaningful relationships at many stages of Americans' lives. Expanding notions of desire, love, and fulfillment have birthed contentious debates in our society, leading to worries about what relationships will persist and provide structure and continuity. These need not be romantic relationships, or at least not solely romantic ones. As men and women are increasingly free to *desire* whom they choose, that freedom must also be expanded to include the right to *love* in more nuanced and expansive ways.[17] Male/female friendships' link to choice and liberty thus remains today. What other cultural and institutional meanings those friendships will take on is an evolving political question.

The growth of social networking sites, particularly Facebook, has opened new questions about the place and importance of friendships in Americans' lives. The term "friend" in the Facebook lexicon encompasses a range of relationships beyond even that familiar to colonial Americans: colleagues, teachers, family, schoolmates, even public figures one has never met can be "friends." But Facebook has also problematized privacy, intimacy, and expectations in friendships. Social scientists are increasingly interested in how technology works as "the architect of our intimacies," in psychologist Sherry Turkle's words, and many offer sobering assessments of the future of in-person relationships and Americans' emotional lives.[18] How social networking will change male/female friendships is as yet unclear. Certainly the expansive definition of friendship in this context makes it simpler for men and women to nominally be "friends" online, making it easier for mixed-sex friends to keep up with the latest news in each other's lives. But this development may do little to change the rules of interaction for men and women in person.

The persistence of friendships between men and women despite the odds against them reminds us of the power of individual choices and emotions. Discourse, popular culture, conventional wisdom—none of them can determine or constrain relationships between people who have the imagination and perhaps courage to see beyond these boundaries. More than two hundred years ago, men and women, including some of the most prominent people of the era, created an expansive form of social and political life in which gender was no barrier and in which the quest for emotional fulfillment defied the rules of convention. Their friendships are a lesson to Americans today about the possibilities for relationships and how we create the fabric of our society.

Notes

INTRODUCTION

1. Margaret Bayard Smith to Anthony Bleecker, November 4, 1823, Margaret Bayard Smith Papers, Library of Congress; Margaret Bayard Smith, *A Winter in Washington, Or, Memoirs of the Seymour Family: In Two Volumes* (New York: Published by E. Bliss & E. White, 1824), 3: 275–79.

2. My understanding of the interplay between gender and power and the formation of gender through relationships is influenced by Joan Scott's seminal article and many gender scholars who have used relationships as an important lens. Joan W. Scott, "Gender: A Useful Category of Historical Analysis," *The American Historical Review* 91, no. 5 (December 1986): 1053–75.

3. "Platonic, adj. and n." *OED Online.* Oxford University Press, http://www.oed.com/view/Entry/145418 (accessed July 22, 2014).

4. For a survey of these meanings, see "Friend," *OED Online.* There is a vast array of scholarship on the meanings and uses of friendship, notably Alan Bray, *The Friend* (Chicago: University of Chicago Press, 2003); Sarah Horowitz, *Friendship and Politics in Post-Revolutionary France* (State College: Penn State University Press, 2013); Horst Hutter, *Politics As Friendship: The Origins of Classical Notions of Politics in the Theory and Practice of Friendship* (Waterloo, OT: Wilfrid Laurier University Press, 1978); Ivy Schweitzer, *Perfecting Friendship: Politics and Affiliation in Early American Literature* (Chapel Hill: University of North Carolina Press, 2006); Allan Silver, "Friendship in Commercial Society: Eighteenth-Century Social Theory and Modern Sociology," *The American Journal of Sociology* 95, no. 6 (May 1990): 1474–1504; Carroll Smith-Rosenberg, "The Female World of Love and Ritual: Relations between Women in Nineteenth-Century America," *Signs* 1, no. 1 (Autumn 1975): 1–29.

5. See, e.g., Caleb Crain, *American Sympathy: Men, Friendship, and Literature in the New Nation* (New Haven: Yale University Press, 2001), 33; Richard Godbeer, *The*

Overflowing of Friendship: Love Between Men and the Creation of the American Republic (Baltimore: Johns Hopkins University Press, 2009), 2–6; Victor Luftig, *Seeing Together: Friendship between the Sexes in English Writing from Mill to Woolf* (Stanford, CA.: Stanford University Press, 1993), 1–7; Smith-Rosenberg, "The Female World of Love and Ritual," 1–7.

6. On women's changing role after the American Revolution, see Nancy F. Cott, *The Bonds of Womanhood: "Woman's Sphere" in New England, 1780–1835* (New Haven: Yale University Press, 1977); Linda K. Kerber, *Women of the Republic: Intellect and Ideology in Revolutionary America* (New York: Norton, 1986); Mary Beth Norton, *Liberty's Daughters: The Revolutionary Experience of American Women, 1750–1800* (Boston, MA: Little, Brown, 1980). On new roles for men, see Lorri Glover, *Southern Sons: Becoming Men in the New Nation* (Baltimore: Johns Hopkins University Press, 2007); Mark E. Kann, *A Republic of Men: The American Founders, Gendered Language, and Patriarchal Politics* (New York: New York University Press, 1998); Dana D. Nelson, *National Manhood: Capitalist Citizenship and the Imagined Fraternity of White Men* (Durham, NC: Duke University Press, 1998); E. Anthony Rotundo, *American Manhood: Transformations in Masculinity from the Revolution to the Modern Era* (New York: Basic Books, 1993). On changes in gendered roles within family structures, see Anya Jabour, *Marriage in the Early Republic: Elizabeth and William Wirt and the Companionate Ideal* (Baltimore: Johns Hopkins University Press, 1998); Jan Lewis, *The Pursuit of Happiness: Family and Values in Jefferson's Virginia* (Cambridge: Cambridge University Press, 1983); Carole Shammas, *A History of Household Government in America* (Charlottesville: University of Virginia Press, 2002).

7. Leora Auslander, *Cultural Revolutions: Everyday Life and Politics in Britain, North America, and France* (Berkeley: University of California Press, 2009), 1, 8; Andrew Cayton, *Love in the Time of Revolution: Transatlantic Literary Radicalism and Historical Change, 1793–1818* (Chapel Hill: Published for the Omohundro Institute of Early American History and Culture, Williamsburg, Virginia, by the University of North Carolina Press, 2013), 33.

8. Sarah Knott, *Sensibility and the American Revolution* (Chapel Hill: Published for the Omohundro Institute of Early American History and Culture, Williamsburg, Virginia, by the University of North Carolina Press, 2009), e.g., 113, 259; Godbeer, *The Overflowing of Friendship*, e.g., 9, 12, 157; Ruth H. Bloch, "Changing Conceptions of Sexuality and Romance in Eighteenth-Century America," *The William and Mary Quarterly*, Third Series, 60, no. 1 (January 2003): 40.

9. Numerous scholars have discussed the basis of early American political life in fraternity; see Godbeer, *The Overflowing of Friendship*; Mark E. Kann, *A Republic of Men: The American Founders, Gendered Language, and Patriarchal Politics* (New York: New York University Press, 1998); Wilson C. McWilliams, *The Idea of Fraternity in America* (Berkeley: University of California Press, 1973); Dana D. Nelson, *National Manhood: Capitalist Citzenship and the Imagined Fraternity of*

White Men, New Americanists (Durham, NC: Duke University Press, 1998). On the Greek ideals of friendship, often referred to by writers in the early republic, see Hutter, *Politics As Friendship*; Schweitzer, *Perfecting Friendship*, 3–39.

10. Some of the key texts on women's political importance as wives and mothers in this era include Catherine Allgor, *Parlor Politics: In Which the Ladies of Washington Help Build a City and a Government* (Charlottesville: University Press of Virginia, 2000); Mary Kelley, *Learning to Stand and Speak: Women, Education, and Public Life in America's Republic* (Chapel Hill: University of North Carolina Press, 2008); Kerber, *Women of the Republic*; Jan Lewis, "The Republican Wife: Virtue and Seduction in the Early Republic," *The William and Mary Quarterly* 44, no. 4 October (1987): 689–721; Rosemarie Zagarri, *Revolutionary Backlash: Women and Politics in the Early American Republic* (Philadelphia: University of Pennsylvania Press, 2007).

11. Elizabeth Maddock Dillon, *The Gender of Freedom: Fictions of Liberalism and the Literary Public Sphere* (Stanford, CA: Stanford University Press, 2004), 116–96; Knott, *Sensibility and the American Revolution*, 123; Lewis, "The Republican Wife"; Linda W. Rosenzweig, *Another Self: Middle-Class American Women and Their Friends in the Twentieth Century* (New York: New York University Press, 1999), 150; Schweitzer, *Perfecting Friendship*, 130.

12. Mary Wollstonecraft, *A Vindication of the Rights of Woman*, ed. Sheila Rowbotham (London: Verso, 2010), 98, 40, 140. For more on Wollstonecraft's ideas about friendship and love, see Cayton, *Love in the Time of Revolution: Transatlantic Literary Radicalism and Historical Change, 1793–1818*.

13. Elizabeth Graeme Fergusson, "Poemata Juvenalia," 1750s–1780s, 131, Library Company of Philadelphia. See also David S. Shields, *Civil Tongues & Polite Letters in British America* (Chapel Hill: Published for the Institute of Early American History and Culture, Williamsburg, Virginia, by the University of North Carolina Press, 1997), 126–40.

14. Margaret Bayard to Samuel Smith, May 3, 1800, Margaret Bayard Smith Papers, Library of Congress.

15. On men's concerns about women's entry into political life in this era, see Susan Branson, *These Fiery Frenchified Dames: Women and Political Culture in Early National Philadelphia* (Philadelphia: University of Pennsylvania Press, 2001); Zagarri, *Revolutionary Backlash*.

16. My thoughts on tactics of subtle resistance stems largely from the work of Bourdieau and de Certeau. See Pierre Bourdieu, *Outline of a Theory of Practice* (Cambridge: Cambridge University Press, 1977); Michel de Certeau, *The Practice of Everyday Life*, trans. Steven Rendall (Berkeley: University of California Press, 1984).

17. John Watson to Susan Livingston Ridley Sedgwick, January 26, 1805, Box 2, Folder 8, Watson Family Papers, The Joseph Downs Collection of Manuscripts and Printed Ephemera, The Winterthur Library.

18. Eric Foner, *The Story of American Freedom* (New York: W. W. Norton & Company, 1999), 16–20; Lawrence Meir Friedman, *The Republic of Choice: Law, Authority, and Culture* (Cambridge, MA: Harvard University Press, 1990), 2. On Jefferson's notion of the "pursuit of happiness," see e.g., Allen Jayne, *Jefferson's Declaration of Independence: Origins, Philosophy, and Theology* (Lexington: University Press of Kentucky, 1998); Lewis, *The Pursuit of Happiness*, xii–xv; Garry Wills, *Inventing America: Jefferson's Declaration of Independence* (New York: Houghton Mifflin Harcourt, 2002), 240–55.

19. Gordon S. Wood, *The Creation of the American Republic, 1776–1787*, First Norton Edition (New York: W. W. Norton & Company, 1972), 70–71.

20. There is a vast literature on the disjunction between ideals of equality and the system of racial slavery of early America, which Edmund Morgan called "The American Paradox." See, e.g., Alexander O. Boulton, "The American Paradox: Jeffersonian Equality and Racial Science," *American Quarterly* 47, no. 3 (September 1995): 467; John P. Diggins, "Slavery, Race, and Equality: Jefferson and the Pathos of the Enlightenment," *American Quarterly* 28, no. 2 (1976): 206; Jack Greene, "All Men Are Created Equal: Some Reflections on the Character of the American Revolution," in *Imperatives, Behaviors and Identities: Essays in Early American Cultural History* (Charlottesville: University of Virginia Press, 1992), 236–67; Winthrop D. Jordan, *White Over Black: American Attitudes Toward the Negro, 1550–1812*, 2nd ed. (Chapel Hill: University of North Carolina Press, 2012); Edmund Morgan, *American Slavery, American Freedom: The Ordeal of Colonial Virginia* (New York: W. W. Norton, 1976). On the exclusion of women from notions of equality, see especially Norma Basch, "Equity vs. Equality: Emerging Concepts of Women's Political Status in the Age of Jackson," *Journal of the Early Republic* 3, no. 3 (Autumn 1983): 297–318 Kerber, *Women of the Republic*; Lucia McMahon, *Mere Equals: The Paradox of Educated Women in the Early American Republic* (Ithaca: Cornell University Press, 2012); Zagarri, *Revolutionary Backlash*.

21. For a theoretical examination of the marriage contract, see Carole Pateman, *The Sexual Contract* (Stanford: Stanford University Press, 1988), 117, 158. On the hierarchical nature of companionate marriage, see Joseph Allen Boone, *Tradition Counter Tradition: Love and the Form of Fiction* (Chicago: University of Chicago Press, 1987), 60; Jabour, *Marriage in the Early Republic*, esp. 4–6; Lewis, "The Republican Wife," 708; Sheila L. Skemp, *First Lady of Letters: Judith Sargent Murray and the Struggle for Female Independence* (Philadelphia: University of Pennsylvania Press, 2009), 37.

22. Jabour, *Marriage in the Early Republic*, 6, 132; McMahon, *Mere Equals*, 91, 117.

23. The other relationship closest to achieving the republic's ideals was the brother/sister relationship; see C. Dallett Hemphill, *Siblings: Brothers and Sisters in American History* (New York: Oxford University Press, 2011). Yet in the absence

of a father, a brother could have legal control over a sister, and their relationship was formed by blood rather than choice.

24. Amanda Foreman, *Georgiana, Duchess of Devonshire* (New York: Random House, 1999), 34, 60, 68; Thomas Foster, "Reconsidering Libertines and Early Modern Heterosexuality: Sex and American Founder Gouverneur Morris," *Journal of the History of Sexuality* 22, no. 1 (January 2013): 72; Sarah C. Maza, *Private Lives and Public Affairs: The Causes Célèbres of Prerevolutionary France* (Berkeley: University of California Press, 1999), 282–86.

25. Adam Smith, *An Inquiry into the Nature and Causes of the Wealth of Nations*, ed. Edwin Cannan, 5th ed. (London: Methuen & Co., Ltd., 1904), V.1.199, http://www.econlib.org/library/Smith/smWN20.html#V.1.199.

26. On fears of female sexuality and its ties to political influence in England, see Katherine Binhammer, "The Sex Panic of the 1790s," *Journal of the History of Sexuality* 6, no. 3 (January 1996): 409–34; Elaine Chalus, *Elite Women in English Political Life, C.1754–1790* (Oxford: Oxford University Press, 2005), 14, 29. On French women's involvement in politics, see Dena Goodman, *The Republic of Letters: A Cultural History of the French Enlightenment* (Ithaca, NY: Cornell University Press, 1994); Steven D. Kale, *French Salons: High Society and Political Sociability from the Old Regime to the Revolution of 1848* (Baltimore: Johns Hopkins University Press, 2004); Joan B. Landes, *Women and the Public Sphere in the Age of the French Revolution* (Ithaca, NY: Cornell University Press, 1900). There are no studies of heterosocial friendship in England in this era, although examples of such friendships are discsussed in Chalus, *Elite Women in English Political Life, C.1754–1790*; Norma Clarke, *Dr. Johnson's Women* (London: Hambledon and London, 2000); Anna Farwell De Koven, *Horace Walpole and Madame Du Deffand; an Eighteenth-Century Friendship* (New York, London: D. Appleton and Company, 1929); Foreman, *Georgiana, Duchess of Devonshire*; Naomi Tadmor, *Family and Friends in Eighteenth-Century England: Household, Kinship, and Patronage* (Cambridge: Cambridge University Press, 2001); Clara Tuite and Claire Russell, eds., *Romantic Sociability: Social Networks and Literary Culture in Britain, 1770–1840* (Cambridge: Cambridge University Press, 2002). There are several studies focusing on heterosocial friendship in France; see Elizabeth Colwill, "Epistolary Passions: Friendship and the Literary Public of Constance de Salm, 1767–1845," *Journal of Women's History* 12, no. 3 (2000): 39–68; Julie Candler Hayes, "Friendship and the Female Moralist," *Studies in Eighteenth-Century Culture* 39(2010): 171–89; Sarah Horowitz, *Friendship and Politics in Post-Revolutionary France* (State College: Penn State University Press, 2014).

27. On the importance of chastity—specifically *female* chastity—to the American republic, see Mark E. Kann, *Taming Passion for the Public Good: Policing Sex in the Early Republic* (New York: New York University Press, 2013); Clare A. Lyons,

Sex Among the Rabble: An Intimate History of Gender & Power in the Age of Revolution, Philadelphia, 1730–1830 (Chapel Hill: Published for the Omohundro Institute of Early American History and Culture, Williamsburg, Virginia, by the University of North Carolina Press, 2006), 288–98.

28. Having set out here that I refer specifically to an elite group of people, I will omit the use of the term "elite" throughout this book. Generalities about these friendships and their meanings do not apply beyond this class. I acknowledge that defining "elite" is difficult in this period and adopt Andrew Schocket's definition of elites as those with "access to capital, use of state power, elite consciousness, and patterns of elite social behavior." See Andrew Schocket, "Thinking about Elites in the Early Republic," *Journal of the Early Republic* 25, no. 4 (Winter 2005): 547–55.

29. Lyons, *Sex Among the Rabble*, 288.

30. While this project does not trace differences across life stages, Michael Monsour's contemporary study includes many observations that hold true for the early republic as well. See Michael Monsour, *Women and Men as Friends: Relationships Across the Life Span in the 21st Century* (Mahwah, NJ: L. Erlbaum, 2002).

31. Michael O'Brien, *Conjectures of Order: Intellectual Life and the American South, 1810–1860* (Chapel Hill: University of North Carolina Press, 2004), 1: 456.

32. Glover, *Southern Sons*, 135; O'Brien, *Conjectures of Order: Intellectual Life and the American South, 1810–1860*, I:408.

33. Zagarri, *Revolutionary Backlash*.

34. Margaret Bayard to Samuel Smith, May 3, 1800, Margaret Bayard Smith Papers, Library of Congress.

35. Margaret Bayard Smith to Susan B. Smith, March 1809, in *The First Forty Years of Washington Society, Portrayed by the Family Letters of Mrs. Samuel Harrison Smith (Margaret Bayard) from the Collection of Her Grandson, J. Henley Smith*, ed. Gaillard Hunt. (New York: C. Scribner's Sons, 1906), 424.

CHAPTER 1

1. Similarly, Naomi Tadmor argues that the notion of "service" was central to demonstrating friendship in eighteenth-century England. Naomi Tadmor, *Family and Friends in Eighteenth-Century England: Household, Kinship, and Patronage* (Cambridge: Cambridge University Press, 2001), 179, 213–15.

2. Numerous works treat each of their stays in Europe; see especially William Howard Adams, *The Paris Years of Thomas Jefferson* (New Haven: Yale University Press, 2000); Edith Belle Gelles, *Portia: The World of Abigail Adams* (Bloomington: Indiana University Press, 1992); Woody Holton, *Abigail Adams* (New York: Free Press, 2009); Brian Steele, "Thomas Jefferson's Gender Frontier," *Journal of American History* 95, no. 1 (June 2008): 17–42. There is little treatment of Abigail's relationships with men besides her husband, but Jefferson's relationships

with women are examined in Jon Kukla, *Mr. Jefferson's Women* (New York: Alfred A. Knopf, 2007); Jan Lewis, "'Those Scenes for Which Alone My Heart Was Made': Affection and Politics in the Age of Jefferson and Hamilton," in *An Emotional History of the United States*, ed. Jan Lewis and Peter N. Stearns (New York: New York University Press, 1998); John P. Kaminski, ed., *Jefferson in Love: The Love Letters Between Thomas Jefferson & Maria Cosway* (Madison, WI: Madison House, 1999); Virginia Scharff, *The Women Jefferson Loved* (New York: Harper, 2010). Only Kukla offers an extended treatment of this particular relationship.

3. There have been three recent biographies of their marriage: G. J. Barker-Benfield, *Abigail and John Adams: The Americanization of Sensibility* (Chicago: University of Chicago Press, 2010); Joseph J. Ellis, *First Family: Abigail and John* (New York: Alfred A. Knopf, 2010); Edith Belle Gelles, *Abigail & John: Portrait of a Marriage* (New York: HarperCollins, 2009).

4. Abigail Adams to Elizabeth Smith Shaw Peabody, February 12, 1796, cited in Holton, *Abigail Adams*, 293.

5. Abigail Adams to Mary Cranch, May 8, 1785, in Charles Francis Adams, ed., *Letters of Mrs. Adams, the Wife of John Adams* (Boston: C. C. Little and J. Brown, 1840), 93.

6. Margaret Bayard Smith, *The First Forty Years of Washington Society, Portrayed by the Family Letters of Mrs. Samuel Harrison Smith (Margaret Bayard) from the Collection of Her Grandson, J. Henley Smith*, ed. Gaillard Hunt (New York: C. Scribner's Sons, 1906), 6–7.

7. Abigail Adams to Thomas Jefferson, June 6, 1785; Jefferson to Abigail Adams, June 21, 1785, in Julian P. Boyd and Barbara Oberg, eds., *The Papers of Thomas Jefferson* (Princeton, NJ: Princeton University Press, 1950—), 8: 173, 239. Hereafter *PTJ*.

8. Thomas Jefferson to Abigail Adams, September 25, 1785, *PTJ*, 8: 548–49.

9. Thomas Jefferson to Abigail Adams, December 21, 1786, *PTJ*, 10: 621.

10. Elaine Forman Crane, "Political Dialogue and the Spring of Abigail's Discontent," *The William and Mary Quarterly*, Third Series, 56, no. 4 (October 1999): 745–74; Holton, *Abigail Adams*, 10, 308.

11. Crane, "Political Dialogue and the Spring of Abigail's Discontent," 746, 757.

12. Kukla, *Mr. Jefferson's Women*, 143; Richard B. Bernstein, *Thomas Jefferson* (New York: Oxford University Press, 2003), 108.

13. Thomas Jefferson to Angelica Schuyler Church, September 21, 1788, *PTJ*, 16: 623–24.

14. Thomas Jefferson to Abigail Adams, December 27, 1785, August 9, 1786, *PTJ*, 9: 129, 10: 202–03.

15. Abigail Adams to Thomas Jefferson, January 29, 1787; Thomas Jefferson to Abigail Adams, February 22, 1787, *PTJ*, 9: 126; 11: 86–88, 174.

16. Thomas Jefferson to Abigail Adams, June 21, 1785 in *PTJ*, 8: 239–42.

17. Abigail Adams to John Adams, December 31, 1796, in *Adams Family Papers: An Electronic Archive*. Massachusetts Historical Society. http://www.masshist.org/digitaladams/.

18. Abigail Adams to John Adams, January 15, 1795 [i.e., 1796], in *Adams Family Papers: An Electronic Archive*. Massachusetts Historical Society. http://www.masshist.org/digitaladams/.

19. Abigail Adams to Thomas Jefferson, May 20, 1804; Thomas Jefferson to Abigail Adams, June 13, 1804; for the complete 1804 exchange, see Lester Jesse Cappon, ed., *The Adams-Jefferson Letters: The Complete Correspondence Between Thomas Jefferson and Abigail and John Adams* (Chapel Hill: Published for the Institute of Early American History and Culture at Williamsburg, Virginia, by the University of North Carolina Press, 1959), 2: 268–80. Note that at the time of the publication of this book, neither the Jefferson nor Adams documentary editions are complete, so letters those projects have yet to publish are cited in Cappon's edition.

20. Thomas Jefferson to Abigail Adams, June 13, 1804; Abigail Adams to Thomas Jefferson, October 25, 1804, in Cappon, *The Adams-Jefferson Letters*, 269, 280.

21. Thomas Jefferson to Benjamin Rush, January 16, 1811, in J. Jefferson Looney, ed., *The Papers of Thomas Jefferson: Retirement Series* (Princeton, NJ: Princeton University Press, 2004), 3: 307. Hereafter *PTJ-RS*.

22. John Adams to Thomas Jefferson, July 15, 1813; Thomas Jefferson to Abigail Adams, August 22, 1813; Abigail Adams to Thomas Jefferson, September 20, 1813; *PTJ-RS*, 6: 297, 437–38, 516–17.

23. Abigail Adams to Thomas Jefferson, December 15, 1816; Thomas Jefferson to Abigail Adams, May 15, 1817; Thomas Jefferson to John Adams, November 13, 1818, in Cappon, *The Adams-Jefferson Letters*, 2: 500, 514, 529. Abigail Adams to Thomas Jefferson, September 20, 1813, *PTJ-RS*, 6: 516–17.

24. See, e.g., Beverley Anne Fehr, *Friendship Processes* (Thousand Oaks, CA: Sage Publications, 1996), 173; Lucia McMahon, *Mere Equals: The Paradox of Educated Women in the Early American Republic* (Ithaca, NY: Cornell University Press, 2012), 45, 79.

25. Carroll Smith-Rosenberg, "The Female World of Love and Ritual: Relations between Women in Nineteenth-Century America," *Signs* 1, no. 1 (Autumn 1975): 14; Carol Lasser, "'Let Us Be Sisters Forever': The Sororal Model of Nineteenth-Century Female Friendship," *Signs* 14(1988): 162–69.

26. This was particularly true for marriages, in which "the woman was heart, the man head." Jan Lewis, *The Pursuit of Happiness: Family and Values in Jefferson's Virginia* (Cambridge: Cambridge University Press, 1983), 199.

27. E T—n, "An Essay on Friendship with Women," *Massachusetts Magazine*, August 1796, 440.

28. John Mifflin to Elzina de la Roche, December 22, 1801, Baron Frederick de la Roche Papers, Maryland Historical Society.

29. Because Mifflin left a detailed journal as a young man, his friendships with men during that time have been used as an example of the intense friendships between men. See Caleb Crain, *American Sympathy: Men, Friendship, and Literature in the New Nation* (New Haven: Yale University Press, 2001), 16–52; Richard Godbeer, *The Overflowing of Friendship: Love Between Men and the Creation of the American Republic* (Baltimore: The Johns Hopkins University Press, 2009), 17–48; Sarah Knott, *Sensibility and the American Revolution* (Chapel Hill: Published for the Omohundro Institute of Early American History and Culture, Williamsburg, Virginia, by the University of North Carolina Press, 2009), 113–23. These authors, however, do not address Mifflin's similarly intimate friendship with Madame de la Roche.

30. John Mifflin to Elzina de la Roche, May 13, 1805, and July 23, 1807, Baron Frederick de la Roche Papers, Maryland Historical Society.

31. Godbeer, *The Overflowing of Friendship*, 10; Crain, *American Sympathy*, 35.

32. Abigail Adams to James Lovell, ca. December 15, 1777, in L. H. Butterfield, ed., *Adams Family Correspondence* (Cambridge, MA: Belknap Press of Harvard University Press, 1963), 370–71.

33. Patty Rogers, *Passionate Spinster: The Diary of Patty Rogers, 1785* (Exeter, NH: Exeter Historical Society, 2001), 160–61.

34. On Channing's attractiveness as a friend to woman, see Megan Marshall, *The Peabody Sisters: Three Women Who Ignited American Romanticism* (Boston, MA: Houghton Mifflin, 2005), 160–61.

35. William Henry Channing, *The Life of William Ellery Channing*, 3rd ed. (Boston, MA: American Unitarian Association, 1880), 609.

36. William Ellery Channing to Eloise Richards Payne, November 22, 1813, William Ellery Channing Papers, Andover-Harvard Theological Library.

37. Eloise Richards Payne to William Ellery Channing, January 8, 1814, John Howard Payne Papers [ca. 1780] –1952, Rare Book Library, Columbia University.

38. Eloise Richards Payne to Catharine Maria Sedgwick, c. 1813, Payne Papers, Rare Book Library, Columbia University.

39. William Ellery Channing to Eloise Richards Payne, November 22, 1813, Channing Papers, Andover-Harvard Theological Library.

40. Eloise Richards Payne to William Ellery Channing, January 8, 1814, Payne Papers, Rare Book Library, Columbia University.

41. William Ellery Channing to Eloise Richards Payne, 1811, William Ellery Channing Papers, Massachusetts Historical Society.

42. William Ellery Channing to Eloise Richards Payne, November 22, 1813, Channing Papers, Andover-Harvard Theological Library.

43. Eloise Richards Payne to William Ellery Channing, October 18, 1811, Payne Papers, Columbia University.

44. William Ellery Channing to Eloise Richards Payne, January 9, 1810, Channing Papers, Andover-Harvard Theological Library.

45. For more on this position, see Shirley Marchalonis, ed., *Patrons and Protégées: Gender, Friendship, and Writing in Nineteenth-Century America* (New Brunswick, NJ: Rutgers University Press, 1998).

46. Eloise Richards Payne to William Ellery Channing, September 24, 1809, January 6, 1813, Payne Papers, Rare Book Library, Columbia University.

47. Channing to Eloise Payne, October 1810, December 6, 1810, early 1811, William Ellery Channing Papers, Massachusetts Historical Society.

48. Eloise Richards Payne to William Ellery Channing, December 19, 1810, Payne Papers, Rare Book Library, Columbia University.

49. William Ellery Channing to Eloise Payne, 1811, William Ellery Channing Papers, Massachusetts Historical Society.

50. William Ellery Channing to Eloise Payne, April 9, 1813; May 21, 1814, William Ellery Channing Papers, Massachusetts Historical Society.

51. Susan H. Irons, "Channing's Influence on Peabody: Self-Culture and the Danger of Egoism," *Studies in the American Renaissance*, 1992, 121–22; Marshall, *The Peabody Sisters*; Bruce A. Ronda, *Elizabeth Palmer Peabody: A Reformer on Her Own Terms* (Cambridge, MA: Harvard University Press, 1999), 77.

52. Irons, "Channing's Influence on Peabody," 132.

53. Irons, "Channing's Influence on Peabody," 122. See also Marshall, *The Peabody Sisters*, 91–93, 215, 275.

54. Judith Sargent married John Stevens in 1769, and John Murray became her friend and religious mentor in the early 1770s. Two years after Stevens died in 1786, Judith married Murray. She is well known among women's historians today for her writings on female equality; see Sheila L. Skemp, *First Lady of Letters: Judith Sargent Murray and the Struggle for Female Independence* (Philadelphia: University of Pennsylvania Press, 2009). For this quote, see Stevens to Murray, November 14, 1774, in Bonnie Hurd Smith, ed., *Mingling Souls upon Paper: An Eighteenth-Century Love Story* (Salem, MA.: Judith Sargent Murray Society, 2007), 41.

55. Judith Sargent Murray to John Murray, December 24, 1780, in Smith, *Mingling Souls upon Paper*, 56.

56. Cynthia A. Kierner, *Scandal at Bizarre: Rumor and Reputation in Jefferson's America* (New York: Palgrave Macmillan, 2004), 96.

57. Lisa Wilson, *Life after Death: Widows in Pennsylvania, 1750–1850* (Philadelphia: Temple University Press, 1992), 152, 157.

58. Bryan to Randolph of Roanoke, April 23, 1819, Materials Concerning John Randolph of Roanoke, 1787–1903, Virginia Historical Society. Delia wrote to John, "If the Estate and myself are successful in our crops I wish the boys to spend next winter with me provided it meets your approbation."

59. Kirsten E. Wood, *Masterful Women: Slaveholding Widows from the American Revolution Through the Civil War* (Chapel Hill: University of North Carolina Press, 2004), 10, 62.

60. Wilson, *Life After Death*, 124.

61. On the friendly language of business correspondence, see Toby L. Ditz, "Shipwrecked; Or, Masculinity Imperiled: Mercantile Representations of Failure and the Gendered Self in Eighteenth-Century Philadelphia," *The Journal of American History* 81, no. 1 (June 1994): 51–80.

62. The best source on Litchfield and the Pierce family is Lynne Templeton Brickley, "Sarah Pierce's Litchfield Female Academy, 1792–1833" (PhD Diss., Harvard University, 1985). Biographical details on all three of the people discussed here, as well as thousands of other Litchfield teachers and students, are also available via the Litchfield Historical Society's database at http://www.litchfieldhistoricalsociety.org/ledger.

63. John Pierce Brace, *More Chronicles of a Pioneer School, from 1792 to 1833*, ed. Emily Noyes Vanderpoel (New York: The Cadmus Book Shop, 1927), 153.

64. Mrs. Asa Gray, "Sketch of Miss Mary Pierce," in *Chronicles of a Pioneer School, from 1792–1833*, ed. Emily Noyes Vanderpoel and Elizabeth Cynthia Barney Buel (Cambridge, MA: Harvard University Press, 1903), 325–26.

65. Brickley, "Sarah Pierce's Litchfield Female Academy, 1792–1833," 16, 402–14, 452.

66. Theophilus Parsons, "Memoir of Charles Greely Loring," in *Proceedings of the Massachusetts Historical Society*, vol. 11 (Boston, MA: The Society, 1869), 288, 64, 282.

67. Brickley, "Sarah Pierce's Litchfield Female Academy, 1792–1833," 498.

68. Mary Pierce to Charles Loring, March 1, 1816, Loring Family Correspondence, Helga J. Ingraham Memorial Library, Litchfield Historical Society. All of the below cited letters between them are from this collection.

69. Charles to Mary, June 29, 1817.

70. Mary to Charles, January 22 and November 17, 1816.

71. Charles to May, June 29, 1817.

72. Gray, "Sketch of Miss Mary Pierce."

73. Mary to Charles, August 15, 1816.

74. Mary to Charles, March 11, 1818.

75. Gray, "Sketch of Miss Mary Pierce."

76. Parsons, "Memoir of Charles Greely Loring," 290, 266.

77. Charles to Mary, August 18, 1817; Mary to Charles, February 4, 1817.

78. Charles to Mary, June 11, 1817.

79. Mary to Charles, July 1817.

80. Charles to Mary, August 1, 1817; Mary to Charles, August 1817.

81. Parsons, "Memoir of Charles Greely Loring," 282.

82. There are three letters from Mary Pierce to Charles Loring in the Charles G. Loring Papers at Houghton Library at Harvard University. The latest of these, item 1127, is conjectured by the archivists to be from the 1850s.

83. Lee S. Cook, "Loring Family Correspondence, 1812–1863," finding aid, Helga J. Ingraham Memorial Library, Litchfield Historical Society. This finding aid lists and summarizes every letter in the collection.

84. Michael Monsour, *Women and Men as Friends: Relationships across the Life Span in the 21st Century* (Mahwah, NJ: L. Erlbaum, 2002), 103, 135.

85. Jane Shedden to John Pierce Brace, May 20, 1813, Litchfield Female Academy Collection, Series 2, Folder 76, Litchfield Historical Society.

86. Eliza Slough to Fielding Lucas, February 16, 1807, Fielding Lucas Collection, Maryland Historical Society.

87. Eliza Slough to Fielding Lucas, August 22, 1808, September 16, 1808, Fielding Lucas Collection, Maryland Historical Society.

88. For more on Rodgers and his courtship of Minerva Denison, see John H. Schroeder, *Commodore John Rodgers: Paragon of the Early American Navy* (Gainesville: University Press of Florida, 2006), 27–55. Note that this author says Pinkney was Rodgers's young sister, when in fact she was only the sister of Rodgers's brother-in-law and the two never referred to each other as siblings.

89. John Rodgers to Ann Pinkney, c. 1803, Rodgers Family Papers, Library of Congress.

90. Ann Pinkney to John Rodgers, May 29, 1803, Rodgers Family Papers, Library of Congress.

91. Ann Pinkney to John Rodgers, January 11, 1804, Rodgers Family Papers, Library of Congress.

92. John Rodgers to Minerva Denison, January 13, 1804, Rodgers Family Papers, Library of Congress.

93. Horst Hutter, *Politics as Friendship: The Origins of Classical Notions of Politics in the Theory and Practice of Friendship* (Waterloo, ON: Wilfrid Laurier University Press, 1978), 11.

94. Women were supposed to be intellectual, but not *too* intellectual; showing too much intelligence could scare off men. See, e.g., Linda K. Kerber, *Women of the Republic: Intellect and Ideology in Revolutionary America* (New York: Norton, 1986), 196–99, 226–28; McMahon, *Mere Equals*, 3–12.

CHAPTER 2

1. On the interplay between texts, particularly novels, and social behavior in early America, see Martha Tomhave Blauvelt, "Women, Words, and Men: Excerpts from the Diary of Mary Guion," *Journal of Women's History* 2, no. 2 (Fall 1990): 17; Andrew Cayton, *Love in the Time of Revolution: Transatlantic Literary Radicalism and Historical Change, 1793–1818* (Chapel Hill: Published for the Omohundro Institute of Early American History and Culture, Williamsburg, Virginia, by the University of North Carolina Press, 2013), 10; Cathy N. Davidson, *Revolution and the Word* (Oxford: Oxford University Press, 1987), 113–23; Rodney Hessinger, *Seduced, Abandoned, and Reborn: Visions of Youth in Middle-Class America, 1780–1850* (Philadelphia: University of Pennsylvania Press, 2005), 8; Jane P. Tompkins, *Sensational Designs: The Cultural Work of American Fiction,*

1790–1860 (New York: Oxford University Press, 1985), xi–xvii. On the larger theoretical questions of how readers engage with texts and the degree to which media influences readers, see Michel De Certeau, "Reading as Poaching." *The Practice of Everyday Life.* Trans. Steven F. Rendall (Berkeley: University of California Press, 1984), 165–76.

2. On emotion and particularly emotional expression as learned rather than innate, see William M. Reddy, *The Navigation of Feeling: A Framework for the History of Emotions* (Cambridge: Cambridge University Press, 2001), x, 35.

3. Sarah Knott, *Sensibility and the American Revolution* (Chapel Hill: Published for the Omohundro Institute of Early American History and Culture, Williamsburg, Virginia, by the University of North Carolina Press, 2009), 20.

4. Julie K. Ellison, *Cato's Tears and the Making of Anglo-American Emotion* (Chicago: University of Chicago Press, 1999), 25.

5. Rosemarie Zagarri, "Morals, Manners, and the Republican Mother," *American Quarterly* 44, no. 2 (June 1, 1992): 198, 202. See also Teresa Anne Murphy, *Citizenship and the Origins of Women's History in the United States* (Philadelphia: University of Pennsylvania Press, 2013).

6. On Americans' fears about the pernicious effects of reading novels and how to guard against them, see Katherine Sarah Gaudet, "Fear of Fiction: Reading and Resisting the Novel in Early America" (PhD diss., University of Chicago, 2011). For studies of how novels were shaped for national audiences, see esp. Joseph Paul Rezek, "Tales from Elsewhere: Fiction at a Proximate Distance in the Anglophone Atlantic, 1800–1850" (PhD diss., University of California, Los Angeles, 2009); Leonard Tennenhouse, "The Americanization of Clarissa," *The Yale Journal of Criticism* 11, no. 1 (Spring 1998): 177–96. On adaptations of other genres for American audiences, see C. Dallett Hemphill, *Bowing to Necessities: A History of Manners in America, 1620–1860* (New York: Oxford University Press, 2002); Murphy, *Citizenship and the Origins of Women's History in the United States.*

7. James Fordyce, *The Character and Conduct of the Female Sex, and the Advantages to Be Derived by Young Men from the Society of Virtuous Women. A Discourse, in Three Parts, Delivered in Monkwell-Street Chapel, January 1, 1776, by James Fordyce, D. D. Author of the Sermons to Young Women, and Addresses to Young Men*, 3rd ed. (Boston, MA: John Gill, 1781), 45.

8. James Fordyce, *Sermons to Young Women* (Philadelphia: Thomas Dobson, 1787), 106, 112–16.

9. Hemphill, *Bowing to Necessities*, 107–13.

10. Ivy Schweitzer, *Perfecting Friendship: Politics and Affiliation in Early American Literature* (Chapel Hill: University of North Carolina Press, 2006), 3, 64–65.

11. Richard Godbeer, *The Overflowing of Friendship: Love Between Men and the Creation of the American Republic* (Baltimore: Johns Hopkins University Press, 2009), 62–66.

12. Hester Chapone, *Letters on the Improvement of the Mind* (London: J. Walter and C. Dilly, 1790), 82–89.

13. "On Friendship," *The Monthly Anthology, and Boston Review Containing Sketches and Reports of Philosophy, Religion, History, Arts, and Manners*, June 1, 1804.

14. II Samuel 1. 23–27 (King James Bible).

15. "On Benevolence and Friendship," *The Intellectual Regale; Or, Ladies' Tea Tray*, January 14, 1815.

16. "Friendship," *Ladies' Portfolio*, January 29, 1820.

17. Schweitzer, *Perfecting Friendship*, 39.

18. Schweitzer, *Perfecting Friendship*, 3–15; Lillian Faderman, *Surpassing the Love of Men: Romantic Friendship and Love Between Women from the Renaissance to the Present* (New York: Morrow, 1981), 66. See Aristotle's *Nicomachean Ethics* or Cicero's *De Amicita* for the most prominent examples.

19. William Alexander, *The History of Women, From the Earliest Antiquity, to the Present Time; Giving an Account of Almost Every Interesting Particular Concerning That Sex, Among All Nations, Ancient and Modern.* (Boston, MA: Joseph Burnstead, 1790), 102.

20. Cited in Lillian Faderman, *Romantic Friendship*, 85.

21. Alexander, *The History of Women, From the Earliest Antiquity, to the Present Time; Giving an Account of Almost Every Interesting Particular Concerning That Sex, Among All Nations, Ancient and Modern*, 102–03.

22. "Female Friendship," *Weekly Visitor, or Ladies' Miscellany*, January 7, 1804.

23. Fordyce, *Sermons to Young Women*, 100.

24. "On Friendship," *Balance and Columbian Repository*, November 13, 1804.

25. "The Friendship of Man," *Ladies Magazine*, October 1829.

26. Caleb Crain, *American Sympathy: Men, Friendship, and Literature in the New Nation* (New Haven: Yale University Press, 2001), 13; Godbeer, *The Overflowing of Friendship*, 11. Both authors point to the example of John Mifflin requesting to see his female friends' letters as a young man in order to pick up the women's sentimental styling. See Crain, 30–31 and Godbeer, 75–76.

27. Henry Home, *Six Sketches on the History of Man* (Philadelphia, 1776), 242.

28. William Christian Lehmann, *Henry Home, Lord Kames, and the Scottish Enlightenment: A Study in National Character and in the History of Ideas* (New York: Springer, 1971), 248; Murphy, *Citizenship and the Origins of Women's History in the United States*, 24.

29. Arianne Chernock, "Cultivating Woman: Men's Pursuit of Intellectual Equality in the Late British Enlightenment," *Journal of British Studies* 45, no. 3 (July 2006): 513.

30. Susan (Mansfield) Huntington, *Memoirs of the Late Mrs. Susan Huntington, of Boston, Mass.*, ed. Benjamin Blydenburg Wisner, 3d ed. (Boston, MA: Crocker and Brewster, 1829), 168.

31. "Women," *The Massachusetts Centinel*, May 5, 1790.

32. There were some sixty-nine American editions of this British-authored text, and it was reprinted in magazines frequently. Hemphill, *Bowing to Necessities*, 108.

33. E T—n, "An Essay on Friendship with Women," *Massachusetts Magazine*, August 1796.

34. Lucia McMahon argues that complementarity between men and women created "mere equality," the idea that women were men's intellectual and social equals but remained naturally distinct. Thus complementarity maintained the politically critical gender difference between men and women. Lucia McMahon, *Mere Equals: The Paradox of Educated Women in the Early American Republic* (Ithaca, NY: Cornell University Press, 2012).

35. Fordyce, *Sermons to Young Women*, 106.

36. On the hardening of the gender binary and its biological bases, see Clare A. Lyons, *Sex Among the Rabble: An Intimate History of Gender & Power in the Age of Revolution, Philadelphia, 1730–1830* (Chapel Hill: Published for the Omohundro Institute of Early American History and Culture, Williamsburg, Virginia, by the University of North Carolina Press, 2006).

37. Jan Lewis, "The Republican Wife: Virtue and Seduction in the Early Republic," *The William and Mary Quarterly* 44, no. 4 (October 1987): 703. On the connection between Scottish Enlightenment philosophy and the republican mother and wife, see Zagarri, "Morals, Manners, and the Republican Mother."

38. Godbeer, *The Overflowing of Friendship*, 177.

39. "On Friendship," *Balance and Columbian Repository*, November 13, 1804.

40. "Thoughts on Cicisbeism," *Farmer's Weekly Museum*, June 12, 1798.

41. *Advice to the Fair Sex in a Series of Letters on Various Subjects Chiefly Describing the Graceful Virtues Which Are Indispensibly Required to Adorn and Perfect the Female Sex . . . and the Contrast: Thereby Showing How to Follow What Is Good and Eshew [sic] What Is Evil* (Philadelphia: Printed for the author, by Robert Cochran, 1803), 27.

42. "The Friendship of Woman," *Ladies Magazine,* December 1829.

43. Mary Wollstonecraft, *Thoughts on the Education of Daughters* (Bristol: Thoemmes, 1995), 88.

44. Joseph Addison and Sir Richard Steele, *The Spectator* (Philadelphia: Printed by Tesson and Lee for Samuel F. Bradford and John Conrad, 1803), no. 400.

45. "On the Happy Influence Arising from Female Society, from Dr. Alexander's History of Women," *Massachusetts Magazine*, 1795.

46. "The Art of Conversation," *Philadelphia Repository and Weekly Register*, August 15, 1801.

47. Samuel Saunter, "The American Lounger," *The Port-Folio*, July 15, 1803.

48. Fordyce, *The Character and Conduct of the Female Sex*, 10, 11, 16, 45, 46.

49. "A Father's Advice to His Daughters: Friendship, Love, and Marriage," *The Christian's, Scholar's, and Farmer's Magazine*, March 1790.

50. Rowson, *Mentoria; or The Young Lady's Friend. In Two Volumes* (Philadelphia: Printed for Robert Campbell, by Samuel Harrison Smith, 1794), 11.

51. On the use of advice literature and seduction novels to warn and teach young women, see Hessinger, *Seduced, Abandoned, and Reborn*, 1–42.

52. Hannah Webster Foster, *The Coquette*, ed. Cathy N. Davidson (New York: Oxford University Press, 1986), 126–27.

53. Foster, *The Coquette*, 128.

54. Elizabeth Dillon also argues that Eliza chooses a circle of friends (although not necessarily male ones) over marriage. See Elizabeth Maddock Dillon, *The Gender of Freedom: Fictions of Liberalism and the Literary Public Sphere* (Stanford, CA: Stanford University Press, 2004), 189.

55. Schweitzer, *Perfecting Friendship*, 107.

56. Caroline Lamb, *Glenarvon* (London: Printed for Henry Colburn and Co., 1816), 2: 124, 192.

57. Lamb, *Glenarvon*, 2: 155.

58. Lamb, *Glenarvon*, 2: 308.

59. Lamb, *Glenarvon*, 3: 82.

60. Susanna Rowson, *Charlotte Temple and Lucy Temple* (New York: Penguin Classics, 1991), 105.

61. For more on the story of Elizabeth Whitman, see Richard Buel, *Joel Barlow: American Citizen in a Revolutionary World* (Baltimore: Johns Hopkins University Press, 2011), 31–44; Bryan Waterman, "Coquetry and Correspondence in Revolutionary-Era Connecticut: Reading Elizabeth Whitman's Letters," *Early American Literature* 46, no. 3 (2011): 541–63; Bryan Waterman, "Elizabeth Whitman's Disappearance and Her 'Disappointment,'" *William and Mary Quarterly* LXVI, no. 2 (April 2009): 325–64.

62. Clara Tuite, "Tainted Love and Romantic Literary Celebrity," *ELH* 74, no. 1 (2007): 59–88.

63. Lewis, "The Republican Wife," 716.

64. For a similar argument on the use of heterosocial friendships in Victorian novels, see Victor Luftig, *Seeing Together: Friendship between the Sexes in English Writing from Mill to Woolf* (Stanford, CA: Stanford University Press, 1993), 14.

65. Mrs. Burke, *Ela: Or the Delusions of the Heart*, English (Boston, MA: Benj. Larking and John W. Folsom, 1790), 28, 46.

66. Robert Bage, *Hermsprong, Or, Man as He Is Not* (Peterborough, ON: Broadview Press, 2002), 77.

67. Fanny Burney, *Evelina*, ed. Stewart J. Cooke (W. W. Norton & Company, 1998), 7–19.

68. Isabelle de Montolieu, *Caroline of Lichtfield*, trans. Thomas Holcroft (New York: re-printed by J. S. Mott, for Evert Duyckinck & Co, 1798), 23.

69. Judith Lowder Newton, *Women, Power, and Subversion: Social Strategies in British Fiction, 1778–1860* (New York: Methuen, 1985), 9, 28.

70. Tony Tanner, *Adultery in the Novel: Contract and Transgression* (Baltimore: Johns Hopkins University Press, 1979), 15.

71. Joseph Allen Boone, *Tradition Counter Tradition: Love and the Form of Fiction* (Chicago: University of Chicago Press, 1987), 78.

72. Katherine Sobba Green, *The Courtship Novel, 1740–1820: A Feminized Genre* (Lexington: University Press of Kentucky, 1991).

73. Susanna Rowson, *The Inquisitor; Or, Invisible Rambler* (Philadelphia: Mathew Carey, 1794), 189.

74. Maria Edgeworth, *Belinda* (New York: Oxford World's Classics, 1999), 78.

75. Edgeworth, *Belinda*, 144.

76. Out of all of Austen's novels, I have chosen *Emma* because that was the only one of her novels published in America contemporaneously with its publication in England. Austen's other novels were available in America by the 1810s, but no others were published in America until after 1830. Charles Beecher Hogan, "Jane Austen and Her Early Public," *The Review of English Studies*, New Series v. 1, no. 1 (January 1950): 53.

77. Ruth Perry, "Interrupted Friendships in Jane Austen's Emma," *Tulsa Studies in Women's Literature* 5, no. 2 (Autumn 1986): 192.

78. Claudia L. Johnson, *Equivocal Beings: Politics, Gender, and Sentimentality in the 1790s: Wollstonecraft, Radcliffe, Burney, Austen* (Chicago: University of Chicago Press, 1995), 201.

79. Jane Austen, *Emma* (New York: Penguin Classics, 1985), 328, 131, 417.

80. Burney, *Evelina*, 260.

81. Burney, *Evelina*, 266.

82. Burney, *Evelina*, 290.

83. Adela Pinch, *Strange Fits of Passion* (Stanford, CA: Stanford University Press, 1996), 56–57.

84. Max Cavitch, "The Man That Was Used Up: Poetry, Particularity, and the Politics of Remembering George Washington," *American Literature* 75, no. 2 (July 3, 2003): 250.

85. Jerome J McGann, *The Poetics of Sensibility: A Revolution in Literary Style* (Oxford: Clarendon Press, 1996), 81.

86. Judith Pascoe, *Romantic Theatricality: Gender, Poetry, and Spectatorship* (Ithaca, NY: Cornell University Press, 1997), 3.

87. Pascoe, *Romantic Theatricality*, 69.

88. See Ashley Cross, "Coleridge and Robinson: Harping on Lyrical Exchange," in *Fellow Romantics: Male and Female British Writers, 1790–1835*, ed. Beth Lau (Farnham, England: Ashgate, 2009), 41; Pascoe, *Romantic Theatricality*, 87; Reggie Allen, "The Sonnets of William Hayley and Gift Exchange," *European Romantic Review* 13 (2002): 383–92.

89. McGann, *The Poetics of Sensibility*, 82.

90. Anna Matilda, "To Della Crusca: The Pen," *The New York Magazine, or Literary Repository*, May 1790, 306.

91. Lavinia, "Lines to the Village Lass," *Massachusetts Magazine*, May 1794.

92. David Paul Nord, "A Republican Literature: A Study of Magazine Reading and Readers in Late Eighteenth-Century New York," *American Quarterly* 40, no. 1 (March 1988): 42–64.

93. Katie Gray, " 'A Brilliant Assemblage of Both Sexes': Youthful Literary Society in the Early Republic" (presented at the Society for Historians of the Early American Republic, Springfield, Illinois, 2009); Knott, *Sensibility and the American Revolution*, 306.

94. Gray, " 'A Brilliant Assemblage of Both Sexes': Youthful Literary Society in the Early Republic"; Susan Branson, "Gendered Strategies for Success in the Early Nineteenth-Century Literary Marketplace: Mary Carr and the 'Ladies' Tea Tray," *Journal of American Studies* 40, no. 1 (2006): 35–51.

95. "To Henry," *The Intellectual Regale; Or, Ladies' Tea Tray*, October 28, 1815, 809.

96. Albert, "The Request: To Stella," *The Philadelphia Minerva*, March 5, 1796.

97. Joseph Allen Boone argues that "the novelistic tradition has served a powerfully conservative function, promoting exaggerated expectations of everlasting bliss that have enforced the subconscious acquiescence of many readers . . . to a limiting position within the social and marital order." See Boone, *Tradition Counter Tradition*, 2.

CHAPTER 3

1. John Paul Jones to the Comtesse of Lowendahl, July 14, 1780, *Papers of John Paul Jones, 1762–1788*, ed. James C. Bradford (Cambridge: Chadwyck-Healey, 1986).

2. These are indeed the same ways in which sexuality figures into modern-day heterosocial friendships; see J. Donald O'Meara, "Cross-Sex Friendship: Four Basic Challenges of an Ignored Relationship," *Sex Roles* 21, no. 7 (1989): 535.

3. On the linkage between romantic love and marriage in the late eighteenth century, see Ruth H. Bloch, "Changing Conceptions of Sexuality and Romance in Eighteenth-Century America," *The William and Mary Quarterly*, Third Series, 60, no. 1 (January 2003): 13–42.

4. Some of the literature on same-sex friendships and sexuality includes Alan Bray, *The Friend* (Chicago: University of Chicago Press, 2003); Caleb Crain, *American Sympathy: Men, Friendship, and Literature in the New Nation* (New Haven: Yale University Press, 2001); Marylynne Diggs, "Romantic Friends or a 'Different Race of Creatures'? The Representation of Lesbian Pathology in Nineteenth-Century America," *Feminist Studies* 21, no. 2 (Summer 1995): 317–40; Lillian Faderman, *Surpassing the Love of Men: Romantic Friendship and Love Between Women from the Renaissance to the Present* (New York: Morrow, 1981); Richard Godbeer, *The Overflowing of Friendship: Love Between Men and the Creation of the American Republic* (Baltimore: Johns Hopkins University Press, 2009); Sharon Marcus, *Between Women: Friendship, Desire, and Marriage in Victorian England* (Princeton,

NJ: Princeton University Press, 2007); Lisa Moore, "'Something More Tender Still than Friendship': Romantic Friendship in Early-Nineteenth-Century England," *Feminist Studies* 18, no. 3 (Autumn 1992): 499–520; Carroll Smith-Rosenberg, "The Female World of Love and Ritual: Relations between Women in Nineteenth-Century America," *Signs* 1, no. 1 (Autumn 1975): 1–29; Donald Yacovone, "Abolitionists and the 'Language of Fraternal Love,'" in *Meanings for Manhood: Constructions of Masculinity in Victorian America*, ed. Mark C. Carnes and Clyde Griffen (Chicago: University of Chicago Press, 1990).

5. This has been a particularly controversial issue for scholars in queer studies; see especially William Benemann, "A Bedpost (Is/Is Not) Only a Bedpost," *Reviews in American History* 37, no. 3 (2009): 338–44.

6. Laura M. Ahearn, *Invitations to Love: Literacy, Love Letters, and Social Change in Nepal* (Ann Arbor: University of Michigan Press, 2001), 52–53; Nicole Eustace, *Passion Is the Gale: Emotion, Power, and the Coming of the American Revolution* (Chapel Hill: Published for the Omohundro Institute of Early American History and Culture, Williamsburg, Virginia, by the University of North Carolina Press, 2008), 11; William M. Reddy, *The Navigation of Feeling: A Framework for the History of Emotions* (Cambridge: Cambridge University Press, 2001), 80.

7. Quoted in Lawrence Stone, *The Family, Sex and Marriage in England 1500–1800*, Abridged ed. (New York: Harper & Row, 1979), 191.

8. The term "structure of feeling" is a concept set out by Raymond Williams as the framework of language for expressing emotion. Raymond Williams, *Marxism and Literature* (Oxford: Oxford University Press, 1977), 128.

9. Laura Ahearn argues that in studying emotions we use what she calls a "practice theory of meaning constraint" and consider how available language "constrains the type and number of meanings that might emerge from an event." This theory builds on Raymond Williams's notion of structures of feeling, which includes the idea that there can be, as Ahearn puts it, "tension between the received interpretation and practical experience." Ahearn, *Invitations to Love*, 52, 56. On the way concepts constrain the possibilities we can imagine, see Ian Hacking, *Historical Ontology* (Cambridge, MA: Harvard University Press, 2004).

10. Phoebe Ellsworth, "Levels of Thoughts and Levels of Emotion" in *The Nature of Emotion: Fundamental Questions*, ed. Paul Ekman and Richard J. Davidson, 192–93, cited in Reddy, *The Navigation of Feeling*, xii. For more on the ways language influences feeling, see Ahearn, *Invitations to Love*, 48–52; Eustace, *Passion Is the Gale*, 12.

11. Lucia McMahon points out that "Friends, courting couples and married couples all employed similar standards and language to describe their most fulfillng relationships." Lucia F. McMahon, "'The Harmony of Social Life': Gender, Education, and Society in the Early Republic" (PhD diss., Rutgers, The State University of New Jersey, 2004), 15.

12. Claude Anne Lopez, *Mon Cher Papa: Franklin and the Ladies of Paris* (New Haven: Yale University Press, 1966), 32.

13. O'Meara, "Cross-Sex Friendship," 533.

14. Ellen K. Rothman, *Hands and Hearts: A History of Courtship in America* (New York: Basic Books, Inc., 1984), 36–37.

15. Megan Marshall, *The Peabody Sisters: Three Women Who Ignited American Romanticism* (Boston, MA: Houghton Mifflin, 2005), 252, 290. Marshall's description of the Peabody women's relationships throughout their lives is masterful; Elizabeth is the focus of the book, and she was friends with William Ellery Channing, Horace Mann, Nathaniel Hawthorne, Bronson Alcott, Ralph Waldo Emerson, and Theodore Parker. Mary Peabody and Horace Mann eventually married in 1843; the youngest Peabody sister, Sophia, married Elizabeth's friend and (likely romantic interest) Nathaniel Hawthorne in 1842.

16. Elizabeth Peabody to Mary Peabody, Saturday night [September 20] to Monday Morning [October 6, 1834], Elizabeth Palmer Peabody Collection, Berg Collection, New York Public Library.

17. Rachel Van Dyke, *To Read My Heart: The Journal of Rachel Van Dyke, 1810–1811*, ed. Lucia McMahon and Deborah Schriver (Philadelphia: University of Pennsylvania Press, 2000), 83–84.

18. Van Dyke, *To Read My Heart*, 197, 244.

19. Martha Tomhave Blauvelt, *The Work of the Heart: Young Women and Emotion, 1780–1830* (Charlottesville: University of Virginia Press, 2007), 8.

20. Marilyn J. Easton, ed., *Passionate Spinster: The Diary of Patty Rogers, 1785* (Exeter, NH: Exeter Historical Society, 2001), 82, 88, 103–04.

21. Isabelle de Montolieu, *Caroline of Lichtfield*, trans. Thomas Holcroft (New York: re-printed by J. S. Mott, for Evert Duyckinck & Co., 1798), 64, 72.

22. Charles Brockden Brown, *Wieland, Or, The Transformation: An American Tale, with Related Texts*, ed. Philip Barnard and Stephen Shapiro (Indianapolis, IN: Hackett Pub. Co., 2009), 66, 140.

23. Joseph Addison and Sir Richard Steele, *The Spectator* (Philadelphia: Printed by Tesson and Lee for Samuel F. Bradford and John Conrad, 1803), no. 380, p. 270.

24. O'Meara, "Cross-Sex Friendship," 534.

25. Thomas Jefferson to Maria Cosway, October 12, 1786, in Julian P. Boyd and Barbara Oberg, eds., *The Papers of Thomas Jefferson* (Princeton, NJ: Princeton University Press, 1950—), 10: 443–55. Jon Kukla devotes an excellent chapter to the relationship in Jon Kukla, *Mr. Jefferson's Women* (New York: Alfred A. Knopf, 2007).

26. For a range of opinions on this topic, see Helen Claire Duprey Bullock, *My Head and My Heart, a Little History of Thomas Jefferson and Maria Cosway*, (New York: G. P. Putnam's Sons, 1945); Andrew Burstein, "Life Follows My Pen: Jefferson, Letter-Writing and the Quest for Imaginative Friendship" (PhD diss., University of Virginia, 1994); John P. Kaminski, ed., *Jefferson in Love: The Love Letters*

Between Thomas Jefferson & Maria Cosway (Madison, WI: Madison House, 1999); Roger G. Kennedy, *Burr, Hamilton, and Jefferson: A Study in Character* (Oxford: Oxford University Press, 2000); Kukla, *Mr. Jefferson's Women*; Virginia Scharff, *The Women Jefferson Loved* (New York: Harper, 2010).

27. On the misplaced modern focus on sexuality and lack of attention to other possible configurations of intimacy, see Bray, *The Friend*, 6–7; Faderman, *Surpassing the Love of Men: Romantic Friendship and Love Between Women from the Renaissance to the Present*, 19; Godbeer, *The Overflowing of Friendship*, 3–7; Smith-Rosenberg, "The Female World of Love and Ritual," 8.

28. Kukla, *Mr. Jefferson's Women*, 102; Kaminski, *Jefferson in Love*, 38.

29. Amanda Foreman makes a similar point about the relationship between Georgiana, Duchess of Devonshire, and the British leader Charles Fox: "If Georgiana was having an affair with Fox [in 1783–1784], it was brief and insignificant compared to their profound friendship." Amanda Foreman, *Georgiana, Duchess of Devonshire* (New York: Random House, 1999), 127.

30. O'Meara, "Cross-Sex Friendship," 535.

31. James Lovell to Abigail Adams, January 13, 1780, in L. H. Butterfield, ed., *Adams Family Correspondence* (Cambridge, MA: Belknap Press of Harvard University Press, 1963), 3: 257.

32. Edith Gelles, "A Virtuous Affair: The Correspondence Between Abigail Adams and James Lovell," *American Quarterly* 39, no. 2 (Summer 1987): 252, 264.

33. Margaret Law Calcott, ed., *Mistress of Riversdale: The Plantation Letters of Rosalie Stier Calvert, 1795–1821* (Baltimore: Johns Hopkins University Press, 1991), 138, 165, 188–89.

34. Calvert wrote openly of her distress as she struggled through nine pregnancies and tried to find a means of birth control. As Susan Klepp has shown, women in this period often tried to limit family size through herbal remedies, periodic abstinence, and coitus interruptus, but the latter two required a husband's cooperation. George Calvert also fathered five children with one known slave mistress, and possibly more children with others. Calcott, *Mistress of Riversdale*, 233, 252–53, 379–81; Susan E. Klepp, *Revolutionary Conceptions: Women, Fertility, and Family Limitation in America, 1760–1820* (Chapel Hill: Published for the Omohundro Institute of Early American History and Culture, Williamsburg, Virginia, by the University of North Carolina Press, 2009), 178–214.

35. Rothman, *Hands and Hearts*, 54.

36. On the shifting ideas about sexual fulfillment and the state's role in policing sexuality, see Richard Godbeer, *Sexual Revolution in Early America* (Baltimore: Johns Hopkins University, 2004); Mark E. Kann, *Taming Passion for the Public Good: Policing Sex in the Early Republic* (New York: New York University Press, 2013). On sex outside of marriage, see Thomas Foster, "Reconsidering Libertines and Early Modern Heterosexuality: Sex and American Founder Gouverneur Morris," *Journal of the History of Sexuality* 22, no. 1 (January 2013); Clare A. Lyons,

Sex Among the Rabble: An Intimate History of Gender & Power in the Age of Revolution, Philadelphia, 1730–1830 (Chapel Hill: Published for the Omohundro Institute of Early American History and Culture, Williamsburg, Virginia, by the University of North Carolina Press, 2006).

37. Richard Beale Davis, ed., *Jeffersonian America: Notes on the United States of America, Collected in the Years 1805–6–7 and 11–12* (Westport, CT: Greenwood Press, 1980), 65.

38. Matthew Ridley to Catherine Livingston, September 22, 1786, Matthew Ridley Papers II, Massachussetts Historical Society.

39. "Love," *Hartford Gazette*, February 17, 1794.

40. Benedict Arnold to Margaret Shippen, April 28, 1778, in Lewis Burd Walker et al., "Life of Margaret Shippen, Wife of Benedict Arnold (continued)," *The Pennsylvania Magazine of History and Biography* 25, no. 1 (1901): 30–31.

41. On companionate marriage, see Nancy F. Cott, *Public Vows: A History of Marriage and the Nation* (Cambridge, MA: Harvard University Press, 2002); Anya Jabour, *Marriage in the Early Republic: Elizabeth and William Wirt and the Companionate Ideal* (Baltimore: Johns Hopkins University Press, 1998); Jan Lewis, "The Republican Wife: Virtue and Seduction in the Early Republic," *The William and Mary Quarterly* 44, no. 4 (October 1987): 689–721.

42. For more examples of this transition, see Jabour, *Marriage in the Early Republic*; Timothy Kenslea, *The Sedgwicks in Love: Courtship, Engagement, and Marriage in the Early Republic* (Boston, MA: Northeastern University Press, 2006); Lucia McMahon, *Mere Equals: The Paradox of Educated Women in the Early American Republic* (Ithaca, NY: Cornell University Press, 2012).

43. Judith Sargent Stevens to Maria Sargent, April 15, 1788, in Bonnie Hurd Smith, ed., *Letters of Loss and Love: Judith Sargent Murray Papers, Letter Book 3* (Massachusetts: Hurd Smith Communications: Judith Sargent Murray Society, 2009), 367–68.

44. Judith Sargent Stevens to Winthrop Sargent, April 18, 1788, in Murray, *Letters of Love and Loss*, 373.

45. Jean-Jacques Rousseau, *Eloisa: A Series of Letters* (London: John Harding, 1810), 3: 198; 2: 141.

46. Johann Wolfgang von Goethe, *The Sorrows and Sympathetic Attachments of Werter* (Philadelphia: Robert Bell, 1784), 108, 111.

47. "Charlotte's Sohlequy to the Manes of Werter," *The American Museum; Or, Repository of Ancient and Modern Fugitive Pieces &c*, February 1787; Laura, "On Reading the Sorrows of Werter," *The Universal Asylum and Columbian Magazine*, October 1790; "The Monitress," *The Emerald*, November 3, 1810; "Novels," *The Atheneum; Or, the Spirit of the English Magazines*, March 15, 1820.

48. "Sorrows of Werter," *Merrimack Magazine and Ladies' Literary Cabinet*, December 14, 1805. For a broader history of the reception of *Werter* in America and its influence on actual suicides, see Richard Bell, *We Shall Be No More: Suicide*

and Self-Government in the Newly United States (Cambridge, MA: Harvard University Press, 2012), 43–80.

49. For the concept of emotional labor, particularly in women, see Blauvelt, *The Work of the Heart*, 12.

50. Easton, *Passionate Spinster*, 58.

51. Ann (Ward) Radcliffe, *The Romance of the Forest* (Boston, MA: G. Clark, 1835), 135.

52. Elizabeth Ann Bayley Seton to Antonio Filicchi, April 20 & 30, 1805, in *Elizabeth Bayley Seton: Collected Writings, Vol. 1*, ed. Judith Metz and Regina Bechtle (Hyde Park: New City Press, 2003), 3: 358, 356.

53. Richard Brookhiser, *Gentleman Revolutionary: Gouverneur Morris, the Rake Who Wrote the Constitution* (New York: Free Press, 2003), 112. See also Foster, "Reconsidering Libertines and Early Modern Heterosexuality: Sex and American Founder Gouverneur Morris," 75, 81–82.

54. Blauvelt, *The Work of the Heart*, 84.

55. Dr. Gregory, *A Father's Legacy to His Daughters* (New York: T. Allen, 1793), 40.

56. "Breach of the marriage promise," *Hampden Patriot*, May 22, 1822.

57. Gregory, *A Father's Legacy to His Daughters*, 43.

58. Maria Edgeworth, *Belinda* (New York: Oxford World's Classics, 1999), 351.

59. Thomas Cogan, *A Philosophical Treatise on the Passions* (London: Printed and sold by S. Hazard, 1802), 151.

60. Mary Wollstonecraft, *A Vindication of the Rights of Woman*, ed. Sheila Rowbotham (London: Verso, 2010).

61. Easton, *Passionate Spinster*, 107.

62. Montolieu, *Caroline of Lichtfield*, 2: 138.

63. Edgeworth, *Belinda*, 78–79.

64. McMahon argues that "friendship and love existed along the same emotional continuum." McMahon, *Mere Equals*, 90.

65. Radcliffe, *The Romance of the Forest*, 135.

66. S. B., "Female Love Forsaken," *The New-York Packet*, December 9, 1790.

67. Karen Lystra, *Searching the Heart: Women, Men, and Romantic Love in Nineteenth-Century America* (New York: Oxford University Press, 1989), 9. On the negotiating power of emotional expressions, see Eustace, *Passion Is the Gale*, 13.

68. Robert Bage, *Hermsprong, Or, Man as He Is Not* (Peterborough, ON: Broadview Press, 2002), 329.

69. William W. Wilkins to Dolley Payne Todd Madison, [1794], in *The Dolley Madison Digital Edition*, ed. Holly C. Shulman (Charlottesville: University of Virginia Press, Rotunda, 2004—).

70. "golden, a." in *OED Online* (Oxford University Press, Second edition, 1989; online version September 2011), http://www.oed.com/view/Entry/79775.

71. Ferdinand Marie Bayard, *Travels of a Frenchman in Maryland and Virginia, with a Description of Philadelphia and Baltimore, in 1791: Or, Travels in the Interior of*

the United States, to Bath, Winchester, in the Valley of the Shenandoah, Etc., Etc., During the Summer of 1791 (Ann Arbor, MI: Edwards Brothers, 1950), 140.

72. Mary Wollstonecraft, *Thoughts on the Education of Daughters, with Reflections on Female Conduct in the More Important Duties of Life* (London: J. Johnson, 1787), 81.

73. G. J. Barker-Benfield, *The Culture of Sensibility: Sex and Society in Eighteenth-Century Britain* (Chicago: University of Chicago Press, 1992), 8, 295; Sarah Knott, *Sensibility and the American Revolution* (Chapel Hill: Published for the Omohundro Institute of Early American History and Culture, Williamsburg, Virginia, by the University of North Carolina Press, 2009), 78–79.

74. Cogan, *A Philosophical Treatise on the Passions*, 7.

75. On "extravagant" or "excessive" displays of feeling in novels of this era, see Adela Pinch, *Strange Fits of Passion* (Stanford, CA: Stanford University Press, 1996).

76. Rousseau, *Eloisa*, 1: 263.

77. Edgeworth, *Belinda*, 144.

78. Rogers, March 19, 1785, *Passionate Spinster*, 58.

79. Virginia Armentrout and James S. Armentrout Jr, eds., *The Diary of Harriet Manigault, 1813–1816* (Philadelphia: The Colonial Dames of America, 1976), 123.

80. Hendrik Hartog, *Man and Wife in America: A History* (Cambridge, MA: Harvard University Press, 2000), 137. The rewards for these cases could be massive, higher even than the net worth of the plaintiff and reaching up to £20,000. See Susan Staves, "Money for Honor: Damages for Criminal Conversation," *Studies in Eighteenth-Century Culture* 11 (1982): 279–97.

81. Lawrence Stone, *Road to Divorce: England 1530–1987* (Oxford: Oxford University Press, 1990), 231–300.

82. Benjmain Rush, "Directions for Conducting a News-Paper," *Weekly Museum*, May 14, 1791.

83. On the use of formulaic, sentimental narratives in such cases in the nineteenth century, see Laura Hanft Korobkin, *Criminal Conversations: Sentimentality and Nineteenth-Century Legal Stories of Adultery* (New York: Columbia University Press, 1998).

84. Pierre C. Van. Wyck, *Jeffers v. Tyson* (New York: Henry C. Southwick, 1808), 8.

85. Again, this was not properly a crim. con. trial but was included in a volume chronicling such trials. "The Trial of the Rev. Mr. James Altham . . . for Adultery, Defamation, and Obscenity 1785 (in Episcopal Court)," in *The Cuckold's Chronicle: Being Select Trials for Adultry [sic], Incest, Imbecility, Ravishment, &c.: Volume I* (Boston, 1798).

86. Andrew Ure, *Case of Divorce of Andrew Ure, M.D. v. Catharine Ure.* (Philadelphia: William Fry, 1821), 16.

87. Mason L. Weems, *God's Revenge Against Adultery, Awfully Exemplified in the Following Cases of American Crim. Con.*, third edition (Philadelphia: Printed for the author, 1818), 10.

88. Rev. Charles Massy, *A report of the trial on an action for damages, brought by the Reverend Charles Massy against the most noble, the Marquis of Headfort, for criminal conversation with plaintiff's wife: damages laid at £.40,000/taken in shorthand by an eminent Barrister* (New York: Printed for and sold by B. Dornin, and P. Byrne, Philadelphia, 1804), 30.

89. "Cadogan v. Cooper," *The Herald* (New York), December 24, 1794.

90. Gregory, *A Father's Legacy to His Daughters*, 39.

91. Wollstonecraft, *Thoughts on the Education of Daughters, with Reflections on Female Conduct in the More Important Duties of Life*, 88–89.

92. Edgeworth, *Belinda*, 144.

93. Eliza Wilkinson to Mary P., September 20, 1782, Eliza Wilkinson Papers, South Caroliniana Library, quoted in Lorri Glover, *All Our Relations: Blood Ties and Emotional Bonds Among the Early South Carolina Gentry* (Baltimore: Johns Hopkins University Press, 2000), 59.

94. Rodney Hessinger, *Seduced, Abandoned, and Reborn: Visions of Youth in Middle-Class America, 1780–1850* (Philadelphia: University of Pennsylvania Press, 2005), 42.

95. William Thompson, *Appeal of One Half the Human Race, Women* (New York: Ayer Publishing, 1970), 84.

96. Hartog, *Man and Wife in America*, 64.

97. Clare Lyons has found that in Philadelphia in the early republic, women most often brought adultery cases. Lyons, *Sex Among the Rabble*, 255.

98. Stone, *The Family, Sex and Marriage in England 1500–1800*, 316–17.

99. Wollstonecraft, *A Vindication of the Rights of Woman*, 186, 181.

100. Stone, *Road to Divorce*, 242.

101. Katherine Binhammer, "The Sex Panic of the 1790s," *Journal of the History of Sexuality* 6, no. 3 (January 1996): 421, 432–33; Lyons, *Sex Among the Rabble*.

102. Edith Gelles, "Gossip: An Eighteenth-Century Case," *Journal of Social History* 22, no. 4 (Summer 1989): 668.

103. Sheila L. Skemp, *First Lady of Letters: Judith Sargent Murray and the Struggle for Female Independence* (Philadelphia: University of Pennsylvania Press, 2009), 164; David S. Shields, *Civil Tongues & Polite Letters in British America* (Chapel Hill: Published for the Institute of Early American History and Culture, Williamsburg, Virginia, by the University of North Carolina Press, 1997), 144; Joanne B. Freeman, *Affairs of Honor: National Politics in the New Republic* (New Haven: Yale University Press, 2001), 77.

104. Cynthia A. Kierner, *Scandal at Bizarre: Rumor and Reputation in Jefferson's America* (New York: Palgrave Macmillan, 2004), 71.

105. Konstantin Dierks, *In My Power: Letter Writing and Communications in Early America* (Philadelphia: University of Pennsylvania Press, 2009), 174; Jay Fliegelman, *Declaring Independence: Jefferson, Natural Language & the Culture of Performance* (Stanford, CA: Stanford University Press, 1993), 59; Joanne B. Freeman,

"Slander, Poison, Whispers, and Fame: Jefferson's 'Anas' and Political Gossip in the Early Republic," *Journal of the Early Republic* 15, no. 1 (1995): 51.

106. Susan (Mansfield) Huntington, *Memoirs of the Late Mrs. Susan Huntington, of Boston, Mass*, ed. Benjamin Blydenburg Wisner, 3d ed (Boston, MA: Crocker and Brewster, 1829), 292.

107. Nelly Custis to Elizabeth Bordley, August 20, 1797, in David L. Ribblett, *Nelly Custis: Child of Mount Vernon* (Mount Vernon, VA: Mount Vernon Ladies Association, 1993), 40–41.

108. A search of the online database Early American Newspapers turned up more than 300 results in this period discussing the Eaton affair.

109. Peggy Eaton, *The Autobiography of Peggy Eaton* (New York: C. Scribner's Sons, 1932), 40.

110. For more on this scandal, see John F. Marszalek, *The Petticoat Affair: Manners, Mutiny, and Sex in Andrew Jackson's White House* (New York: Free Press, 1997).

111. Relationships discussed in this project in which boundaries and/or public perception were problematic include: Fielding Lucas and Eliza Slough; Margaret Bayard Smith and Anthony Bleecker; Benjamin Franklin and a number of female friends; Thomas Jefferson and Maria Cosway; Abigail Adams and James Lovell; Nelly Custis and George Washington Lafayette; Sarah Apthorp Morton and Gilbert Stuart; Anna Maria Coale and Samuel Ewing; Rebecca Gratz and John E. Hall; Elizabeth Bayley Seton and Antonio Filicchi; John Farmer and Lucy Spalding; Judith Sargent Stevens and John Murray; Patty Rogers and Samuel Tenney; Rachel Van Dyke and Ebenezer Grovesnor; Harry Sedgwick and the "Friendlies"; Rosalie Stier Calvert and Augustus John Foster; Annis Boudinot Stockton and Benjamin Young Prime; Nancy Shippen and Louis Otto; Elizabeth Kennon and the Mordecai brothers.

112. Deborah Norris to Sally Fisher, nd, in Sally Fisher Dawes, ed., "The Norris-Fisher Correspondence: A Circle of Friends, 1779–82," *Delaware History* 6 (1955): 215.

113. Lyons, *Sex Among the Rabble*, 288–89.

CHAPTER 4

1. William Ellery Channing to Eloise Payne, April 1809, William Ellery Channing Papers, Massachusetts Historical Society.

2. J. Donald O'Meara, "Cross-Sex Friendship: Four Basic Challenges of an Ignored Relationship," *Sex Roles* 21, no. 7 (1989): 537.

3. In his study of the challenges of heterosocial friendships, sociologist J. Donald O'Meara argues that men and women today have to employ strategies to show those around them that the relationship is not sexual. This observation, as well as many others by sociologists who have written on this topic, also held true for the Early Republic. O'Meara, "Cross-Sex Friendship," 530. For more on this point, see Chapter 2 on heterosocial friendship and sensibility literature.

4. Graham Allan argues that this is what cross-gender friends do today. Graham A. Allan, *Friendship: Developing a Sociological Perspective* (New York: Harvester Wheatsheaf, 1989), 83.

5. Pierre Bourdieu refers to such manuevers as "strategies." Pierre Bourdieu, *Outline of a Theory of Practice* (Cambridge: Cambridge University Press, 1977), 9–13; David Swartz, *Culture & Power: The Sociology of Pierre Bourdieu* (Chicago: University of Chicago Press, 1997), 98–100.

6. Carroll Smith-Rosenberg makes this point about pairs of female friends. Carroll Smith-Rosenberg, "The Female World of Love and Ritual: Relations between Women in Nineteenth-Century America," *Signs* 1, no. 1 (Autumn 1975): 11.

7. Sarah Knott, *Sensibility and the American Revolution* (Chapel Hill: Published for the Omohundro Institute of Early American History and Culture, Williamsburg, Virginia, by the University of North Carolina Press, 2009), e.g., 113, 259; Richard Godbeer, *The Overflowing of Friendship: Love Between Men and the Creation of the American Republic* (Baltimore: Johns Hopkins University Press, 2009), e.g., 9, 12, 157.

8. Lucia McMahon argues that because friendship and romantic love shared similar goals and language, they could both occur within heterosocial circles like salons. Lucia F. McMahon, "'The Harmony of Social Life': Gender, Education, and Society in the Early Republic" (PhD diss., Rutgers, The State University of New Jersey, 2004), 21, 167.

9. Lynne Templeton Brickley, "Sarah Pierce's Litchfield Female Academy, 1792–1833" (PhD diss., Harvard University, 1985); Charlene M. Boyer Lewis, *Ladies and Gentlemen on Display: Planter Society at the Virginia Springs, 1790–1860* (Charlottesville: University Press of Virginia, 2001).

10. For more on heterosociability and romance among young people, see Katherine Gray, "Mixed Company: Youth in Philadelphia, 1750–1815" (PhD diss., Johns Hopkins University, 2011).

11. C. Dallett Hemphill, *Bowing to Necessities: A History of Manners in America, 1620–1860* (New York: Oxford University Press, 2002), 109, 191. Novels and advice literature warned women that if a man and woman were alone, the man could take advantage of the woman. See, e.g., Hannah Webster Foster, *The Coquette*, ed. Cathy N. Davidson (New York: Oxford University Press, 1986).

12. Christine Stansell, *City of Women: Sex and Class in New York, 1789–1860* (New York: Knopf, 1986), 27.

13. For a good overview of British, French, and American salons, see Susan M. Stabile, "Salons and Power in the Era of the Revolution: From Literary Coteries to Epistolary Enlightenment," in *Benjamin Franklin and Women*, ed. Larry E. Tise (University Park: Pennsylvania State University Press, 2000), 129–48. On defusing sexual tensions among friends of the opposite sex within salon culture, see David S. Shields, *Civil Tongues & Polite Letters in British America* (Chapel Hill: Published for the Institute of Early American History and Culture, Williamsburg, Virginia, by the University of North Carolina Press, 1997), 45.

14. For a similar conclusion regarding French Enlightenment salons, see Dena Goodman, *The Republic of Letters: A Cultural History of the French Enlightenment* (Ithaca, NY: Cornell University Press, 1994), 83.

15. For a more in-depth discussion of Washington social life, see Cassandra Good, "Capital Manners: Etiquette, Politics, and Identity in Early Washington City" (MA Thesis, George Washington University, 2004).

16. Catherine O'Donnell Kaplan, *Men of Letters in the Early Republic: Cultivating Forums of Citizenship* (Chapel Hill: Published for the Omohundro Institute of Early American History and Culture, Williamsburg, Virginia, by the The University of North Carolina Press, 2008), 204.

17. O'Donnell, *Men of Letters*, 36.

18. Margaret Bayard to Samuel Harrison Smith, May 3, 1800, Papers of Margaret Bayard Smith, Library of Congress.

19. Bayard to Samuel Harrison Smith, May 3, 1800, Papers of Margaret Bayard Smith.

20. On the value of conversation for Bayard and her circle, see Fredrika Teute, "A 'Republic of Intellect': Conversation and Criticism among the Sexes in 1790s New York," in *Revising Charles Brockden Brown: Culture, Politics, and Sexuality in the Early Republic*, ed. Philip Barnard, Mark Kamrath, and Stephen Shapiro (Knoxville: University of Tennessee Press, 2004), 149–81.

21. Bryan Waterman, *Republic of Intellect: The Friendly Club of New York City and the Making of American Literature* (Baltimore: Johns Hopkins University Press, 2007), 136.

22. Rosemarie Zagarri, *A Woman's Dilemma: Mercy Otis Warren and the American Revolution* (Wheeling, IL: Harlan Davidson, 1995), 88–89.

23. Abigail Adams to Mercy Otis Warren, December 30, 1812; Warren to Adams, January 26, 1813, in Charles F. Adams, ed., *Correspondence Between John Adams and Mercy Warren*, Collections of the Massachusetts Historical Society; Ser. 5, v. 4. (New York: Arno Press, 1972), 502–03.

24. This is true in part because, as Lori Ginzburg argues, religious and sexual fidelity were connected, such that irreligion was linked with sexual deviance—and presumably the inverse was true as well. Lori Ginzberg, " 'The Hearts of Your Readers Will Shudder': Fanny Wright, Infidelity, and American Freethought," *American Quarterly* 46, no. 2 (June 1994): 216.

25. Godbeer, *The Overflowing of Friendship*, 84; Elizabeth Ann Bayley Seton, *Elizabeth Bayley Seton: Collected Writings*, ed. Judith Metz and Regina Bechtle (Hyde Park: New City Press, 2000), 325.

26. Rosemary Rader, *Breaking Boundaries: Male/Female Friendship in Early Christian Communities* (New York: Paulist Press, 1983), 4.

27. Godbeer, *The Overflowing of Friendship*, 63–66.

28. Godbeer, *Overflowing of Friendship*, 84; Christine Leigh Heyrman, *Southern Cross: The Beginnings of the Bible Belt* (New York: Knopf, 1997); Susan Juster,

Disorderly Women: Sexual Politics & Evangelicalism in Revolutionary New England (Ithaca, NY: Cornell University Press, 1994), 104; Cynthia Lynn Lyerly, "A Tale of Two Patriarchs; Or, How a Eunuch and a Wife Created a Family in the Church," *Journal of Family History* 28, no. 4 (October 2003): 503.

29. William Ellery Channing to Catharine Maria Sedgwick, January 11, 1827, William Ellery Channing Papers, Massachusetts Historical Society.

30. *Elizabeth Bayley Seton: Collected Writings*, ed. Regina M. Bechtle and Judith Metz (Hyde Park: New City Press, 2000-2002).

31. Sarah Hawkes and Richard Cecil, *Memoirs of Mrs. Hawkes, Including Remarks and Extracts From Sermons and Letters of R. Cecil* (London: Hatchard and Son, L. and G. Seeley; Nisbet and Co. Shaw, &c., 1838), 207, 274.

32. Bloch, "Changing Conceptions of Sexuality and Romance in Eighteenth-Century America," 30; Robert Kent Nelson, "Society of Souls: Spirit, Friendship, and the Antebellum Reform Imagination" (PhD diss., The College of William and Mary, 2006), 11.

33. Judith Sargent Murray to John Murray, November 14, 1774, in Bonnie Hurd Smith, ed., *Mingling Souls Upon Paper: An Eighteenth-Century Love Story* (Salem, MA: Judith Sargent Murray Society, 2007), 42.

34. Nancy Andrews album (RI, 1821), John Hay Library, Brown University.

35. Jerry William Frost, *The Quaker Family in Colonial America: A Portrait of the Society of Friends* (New York: St. Martin's Press, 1973), 14–15.

36. Helen Plant, "'Subjective Testimonies': Women Quaker Ministers and Spiritual Authority in England: 1750–1825," *Gender & History* 15, no. 2 (2003): 310. For broader accounts on female ministry, see Catherine A. Brekus, *Strangers & Pilgrims: Female Preaching in America, 1740–1845* (Chapel Hill: University of North Carolina Press, 1998); Rebecca Larson, *Daughters of Light: Quaker Women Preaching and Prophesying in the Colonies and Abroad, 1770–1775* (New York: Knopf, 1999); Phyllis Mack, *Visionary Women: Ecstatic Prophecy in Seventeenth-Century England* (Berkeley: University of California Press, 1992).

37. Rufus Matthew Jones, *The Later Periods of Quakerism* (London: Macmillan and Co., Limited, 1921), 1: 65–68.

38. John Dollin to Patience Greene Brayton, February 2, 1787, in *A Short Account of the Life and Religious Labours of Patience Brayton Late of Swansey, in the State of Massachusetts* (New Bedford [Mass.]: Printed by Abraham Shearman, June 1801), 120.

39. Thomas Ross to Rebecca Jones, January 25, 1785, in Rebecca Jones, *Memorials of Rebecca Jones* (Philadelphia: H. Longstreth, 1849), 94.

40. Esther Tuke to George Churchman, August 8, 1794, Emlen Family Papers, 1796–1866, Friends Historical Library, Swarthmore College.

41. Sarah Crabtree, "'A Beautiful and Practical Lesson of Jurisprudence': The Transatlantic Quaker Ministry in an Age of Revolution," *Radical History Review,*

no. 99 (Fall 2007): 51–79; Frost, *The Quaker Family in Colonial America: A Portrait of the Society of Friends*, 5. Crabtree calculates that there were seventy-six Quaker ministers who crossed the Atlantic between 1750 and 1820, thirty-six of whom were women. This total is in addition to the many more who traveled within America.

42. Amanda E. Herbert, "Companions in Preaching and Suffering: Itinerant Female Quakers in the Seventeenth- and Eighteenth-Century British Atlantic World," *Early American Studies* 9, no. 1 (2011): 103. While most secondary literature on female ministers discusses their having female companions, there is little attention to male friends who escorted these women.

43. Brayton, *A Short Account of the Life and Religious Labours of Patience Brayton Late of Swansey, in the State of Massachusetts*, 24, 46, 89, 94.

44. Elizabeth Foulke to William Jackson, August 15, 1798, Jackson-Conard Family Papers, 1748–1910, Friends Historical Library, Swarthmore College.

45. Jones, *Memorials of Rebecca Jones*, 350.

46. Phoebe Prior to William Jackson, July 7, 1787, Jackson-Conard Family Papers.

47. Anne Hart to John Stanford, March 12, 1810, Anne Hart/Reverend John Stanford Correspondence 1804–1811, New Jersey Historical Society.

48. Hawkes and Cecil, *Memoirs of Mrs. Hawkes, Including Remarks and Extracts From Sermons and Letters of R. Cecil*, 304.

49. Ann Douglas, *The Feminization of American Culture* (New York: Anchor Books, 1977).

50. Heyrman, *Southern Cross*, 169.

51. William Henry Channing, *The Life of William Ellery Channing*, 3rd ed. (Boston: American Unitarian Association, 1880), 659–60.

52. Isabella Graham and Divie Bethune, *The Power of Faith: Exemplified in the Life and Writings of the Late Mrs. Isabella Graham* (New York: American Tract Society, 1843), 93.

53. Hawkes and Cecil, *Memoirs of Mrs. Hawkes, Including Remarks and Extracts From Sermons and Letters of R. Cecil*, 38.

54. Graham and Bethune, *The Power of Faith*, 90.

55. Anne Hart to Reverend Stanford, March 12, 1810, Anne Hart/Reverend John Stanford Correspondence.

56. Sarah Wentworth Morton, *My Mind and Its Thoughts, in Sketches, Fragments, and Essays* (Delmar, NY: Scholars' Facsimiles & Reprints, 1975), 235.

57. Sarah Jones to Jeremiah Minter, January 25, 1790, *Devout letters, or, Letters spiritual and friendly*, ed. Jeremiah Minter (Alexandria: Samuel Snowden, 1804), 11.

58. Lyerly, "A Tale of Two Patriarchs; or, How a Eunuch and a Wife Created a Family in the Church." For a few examples of scandals with evangelical ministers in the 1830s, see Teresa Anne Murphy, *Ten hours' labor: religion, reform, and gender in early New England* (Ithaca: Cornell University Press, 1992), 97–100.

59. Heyrman, *Southern Cross*, 26.

60. Irene Quenzler Brown, "Death, Friendship, and Female Identity During New England's Second Great Awakening," *Journal of Family History* 12, no. 4 (October 1987): 370.

61. Jay Fliegelman, *Prodigals and Pilgrims* (Cambridge: Cambridge University Press, 1985); Jan Lewis, "The Republican Wife: Virtue and Seduction in the Early Republic," *The William and Mary Quarterly* 44, no. 4 (October 1987): 689–721.

62. Ivy Schweitzer, *Perfecting Friendship: Politics and Affiliation in Early American Literature* (Chapel Hill: University of North Carolina Press, 2006), 9; Godbeer, *The Overflowing of Friendship*, 82; Nancy F. Cott, *Public Vows: A History of Marriage and the Nation* (Cambridge, MA: Harvard University Press, 2002), 10.

63. This is a characterization of friendship in both this era and across time. See, e.g., Robert Brain, *Friends and Lovers* (New York: Basic Books, 1976); Richard Godbeer, *The Overflowing of Friendship: Love between Men and the Creation of the American Republic* (Baltimore: Johns Hopkins University Press, 2009); Horst Hutter, *Politics As Friendship: The Origins of Classical Notions of Politics in the Theory and Practice of Friendship* (Waterloo, ON: Wilfrid Laurier University Press, 1978); Sarah Knott, *Sensibility and the American Revolution* (Chapel Hill: University of North Carolina Press, 2009); Ivy Schweitzer, *Perfecting Friendship: Politics and Affiliation in Early American Literature* (Chapel Hill: University of North Carolina Press, 2006).

64. Glenn Hendler, *Public Sentiments: Structures of Feeling in Nineteenth-Century American Literature* (Chapel Hill: University of North Carolina Press, 2001), 125.

65. C. Dallett Hemphill, *Siblings: Brothers and Sisters in American History* (New York: Oxford University Press, 2011), 6.

66. Sarah Horowitz, "States of Intimacy: Friendship and the Remaking of French Political Elites, 1815–1848" (PhD diss., University of California at Berkeley, 2008), 139.

67. On the egalitarian nature of same and cross-sex sibling relationships, see Lorri Glover, *All Our Relations: Blood Ties and Emotional Bonds Among the Early South Carolina Gentry* (Baltimore: Johns Hopkins University Press, 2000), 61; Hemphill, *Siblings: Brothers and Sisters in American History*, 7, 26, 89, 124.

68. Hemphill, *Siblings: Brothers and Sisters in American History*, 74.

69. E. Anthony Rotundo, *American Manhood: Transformations in Masculinity from the Revolution to the Modern Era* (New York: Basic Books, 1993), 93.

70. Elizabeth Slough to Fielding Lucas, September 16, 1808, Fielding Lucas Collection, Maryland Historical Society.

71. Hemphill, *Siblings: Brothers and Sisters in American History*, 118–19.

72. Eloise Richards Payne to Catherine Maria Sedgwick, January 18, 1813, John Howard Payne Papers, Rare Book Library, Columbia University.

73. Nelly Custis to Elizabeth Bordley, August 20, 1797, in David L. Ribblett, *Nelly Custis: Child of Mount Vernon* (Mount Vernon, VA: Mount Vernon Ladies

Association, 1993), 40–41. Original letter in the collection of the Mount Vernon Ladies' Association.

74. Undated draft to Rev. John Henry Hobart from Seton, *Elizabeth Bayley Seton*, 1: 305.

75. Elizabeth Bayley Seton to Antonio Filicchi, April 6, 1805, *Elizabeth Bayley Seton*, 1: 351.

76. "LOVE and FRIENDSHIP Reconciled: A Colloquy: Occasioned by a Lady's Corresponding with a Gentleman, under a Seal Representative of Friendship," *The Boston Gazette, and the Country Journal*, June 6, 1785.

77. William W. Wilkins to Dolley Payne Todd Madison, [1794]; William W. Wilkins to Dolley Payne Todd Madison, August 22, 1794; in *The Dolley Madison Digital Edition*, ed. Holly C. Shulman (Charlottesville: University of Virginia Press, Rotunda, 2004).

78. Ribblett, *Nelly Custis: Child of Mount Vernon*, 70.

79. Lafayette to Custis, October 20, 1824; October 29, 1826; October 30, 1826. Eliza Custis-Lafayette Correspondence, 1778–1828, Maryland Historical Society.

80. Lafayette to Custis, August 28, 1828, Eliza Custis-Lafayette Correspondence, 1778–1828.

81. Patricia Brady, ed., *George Washington's Beautiful Nelly: The Letters of Eleanor Parke Custis Lewis to Elizabeth Bordley Gibson, 1794–1851* (Columbia: University of South Carolina Press, 1991), 166–67.

82. Claude Anne Lopez, *Mon Cher Papa: Franklin and the Ladies of Paris* (New Haven: Yale University Press, 1966), 243.

83. Jan Lewis, "Sex and the Married Man: Benjamin Franklin's Families," in *Benjamin Franklin and Women*, ed. Larry E. Tise (University Park: The Pennsylvania State University Press, 2000), 81, 72, 74.

84. Claude Anne Lopez, "Three Women, Three Styles: Catharine Ray, Polly Hewson, and Georgiana Shipley," in *Benjamin Franklin and Women*, ed. Larry E. Tise (University Park: Pennsylvania State University Press, 2000), 53.

85. Lewis, "Sex and the Married Man: Benjamin Franklin's Families," 75.

86. Lopez, *Mon Cher Papa: Franklin and the Ladies of Paris*, 40.

87. Brian Joseph Connolly, "'Every Family Become a School of Abominable Impurity': Incest and Theology in the Early Republic," *Journal of the Early Republic*, 30, no. 3 (Fall 2010): 413, 431–32.

88. Hendler, *Public Sentiments*.

89. Hendler, *Public Sentiments*, 125.

90. R. Claiborne to Marcia Burns, [1802], Van Ness Papers, Box 2, folder 1, New-York Historical Society.

91. R. Claiborne to [J. P.?] Van Ness, December 12, 1803, Van Ness Papers, Box 2, folder 1, New-York Historical Society.

92. Augustus Foster to his mother, July 3, 1805, Augustus John Foster Papers, Library of Congress; transcribed in Marilyn K. Parr, "Augustus John Foster and

the 'Washington Wilderness': Personal Letters of a British Diplomat" (PhD diss., George Washington University, 1987), 131.

93. Jane Minot to Harry Sedgwick, January 28, 1817, Sedgwick papers, Box 17, folder 21, Massachusetts Historical Society. On this social circle, see Timothy Kenslea, *The Sedgwicks in Love: Courtship, Engagement, and Marriage in the Early Republic* (Boston, MA: Northeastern University Press, 2006).

94. John Farmer to Isaac Spalding, May 5, 1828, in John Farmer Correspondence, New Hampshire Historical Society. I am indebted to Alea Henle for discovering and transcribing this correspondence.

95. Mary Telfair to Mary Few, January 14, [1814/1815?], in Betty Wood, *Mary Telfair to Mary Few: Selected Letters, 1802–1844* (Athens, GA: University of Georgia Press, 2007), 253.

96. William Thompson, *Appeal of One Half the Human Race, Women* (New York: Ayer Publishing, 1970), 84.

97. For a comparison between the rhetoric and reality of companionate marriage in this era, see Anya Jabour, *Marriage in the Early Republic: Elizabeth and William Wirt and the Companionate Ideal* (Baltimore: Johns Hopkins University Press, 1998); Lewis, "The Republican Wife." Also see Cott, *Public Vows*, 17.

98. Hendrik Hartog, *Man and Wife in America: A History* (Cambridge, MA: Harvard University Press, 2000), 98–109.

99. Thompson, *Appeal of One Half the Human Race, Women*, 83. See also Abbie L. Cory, "Wheeler and Thompson's Appeal: The Rhetorical Re-Visioning of Gender," *New Hibernia Review* 8, no. 2 (2004), 106–20.

100. Clare Midgley, "British Abolition and Feminism in Transatlantic Perspective," in *Women's Rights and Transatlantic Antislavery in the Era of Emancipation*, ed. Kathryn Kish Sklar and James Brewer Stewart (New Haven: Yale University Press, 2007), 127, 130.

101. William Godwin, *An Enquiry Concerning Political Justice: and its Influence on General Virtue and Happiness* (Dublin: Printed for Luke White, 1793), 381.

102. John Farmer to Lucy Spalding, March 19, 1829, John Farmer Correspondence.

103. Ethel Armes, ed., *Nancy Shippen, Her Journal Book; the International Romance of a Young Lady of Fashion of Colonial Philadelphia with Letters to Her and About Her* (New York: B. Blom, 1968), 145.

104. Armes, *Nancy Shippen, Her Journal Book,* 271.

105. This, indeed, is Richard Godbeer's argument, and he focuses almost exclusively on male friendships. Godbeer, *The Overflowing of Friendship*.

106. For a discussion of the changing roles and responsibilities of men who became husbands in early New England, see Anne S. Lombard, *Making Manhood: Growing up Male in Colonial New England* (Cambridge, MA: Harvard University Press, 2003), 98–119, 170. For a sociological perspective, particularly on how becoming a husband affects friendships, see Michael Monsour, *Women and Men*

as Friends: Relationships Across the Life Span in the 21st Century (Mahwah, NJ: L. Erlbaum, 2002), 9; Allan, *Friendship*, 41.

107. Benjamin Franklin to Catharine Ray, September 11, 1755, in Leonard W. Labaree et al., eds., *The Papers of Benjamin Franklin* (New Haven: Yale University Press, 1959—), 6: 184.

108. On single women in colonial and early national America, see Lee Chambers-Schiller, *Liberty, a Better Husband: Single Women in America: The Generations of 1780–1840* (New Haven: Yale University Press, 1984); Karin A. Wulf, *Not All Wives: Women of Colonial Philadelphia* (Ithaca: Cornell University Press, 2000).

109. For more on these relationships, see Chapter 6.

110. William Eustis to David Cobb, November 16, 1794, David Cobb Papers, microfilm reel 1, Massachusetts Historical Society, cited in Carrie Rebora Barratt and Ellen G. Miles, *Gilbert Stuart* (New York: Metropolitan Museum of Art, 2004), 293. Cobb was involved in Maine transactions, perhaps with Knox's family.

111. Eleanor Pearson DeLorme, "The Swan Commissions: Four Portraits by Gilbert Stuart," *Wintherthur Portfolio* 14, no. 4 (1979): 392–95.

112. Elizabeth and Jerome met and married after a short acquaintance in 1803. When Jerome returned to Europe to safeguard his political status with his brother in 1805, Napoleon had the marriage annulled and arranged for Jerome to marry Princess Catharine of Wurtenberg. Elizabeth struggled with the French government and Jerome to maintain custody and financial support for her son with Jerome, and she never remarried. There are two new biographies on Elizabeth; see Carol Berkin, *Wondrous Beauty: The Life and Adventures of Elizabeth Patterson Bonaparte* (New York: Knopf, 2014); Charlene M. Boyer Lewis, *Elizabeth Patterson Bonaparte: An American Aristocrat in the Early Republic* (Philadelphia: University of Pennsylvania Press, 2012). Also see Claude Bourguignon-Frasseto, *Betsy Bonaparte: The Belle of Baltimore* (Baltimore: Maryland Historical Society, 2003); Helen J. Burn, *Betsy Bonaparte* (Baltimore: Maryland Historical Society, 2010); Eugène Lemoine Didier, *The Life and Letters of Madame Bonaparte* (New York: C. Scribner's sons, 1879); Annie Middleton Leakin Sioussat, *Old Baltimore* (New York: The Macmillan Company, 1931), 160–205.

113. Elizabeth Patterson Bonaparte Papers, Maryland Historical Society. On her many male friends and admirers, see Lewis, *Elizabeth Patterson Bonaparte*, 127–32.

114. See Eliza Custis and David Bailie Warden, Custis-Lee Family Papers, 1700-Circa 1928 (bulk 1770–1870), Library of Congress.

115. See Anne M. Ousterhout, *The Most Learned Woman in America: A Life of Elizabeth Graeme Fergusson* (University Park: Pennsylvania State University Press, 2004).

116. Elizabeth Graeme Fergusson to Benjamin Rush, September 24, 1793, Benjamin Rush Papers, v. 40, p. 60, Library Company of Philadelphia.

117. Annis Boudinot Stockton, *Only for the Eye of a Friend: The Poems of Annis Boudinot Stockton*, ed. Carla Mulford (Charlottesville: University Press of Virginia, 1995), 26–27.

118. Lisa Wilson, *Life After Death: Widows in Pennsylvania, 1750–1850* (Philadelphia: Temple University Press, 1992), 5.

119. Kirsten E. Wood, *Masterful Women: Slaveholding Widows from the American Revolution Through the Civil War* (Chapel Hill: University of North Carolina Press, 2004), 93–94.

120. Scholars on women in the South during this period argue that women were more socially isolated there than in the North. See, e.g., Catherine Kerrison, *Claiming the Pen: Women and Intellectual Life in the Early American South* (Ithaca, NY: Cornell University Press, 2006), 182–83; Cynthia A. Kierner, *Beyond the Household: Women's Place in the Early South, 1700–1835* (Ithaca, NY: Cornell University Press, 1998), 6; Lewis, *Ladies and Gentlemen on Display*, 9, 123.

121. John Randolph to General Forman, April 2, 1816, "Letters of John Randolph, of Roanoke, to General Thomas Marsh Forman," *The Virginia Magazine of History and Biography* 49, no. 3 (July 1941): 206.

122. Delia Bryan to John Randolph, December 6, 1819, John Randolph Letters, p. 122, Virginia Historical Society.

123. Cynthia A. Kierner, *Scandal at Bizarre: Rumor and Reputation in Jefferson's America* (New York: Palgrave Macmillan, 2004), 92; E. F. Ellet, *The Court Circles of the Republic: Or, the Beauties and Celebrities of the Nation: Illustrating Life and Society Under Eighteen Presidents; Describing the Social Features of the Successive Administrations from Washington to Grant* (Philadelphia: Philadelphia Pub. Co, 1870), 78–79.

124. Randolph to Forman, February 13, 1826, "Letters of John Randolph, of Roanoke, to General Thomas Marsh Forman," 211.

125. Benjamin Franklin to Margaret Stevenson, January 25, 1779, in *Papers of Benjamin Franklin*, 28: 421.

126. Lopez, "Three Women, Three Styles: Catharine Ray, Polly Hewson, and Georgiana Shipley," 55.

127. Anne Plumptre, *Antoinette Percival. A Novel.: [Two Lines from Pope]* (Philadelphia: Mathew Carey, 1800), 39.

128. Erving Goffman, *Relations in Public: Microstudies of the Public Order* (New York: Basic Books, 1971), x.

CHAPTER 5

1. Ethel Armes, ed., *Nancy Shippen, Her Journal Book; the International Romance of a Young Lady of Fashion of Colonial Philadelphia with Letters to Her and About Her* (New York: B. Blom, 1968), 191.

2. E. H. Smith to Idea Strong, Late March 1796, in *The Diary of Elihu Hubbard Smith (1771–1798)*, in *Memoirs of the American Philosophical Society* v.95 (Philadelphia: American Philosophical Society, 1973), 147.

3. Konstantin Dierks, *In My Power: Letter Writing and Communications in Early America* (Philadelphia: University of Pennsylvania Press, 2009), 160.

4. On the materiality of letters, see William Merrill Decker, *Epistolary Practices: Letter Writing in America Before Telecommunications* (Chapel Hill: University of North Carolina Press, 1998), 37–47; Nigel Hall, "The Materiality of Letter Writing: A Nineteenth-Century Perspective," in *Letter Writing as a Social Practice*, ed. David Barton and Nigel Hall (Philadelphia: John Benjamins, 2000), 83–108.

5. I take the theoretical lens here of Michel de Certeau, *The Practice of Everyday Life*, trans. Steven Rendall (Berkeley: University of California Press, 1984).

6. See e.g., Michael O'Brien, *Conjectures of Order: Intellectual Life and the American South, 1810–1860*, (Chapel Hill: University of North Carolina Press, 2004), 1: 441; Barbara Maria Zaczek, *Censored Sentiments: Letters and Censorship in Epistolary Novels and Conduct Material* (Newark: University of Delaware Press, 1997), 23.

7. Eve Tavor Bannet, *Empire of Letters: Letter Manuals and Transatlantic Correspondence, 1688–1820* (Cambridge: Cambridge University Press, 2005), 259.

8. Elizabeth Slough to Fielding Lucas, June 1, 1807, Fielding Lucas Collection, Maryland Historical Society.

9. Decker, *Epistolary Practices*, 46; Dena Goodman, *Becoming a Woman in the Age of Letters* (Ithaca: Cornell University Press, 2009), 157–94; Susan M. Stabile, *Memory's Daughters: The Material Culture of Remembrance in Eighteenth-Century America* (Ithaca: Cornell University Press, 2004), 84–87.

10. Benjamin Franklin to Catharine Ray, March–April 1755, in Leonard W. Labaree et al., eds., *The Papers of Benjamin Franklin* (New Haven: Yale University Press, 1959), 5: 536–37.

11. On the expansion of letter writing in the eighteenth century, see Dierks, *In My Power*.

12. Abigail Adams to James Lovell, February 13, 1780, in L. H. Butterfield, ed., *Adams Family Correspondence* (Cambridge, MA: Belknap Press of Harvard University Press, 1963), 3: 274.

13. Dierks, *In My Power*, 150.

14. H. Dilworth, *The Complete Letter Writer, Or, Young Secretary's Instructor: Containing a Great Variety of Letters on Friendship, Duty, Love, Marriage, Amusement, Business, &c. to Which Is Prefixed, Plain Instructions for Writing Letters on All Occasions by H. Dilworth* (New Haven: Sidney's Press, for Increase Cooke, 1809), introduction.

15. Dierks, *In My Power*, 142–77; Karen Lystra, *Searching the Heart: Women, Men, and Romantic Love in Nineteenth Century America* (New York: Oxford University Press, 1989), 124.

16. Lystra, *Searching the Heart*, 14.

17. *The Complete American Letter-Writer: Containing Letters on Trade & Merchandize Also Letters on Familiar & Interesting Subjects* (Ostego, NY: Printed by H. & E. Phinney, Jun., 1808), 95.

18. Elizabeth Frank, *Classical English Letter-Writer, Or, Epistolary Selections Designed to Improve Young Persons in the Art of Letter-Writing and in the Principles of Virtue and Piety by the Author of Lessons for Young Persons in Humble Life* (Philadelphia: Caleb Richardson, 1816), 97.

19. Richard Bushman, *The Refinement of America* (New York: Vintage Books, 1993), 288–89.

20. Hannah Webster Foster, *The Coquette*, ed. Cathy N. Davidson (New York: Oxford University Press, 1986), 47.

21. On the convention of same-sex friends' use of emotional and even romantic language in letters, see Dierks, *In My Power*, 168–70; Anya Jabour, "Male Friendship and Masculinity in the Early National South: William Wirt and His Friends," *Journal of the Early Republic* 20, no. 1 (Spring 2000): 91–92.

22. Daniel Webster to James Bingham, December 28, 1800, quoted in Richard Godbeer, *The Overflowing of Friendship: Love between Men and the Creation of the American Republic* (Baltimore: Johns Hopkins University Press, 2009), 50.

23. William Wirt to Dabney Carr, December 18, 1811, quoted in Jabour, "Male Friendship and Masculinity in the Early National South: William Wirt and His Friends," 93.

24. Eliza Schlatter to Sophie DuPont, August 24, 1834, quoted in Carroll Smith-Rosenberg, "The Female World of Love and Ritual: Relations between Women in Nineteenth-Century America," *Signs* 1, no. 1 (Autumn 1975): 26.

25. Elihu Hubbard Smith to Sally Pierce, June 9, 1797, in *The Diary of Elihu Hubbard Smith* (1771–1798), 324.

26. Lystra, *Searching the Heart*, 19–20.

27. I base this generalization upon the approximately eighty manuscript collections and published volumes of letters I examined.

28. Bannet, *Empire of Letters*, 66.

29. John Rodgers to Ann Pinkney, c. 1803, Rodgers Family Papers, Library of Congress.

30. He refers here to Elizabeth's friend, the famous British author Lady Sydney Morgan.

31. Horace Holley to Elizabeth Patterson Bonaparte, April 2, 1818, Box 4, Elizabeth Patterson Bonaparte Papers, Maryland Historical Society.

32. On their meeting during his travels in Baltimore, see Charlene M. Boyer Lewis, *Elizabeth Patterson Bonaparte: An American Aristocrat in the Early Republic* (Philadelphia: University of Pennsylvania Press, 2012), 47–49.

33. Simon Le Blanc, *Report of a Cause Between Joseph Foster, Plaintiff, against Miss Esther Mellish, Defendant, for a Breach of Promise of Marriage; Tried in the Court*

of King's Bench, at Westminster, on Tuesday the 23d Feb. 1802 (London: Printed for J. Ridgway, No. 1, York Street, St. James's Square, 1802), 7–8.

34. James Lovell to Abigail Adams, July 16, 1779, in Butterfield, *Adams Family Correspondence*, 3: 212.

35. *Elizabeth Bayley Seton: Collected Writings*, ed. Judith Metz and Regina Bechtle (Hyde Park: New City Press, 2000).

36. Bryan Waterman, "Coquetry and Correspondence in Revolutionary-Era Connecticut: Reading Elizabeth Whitman's Letters," *Early American Literature* 46, no. 3 (2011): 541–63.

37. I see this accretion of cultural norms through practice via the lens of Bourdieu. See Pierre Bourdieu, *Outline of a Theory of Practice* (Cambridge: Cambridge University Press, 1977).

38. Samuel Ewing to Mary Abigail Willing Coale, August 1, 1803, Coale Collection in Redwood Collection, Maryland Historical Society.

39. Matthew Ridley to Catherine Livingston, March 26, 1783, Box 2, Matthew Ridley Papers II, Massachusetts Historical Society.

40. Morton to Joseph Dennie, March 27, 1797, in Emily Pendleton, *Philenia: The Life and Works of Sarah Wentworth Morton, 1759–1846* (Orono, Maine: Printed at the University Press, 1931), 74.

41. R. Claiborne to Major J. P. Van Ness, July 26, 1802[?], Van Ness Papers 1743–1951, New-York Historical Society.

42. Aaron Burr to Mrs. Gordon, March 11, 1809, in *The Private Journal of Aaron Burr, During His Residence of Four Years in Europe; with Selections from His Correspondence* (New York: Harper & Brothers, 1838), 133.

43. John Farmer to Isaac Spalding, May 5, 1828, John Farmer Correspondence, New Hampshire Historical Society.

44. John Farmer to Lucy Spalding, March 19, 1829, John Farmer Correspondence.

45. John Farmer to Lucy Spalding, September 5, 1836, John Farmer Correspondence.

46. John Farmer to Lucy and Isaac Spalding, October 12, 1829, John Farmer Correspondence.

47. John Farmer to Lucy and Isaac Spalding, October 12, 1829, John Farmer Correspondence.

48. Elizabeth Powel to Bushrod Washington, January 1, 1785, Papers of George Washington, Mount Vernon Ladies Association.

49. Elizabeth Powel to Bushrod Washington, June 22, 1785, Series III, Box 2, Powel Family Papers, Historical Society of Pennsylvania. Powel wrote Bushrod's mother Hannah a long letter in 1783 reporting on him and describing him as a "most amiable youth." Elizabeth Powel to Hannah Bushrod Washington, April 17, 1783, Papers of George Washington, Mount Vernon Ladies Association.

50. Elizabeth Powel to Bushrod Washington, June 22, 1785, Series III, Box 2, Powel Family Papers, Historical Society of Pennsylvania.

51. Elizabeth Powel to Bushrod Washington, April 4, 1789, Papers of George Washington, Mount Vernon Ladies Association. Bushrod's uncle, George Washington, signed his letters to Powel in quite warm terms, e.g., "I am always Yours." George Washington to Elizabeth Powel, December 4, 1798, in *Papers of George Washington: Retirement Series* (Charlottesville: University Press of Virginia, 1999), 3: 244.

52. Bushrod Washington to [Nancy Shippen], April 28, 1784, Shippen Family Papers, 1671–1936, Library of Congress.

53. Samuel Ewing to Mary Abigail Willing Coale, August 1, 1803, Coale Collection in Redwood Collection, Maryland Historical Society.

54. Watson probably means "platonism," referring to platonic love.

55. John Watson to Susan Livingston Ridley Sedgwick, January 26, 1805, Box 2, Folder 8, Watson Family Papers, The Joseph Downs Collection of Manuscripts and Printed Ephemera, The Winterthur Library. Thanks to Whitney Martinko for finding this letter.

56. Dianne Ashton, *Rebecca Gratz: Women and Judaism in Antebellum America* (Detroit: Wayne State University Press, 1997), 81–82. Note that John Hall was in fact Samuel Ewing's nephew, although close to Samuel's age.

57. J[ohn] E. H[all] to Rebecca Gratz, December 3, 1806, folder 31–1, Gratz Family Papers, American Philosophical Society.

58. Bannet, *Empire of Letters*, 44, 46; Bruce Redford, *The Converse of the Pen: Acts of Intimacy in the Eighteenth-Century Familiar Letter* (Chicago: University of Chicago Press, 1986), 1–4.

59. Redford, *The Converse of the Pen*, 1. Redford's entire book is based upon this notion.

60. John E. Hall to Rebecca Gratz, May 8, 1807, folder 29–4, Gratz Family Papers, American Philosophical Society.

61. Elihu Hubbard Smith to Idea Strong, Late March 1796, in *The Diary of Elihu Hubbard Smith (1771–1798)*, in *Memoirs of the American Philosophical Society* v.95 (Philadelphia: American Philosophical Society, 1973), 147.

62. Bannet, *Empire of Letters*, 68.

63. Samuel Ewing to Mary Abigail Willing Coale, August 1, 1803, Coale Collection in Redwood Collection, Maryland Historical Society.

64. Abigail Adams to James Lovell, September 3, 1780, in Butterfield, *Adams Family Correspondence*, 3: 408.

65. Maria Cosway to Thomas Jefferson, July 15, 1788, in Julian P. Boyd and Barbara Oberg, eds., *The Papers of Thomas Jefferson* (Princeton: Princeton University Press, 1950—), 13: 360.

66. Decker, *Epistolary Practices*, 51.

67. Bannet, *Empire of Letters*, 60.

68. Elizabeth Graham Fergusson to Benjamin Rush, undated poem, Papers of Benjamin Rush, 40:12, Library Company of Philadelphia.

69. Pierre Bourdieu, *Practical Reason: On the Theory of Action*, trans. Randall Johnson (Stanford: Stanford University Press, 1998), 94, 102.

70. Goodman, *Becoming a Woman in the Age of Letters*, 3.

CHAPTER 6

1. Marcel Mauss, *The Gift: The Form and Reason for Exchange in Archaic Societies* (New York: W. W. Norton & Company, 2000), 14. Mauss published the pioneering anthropological study on gift-giving in French in 1924, spawning a considerable body of theory on the topic. An excellent compilation of important modern commentaries on Mauss's theory as well as an extensive bibliography is Alan D. Schrift, *The Logic of the Gift: Toward an Ethic of Generosity* (New York: Routledge, 1997). My own interpretations have been influenced by Pierre Bourdieu's *Practical Reason: On the Theory of Action*, trans. Randall Johnson (Stanford: Stanford University Press, 1998). Historians of early America who write about gift exchange generally focus on the importance of the practice in Native American communities, particularly in terms of diplomatic relations with local imperial powers. See e.g., David Murray, *Indian Giving: Economies of Power in Indian-White Exchanges* (Amherst: University of Massachusetts Press, 2000).

2. Pierre Bourdieu, *Practical Reason: On the Theory of Action*, trans. Randall Johnson (Palo Alto: Stanford University Press, 1998), 94; Alan Bray, *The Friend* (Chicago: University of Chicago Press, 2003), 150.

3. Judith Sargent Murray to John Murray, July 9, 1784, in Bonnie Hurd Smith, ed., *Mingling Souls Upon Paper: An Eighteenth-Century Love Story* (Salem, MA: Judith Sargent Murray Society, 2007).

4. As Leora Auslander writes, "Objects take on meanings, and their capacity to effect historical change, through social relations. Objects are dreamed of, invented, produced, sold, bought, used, and destroyed by people. People are both free and constrained in their intervention into the lives of these objects." Leora Auslander, *Cultural Revolutions: Everyday Life and Politics in Britain, North America, and France* (Berkeley: University of California Press, 2009), 14.

5. *The Complete American Letter-Writer: Containing Letters on Trade & Merchandize Also Letters on Familiar & Interesting Subjects* (Ostego, NY: Printed by H. & E. Phinney, Jun., 1808), 91–94.

6. Jonathan Richardson, "An Essay on the Theory of Painting," in *The Works of Jonathan Richardson* (Whitehall: T. and J. Egerton, 1972), 10.

7. Marcia R. Pointon, *Hanging the Head: Portraiture and Social Formation in Eighteenth-Century England* (New Haven: Published for the Paul Mellon Centre for Studies in British Art by Yale University Press, 1993), 143.

8. Marcia R. Pointon, *Strategies for Showing: Women, Possession, and Representation in English Visual Culture, 1665–1800* (Oxford: Oxford University Press, 1997), 205.

9. Shearer West, *Portraiture* (Oxford: Oxford University Press, 2004), 60.

10. Mauss, *The Gift*, 46.

11. Ellen G. Miles, telephone interview, February 3, 2010. Miles, one of the foremost experts on early American portraiture, sees Benjamin Franklin as perhaps the only exception here.

12. Ellen G. Miles, "'I Have Resolved to Sit No More;' Washington and Artists' Ambitions, 1776–1800" (presented at the Initiatives in Art and Culture: Celebrity in American Art, 1790–Present, New-York Historical Society, 2009), 10.

13. Charles Coleman Sellers, *Benjamin Franklin in Portraiture* (New Haven: Yale University Press, 1962), 35.

14. Georgiana Shipley to Benjamin Franklin, May 1, 1779, February 3, 1780, in Barbara Oberg et al., eds., *The Papers of Benjamin Franklin* (New Haven: Yale University Press, 1959), 29: 408; 31: 444–45.

15. Miles, "'I Have Resolved to Sit No More;' Washington and Artists' Ambitions, 1776–1800," 3.

16. Ellen G. Miles, *George and Martha Washington: Portraits from the Presidential Years* (Washington, DC: Smithsonian Institution, National Portrait Gallery, 1999), 19–20; Miles, "'I Have Resolved to Sit No More;' Washington and Artists' Ambitions, 1776–1800."

17. Miles, "'I Have Resolved to Sit No More;' Washington and Artists' Ambitions, 1776–1800," 3. Miles argues that if Washington commissioned the portrait, it shows us how he would have wanted himself to be portrayed.

18. On Trumbull's portraits of Jefferson, see Gaye Wilson, "'Behold me at length on the vaunted scene of Europe:' Thomas Jefferson and the Creation of an American Image Abroad" in *Old World, New World: America and Europe in the Age of Jefferson*, ed. Leonard Sadosky, Peter Nicolaisen, Peter S. Onuf, and Andrew J. O'Shaughnessy (Charlottesville: University of Virginia Press, 2010).

19. Trumbull to Jefferson, March 6, 1788; Cosway to Jefferson, March 7, 1788; Church to Jefferson, July 21, 1788, in Julian P. Boyd and Barbara Oberg, eds., *The Papers of Thomas Jefferson* (Princeton: Princeton University Press, 1950—), 12: 647, 645; 13: 391. Jefferson never appears to have said anything to Trumbull about whether to make the paintings for the women, so it is likely the women paid for the portraits or Trumbull painted them as a gift.

20. Elizabeth Cometti, "Maria Cosway's Rediscovered Miniature of Jefferson," William and Mary Quarterly 9 (April 1952), 152–155.

21. Miles, interview. The provenance records at MFA show it as being owned first by Stuart and then by Morton's granddaughter. Miles says there is insufficient evidence to determine for whom this portrait was created.

22. Paul S. Harris, "Gilbert Stuart and a Portrait of Mrs. Sarah Apthorp Morton," *Winterthur Portfolio* I (1964): 216. This portrait is now owned by the Winterthur Museum.

23. A pentimento is a sign of an earlier form that has been painted over but still shows faintly.

24. Curatorial discussion notes, Worcester Art Museum, http://www.worcesterart. org/Collection/Early_American/Artists/stuart/sarah/painting.html.

25. Published in Samuel Saunter, "The American Lounger No. LXIV," *The Port-Folio*, June 18, 1803. "Samuel Saunter" was Morton's friend, the writer Joseph Dennie, according to the Worcester Art Museum essay.

26. Eleanor Pearson DeLorme, "The Swan Commissions: Four Portraits by Gilbert Stuart," *Wintherthur Portfolio* 14, no. 4 (1979): 361, 368.

27. Carrie Rebora Barratt and Ellen G. Miles, *Gilbert Stuart* (New York: Metropolitan Museum of Art, 2004), 293.

28. Barratt and Miles, *Gilbert Stuart*, 293.

29. Robin Jaffee Frank, *Love and Loss: American Portrait and Mourning Miniatures* (New Haven: Yale University Art Gallery, 2000), 34. No scholarship about exchange of miniatures between cross-sex friends exists outside of work on individual examples, and thus the conclusion here is my own. I am indebted to art historian Ann Verplanck for her advice in writing about miniatures.

30. Benjamin Franklin to Jane Mecom, October 25, 1779, in *Papers of Benjamin Franklin*, 30: 583.

31. Jean-Jacques Rousseau, Eloisa: *A Series of Letters* (London: John Harding, 1810), 12–13.

32. Charles Willson Peale to Rembrandt Peale, July 23, 1820, quoted in Anne Sue Hirshorn, "Legacy of Ivory: Anna Claypoole Peale's Portrait Miniatures," *Bulletin of the Detriot Institute of Arts* 64, no. 4 (1989): 25.

33. Quoted in Evan Thomas, *John Paul Jones: Sailor, Hero, Father of the American Navy* (New York: Simon & Schuster, 2003), 220–21.

34. M. Mac Dermot Crawford, *The Sailor Whom England Feared: Being the Story of John Paul Jones, Scotch Naval Adventurer and Admiral in the American and Russian Fleets* (London: E. Nash, 1913), 106; Samuel Eliot Morison, *John Paul Jones: A Sailor's Biography*, 333–339.

35. John Paul Jones to Comtesse de Lowendahl, June 7, 1780, Letter 1100 in *Papers of John Paul Jones*, 1762–1788, ed. James C. Bradford (Cambridge: Chadwyck-Healey, 1986).

36. John Paul Jones to Comtesse de Lowendahl, July 14, 1780, Letter 1155, *Papers of John Paul Jones*.

37. Chris Packard, "Self-Fashioning in Sarah Goodridge's Self-Portraits," Common-Place 4, no. 1 (October 2003), http://www.common-place.org/vol-04/no-01/lessons/.

38. Frank Goodyear, "Reclaiming the Female Nude: Sarah Goodridge's 'Beauty Revealed'" (unpublished seminar paper, University of Texas at Austin, 1995), 8. Many thanks to Goodyear for bringing this portrait to my attention at the very beginning of this project.

39. Pointon, *Strategies for Showing*, 205. Pointon argues that for a man to own a portrait of his wife was to doubly show his ownership of her body.

40. Samuel Hopkins Adams, *The Godlike Daniel* (New York: Sears Publishing Company, Inc., 1930), 160.

41. Adams, *The Godlike Daniel*, 160.

42. Goodyear, "Reclaiming the Female Nude: Sarah Goodridge's 'Beauty Revealed,'" 5.

43. Anne Ayer Verplanck, "Facing Philadelphia: The Social Functions of Silhouettes, Miniatures, and Daguerreotypes, 1760–1860" (PhD diss., The College of William and Mary, 1996), 4, 71–83.

44. Advertisement in the *Aurora*, Dec. 28, 1802, cited in Anne Ayer Verplanck, "Facing Philadelphia: The Social Functions of Silhouettes, Miniatures, and Daguerreotypes, 1760–1860" (PhD diss., The College of William and Mary, 1996), 88.

45. John Quincy Adams diary, March 4, 1829, Adams Family Papers, Massachusetts Historical Society.

46. Mary E. Roberdeau autograph album, Historical Society of Pennsylvania.

47. Helen Sheumaker, *Love Entwined: The Curious History of Hairwork in America* (Philadelphia: University of Pennsylvania Press, 2007), vii, 29.

48. The best example of uses of hair of the deceased in jewelry are at the Winterthur Museum and Library; for an album example, see Mary Mansfield Peck Album, Litchfield Female Academy Collection, Litchfield Historical Society.

49. Marquis de Lafayette to Eliza Custis, October 20, 1824, Eliza Custis-Lafayette Correspondence, 1778–1828, Maryland Historical Society.

50. Eleanor Parke Custis Lewis to Elizabeth Bordley, November 24, 1824, *George Washington's Beautiful Nelly the Letters of Eleanor Parke Custis Lewis to Elizabeth Bordley Gibson, 1794–1851*, ed. Patricia Brady (Columbia, SC: University of South Carolina Press, 1991).

51. Margaret Cockburn Conkling, *Memoirs of the Mother and Wife of Washington* (Auburn, NY: Derby, Miller, and Company, 1850), 158.

52. The first two pieces are at the Mount Vernon Ladies' Association; the third is at Winterthur Museum and Library. Thanks to Laura Simo for providing curatorial information on the Mount Vernon pieces.

53. Abigail Adams to Mercy Otis Warren, December 30, 1812; Mercy Otis Warren to Abigail Adams, January 26, 1813, in Charles F. Adams, ed., *Correspondence Between John Adams and Mercy Warren*, Collections of the Massachusetts Historical Society; Ser. 5, v. 4. (New York: Arno Press, 1972), 502–03.

54. John Swanwick, *Poems on Several Occasions* (Philadelphia: F. and R. Bailey, 1797), 37.

55. John Quincy Adams to Mary Roberdeau, October 23, 1832, Adams Family Papers, Massachusetts Historical Society.

56. Martha Washington to David Humphreys, June 26, 1797, in George Washington Family Letters, Library of Congress.

57. The desk was once part of the Edmund Law Rogers Smith collection and was sold to a collector in Alabama. It remains in private hands and was featured on the PBS show "Antiques Roadshow" on May 26, 2007. See http://www.pbs.org/wgbh/roadshow/tg/lapdesk.html.

58. David S. Shields, *Civil Tongues & Polite Letters in British America* (Chapel Hill: Published for the Institute of Early American History and Culture, Williamsburg, Virginia, by the University of North Carolina Press, 1997), xxvii.

59. For studies of exchanges of poetry among groups of friends in this era, see Reggie Allen, "The Sonnets of William Hayley and Gift Exchange," *European Romantic Review* 13 (2002): 383–92; Mark Schoenfield, "Private Souvenirs: Exchanges among Byron's Southwell Set," *Wordsworth Circle* 39, no. Winter–Spring (2008): 30–34; Lauren Wallis, " 'To Form a New World, New Systems Create': Margaret Lowther Page's Poetic Revisions of Women's Roles in the Early Republic" (MA Thesis, University of North Carolina at Greensboro, 2010).

60. Annis Boudinot Stockton, *Only for the Eye of a Friend: The Poems of Annis Boudinot Stockton*, ed. Carla Mulford (Charlottesville: University Press of Virginia, 1995), 119.

61. George Washington to Annis Boudinot Stockton, September 2, 1783, in *The Writings of George Washington from the Original Manuscript Sources, 1745–1799*, ed. John C. Fitzpatrick. Online edition, Library of Congress.

62. Stockton, *Only for the Eye of a Friend*, 144; George Washington to Annis Boudinot Stockton, August 31, 1788, in W. W. Abbot et al., eds., *The Papers of George Washington: Confederation Series* (Charlottesville: University of Virginia Press, 1992), 6: 496–98.

63. Elizabeth Graeme Fergusson Papers, Library Company of Philadelphia; *Papers of George Washington*, Presidential Series, 12: 239–242.

64. Elizabeth Graham Fergusson to Benjamin Rush, undated poem, Papers of Benjamin Rush, 40:12, Library Company of Philadelphia.

65. Swanwick, *Poems on Several Occasions*.

66. Roland M. Baumann, "John Swanwick: Spokesman for 'Merchant-Republicanism' in Philadelphia, 1790–1798," *The Pennsylvania Magazine of History and Biography* 97, no. 2 (April 1, 1973): 139–40; James Carey, *He Wou'd Be a Poet; Or, "Nature Will Be Nature Still." An Heroic Poem: To Which Is Annexed a Thanksgiving Epistle on Electioneering Success. By Geoffry Touchstone* (Philadelphia: Printed for the author, 1796).

67. Robert Gilmor, "To Miss Patterson on her birthday the 6 February 1802," Box 9, Elizabeth Patterson Bonaparte Papers, Maryland Historical Society.

68. W. K. McNeil, "The Autograph Album Custom: A Tradition and Its Scholarly Treatment," *Keystone Folklore Quarterly*, Spring 1968, 29.

69. See, e.g., Caroline M. Northam Album (Newport, RI, 1819); Bathsheba Barton album (Weston, MA., 1818); Caroline's album (Providence, RI, 1809), in John Hay Library, Brown University.

70. The few works of scholarship on friendship albums treat them as part of women's domestic culture; see Erica R. Armstrong, "A Mental and Moral Feast: Reading, Writing, and Sentimentality in Black Philadelphia," *Journal of Women's History* 16, no. 1 (2004): 78–102; Todd Steven Gernes, "Recasting the Culture of Ephemera: Young Women's Literary Culture in Nineteenth-Century America" (PhD diss., Brown University, 1992); Anya Jabour, "Albums of Affection: Female Friendship and Coming of Age in Antebellum Virginia," *Virginia Magazine of History and Biography* 107, no. 2 (1999): 125–58.

71. Philo P., "Ladies department," *Christian Secretary*, March 17, 1827.

72. "Definition of a Ladies' Album," *Boston Medical Intelligencer*, January 9, 1827.

73. P., "Ladies Department."

74. Adela Pinch makes a similar argument about the poet Charlotte Smith's poetry, which Pinch sees as a combination of the personal and the conventional, just as greeting cards are. Certain poetry, Pinch argues, can be simultaneously personal and conventional. Adela Pinch, *Strange Fits of Passion* (Stanford: Stanford University Press, 1996), 69.

75. Israel Izzard, "Original Communications: Crumbs of Advice for the Ladies," *The New—England Galaxy and United States Literary Advertiser*, September 2, 1825.

76. P., "Ladies Department."

77. Susan M. Stabile, *Memory's Daughters: The Material Culture of Remembrance in Eighteenth-Century America* (Ithaca: Cornell University Press, 2004), 82–85.

78. The original source for this poem is Mary Balfour, *Hope, a Poetical Essay; with Various Other Poems* (Belfast: Smyth and Lyons, 1810).

79. Armstrong, "A Mental and Moral Feast," 83, 85.

80. Elizabeth Dodge Album, 1824–1837, New Jersey Historical Society.

81. This vision of womanhood is similar to the "cult of true womanhood" that Barbara Welter identified as beginning in the 1820s. Barbara Welter, "The Cult of True Womanhood: 1820–1860," *American Quarterly* 18, no. 2, part 1 (Summer 1966): 151–74.

82. P., "Ladies Department."

83. "The Confessions of an Album Writer," *The Ladies Garland*, September 29, 1827.

84. For a short biography of LeVert, see the Alabama Women's Hall of Fame, http://www.awhf.org/levert.html.

85. "Octavia Walton Le Vert Album," Edgar Allan Poe papers, 1827–1908, Rare Book & Manuscript Library, Columbia University.

86. "Remember Me," *The New-York Mirror: A Weekly Gazette of Literature and the Fine Arts*, May 27, 1826.

87. Mary E. Roberdeau autograph album, Historical Society of Pennsylvania.

88. Nancy Andrews album (RI, 1821), John Hay Library, Brown University.

89. Malcolm, "Lines Written in a Lady's Album," *The New-York Mirror*, March 31, 1827.

90. Mary Mansfield Peck Album, Litchfield Female Academy Collection, Litchfield Historical Society. For biographical information on Litchfield residents, see the Litchfield Ledger at http://www.litchfieldhistoricalsociety.org/ledger.

91. See Loyd Haberly, *Pursuit of the Horizon: A Life of George Catlin Painted & Recorder of the American Indian* (New York: The Macmillan Company, 1948), 21, 81; Edward Deering Mansfield, *Personal Memories, Social, Political, and Literary: With Sketches of Many Noted People, 1803–1843* (R. Clarke & co., 1879), 129–30.

92. Edward Deering Mansfield, Personal Memories, Social, Political, and Literary: With Sketches of Many Noted People, 1803–1843 (R. Clarke & co., 1879), 130.

93. Benita Eisler, *Byron: Child of Passion, Fool of Fame* (New York: Vintage Books, 2000), 255; George Gordon Byron, "Mediterranean Poems," ed. Peter Cochran, 12, http://petercochran.files.wordpress.com/2009/03/mediterranean_poems.pdf.

94. Parthenon, "Ladies' Albums," *The Escritoir; Or, Masonic and Miscellaneous Album*, December 16, 1826.

CHAPTER 7

1. There are no comprehensive studies documenting the extent of political office-holding by elite men in this period, but several factors suggest why so many men held political office at various points in their careers. First, very few men were career politicians at this time, with many spending several years serving in state or national office before returning to their work as lawyers, doctors, and so on. Second, a pre-Revolution sense of duty on the part of the wealthy to serve their communities (and in turn, further their own property interests) persisted in this period. Finally, offices became available rather frequently as a result of short-term service; for example, some nine hundred men served in Congress from 1790–1830. On the first two points here, see Alan Taylor, "From Fathers to Friends of the People: Political Personas in the Early Republic," *Journal of the Early Republic* 11, no. 4 (Winter 1991): 465–91. On the final point, see James Sterling Young, *The Washington Community, 1800–1828* (New York: Columbia University Press, 1966), 67–69, 88; Rosemarie Zagarri, "The Family Factor: Congressmen, Turn-over, and the Burden of Public Service in the Early American Republic," *Journal of the Early Republic* 33, no. 2 (n.d.): 286.

2. While this era had what is called the "first party system," institutionalized political parties did not come into being until the late 1820s with the second party system. See Ronald P. Formisano, "Deferential-Participant Politics: The Early Republic's Political Culture, 1789–1840," *American Political Science Review* 68, no. 2 (June 1974): 473–87; Joanne B. Freeman, *Affairs of Honor: National Politics in the New Republic* (New Haven: Yale University Press, 2001), 8.

3. Barbara G. Carson, *Ambitious Appetites: Dining, Behavior, and Patterns of Consumption in Federal Washington* (Washington, D.C.: AIA Press, 1990), 4.

4. Freeman, *Affairs of Honor*, 53.

5. Much of the debate over the public/private spheres paradigm has been fostered by readings of Jurgen Habermas's *The Structural Transformation of the Public Sphere*, published in 1962 but not translated into English until 1989. His usage of the term "public sphere" is often conflated with the public sphere of the public/private spheres paradigm, but this is an inaccurate application of his terminology. Habermas identifies an inauthentic public sphere; an intimate, private sphere; and an authentic public sphere of private individuals in the middle. I agree with many gender scholars that Habermas's terminology (which does not consider gender and is ahistorical) is not constructive for current scholarship (see, e.g.,

Dena Goodman, "Public Sphere and Private Life: Toward a Synthesis of Current Historiographical Approaches to the Old Regime," *History and Theory* 31, No. 1 (February 1992), 1–20). On the inapplicability of the separate spheres paradigm for the early republic, see Linda K. Kerber et al., "Beyond Roles, Beyond Spheres: Thinking about Gender in the Early Republic," *The William and Mary Quarterly*, Third Series, 46, no. 3 (July 1989): 565–85; Linda K. Kerber, "Separate Spheres, Female Worlds, Woman's Place: The Rhetoric of Women's History," *The Journal of American History* 75, no. 1 (June 1988): 9–39; Carol Lasser, "Beyond Separate Spheres: The Power of Public Opinion," *Journal of the Early Republic* 21, no. 1 (Spring 2001): 115–23. Several scholars have also explained the lack of separate spheres and the heterosocial nature of Washington City; see Catherine Allgor, *Parlor Politics: In Which the Ladies of Washington Help Build a City and a Government* (Charlottesville: University Press of Virginia, 2000); Jan Lewis, "Politics and the Ambivalence of the Private Sphere: Women in Early Washington, D.C.," and Fredrika Teute, "Roman Matron on the Banks of Tiber Creek: Margaret Bayard Smith and the Politicization of Spheres in the Nation's Capital," in *A Republic for the Ages: The United States Capitol and the Political Culture of the Early Republic*, ed. Kenneth Bowling (Charlottesville: Published for the United States Capitol Historical Society by the University of Virginia Press, 1999). My understanding of social life in Washington is expanded upon in Cassandra Good, "Capital Manners: Etiquette, Politics, and Identity in Early Washington City" (MA Thesis, George Washington University, 2004).

6. Margaret Bayard Smith to Mrs. Kirkpatrick, Washington, March 13, 1814, in Margaret Bayard Smith, *The First Forty Years of Washington Society, Portrayed by the Family Letters of Mrs. Samuel Harrison Smith (Margaret Bayard) from the Collection of Her Grandson, J. Henley Smith*, ed. Gaillard Hunt (New York: C. Scribner's Sons, 1906), 95–96.

7. Frances Eleanor Trollope, *Domestic Manners of the Americans*, ed. Donald Smalley (New York: Alfred A. Knopf, 1949), 230.

8. Judith Page Rives to Dolley Payne Madison, Washington, January 26, 1829, David B. Mattern and Holly C. Shulman, eds., *The Selected Letters of Dolley Payne Madison* (Charlottesville: University of Virginia Press, 2003), 276.

9. Smith, *The First Forty Years of Washington Society, Portrayed by the Family Letters of Mrs. Samuel Harrison Smith (Margaret Bayard) from the Collection of Her Grandson, J. Henley Smith*, 148–49.

10. Judith S. Graham et al., eds., *Diary and Autobiographical Writings of Louisa Catherine Adams* (Cambridge, MA: The Belknap Press of Harvard University Press, 2013), 2: 459.

11. Abigail Adams to Elizabeth Smith Shaw Peabody, February 12, 1796, cited in Woody Holton, *Abigail Adams* (New York: Free Press, 2009), 293.

12. Graham et al., *Diary and Autobiographical Writings of Louisa Catherine Adams*, 2: 659.

13. Elizabeth Powel to Bushrod Washington, June 22, 1785, Series III, Box 2, Powel Family Papers, Historical Society of Pennsylvania. Powel is referring in particular to cultivating the friendship of Bushrod's uncle, George Washington, who was a close friend of Powel's.

14. George Washington to Annis Boudinot Stockton, August 31, 1788, *George Washington Papers: Confederation Series*, 6: 497.

15. John Adams to James Warren, September 26, 1775; to Mercy Otis Warren, April 16, 1776, *Papers of John Adams*, 3: 168, 4: 123–25.

16. This is a term that was both used at the time and historiographically in Rosemarie Zagarri, *Revolutionary Backlash: Women and Politics in the Early American Republic* (Philadelphia: University of Pennsylvania Press, 2007), 5.

17. Linda K. Kerber, *Women of the Republic: Intellect and Ideology in Revolutionary America* (New York: Norton, 1986), 80.

18. Louisa Catherine Adams to Joseph Hopkinson, January 5, 1823, Hopkinson Family Papers, volume 12, Historical Society of Pennsylvania.

19. Dolley Madison to Thomas Parke, February 10, 1807, in *The Dolley Madison Digital Edition*, ed. Holly C. Shulman (Charlottesville: University of Virginia Press, Rotunda, 2004–).

20. "Strictures on Female Education," *The Columbian Magazine; Comprehending Ecclesiastical History, Morality, Religion, and Other Useful and Interesting Matter* 1, no. 5 (August 1806): 179; "Observations on Female Politicians," *Philadelphia Repository and Weekly Register* 1, no. 2 (November 22, 1800): 4; "Remarks on Female Politicians," *The Monthly Magazine, and American Review* 3, no. 6 (December 1800): 416.

21. Brown here echoes his narrator in his story *Alcuin*, which he had probably written in 1796 or 1797. Alcuin asks a woman what party she was in and she, like Smith, responds that it was foolish to ask a woman such a question. The piece continues on with a discussion of women's exclusion from politics, although scholars have debated what Brown's personal opinion on the subject was. See Charles Brockden Brown, *Alcuin: A Dialogue*, ed. Cynthia A. Kierner (New York: Rowman & Littlefield, 1995), 31–32.

22. My interpretation differs from the authors of two recent books on Jefferson's relationships with women; see Jon Kukla, *Mr. Jefferson's Women* (New York: Alfred A. Knopf, 2007); Virginia Scharff, *The Women Jefferson Loved* (New York: Harper, 2010).

23. Thomas Jefferson to Anne Willing Bingham, May 11, 1788, *Papers of Thomas Jefferson*, 13: 151–52.

24. On Jefferson's reliance on female friends, particularly Church, for a refuge from politics, see Jan Lewis, "'Those Scenes for Which Alone My Heart Was Made': Affection and Politics in the Age of Jefferson and Hamilton," in *An Emotional History of the United States*, ed. Jan Lewis and Peter N. Stearns (New York: New York University Press, 1998).

25. Elaine Chalus, *Elite Women in English Political Life, C.1754–1790* (Oxford: Oxford University Press, 2005); Judith Schneid Lewis, *Sacred to Female*

Patriotism: Gender, Class, and Politics in Late Georgian Britain (New York: Routledge, 2003).

26. Dena Goodman, *The Republic of Letters: A Cultural History of the French Enlightenment* (Ithaca: Cornell University Press, 1994); Steven D. Kale, *French Salons: High Society and Political Sociability from the Old Regime to the Revolution of 1848* (Baltimore: Johns Hopkins University Press, 2004); Joan B. Landes, *Women and the Public Sphere in the Age of the French Revolution* (Ithaca: Cornell University Press, 1988).

27. William Seward, *Anecdotes of Some Distinguished Persons: Chiefly of the Present and Two Preceding Centuries* (London: T. Cadell Jun. and W. Davies, 1795), 3: 345.

28. On how Jefferson in particular formed his views on women's political participation in response to his experiences in France, see Brian Steele, "Thomas Jefferson's Gender Frontier," *Journal of American History* 95, no. 1 (June 2008): 17–42.

29. Mercy Otis Warren to Catharine Macaulay, December 1774 in Kate Davies, *Catharine Macaulay and Mercy Otis Warren: The Revolutionary Atlantic and the Politics of Gender* (Oxford: Oxford University Press, 2005), 1.

30. John Adams to James Warren, June 25, 1774; James and Mercy Otis Warren to John Adams, July 14, 1774, *Papers of John Adams*, 2: 99–100, 106–09.

31. On Trist's friendship with Jefferson and her expression of political opinions to him, see Cynthia A. Kierner, *Martha Jefferson Randolph, Daughter of Monticello: Her Life and Times* (Chapel Hill: University of North Carolina Press, 2012), 41–43, 112.

32. Elizabeth House Trist to Thomas Jefferson, March 1, 180[1], *Papers of Thomas Jefferson*, 33: 115.

33. See, e.g., Nancy Isenberg, *Fallen Founder: The Life of Aaron Burr* (New York: Penguin, 2007), 267–365; Andro Linklater, *An Artist in Treason: The Extraordinary Double Life of General James Wilkinson* (New York: Walker Publishing Company, 2010); Buckner F. Melton, *Aaron Burr: Conspiracy to Treason* (New York: John Wiley & Sons, 2001).

34. Elizabeth House Trist to Thomas Jefferson, October 27, 1807, Nicholas P. Trist Papers, Southern Historical Collection.

35. "Strictures on Female Education."

36. Zagarri, *Revolutionary Backlash*, 113.

37. Hannah Mather Crocker, *Observations on the Real Rights of Women with Their Appropriate Duties: Agreeable to Scripture, Reason and Common Sense* (Boston: Printed for the author, 1818), 15–16.

38. Pierre-Joseph Boudier de Villemert, *The Friend of Women*, trans. Alexander Morrice (Philadelphia: John Conrad & Company, 1803), 21–22, 35.

39. Jane Mansbridge, "Reconstructing Democracy," in *Revisioning the Political: Feminist Reconstructions of Traditional Concepts in Western Political Theory*, ed. Nancy J. Hirschmann and Christine Di Stefano, (Boulder, CO: Westview Press, 1996), 118.

40. Eliza Lea album, Library Company of Philadelphia.

41. Abigail Adams to John Adams, May 7, 1776, L. H. Butterfield, ed., *Adams Family Correspondence* (Cambridge: Belknap Press of Harvard University Press, 1963), 1: 403.

42. Abigail Adams to Elbridge Gerry, July 20, 1781; Gerry to Adams, July 30, 1781, *Adams Family Correspondence*, 4: 183–84, 189–90.

43. Elizabeth Powel to George Washington, November 17, 1792, *Papers of George Washington*, Presidential Series, 11: 395–97.

44. "Conversations with the President," February 7, 1793, in *Miscellany*, ed. Merill D. Peterson.

45. Allgor, *Parlor Politics*, 128–44.

46. Allgor, *Parlor Politics*, 128–30; Gordon S. Wood, *The Radicalism of the American Revolution* (New York: Random House, 1992), 174–75

47. Lewis, *Sacred to Female Patriotism*, 66–68, 82–86.

48. Allgor, *Parlor Politics*, 128–37.

49. Lovell to John Adams, April 12, 1789, Adams Papers, Massachusetts Historical Society; Lovell to Abigail Adams, April 12, 1789; Abigail Adams to John Adams; to Lovell, April 22, 1789, *Adams Family Correspondence*, 8: 331, 333, 335.

50. Elizabeth House Trist to Thomas Jefferson, March 6, 1802, *Papers of Thomas Jefferson*, 37: 17.

51. Catharine Greene to Alexander Hamilton, May 30, 1790, in Harold C. Syrett et al., eds., *Papers of Alexander Hamilton* (New York: Columbia University Press, 1961–987), 6: 448.

52. Anthony Morris to Dolley Madison, July 20, 1812, in *The Dolley Madison Digital Edition*.

53. Phoebe Pemberton Morris to Dolley Madison, March 7, 1814, in *The Dolley Madison Digital Edition*.

54. Alexander Hamilton to Angelica Schuyler Church, January 31, 1791, *Papers of Alexander Hamilton*, 7: 608. My interpretation here differs from Jan Lewis's argument that Hamilton and Jefferson's denials of patronage requests to Angelica Schuyler Church meant these men would not recognize the power of women to obtain offices for friends and family. Lewis believes that this implied that "Friendship was divested of its instrumental, political dimension." However, the continuing usage of patronage to fill offices in this period suggests that politicians simply decided on a case-by-case basis when to grant requests. See Lewis, " 'Those Scenes for Which Alone My Heart Was Made': Affection and Politics in the Age of Jefferson and Hamilton," 60–61.

55. John Adams to Mercy Otis Warren, May 29, 1789, in Charles F. Adams, ed., *Correspondence Between John Adams and Mercy Warren*, Collections of the Massachusetts Historical Society; Ser. 5, v. 4. (New York: Arno Press, 1972), 314.

56. Rosemarie Zagarri, *A Woman's Dilemma: Mercy Otis Warren and the American Revolution* (Wheeling, IL: Harlan Davidson, 1995), 126.

57. See, e.g., Susan Dunn, *Jefferson's Second Revolution: The Election Crisis of 1800 and the Triumph of Republicanism* (New York: Houghton Mifflin Harcourt, 2004), 246; Gaillard Hunt, "Office-Seeking During Jefferson's Administration," *American Historical Review* 3, no. 2 (1898): 270–91; Leonard White, *The Jeffersonians: A Story in Administrative History, 1801–1829* (New York: The Macmillan Company, 1951), 347–67.

58. John Randolph to James Monroe, December 5, 1806, in Daniel Preston and Cassandra Good, eds., *The Papers of James Monroe: Selected Correspondence and Papers, 1803–1811* (New York: ABC-CLIO, 2014), 5: 549.

59. Richard R. John, "Affairs of Office: The Executive Departments, the Election of 1828, and the Making of the Democratic Party," in *The Democratic Experiment: New Directions in American Political History*, ed. Meg Jacobs, William J. Novak, and Julian Zelizer (Princeton, NJ: Princeton University Press, 2003), 50–84; Young, *The Washington Community, 1800–1828*, 174–76, 194–95.

60. Catherine Allgor, "Federal Patronage in the Early Republic: The Role of Women in Washington, D.C.," in *Establishing Congress: The Removal to Washington, D.C., and the Election of 1800*, ed. Donald R. Kennon and Kenneth R. Bowling (Athens: Ohio University Press, 2005), 104.

61. Allgor, *Parlor Politics*, 144.

62. Eleanor Parke Custis Lewis to Elizabeth Bordley, November 24, 1824; December 22, 1824, *George Washington's Beautiful Nelly: The Letters of Eleanor Parke Custis Lewis to Elizabeth Bordley Gibson, 1794–1851*, ed. Patricia Brady (Columbia: University of South Carolina Press, 1991), 157, 159.

63. Elizabeth House Trist to Thomas Jefferson, August 13, 1802; October 24, 1801; *Papers of Thomas Jefferson*, 35: 82, 499–500.

64. Elizabeth House Trist to Thomas Jefferson, March 6, 1802; Jefferson to Trist, March 20, 1802; *Papers of Thomas Jefferson*, 37: 16–18, 98–99.

65. Edgar Stanton Maclay, ed., *Journal of William Maclay, United States Senator from Pennsylvania, 1789–1791* (New York: D. A. Appleton and Company, 1890), 299–300.

66. *Journal of William Maclay*, 74.

67. George Logan to Deborah Norris Logan, July 26 & 28, 1798, Logan Papers, 7: 34–35, Historical Society of Pennsylvania.

68. Susan Branson, *These Fiery Frenchified Dames: Women and Political Culture in Early National Philadelphia* (Philadelphia: University of Pennsylvania Press, 2001), 91–95.

69. Joel Barlow to Dolley Madison, December 21, 1811, in *The Dolley Madison Digital Edition*.

70. Joseph Hopkinson to Louisa Catherine Adams, January 1, 1823, in Charles F. Adams, *Memoirs of John Quincy Adams, Comprising Portions of His Diary from*

1795 to 1848 (Philadelphia: J. B. Lippincott Company, 1874), 6: 130–32. The document John Quincy Adams wrote in response is published in this volume, pages 132–37.

71. Edith Belle Gelles, *Abigail & John: Portrait of a Marriage* (New York: Harper Collins, 2009), 244.

72. Abigail Adams to Elbridge Gerry, June 6, 1797; Gerry to Adams, July 14, 1797, Adams Papers, Massachusetts Historical Society.

73. Burr to Mrs.—, April 25, 1809, in Aaron Burr, *The Private Journal of Aaron Burr, During His Residence of Four Years in Europe; with Selections from His Correspondence* (New York: Harper & Brothers, 1838), 212.

74. Eliza Parke Custis Law to David Bailie Warden, November 7, 1814, Custis-Lee Papers, Library of Congress.

75. Edith Gelles, "A Virtuous Affair: The Correspondence Between Abigail Adams and James Lovell," *American Quarterly* 39, no. 2 (Summer 1987): 257.

76. Abigail Adams to James Lovell, December 13, 1779; Abigail Adams to James Lovell; January 4, 1779, in Butterfield, ed., *Adams Family Correspondence*, 3: 249, 147–48.

77. Alexander Hamilton to Catherine Livingston, April 11, 1777, May 1777, *Papers of Alexander Hamilton*, 1: 225–27, 258–60.

78. Samuel Southard to Margaret Bayard Smith, February 9, 1823, Margaret Bayard Smith Papers, Library of Congress.

79. Margaret Bayard Smith to Mrs. Kirkpatrick, March 12, 1825, in Smith, *The First Forty Years of Washington Society*, 203.

80. Katherine Binhammer, "The Sex Panic of the 1790s," *Journal of the History of Sexuality* 6, no. 3 (January 1996): 409–34; Zagarri, *Revolutionary Backlash*, 111–13.

81. John Randolph to James Monroe, September 16, 1806, in *Papers of James Monroe*, 5: 532.

82. Irving Brant, *James Madison* (New York: Bobbs-Merrill, 1956), 4: 243, 6: 244.

83. Richard Alsop, *The Political Green-House, for the Year 1798. Addressed to the Readers of the Connecticut Courant, January 1st, 1799.* (Hartford, CT: Hudson & Goodwin, 1799); Branson, *These Fiery Frenchified Dames*, 91–95.

84. Deborah Norris Logan, "Transaction's on the Farm & memoranda of various matters commencing June 12th 1798 . . . ," 23, in Logan Papers, v. 62, Historical Society of Pennsylvania.

85. John Murdock, *The Politicians; Or, A State of Things.* (Philadelphia: Printed for the author, 1798).

86. John F. Marszalek, *The Petticoat Affair: Manners, Mutiny, and Sex in Andrew Jackson's White House* (New York: Free Press, 1997). Also see Allgor, *Parlor Politics*, 190-238.

87. Margaret O. Eaton, *The Autobiography of Peggy Eaton* (New York: Ayer Co. Pub., 1980), 47, 124.

88. *New York Enquirer*, March 13, 1829, quoted in Marszalek, *The Petticoat Affair*.

89. *The Farmer's Cabinet* (Amherst, NH), July 9, 1831.

90. Dorothy Emmet, "The Concept of Power: The Presidential Address," *Proceedings of the Aristotelian Society*, New Series, 54 (1953-1954): 10.

91. Emmet, "The Concept of Power," 9–10. Emmet draws here on Mary Parker Follett's 1934 posthumous collection of papers, *Dynamic Administration*.

92. Mansbridge, "Reconstructing Democracy," 118.

AFTERWORD

1. Thomas Jefferson to Angelica Schuyler Church, August 17, 1788, Julian P. Boyd and Barbara Oberg, eds., *The Papers of Thomas Jefferson* (Princeton, NJ: Princeton University Press, 1950—), 13: 520–521.

2. Catherine Allgor, *Parlor Politics: In Which the Ladies of Washington Help Build a City and a Government* (Charlottesville: University Press of Virginia, 2000); Dena Goodman, "Public Sphere and Private Life: Toward a Synthesis of Current Historiographical Approaches to the Old Regime," *History and Theory* 31, no. 1 (February 1992): 1–20; Linda K. Kerber et al., "Beyond Roles, Beyond Spheres: Thinking about Gender in the Early Republic," *The William and Mary Quarterly*, Third Series, 46, no. 3 (July 1989): 565–85; Carol Lasser, "Beyond Separate Spheres: The Power of Public Opinion," *Journal of the Early Republic* 21, no. 1 (Spring 2001): 115–23; Rosemarie Zagarri, *Revolutionary Backlash: Women and Politics in the Early American Republic* (Philadelphia: University of Pennsylvania Press, 2007).

3. Zagarri, *Revolutionary Backlash*, 165, 185. Many scholars have traced the emerging discourses of biological gender difference in this era; see especially Thomas Walter Laqueur, *Making Sex: Body and Gender from the Greeks to Freud* (Cambridge, MA: Harvard University Press, 1990); Clare A. Lyons, *Sex Among the Rabble: An Intimate History of Gender & Power in the Age of Revolution, Philadelphia, 1730–1830* (Chapel Hill: Published for the Omohundro Institute of Early American History and Culture, Williamsburg, Virginia, by the University of North Carolina Press, 2006).

4. As Hofstadter explains, "Party unity was the democrat's answer to the aristocrat's wealth, prestige, and connections." Richard Hofstadter, *The Idea of a Party System: The Rise of Legitimate Opposition in the United States, 1780–1840* (Berkeley: University of California Press, 1969), 246. On shifts in how patronage worked, see Ronald P. Formisano, "Deferential-Participant Politics: The Early Republic's Political Culture, 1789–1840," *American Political Science Review* 68, no. 2 (June 1974): 473–87. On how the second party system led to women's exclusion from politics, see Zagarri, *Revolutionary Backlash*, 6–8, 134.

5. Sarah Knott, *Sensibility and the American Revolution* (Chapel Hill: Published for the Omohundro Institute of Early American History and Culture, Williamsburg, Virginia, by the University of North Carolina Press, 2009), 306.

6. Rodney Hessinger, *Seduced, Abandoned, and Reborn: Visions of Youth in Middle-Class America, 1780–1850* (Philadelphia: University of Pennsylvania Press, 2005), 42; Helen Sheumaker, *Love Entwined: The Curious History of Hairwork in America* (Philadelphia: University of Pennsylvania Press, 2007) ix. The precise dating is based on my own research, but accords with the start date literary scholars use for the literature of sentimentalism, see, e.g., Nina Baym, *Woman's Fiction: A Guide to Novels By and about Women in America, 1820-1870* (Urbana: University of Illinois Press, 1993). While earlier secondary literature on sensibility has used the terms "sensibility" and "sentimentalism" interchangeably, more recent scholarship like Hessinger's makes a clear distinction. I use that distinction here, although with the caveat that the word "sentimental" is used as an adjective in describing both cultures.

7. Richard Godbeer, *The Overflowing of Friendship: Love Between Men and the Creation of the American Republic* (Baltimore: The Johns Hopkins University Press, 2009), 195; Ivy Schweitzer, *Perfecting Friendship: Politics and Affiliation in Early American Literature* (Chapel Hill: University of North Carolina Press, 2006), 64.

8. Shirley Marchalonis, ed., *Patrons and Protégées: Gender, Friendship, and Writing in Nineteenth-Century America* (New Brunswick, NJ: Rutgers University Press, 1998); Iris A. Nelson, "Eliza Caldwell Browning: Lincoln's Loyal Confidante," *Journal of Illinois History* 9, no. 1 (March 2006): 23–42; Brenda Wineapple, *White Heat: The Friendship of Emily Dickinson and Thomas Wentworth Higginson,* (New York: Knopf, 2008).

9. William Deresiewicz, "A Man. A Woman. Just Friends?" *The New York Times,* April 7, 2012, http://www.nytimes.com/2012/04/08/opinion/sunday/a-man-a-woman-just-friends.html.

10. See, e.g., Juliet Lapidos, "Strictly Platonic," *Slate,* September 2010, http://www.slate.com/articles/life/strictly_platonic.html; Michael Monsour, *Women and Men as Friends: Relationships Across the Life Span in the 21st Century* (Mahwah, NJ: L. Erlbaum, 2002), 142, 150; J. Donald O'Meara, "Cross-Sex Friendship: Four Basic Challenges of an Ignored Relationship," *Sex Roles* 21, no. 7 (1989): 525–43; Linda W. Rosenzweig, *Another Self: Middle-Class American Women and Their Friends in the Twentieth Century* (New York: New York University Press, 1999), 150.

11. Nora Ephron, Rob Reiner, Andrew Scheinman, *When Harry Met Sally,* directed by Rob Reiner (1989; Beverly Hills, CA: MGM Home Entertainment, 2001), DVD.

12. For a recent and widely reported example, see Adrian F. Ward, "Men and Women Can't Be 'Just Friends,'" Scientific American, October 23, 2012, http://www.scientificamerican.com/article.cfm?id=men-and-women-cant-be-just-friends.

13. Ephron et al., *When Harry Met Sally,* DVD.

14. There is a vast literature on marriage in the twentieth century; see Kristen Celello, *Making Marriage Work* (Chapel Hill: University of North Carolina Press, 2012);

Stephanie Coontz, *Marriage, A History: From Obedience to Intimacy or How Love Conquered Marriage* (New York: Penguin, 2006); Nancy F. Cott, *Public Vows: A History of Marriage and the Nation* (Cambridge, MA: Harvard University Press, 2002); Christina Simmons, *Making Marriage Modern: Women's Sexuality from the Progressive Era to World War II* (New York: Oxford University Press, 2009). I have been particularly influenced by conversations over the years with William Kuby; see William M. Kuby, "Conjugal Misconduct: Dubious Vows, Unlawful Wedlock, and the Margins of Marital Propriety in the United States, 1900–1940" (PhD diss., University of Pennsylvania, 2011).

15. Margaret Drabble, *The Realms of Gold* (New York: Ballantine Books, 1975), 37.

16. On the importance of language in structuring heterosocial friendship today, see Victor Luftig, *Seeing Together: Friendship Between the Sexes in English Writing from Mill to Woolf* (Stanford: Stanford University Press, 1993), 219, 222.

17. Deresiewicz, "A Man. A Woman. Just Friends?"

18. For the quote, see Sherry Turkle, *Alone Together: Why We Expect More from Technology and Less from Each Other* (New York: Basic Books, 2012), 1. Also see, e.g., Nancy K. Baym, *Personal Connections in the Digital Age* (Malden, MA: Polity Press, 2010); Deborah Chambers, *Social Media and Personal Relationships: Online Intimacies and Networked Friendship* (New York: Palgrave Macmillan, 2013); Alexander Lambert, *Intimacy and Friendship on Facebook* (New York: Palgrave Macmillan, 2013).

Bibliography

MANUSCRIPT COLLECTIONS

American Philosophical Society
Eastwick Collection
Gratz Family Papers

Georgia Historical Society
Daniel Mulford Papers
Forman, Bryan, and Screven Family Papers
Houston Family Papers

Friends Historical Collection, Swarthmore College
Emlen Family Papers
Jackson-Conard Family Papers

Historical Society of Pennsylvania
Ann Head Warder Papers
Deborah Norris Logan Diaries
Hopkinson Family Papers
John F. Watson Letterbook
Logan Family Papers, 1698–1842
Logan Papers, 1664–1871
Loudon Papers
Powel Family Papers
R. R. Logan Collection
Shippen Family Papers
Watson Family Papers
Wharton Family Papers

Library Company of Philadelphia
Benjamin Rush Papers
Elizabeth Graeme Fergusson Commonplace Books

Library of Congress
Custis-Lee Family Papers, 1700–Circa 1928
David Bailie Warden Papers
George Washington Papers (online edition)
Margaret Bayard Smith Papers
Rodgers Family Papers
Shippen Family Papers
Sir Augustus John Foster Papers
Thomas Jefferson Papers (online edition)

Litchfield Historical Society
George Younglove Cutler Album
Laura Maria Wolcott Rankin Diary
Litchfield Female Academy Collection
Loring Family Correspondence

Maryland Historical Society
Baron Frederick Franck de la Roche papers
Coale Collection
Eliza Custis-Lafayette Correspondence, 1778–1828
Elizabeth Patterson Bonaparte Papers
Fielding Lucas Collection
Harper Letters, 1801–1912
J. H. B. Latrobe Papers
Redwood Collection
Thomas Law Family Papers
Warden Papers

Massachusetts Historical Society
Elbridge Gerry Papers
Matthew Ridley Papers II
Sedgwick Family Papers
William Ellery Channing Papers

Mount Vernon Ladies' Association
Bushrod Washington Papers

New Hampshire Historical Society
John Farmer Papers

New Jersey Historical Society
Anne Hart/Reverend John Stanford Correspondence 1804–1811

New-York Historical Society
Albert Gallatin Papers

Jumel Family Papers
Van Ness Papers

Rare Book and Manuscript Library, Columbia University
John Howard Payne Papers

Southern Historical Collection, University of North Carolina
Arnold and Screven Family Papers
Caroline Elizabeth Burgwin Clitherall Diaries
Dillon and Polk Family Papers
Ernest Haywood Collection
Nicholas Philip Trist Papers

Special Collections, University of Virginia Library
Papers of Angelica Schuyler Church (online edition)

Virginia Historical Society
Elizabeth Coles Diary
Elizabeth House Trist Papers
John Randolph Letters
Kennon Family Papers

Winterthur Library
Watson Family Papers

FRIENDSHIP ALBUMS (BY NAME OF OWNER)

American Antiquarian Society
Ann Turnbull
Caroline Turnbull
Eliza J. W. Millen
Emily Clark
Hannah S. Haskell Smith
J. Cowen
William Bannister

Connecticut Historical Society
Albert M. Fish
Almira Dorr
Caroline Whittlesey
Eber Carpenter
Elizabeth Dorr Williams
Elizabeth Warden Healey
Katherine Kellogg

Martha Phelps
Mary C. Wells

Friends Historical Collection, Swarthmore College
Album Collection

Historical Society of Pennsylvania
Anna G. Johnson
Elizabeth C. Clemson
Margaret Shippen
Mary E. Roberdeau
Rebecca F. Taylor

John Hay Library, Brown University
Abigail A. Bomer
Alexander (Boston, Mass.)
Ann Oleson
Anna Potter
Bathsheba Barton
Betsy Brown
Caroline M. Northam
Caroline (Providence, R.I.)
Hannah C. Walker
Jacob R. Huntington
James L. F. Crombie
Lizzie L. Davis
Malvina Gardiner
Mary A. Sawyer
Mary R. Jones
Nancy Andrews
Nancy Curtis
Sarah Franklin
Sarah Knight
Sophia H. Bradley

Library Company of Philadelphia
Amy Matilda Cassey
Eliza Lea
Mary Anne Dickerson
Mary Goddard

Litchfield Historical Society
Margaret C. Bolles Garrett
Jane R. Lewis
Louisa C. Phelps
Mary Peck Mansfield

Maryland Historical Society
Lucy Holmes Balderston Album, 1826–1848

New Jersey Historical Society
Elizabeth Dodge

Rare Book and Manuscript Library, Columbia University
Octavia Walton Le Vert Album

MUSEUM COLLECTIONS

Litchfield Historical Society
Mount Vernon Ladies' Association
Museum of Fine Arts-Boston
National Portrait Gallery
Smithsonian American Art Museum
Winterthur Museum and Library
Worcester Museum of Art

DOCUMENTARY EDITIONS OF MANUSCRIPTS

Abbot, W. W., Dorothy Twohig, Philander D. Chase, Theodore J. Crackel, eds. *The Papers of George Washington*. Charlottesville: University of Virginia Press, 1987-.

Adams, Charles F., ed. *Correspondence between John Adams and Mercy Warren*. Collections of the Massachusetts Historical Society; Ser. 5, v. 4. New York: Arno Press, 1972.

Adams, Charles F., ed. *Letters of Mrs. Adams, the Wife of John Adams*. Boston: C. C. Little and J. Brown, 1840.

Adams, Charles F., ed. *Memoirs of John Quincy Adams, Comprising Portions of His Diary from 1795 to 1848*. Philadelphia: J. B. Lippincott Company, 1874.

Armentrout, Virginia, and James S. Armentrout Jr., eds. *The Diary of Harriet Manigault, 1813–1816*. Philadelphia: The Colonial Dames of America, 1976.

Armes, Ethel, ed. *Nancy Shippen, Her Journal Book; the International Romance of a Young Lady of Fashion of Colonial Philadelphia with Letters to Her and About Her*. New York: B. Blom, 1968.

Boyd, Julian P., and Barbara Oberg, et al., eds. *The Papers of Thomas Jefferson*. Princeton: Princeton University Press, 1950-.

Bradford, James C., ed. *Papers of John Paul Jones, 1762–1788*. Cambridge, U.K.: Chadwyck-Healey, 1986.

Brady, Patricia, ed. *George Washington's Beautiful Nelly: The Letters of Eleanor Parke Custis Lewis to Elizabeth Bordley Gibson, 1794–1851*. Columbia, S.C.: University of South Carolina Press, 1991.

Butterfield, L. H., ed. *Adams Family Correspondence*. Cambridge: Belknap Press of Harvard University Press, 1963-.

Calcott, Margaret Law, ed. *Mistress of Riversdale: The Plantation Letters of Rosalie Stier Calvert, 1795–1821*. Baltimore: Johns Hopkins University Press, 1991.

Cappon, Lester Jesse, ed. *The Adams-Jefferson Letters: The Complete Correspondence Between Thomas Jefferson and Abigail and John Adams*. Chapel Hill: Published for the Institute of Early American History and Culture at Williamsburg, Virginia, by the University of North Carolina Press, 1959.

Davis, Richard Beale, ed. *Jeffersonian America: Notes on the United States of America, Collected in the Years 1805–6–7 and 11–12*. Westport, Conn.: Greenwood Press, 1980.

Dawes, Sally Fisher, ed. "The Norris-Fisher Correspondence: A Circle of Friends, 1779–82." *Delaware History* 6 (1955): 187–232.

Easton, Marilyn J., ed. *Passionate Spinster: The Diary of Patty Rogers, 1785*. Exeter, N.H.: Exeter Historical Society, 2001.

Graham, Judith S., Beth Luey, Margaret A. Hogan, and C. James Taylor, eds. *Diary and Autobiographical Writings of Louisa Catherine Adams*. Cambridge: The Belknap Press of Harvard University Press, 2013.

Kaminski, John P., ed. *Jefferson in Love: The Love Letters Between Thomas Jefferson & Maria Cosway*. Madison, Wis.: Madison House, 1999.

Labaree, Leonard W., Barbara Oberg, Ellen Cohn, et al., eds. *The Papers of Benjamin Franklin*. New Haven: Yale University Press, 1959-.

Looney, J. Jefferson et al., eds. *The Papers of Thomas Jefferson: Retirement Series*. Princeton: Princeton University Press, 2004-.

Maclay, Edgar Stanton, ed. *Journal of William Maclay, United States Senator from Pennsylvania, 1789–1791*. New York: D. A. Appleton and Company, 1890.

McMahon, Lucia, and Deborah Schriver, eds. *To Read My Heart: The Journal of Rachel Van Dyke, 1810–1811*. Philadelphia: University of Pennsylvania Press, 2000.

Metz, Judith, and Regina Bechtle, eds. *Elizabeth Bayley Seton: Collected Writings*.

Mulford, Carla, ed. *Only for the Eye of a Friend: The Poems of Annis Boudinot Stockton*. Charlottesville: University Press of Virginia, 1995.

Parr, Marilyn K., ed. "Augustus John Foster and the 'Washington Wilderness': Personal Letters of a British Diplomat." PhD Diss., George Washington University, 1987.

Pendleton, Emily. *Philenia: The Life and Works of Sarah Wentworth Morton, 1759–1846*. Orono, Maine: Printed at the University press, 1931.

Preston, Daniel, and Cassandra Good, eds. *The Papers of James Monroe: Selected Correspondence and Papers, 1803–1811*. New York: ABC-CLIO, 2014.

Randolph, John. "Letters of John Randolph, of Roanoke, to General Thomas Marsh Forman." *The Virginia Magazine of History and Biography* 49, no. 3 (July 1941): 201–16.

Smith, Bonnie Hurd. *Letters of Loss and Love: Judith Sargent Murray Papers, Letter Book 3*. Massachusetts: Hurd Smith Communications: Judith Sargent Murray Society, 2009.

Smith, Bonnie Hurd, ed. *Mingling Souls Upon Paper: An Eighteenth-Century Love Story*. Salem, Mass.: Judith Sargent Murray Society, 2007.

Smith, E. H. *The Diary of Elihu Hubbard Smith (1771–1798). Memoirs of the American Philosophical Society* v.95. Philadelphia: American Philosophical Society, 1973.

Smith, Margaret Bayard. *The First Forty Years of Washington Society, Portrayed by the Family Letters of Mrs. Samuel Harrison Smith (Margaret Bayard) from the Collection of Her Grandson, J. Henley Smith.* Edited by Gaillard Hunt. New York: C. Scribner's Sons, 1906.

Wood, Betty, ed. *Mary Telfair to Mary Few: Selected Letters, 1802–1844.* Athens, Ga.: University of Georgia Press, 2007.

PUBLISHED PRIMARY SOURCES

Addison, Joseph, and Sir Richard Steele. *The Spectator.* Philadelphia: Printed by Tesson and Lee for Samuel F. Bradford and John Conrad, 1803.

Advice to the Fair Sex in a Series of Letters on Various Subjects Chiefly Describing the Graceful Virtues Which Are Indispensibly Required to Adorn and Perfect the Female Sex . . . and the Contrast: Thereby Showing How to Follow What Is Good and Eshew [sic] What Is Evil. Philadelphia: Printed for the author, by Robert Cochran, 1803.

Albert. "The Request: To Stella." *The Philadelphia Minerva,* March 5, 1796.

Alexander, William. *The History of Women, From the Earliest Antiquity, to the Present Time; Giving an Account of Almost Every Interesting Particular Concerning That Sex, Among All Nations, Ancient and Modern.* Boston: Joseph Burnstead, 1790.

Alsop, Richard. *The Political Green-House, for the Year 1798. Addressed to the Readers of the Connecticut Courant, January 1st, 1799.* Hartford, Conn.: Hudson & Goodwin, 1799.

Anna Matilda. "To Della Crusca: The Pen." *The New York Magazine, or Literary Repository,* May 1790.

Austen, Jane. *Emma.* New York: Penguin Classics, 1985.

Bage, Robert. *Hermsprong, Or, Man as He Is Not.* Peterborough, Ont.: Broadview Press, 2002.

B., S. "Female Love Forsaken." *The New-York Packet,* December 9, 1790.

Balfour, Mary. *Hope, a Poetical Essay; with Various Other Poems.* Belfast: Smyth and Lyons, 1810.

Bayard, Ferdinand Marie. *Travels of a Frenchman in Maryland and Virginia, with a Description of Philadelphia and Baltimore, in 1791: Or, Travels in the Interior of the United States, to Bath, Winchester, in the Valley of the Shenandoah, Etc., Etc., During the Summer of 1791.* Ann Arbor: Edwards Brothers, 1950.

Brace, John Pierce. *More Chronicles of a Pioneer School, from 1792 to 1833.* Edited by Emily Noyes Vanderpoel. New York: The Cadmus Book Shop, 1927.

Brayton, Patience Greene. *A Short Account of the Life and Religious Labours of Patience Brayton Late of Swansey, in the State of Massachusetts.* New Bedford [Mass.]: Printed by Abraham Shearman, June 1801.

"Breach of the Marriage Promise." *Hampden Patriot,* May 22, 1822.

Brown, Charles Brockden. *Alcuin: A Dialogue.* Edited by Cynthia A. Kierner. New York: Rowman & Littlefield, 1995.

Brown, Charles Brockden. *Wieland, Or, The Transformation: An American Tale, with Related Texts*. Edited by Philip Barnard and Stephen Shapiro. Indianapolis: Hackett Pub. Co., 2009.

Burke, Mrs. *Ela: Or The Delusions of the Heart*. English. Boston: Benj. Larking and John W. Folsom, 1790.

Burney, Fanny. *Evelina*. Edited by Stewart J. Cooke. W. W. Norton & Company, 1998.

Burr, Aaron. *The Private Journal of Aaron Burr, During His Residence of Four Years in Europe; with Selections from His Correspondence*. New York: Harper & Brothers, 1838.

Byron, George Gordon Byron. "Mediterranean Poems." Edited by Peter Cochran. Accessed August 28, 2011. http://petercochran.files.wordpress.com/2009/03/mediterranean_poems.pdf.

Carey, James. *He Wou'd Be a Poet; Or, "Nature Will Be Nature Still." An Heroic Poem: To Which Is Annexed a Thanksgiving Epistle on Electioneering Success. By Geoffry Touchstone*. Philadelphia: Printed for the author, 1796.

Chapone, Hester. *Letters on the Improvement of the Mind*. London: J. Walter and C. Dilly, 1790.

"Charlotte's Sohlequy to the Manes of Werter." *The American Museum; Or, Repository of Ancient and Modern Fugitive Pieces &c*, February 1787.

Cogan, Thomas. *A Philosophical Treatise on the Passions*. London: Printed and sold by S. Hazard, 1802.

Crocker, Hannah Mather. *Observations on the Real Rights of Women with Their Appropriate Duties: Agreeable to Scripture, Reason and Common Sense*. Boston: Printed for the author, 1818.

"Definition of a Ladies' Album." *Boston Medical Intelligencer*, January 9, 1827.

Dilworth, H. *The Complete Letter Writer, Or, Young Secretary's Instructor: Containing a Great Variety of Letters on Friendship, Duty, Love, Marriage, Amusement, Business, &c. to Which Is Prefixed, Plain Instructions for Writting Letters on All Occasions by H. Dilworth*. New Haven: Sidney's Press, for Increase Cooke, 1809.

E. "Remarks on Female Politicians." *The Monthly Magazine, and American Review* 3, no. 6 (December 1800): 416.

Eaton, Peggy. *The Autobiography of Peggy Eaton*. New York: C. Scribner's Sons, 1932.

Edgeworth, Maria. *Belinda*. New York: Oxford World's Classics, 1999.

"Female Friendship." *Weekly Visitor, or Ladies' Miscellany*, January 7, 1804.

Fordyce, James. *Sermons to Young Women*. Philadelphia: Thomas Dobson, 1787.

Fordyce, James. *The Character and Conduct of the Female Sex, and the Advantages to Be Derived by Young Men from the Society of Virtuous Women. A Discourse, in Three Parts, Delivered in Monkwell-Street Chapel, January 1, 1776, by James Fordyce, D. D. Author of the Sermons to Young Women, and Addresses to Young Men*. 3rd ed. Boston: John Gill, 1781.

Foster, Hannah Webster. *The Coquette* Ed. by Cathy N. Davidson. New York: Oxford University Press, 1986.

Frank, Elizabeth. *Classical English Letter-Writer, Or, Epistolary Selections Designed to Improve Young Persons in the Art of Letter-Writing and in the Principles of Virtue and Piety by the Author of Lessons for Young Persons in Humble Life.* Philadelphia: Caleb Richardson, 1816.

"Friendship." *Ladies' Portfolio,* January 29, 1820.

Godwin, William. *An Enquiry Concerning Political Justice: And Its Influence on General Virtue and Happiness.* Dublin: Printed for Luke White, 1793.

Goethe, Johann Wolfgang von. *The Sorrows and Sympathetic Attachments of Werter.* Philadelphia: Robert Bell, 1784.

Graham, Isabella, and Divie Bethune. *The Power of Faith: Exemplified in the Life and Writings of the Late Mrs. Isabella Graham.* New York: American Tract Society, 1843.

Gray, Mrs. Asa. "Sketch of Miss Mary Pierce." In *Chronicles of a Pioneer School, from 1792–1833,* edited by Emily Noyes Vanderpoel and Elizabeth Cynthia Barney Buel, 325–26. Cambridge, Mass.: University Press, 1903.

Gregory, Dr. *A Father's Legacy to His Daughters.* New York: T. Allen, 1793.

Hawkes, Sarah, and Richard Cecil. *Memoirs of Mrs. Hawkes, Including Remarks and Extracts From Sermons and Letters of R. Cecil.* London: Hatchard and Son, L. and G. Seeley; Nisbet and Co. Shaw, &c., 1838.

Home, Henry. *Six Sketches on the History of Man.* Philadelphia, 1776.

Huntington, Susan (Mansfield). *Memoirs of the Late Mrs. Susan Huntington, of Boston, Mass.* Edited by Benjamin Blydenburg Wisner. 3d ed. Boston: Crocker and Brewster, 1829.

Izzard, Israel. "Original Communications: Crumbs of Advice for the Ladies." *The New—England Galaxy and United States Literary Advertiser,* September 2, 1825.

Jones, Rebecca. *Memorials of Rebecca Jones.* Philadelphia: H. Longstreth, 1849.

Jones, Rufus Matthew. *The Later Periods of Quakerism.* Vol. I. London: Macmillan and Co., Limited, 1921.

Jones, Sarah. *Devout Letters, Or, Letters Spiritual and Friendly.* Edited by Jeremiah Minter. Alexandria: Samuel Snowden, 1804.

Lamb, Caroline. *Glenarvon.* London: Printed for Henry Colburn and Co., 1816.

Laura. "On Reading the Sorrows of Werter." *The Universal Asylum and Columbian Magazine,* October 1790.

Lavinia. "Lines to the Village Lass." *Massachussetts Magazine,* May 1794.

Le Blanc, Simon. *Report of a Cause Between Joseph Foster, Plaintiff, against Miss Esther Mellish, Defendant, for a Breach of Promise of Marriage; Tried in the Court of King's Bench, at Westminster, on Tuesday the 23d Feb. 1802.* London: Printed for J. Ridgway, No. 1, York Street, St. James's Square, 1802.

"Love." *Hartford Gazette,* February 17, 1794.

"LOVE and FRIENDSHIP Reconciled: A Colloquy: Occasioned by a Lady's Corresponding with a Gentleman, under a Seal Representative of Friendship." *The Boston Gazette, and the Country Journal,* June 6, 1785.

Malcolm. "Lines Written in a Lady's Album." *The New-York Mirror,* March 31, 1827.

Mansfield, Edward Deering. *Personal Memories, Social, Political, and Literary: With Sketches of Many Noted People, 1803–1843*. R. Clarke & Co., 1879.

Massy, Rev. Charles. *A Report of the Trial on an Action for Damages, Brought by the Reverend Charles Massy against the Most Noble, the Marquis of Headfort, for Criminal Conversation with Plaintiff's Wife :damages Laid at £.40,000/taken in Short-Hand by an Eminent Barrister*. New York: Printed for and sold by B. Dornin, and P. Byrne, Philadelphia, 1804.

Montolieu, Isabelle de. *Caroline of Litchfield*. Translated by Thomas Holcroft. New York: reprinted by J. S. Mott, for Evert Duyckinck & Co, 1798.

Morton, Sarah Wentworth. *My Mind and Its Thoughts, in Sketches, Fragments, and Essays*. Delmar, N.Y.: Scholars' Facsimiles & Reprints, 1975.

"Novels." *The Atheneum; Or, the Spirit of the English Magazines*, March 15, 1820.

"Observations on Female Politicians." *Philadelphia Repository and Weekly Register* 1, no. 2 (November 22, 1800): 4.

"On Benevolence and Friendship." *The Intellectual Regale; Or, Ladies' Tea Tray*, January 14, 1815.

"On Friendship." *Balance and Columbian Repository*, November 13, 1804.

"On Friendship." *The Monthly Anthology, and Boston Review Containing Sketches and Reports of Philosophy, Religion, History, Arts, and Manners*, June 1, 1804.

"On the Happy Influence Arising from Female Society, from Dr. Alexander's History of Women." *Massachussetts Magazine*, 1795.

P., Philo. "Ladies Department." *Christian Secretary*, March 17, 1827.

Parsons, Theophilus. "Memoir of Charles Greely Loring." In *Proceedings of the Massachusetts Historical Society*, 11:263–91 Boston: The Society, 1869.

Parthenon. "Ladies' Albums." *The Escritoir; Or, Masonic and Miscellaneous Album*, December 16, 1826.

Plumptre, Anne. *Antoinette Percival. A Novel: [Two Lines from Pope]*. Philadelphia: Mathew Carey, 1800.

Radcliffe, Ann (Ward). *The Romance of the Forest*. Boston: G. Clark, 1835.

"Remember Me." *The New-York Mirror: A Weekly Gazette of Literature and the Fine Arts*, May 27, 1826.

Richardson, Jonathan. "An Essay on the Theory of Painting." In *The Works of Jonathan Richardson*. Whitehall: T. and J. Egerton, 1972.

Rousseau, Jean-Jacques. *Eloisa: A Series of Letters*. London: John Harding, 1810.

Rowson, Susanna. *Charlotte Temple and Lucy Temple*. Edited by Ann Douglas New York: Penguin Classics, 1991.

Rowson, Susanna. *Mentoria; or The Young Lady's Friend. In Two Volumes*. Philadelphia: Printed for Robert Campbell, by Samuel Harrison Smith, 1794.

Rowson, Susanna. *The Inquisitor; Or, Invisible Rambler*. Philadelphia: Matthew Carey, 1794.

Rush, Benjmain. "Directions for Conducting a News-Paper." *Weekly Museum*, May 14, 1791.

Saunter, Samuel. "The American Lounger." *The Port-Folio*, July 15, 1803.

Saunter, Samuel. "The American Lounger No. LXIV." *The Port-Folio*, June 18, 1803.

Seward, William. *Anecdotes of Some Distinguished Persons: Chiefly of the Present and Two Preceding Centuries*. London: T. Cadell Jun. and W. Davies, 1795.

Smith, Margaret Bayard. *A Winter in Washington, Or, Memoirs of the Seymour Family: In Two Volumes*. New York: Published by E. Bliss & E. White, 1824.

"Sorrows of Werter." *Merrimack Magazine and Ladies' Literary Cabinet*, December 14, 1805.

"Strictures on Female Education." *The Columbian Magazine; Comprehending Ecclesiastical History, Morality, Religion, and Other Useful and Interesting Matter* 1, no. 5 (August 1806): 179.

Swanwick, John. *Poems on Several Occasions*. Philadelphia: F. and R. Bailey, 1797.

T—n, E. "An Essay on Friendship with Women." *Massachusetss Magazine*, August 1796.

"The Art of Conversation." *Philadelphia Repository and Weekly Register*, August 15, 1801.

The Complete American Letter-Writer: Containing Letters on Trade & Merchandize: Also Letters on Familiar & Interesting Subjects. Ostego, N.Y.: Printed by H. & E. Phinney, Jun., 1808.

"The Confessions of an Album Writer." *The Ladies Garland*, September 29, 1827.

The Cuckold's Chronicle: Being Select Trials for Adultry [sic], Incest, Imbecility, Ravishment, &c.: Volume I. Boston, 1798.

"The Monitress." *The Emerald*, November 3, 1810.

Thompson, William. *Appeal of One Half the Human Race, Women*. New York: Ayer Publishing, 1970.

"Thoughts on Cicisbeism." *Farmer's Weekly Museum*, June 12, 1798.

"To Henry." *The Intellectual Regale; Or, Ladies' Tea Tray*, October 28, 1815.

Trollope, Frances Eleanor. *Domestic Manners of the Americans*. Edited by Donald Smalley. New York: Alfred A. Knopf, 1949.

Ure, Andrew. *Case of Divorce of Andrew Ure, M.D. v. Catharine Ure*. Philadelphia: William Fry, 1821.

Villemert, Pierre-Joseph Boudier de. *The Friend of Women*. Translated by Alexander Morrice. Philadelphia: John Conrad & Company, 1803.

Weems, Mason L. *God's Revenge Against Adultery, Awfully Exemplified in the Following Cases of American Crim. Con*. Third edition. Philadelphia: Printed for the author, 1818.

Wollstonecraft, Mary. *A Vindication of the Rights of Woman*. Edited by Sheila Rowbotham. London: Verso, 2010.

Wollstonecraft, Mary. *Thoughts on the Education of Daughters, with Reflections on Female Conduct in the More Important Duties of Life*. London: J. Johnson, 1787.

"Women." *The Massachusetts Centinal*, May 5, 1790.

Wyck, Pierre C. Van. *Jeffers v. Tyson*. New York: Henry C. Southwick, 1808.

SECONDARY SOURCES

Adams, Samuel Hopkins. *The Godlike Daniel*. New York: Sears Publishing Company, Inc., 1930.

Adams, William Howard. *The Paris Years of Thomas Jefferson*. New Haven: Yale University Press, 2000.

Ahearn, Laura M. *Invitations to Love: Literacy, Love Letters, and Social Change in Nepal*. Ann Arbor: University of Michigan Press, 2001.

Allan, Graham A. *Friendship: Developing a Sociological Perspective*. New York: Harvester Wheatsheaf, 1989.

Allen, Reggie. "The Sonnets of William Hayley and Gift Exchange." *European Romantic Review* 13 (2002): 383–92.

Allgor, Catherine. *A Perfect Union: Dolley Madison and the Creation of the American Nation*. New York: Henry Holt & Co., 2006.

Allgor, Catherine. "Federal Patronage in the Early Republic: The Role of Women in Washington, D.C." In *Establishing Congress: The Removal To Washington, D.C., And The Election Of 1800*, edited by Donald R. Kennon and Kenneth R. Bowling, 102–27. Athens, Ohio: Ohio University Press, 2005.

Allgor, Catherine. *Parlor Politics: In Which the Ladies of Washington Help Build a City and a Government*. Charlottesville: University Press of Virginia, 2000.

Armstrong, Erica R. "A Mental and Moral Feast: Reading, Writing, and Sentimentality in Black Philadelphia." *Journal of Women's History* 16, no. 1 (2004): 78–102.

Auslander, Leora. *Cultural Revolutions: Everyday Life and Politics in Britain, North America, and France*. Berkeley: University of California Press, 2009.

Bannet, Eve Tavor. *Empire of Letters: Letter Manuals and Transatlantic Correspondence, 1688–1820*. Cambridge, UK: Cambridge University Press, 2005.

Barker-Benfield, G. J. *Abigail and John Adams: The Americanization of Sensibility*. Chicago: University of Chicago Press, 2010.

Barker-Benfield, G. J. *The Culture of Sensibility: Sex and Society in Eighteenth-Century Britain*. Chicago: University of Chicago Press, 1992.

Barratt, Carrie Rebora, and Ellen G. Miles. *Gilbert Stuart*. New York: Metropolitan Museum of Art, 2004.

Basch, Norma. "Equity vs. Equality: Emerging Concepts of Women's Political Status in the Age of Jackson." *Journal of the Early Republic* 3, no. 3 (Autumn 1983): 297–318.

Baumann, Roland M. "John Swanwick: Spokesman for 'Merchant-Republicanism' in Philadelphia, 1790–1798." *The Pennsylvania Magazine of History and Biography* 97, no. 2 (April 1, 1973): 131–82.

Baym, Nancy K. *Personal Connections in the Digital Age*. Malden, MA: Polity Press, 2010.

Baym, Nina. *Woman's Fiction: A Guide to Novels by and About Women in America, 1820–1870*. Urbana: University of Illinois Press, 1993.

Bell, Richard. *We Shall Be No More: Suicide and Self-Government in the Newly United States*. Cambridge, MA: Harvard University Press, 2012.

Benemann, William. "A Bedpost (Is/Is Not) Only a Bedpost." *Reviews in American History* 37, no. 3 (2009): 338–44.

Berkin, Carol. *Wondrous Beauty: The Life and Adventures of Elizabeth Patterson Bonaparte*. New York: Knopf, 2014.

Bernstein, Richard B. *Thomas Jefferson*. New York: Oxford University Press, 2003.

Binhammer, Katherine. "The Sex Panic of the 1790s." *Journal of the History of Sexuality* 6, no. 3 (January 1996): 409–34.

Blauvelt, Martha Tomhave. *The Work of the Heart: Young Women and Emotion, 1780–1830*. Charlottesville: University of Virginia Press, 2007.

Blauvelt, Martha Tomhave. "Women, Words, and Men: Excerpts from the Diary of Mary Guion." *Journal of Women's History* 2, no. 2 (Fall 1990): 177–84.

Bloch, Ruth H. "Changing Conceptions of Sexuality and Romance in Eighteenth-Century America." *The William and Mary Quarterly*, Third Series, 60, no. 1 (January 2003): 13–42.

Boone, Joseph Allen. *Tradition Counter Tradition: Love and the Form of Fiction*. Chicago: University of Chicago Press, 1987.

Boulton, Alexander O. "The American Paradox: Jeffersonian Equality and Racial Science." *American Quarterly* 47, no. 3 (September 1995): 467.

Bourdieu, Pierre. *Outline of a Theory of Practice*. Cambridge, U.K.: Cambridge University Press, 1977.

Bourdieu, Pierre. *Practical Reason: On the Theory of Action*. Translated by Randall Johnson. Palo Alto: Stanford University Press, 1998.

Bourguignon-Frasseto, Claude. *Betsy Bonaparte: The Belle of Baltimore*. Baltimore: Maryland Historical Society, 2003.

Brain, Robert. *Friends and Lovers*. New York: Basic Books, 1976.

Branson, Susan. "Gendered Strategies for Success in the Early Nineteenth-Century Literary Marketplace: Mary Carr and the 'Ladies' Tea Tray." *Journal of American Studies* 40, no. 1 (2006): 35–51.

Branson, Susan. *These Fiery Frenchified Dames: Women and Political Culture in Early National Philadelphia*. Philadelphia: University of Pennsylvania Press, 2001.

Brant, Irving. *James Madison*. New York: Bobbs-Merrill, 1956.

Bray, Alan. *The Friend*. Chicago: University of Chicago Press, 2003.

Brekus, Catherine A. *Strangers & Pilgrims: Female Preaching in America, 1740–1845*. Chapel Hill: University of North Carolina Press, 1998.

Brickley, Lynne Templeton. "Sarah Pierce's Litchfield Female Academy, 1792–1833." PhD Diss., Harvard University, 1985.

Brookhiser, Richard. *Gentleman Revolutionary: Gouverneur Morris, the Rake Who Wrote the Constitution*. New York: Free Press, 2003.

Brown, Irene Quenzler. "Death, Friendship, and Female Identity During New England's Second Great Awakening." *Journal of Family History* 12, no. 4 (October 1987): 367–87.

Buel, Richard. *Joel Barlow: American Citizen in a Revolutionary World*. Baltimore: Johns Hopkins University Press, 2011.

Bullock, Helen Claire Duprey. *My Head and My Heart, a Little History of Thomas Jefferson and Maria Cosway.* New York: G. P. Putnam's Sons, 1945.

Burn, Helen J. *Betsy Bonaparte.* Baltimore: Maryland Historical Society, 2010.

Burstein, Andrew. "Life Follows My Pen: Jefferson, Letter-Writing and the Quest for Imaginative Friendship." PhD Diss., University of Virginia, 1994.

Bushman, Richard. *The Refinement of America.* New York: Vintage Books, 1993.

Carson, Barbara G. *Ambitious Appetites: Dining, Behavior, and Patterns of Consumption in Federal Washington.* Washington, D.C.: AIA Press, 1990.

Cavitch, Max. "The Man That Was Used Up: Poetry, Particularity, and the Politics of Remembering George Washington." *American Literature* 75, no. 2 (July 3, 2003): 247–74.

Cayton, Andrew. *Love in the Time of Revolution: Transatlantic Literary Radicalism and Historical Change, 1793–1818.* Chapel Hill: Published for the Omohundro Institute of Early American History and Culture, Williamsburg, Virginia, by the University of North Carolina Press, 2013.

Chalus, Elaine. *Elite Women in English Political Life, C.1754–1790.* Oxford: Oxford University Press, 2005.

Chambers, Deborah. *Social Media and Personal Relationships: Online Intimacies and Networked Friendship.* New York: Palgrave Macmillan, 2013.

Chambers-Schiller, Lee. *Liberty, a Better Husband: Single Women in America: The Generations of 1780–1840.* New Haven: Yale University Press, 1984.

Channing, William Henry. *The Life of William Ellery Channing.* 3rd ed. Boston: American Unitarian Association, 1880.

Chernock, Arianne. "Cultivating Woman: Men's Pursuit of Intellectual Equality in the Late British Enlightenment." *Journal of British Studies* 45, no. 3 (July 2006): 511–31.

Clarke, Norma. *Dr. Johnson's Women.* London: Hambledon and London, 2000.

Colwill, Elizabeth. "Epistolary Passions: Friendship and the Literary Public of Constance de Salm, 1767–1845." *Journal of Women's History* 12, no. 3 (2000): 39–68.

Cometti, Elizabeth. "Maria Cosway's Rediscovered Miniature of Jefferson," *William and Mary Quarterly* 9 (April 1952): 152–55.

Conkling, Margaret Cockburn. *Memoirs of the Mother and Wife of Washington.* Auburn, N.Y.: Derby, Miller, and Company, 1850.

Connolly, Brian Joseph. "'Every Family Become a School of Abominable Impurity': Incest and Theology in the Early Republic." *Journal of the Early Republic* 30, no. 3 (Fall 2010): 413–22.

Coontz, Stephanie. *Marriage, A History: From Obedience to Intimacy or How Love Conquered Marriage.* New York: Penguin, 2006.

Cory, Abbie L. "Wheeler and Thompson's Appeal: The Rhetorical Re-Visioning of Gender." *New Hibernia Review* 8, no. 2 (2004): 106–20.

Cott, Nancy F. *Public Vows: A History of Marriage and the Nation.* Cambridge: Harvard University Press, 2002.

Cott, Nancy F. *The Bonds of Womanhood: "Woman's Sphere" in New England, 1780–1835.* New Haven: Yale University Press, 1977.

Crabtree, Sarah. "'A Beautiful and Practical Lesson of Jurisprudence': The Transatlantic Quaker Ministry in an Age of Revolution." *Radical History Review*, no. 99 (Fall 2007): 51–79.

Crain, Caleb. *American Sympathy: Men, Friendship, and Literature in the New Nation.* New Haven: Yale University Press, 2001.

Crane, Elaine Forman. "Political Dialogue and the Spring of Abigail's Discontent." *The William and Mary Quarterly*, Third Series, 56, no. 4 (October 1999): 745–74.

Cross, Ashley. "Coleridge and Robinson: Harping on Lyrical Exchange." In *Fellow Romantics: Male and Female British Writers, 1790–1835*, edited by Beth Lau. Farnham, England: Ashgate, 2009.

Davidson, Cathy N. *Revolution and the Word.* Oxford: Oxford University Press, 1987.

Davies, Kate. *Catharine Macaulay and Mercy Otis Warren: The Revolutionary Atlantic and the Politics of Gender.* Oxford: Oxford University Press, 2005.

De Certeau, Michel. *The Practice of Everyday Life.* Translated by Steven Rendall. Berkeley: University of California Press, 1984.

Decker, William Merrill. *Epistolary Practices: Letter Writing in America Before Telecommunications.* Chapel Hill: University of North Carolina Press, 1998.

De Koven, Anna Farwell. *Horace Walpole and Madame Du Deffand; an Eighteenth-Century Friendship.* New York, London: D. Appleton and Company, 1929.

DeLorme, Eleanor Pearson. "The Swan Commissions: Four Portraits by Gilbert Stuart." *Wintherthur Portfolio* 14, no. 4 (1979): 361–95.

Deresiewicz, William. "A Man. A Woman. Just Friends?" *The New York Times*, April 7, 2012.

Didier, Eugène Lemoine. *The Life and Letters of Madame Bonaparte.* C. Scribner's Sons, 1879.

Dierks, Konstantin. *In My Power: Letter Writing and Communications in Early America.* Philadelphia: University of Pennsylvania Press, 2009.

Diggins, John P. "Slavery, Race, and Equality: Jefferson and the Pathos of the Enlightenment." *American Quarterly* 28, no. 2 (1976): 206.

Diggs, Marylynne. "Romantic Friends or a 'Different Race of Creatures'? The Representation of Lesbian Pathology in Nineteenth-Century America." *Feminist Studies* 21, no. 2 (Summer 1995): 317–40.

Dillon, Elizabeth Maddock. *The Gender of Freedom: Fictions of Liberalism and the Literary Public Sphere.* Stanford, Calif.: Stanford University Press, 2004.

Ditz, Toby L. "Shipwrecked; Or, Masculinity Imperiled: Mercantile Representations of Failure and the Gendered Self in Eighteenth-Century Philadelphia." *The Journal of American History* 81, no. 1 (June 1994): 51–80.

Drabble, Margaret. *The Realms of Gold.* New York: Ballantine Books, 1975.

Dunn, Susan. *Jefferson's Second Revolution: The Election Crisis of 1800 and the Triumph of Republicanism.* New York: Houghton Mifflin Harcourt, 2004.

Eisler, Benita. *Byron: Child of Passion, Fool of Fame*. New York: Vintage Books, 2000.

Ellet, E. F. *The Court Circles of the Republic: Or, the Beauties and Celebrities of the Nation: Illustrating Life and Society Under Eighteen Presidents; Describing the Social Features of the Successive Administrations from Washington to Grant*. Philadelphia: Philadelphia Pub. Co., 1870.

Ellis, Joseph J. *First Family: Abigail and John*. New York: Alfred A. Knopf, 2010.

Ellison, Julie K. *Cato's Tears and the Making of Anglo-American Emotion*. Chicago: University of Chicago Press, 1999.

Emmet, Dorothy. "The Concept of Power: The Presidential Address." *Proceedings of the Aristotelian Society*, New Series, 54 (1954 1953): 1–26.

Eustace, Nicole. *Passion Is the Gale: Emotion, Power, and the Coming of the American Revolution*. Chapel Hill: Published for the Omohundro Institute of Early American History and Culture, Williamsburg, Virginia, by the University of North Carolina Press, 2008.

Faderman, Lillian. *Surpassing the Love of Men: Romantic Friendship and Love Between Women from the Renaissance to the Present*. New York: Morrow, 1981.

Fehr, Beverley Anne. *Friendship Processes*. Thousand Oaks, Calif.: Sage Publications, 1996.

Fliegelman, Jay. *Declaring Independence: Jefferson, Natural Language & the Culture of Performance*. Stanford: Stanford University Press, 1993.

Fliegelman, Jay. *Prodigals and Pilgrims*. Cambridge: Cambridge University Press, 1985.

Foner, Eric. *The Story of American Freedom*. New York: W. W. Norton & Company, 1999.

Foreman, Amanda. *Georgiana, Duchess of Devonshire*. New York: Random House, 1999.

Formisano, Ronald P. "Deferential-Participant Politics: The Early Republic's Political Culture, 1789–1840." *American Political Science Review* 68, no. 2 (June 1974): 473–87.

Foster, Thomas. "Reconsidering Libertines and Early Modern Heterosexuality: Sex and American Founder Gouverneur Morris." *Journal of the History of Sexuality* 22, no. 1 (January 2013).

Frank, Robin Jaffee. *Love and Loss: American Portrait and Mourning Miniatures*. New Haven: Yale University Art Gallery, 2000.

Freeman, Joanne B. *Affairs of Honor: National Politics in the New Republic*. New Haven: Yale University Press, 2001.

Freeman, Joanne B. "Slander, Poison, Whispers, and Fame: Jefferson's 'Anas' and Political Gossip in the Early Republic." *Journal of the Early Republic* 15, no. 1 (1995): 25–57.

Friedman, Lawrence Meir. *The Republic of Choice: Law, Authority, and Culture*. Cambridge, MA: Harvard University Press, 1990.

Frost, Jerry William. *The Quaker Family in Colonial America: A Portrait of the Society of Friends*. New York: St. Martin's Press, 1973.

Gaudet, Katherine Sarah. "Fear of Fiction: Reading and Resisting the Novel in Early America." PhD Diss., The University of Chicago, 2011.

Gelles, Edith. "A Virtuous Affair: The Correspondence Between Abigail Adams and James Lovell." *American Quarterly* 39, no. 2 (Summer 1987): 252–69.

Gelles, Edith. *Abigail & John: Portrait of a Marriage.* New York: HarperCollins, 2009.

Gelles, Edith. "Gossip: An Eighteenth-Century Case." *Journal of Social History* 22, no. 4 (Summer 1989): 667–83.

Gelles, Edith. *Portia: The World of Abigail Adams.* Bloomington: Indiana University Press, 1992.

Gernes, Todd Steven. "Recasting the Culture of Ephemera: Young Women's Literary Culture in Nineteenth-Century America." PhD Diss., Brown University, 1992.

Ginzberg, Lori. " 'The Hearts of Your Readers Will Shudder': Fanny Wright, Infidelity, and American Freethought." *American Quarterly* 46, no. 2 (June 1994): 195–226.

Glover, Lorri. *All Our Relations: Blood Ties and Emotional Bonds Among the Early South Carolina Gentry.* Baltimore: Johns Hopkins University Press, 2000.

Glover, Lorri. *Southern Sons: Becoming Men in the New Nation.* Baltimore: Johns Hopkins University Press, 2007.

Godbeer, Richard. *Sexual Revolution in Early America.* Baltimore: Johns Hopkins University Press, 2004.

Godbeer, Richard. *The Overflowing of Friendship: Love Between Men and the Creation of the American Republic.* Baltimore: Johns Hopkins University Press, 2009.

Goffman, Erving. *Relations in Public: Microstudies of the Public Order.* New York: Basic Books, 1971.

Goffman, Erving. *The Presentation of Self in Everyday Life.* Edinburgh: University of Edinburgh, Social Sciences Research Centre, 1956.

Good, Cassandra. "Capital Manners: Etiquette, Politics, and Identity in Early Washington City." MA Thesis, George Washington University, 2004.

Good, Cassandra. "Friendly Relations: Situating Friendships Between Men and Women in the Early American Republic." *Gender & History* 24, no. 1 (April 2012): 18–34.

Goodman, Dena. *Becoming a Woman in the Age of Letters.* Ithaca: Cornell University Press, 2009.

Goodman, Dena. "Public Sphere and Private Life: Toward a Synthesis of Current Historiographical Approaches to the Old Regime." *History and Theory* 31, no. 1 (February 1992): 1–20.

Goodman, Dena. *The Republic of Letters: A Cultural History of the French Enlightenment.* Ithaca, N.Y.: Cornell University Press, 1994.

Goodyear, Frank. "Reclaiming the Female Nude: Sarah Goodridge's 'Beauty Revealed.'" Seminar Paper, University of Texas at Austin, 1995.

Gray, Katie. " 'A Brilliant Assemblage of Both Sexes': Youthful Literary Society in the Early Republic." Society for Historians of the Early American Republic Annual Conference, Springfield, Illinois, 2009.

Green, Katherine Sobba. *The Courtship Novel, 1740–1820: A Feminized Genre.* Lexington: University Press of Kentucky, 1991.

Greene, Jack. "All Men Are Created Equal: Some Reflections on the Character of the American Revolution." In *Imperatives, Behaviors and Identities: Essays in Early American Cultural History*, 236–67. Charlottesville: University of Virginia Press, 1992.

Haberly, Loyd. *Pursuit of the Horizon: A Life of George Catlin Painted & Recorder of the American Indian.* New York: The Macmillan Company, 1948.

Hacking, Ian. *Historical Ontology.* Cambridge, MA: Harvard University Press, 2004.

Hall, Nigel. "The Materiality of Letter Writing: A Nineteenth-Century Perspective." In *Letter Writing as a Social Practice*, edited by David Barton and Nigel Hall, 83–108. Philadelphia: John Benjamins, 2000.

Harris, Paul S. "Gilbert Stuart and a Portrait of Mrs. Sarah Apthorp Morton." *Wintherthur Portfolio* I (1964): 198–220.

Hartog, Hendrik. *Man and Wife in America: A History.* Cambridge, Mass.: Harvard University Press, 2000.

Hayes, Julie Candler. "Friendship and the Female Moralist." *Studies in Eighteenth-Century Culture* 39 (2010): 171–89.

Hemphill, C. Dallett. *Bowing to Necessities: A History of Manners in America, 1620–1860.* New York: Oxford University Press, 2002.

Hemphill, C. Dallett. *Siblings: Brothers and Sisters in American History.* New York: Oxford University Press, 2011.

Hendler, Glenn. *Public Sentiments: Structures of Feeling in Nineteenth-Century American Literature.* Chapel Hill: University of North Carolina Press, 2001.

Herbert, Amanda E. "Companions in Preaching and Suffering: Itinerant Female Quakers in the Seventeenth- and Eighteenth-Century British Atlantic World." *Early American Studies* 9, no. 1 (2011): 100–40.

Hessinger, Rodney. *Seduced, Abandoned, and Reborn: Visions of Youth in Middle-Class America, 1780–1850.* Philadelphia: University of Pennsylvania Press, 2005.

Heyrman, Christine Leigh. *Southern Cross: The Beginnings of the Bible Belt.* New York: Knopf, 1997.

Hirshorn, Anne Sue. "Legacy of Ivory: Anna Claypoole Peale's Portrait Miniatures." *Bulletin of the Detroit Institute of Arts* 64, no. 4 (1989): 16–27.

Hofstadter, Richard. *The Idea of a Party System: The Rise of Legitimate Opposition in the United States, 1780–1840.* Berkeley: University of California Press, 1969.

Hogan, Charles Beecher. "Jane Austen and Her Early Public." *The Review of English Studies* New Series v. 1, no. 1 (January 1950): 39–54.

Holton, Woody. *Abigail Adams.* New York: Free Press, 2009.

Horowitz, Sarah. *Friendship and Politics in Post-Revolutionary France.* State College Penn State University Press, 2014.

Horowitz, Sarah. "States of Intimacy: Friendship and the Remaking of French Political Elites, 1815–1848." PhD Diss., University of California at Berkeley, 2008.

Hunt, Gaillard. "Office-Seeking During Jefferson's Administration." *American Historical Review* 3, no. 2 (1898): 270–91.

Hutter, Horst. *Politics as Friendship: The Origins of Classical Notions of Politics in the Theory and Practice of Friendship.* Waterloo, Ont.: Wilfrid Laurier University Press, 1978.

Irons, Susan H. "Channing's Influence on Peabody: Self-Culture and the Danger of Egoism." *Studies in the American Renaissance* 32, 1992, 121–35.

Isenberg, Nancy. *Fallen Founder: The Life of Aaron Burr.* New York: Penguin, 2007.

Jabour, Anya. "Albums of Affection: Female Friendship and Coming of Age in Antebellum Virginia." *Virginia Magazine of History and Biography* 107, no. 2 (1999): 125–58.

Jabour, Anya. "Male Friendship and Masculinity in the Early National South: William Wirt and His Friends." *Journal of the Early Republic* 20, no. 1 (Spring 2000): 81–111.

Jabour, Anya. *Marriage in the Early Republic: Elizabeth and William Wirt and the Companionate Ideal.* Baltimore: The Johns Hopkins University Press, 1998.

Jayne, Allen. *Jefferson's Declaration of Independence: Origins, Philosophy, and Theology.* Lexington: University Press of Kentucky, 1998.

John, Richard R. "Affairs of Office: The Executive Departments, the Election of 1828, and the Making of the Democratic Party." In *The Democratic Experiment: New Directions in American Political History*, edited by Meg Jacobs, William J. Novak, and Julian Zelizer, 50–84. Princeton: Princeton University Press, 2003.

Johnson, Claudia L. *Equivocal Beings: Politics, Gender, and Sentimentality in the 1790s: Wollstonecraft, Radcliffe, Burney, Austen.* Chicago: University of Chicago Press, 1995.

Jordan, Winthrop D. *White Over Black: American Attitudes Toward the Negro, 1550–1812.* 2nd ed. Chapel Hill: University of North Carolina Press, 2012.

Juster, Susan. *Disorderly Women: Sexual Politics & Evangelicalism in Revolutionary New England.* Ithaca: Cornell University Press, 1994.

Kale, Steven D. *French Salons: High Society and Political Sociability from the Old Regime to the Revolution of 1848.* Baltimore: Johns Hopkins University Press, 2004.

Kann, Mark E. *A Republic of Men: The American Founders, Gendered Language, and Patriarchal Politics.* New York: New York University Press, 1998.

Kann, Mark E. *Taming Passion for the Public Good: Policing Sex in the Early Republic.* New York: New York University Press, 2013.

Kaplan, Catherine O'Donnell. *Men of Letters in the Early Republic: Cultivating Forums of Citizenship.* Chapel Hill: Published for the Omohundro Institute of Early American History and Culture, Williamsburg, Virginia, by the University of North Carolina Press, 2008.

Kelly, Catherine E. *In the New England Fashion: Reshaping Women's Lives in the Nineteenth Century.* Ithaca: Cornell University Press, 1999.

Kelley, Mary. *Learning to Stand and Speak: Women, Education, and Public Life in America's Republic.* Chapel Hill: University of North Carolina Press, 2008.

Kennedy, Roger G. *Burr, Hamilton, and Jefferson: A Study in Character.* Oxford: Oxford University Press, 2000.

Kenslea, Timothy. *The Sedgwicks in Love: Courtship, Engagement, and Marriage in the Early Republic.* Boston: Northeastern University Press, 2006.

Kerber, Linda K. "Separate Spheres, Female Worlds, Woman's Place: The Rhetoric of Women's History." *The Journal of American History* 75, no. 1 (June 1988): 9–39.

Kerber, Linda K. *Women of the Republic: Intellect and Ideology in Revolutionary America.* New York: Norton, 1986.

Kerber, Linda K., Nancy F. Cott, Robert Gross, Lynn Hunt, Carroll Smith-Rosenberg, and Christine M. Stansell. "Beyond Roles, Beyond Spheres: Thinking about Gender in the Early Republic." *The William and Mary Quarterly*, Third Series, 46, no. 3 (July 1989): 565–85.

Kerrison, Catherine. *Claiming the Pen: Women and Intellectual Life in the Early American South.* Ithaca: Cornell University Press, 2006.

Kierner, Cynthia A. *Beyond the Household: Women's Place in the Early South, 1700–1835.* Ithaca: Cornell University Press, 1998.

Kierner, Cynthia A. *Martha Jefferson Randolph, Daughter of Monticello: Her Life and Times.* Chapel Hill: University of North Carolina Press, 2012.

Kierner, Cynthia A. *Scandal at Bizarre: Rumor and Reputation in Jefferson's America.* New York: Palgrave Macmillan, 2004.

Klepp, Susan E. *Revolutionary Conceptions: Women, Fertility, and Family Limitation in America, 1760–1820.* Chapel Hill: Published for the Omohundro Institute of Early American History and Culture, Williamsburg, Virginia, by the University of North Carolina Press, 2009.

Knott, Sarah. *Sensibility and the American Revolution.* Chapel Hill: Published for the Omohundro Institute of Early American History and Culture, Williamsburg, Virginia, by the University of North Carolina Press, 2009.

Korobkin, Laura Hanft. *Criminal Conversations: Sentimentality and Nineteenth-Century Legal Stories of Adultery.* New York: Columbia University Press, 1998.

Kramer, Lloyd. *Lafayette in Two Worlds.* Chapel Hill: University of North Carolina Press, 1999.

Kuby, William M. "Conjugal Misconduct: Dubious Vows, Unlawful Wedlock, and the Margins of Marital Propriety in the United States, 1900–1940." PhD Diss., University of Pennsylvania, 2011.

Kukla, Jon. *Mr. Jefferson's Women.* New York: Alfred A. Knopf, 2007.

Lambert, Alexander. *Intimacy and Friendship on Facebook.* New York: Palgrave Macmillan, 2013.

Landes, Joan B. *Women and the Public Sphere in the Age of the French Revolution.* Ithaca: Cornell University Press, 1988.

Lapidos, Juliet. "Strictly Platonic." *Slate*, September 2010. http://www.slate.com/articles/life/strictly_platonic.html.

Laqueur, Thomas Walter. *Making Sex: Body and Gender from the Greeks to Freud.* Cambridge, MA: Harvard University Press, 1990.

Larson, Rebecca. *Daughters of Light: Quaker Women Preaching and Prophesying in the Colonies and Abroad, 1770–1775.* New York: Knopf, 1999.

Lasser, Carol. "Beyond Separate Spheres: The Power of Public Opinion." *Journal of the Early Republic* 21, no. 1 (Spring 2001): 115–23.

Lasser, Carol. "'Let Us Be Sisters Forever': The Sororal Model of Nineteenth-Century Female Friendship." *Signs* 14 (1988): 158–81.

Lehmann, William Christian. *Henry Home, Lord Kames, and the Scottish Enlightenment: A Study in National Character and in the History of Ideas.* New York: Springer, 1971.

Lewis, Charlene M. Boyer. *Elizabeth Patterson Bonaparte: An American Aristocrat in the Early Republic.* Philadelphia: University of Pennsylvania Press, 2012.

Lewis, Charlene M. Boyer. *Ladies and Gentlemen on Display: Planter Society at the Virginia Springs, 1790–1860.* Charlottesville: University Press of Virginia, 2001.

Lewis, Jan. "Politics and the Ambivalence of the Private Sphere: Women in Early Washington, D.C." In *A Republic for the Ages: The United States Capitol and the Political Culture of the Early Republic,* edited by Kenneth Bowling. Charlottesville: Published for the United States Capitol Historical Society by the University of Virginia Press, 1999.

Lewis, Jan. "Sex and the Married Man: Benjamin Franklin's Families." In *Benjamin Franklin and Women,* edited by Larry E. Tise. University Park: Pennsylvania State University Press, 2000.

Lewis, Jan. *The Pursuit of Happiness: Family and Values in Jefferson's Virginia.* Cambridge: Cambridge University Press, 1983.

Lewis, Jan. "The Republican Wife: Virtue and Seduction in the Early Republic." *The William and Mary Quarterly* 44, no. 4 (October 1987): 689–721.

Lewis, Jan. "'Those Scenes for Which Alone My Heart Was Made': Affection and Politics in the Age of Jefferson and Hamilton." In *An Emotional History of the United States,* edited by Jan Lewis and Peter N. Stearns. New York: New York University Press, 1998.

Lewis, Judith Schneid. *Sacred to Female Patriotism: Gender, Class, and Politics in Late Georgian Britain.* New York: Routledge, 2003.

Linklater, Andro. *An Artist in Treason: The Extraordinary Double Life of General James Wilkinson.* New York: Walker Publishing Company, 2010.

Lombard, Anne S. *Making Manhood: Growing up Male in Colonial New England.* Cambridge, MA: Harvard University Press, 2003.

Lopez, Claude Anne. *Mon Cher Papa: Franklin and the Ladies of Paris.* New Haven: Yale University Press, 1966.

Lopez, Claude Anne. "Three Women, Three Styles: Catharine Ray, Polly Hewson, and Georgiana Shipley." In *Benjamin Franklin and Women,* edited by Larry E. Tise. University Park, Pa.: Pennsylvania State University Press, 2000.

Luftig, Victor. *Seeing Together: Friendship Between the Sexes in English Writing from Mill to Woolf.* Stanford: Stanford University Press, 1993.

Lyerly, Cynthia Lynn. "A Tale of Two Patriarchs; Or, How a Eunuch and a Wife Created a Family in the Church." *Journal of Family History* 28, no. 4 (October 2003): 490–509.

Lyons, Clare A. *Sex Among the Rabble: An Intimate History of Gender & Power in the Age of Revolution, Philadelphia, 1730–1830*. Chapel Hill: Published for the Omohundro Institute of Early American History and Culture, Williamsburg, Virginia, by the University of North Carolina Press, 2006.

Lystra, Karen. *Searching the Heart: Women, Men, and Romantic Love in Nineteenth-Century America*. New York: Oxford University Press, 1989.

Mack, Phyllis. *Visionary Women: Ecstatic Prophecy in Seventeenth-Century England*. Berkeley: University of California Press, 1992.

Mansbridge, Jane. "Reconstructing Democracy." In *Revisioning the Political: Feminist Reconstructions of Traditional Concepts in Western Political Theory*, edited by Nancy J. Hirschmann and Christine Di Stefano. Feminist Theory and Politics. Boulder, Colo.: Westview Press, 1996.

Marchalonis, Shirley, ed. *Patrons and Protégées: Gender, Friendship, and Writing in Nineteenth-Century America*. New Brunswick: Rutgers University Press, 1998.

Marcus, Sharon. *Between Women: Friendship, Desire, and Marriage in Victorian England*. Princeton: Princeton University Press, 2007.

Mauss, Marcel. *The Gift: The Form and Reason for Exchange in Archaic Societies*. New York: W. W. Norton & Company, 2000.

Maxey, David W. *A Portrait of Elizabeth Willing Powel (1743–1830)*. Transactions of the American Philosophical Society. Philadelphia: American Philosophical Society, 2006.

Maza, Sarah C. *Private Lives and Public Affairs: The Causes Célèbres of Prerevolutionary France*. Berkeley: University of California Press, 1999.

McGann, Jerome J. *The Poetics of Sensibility: A Revolution in Literary Style*. Oxford: Clarendon Press, 1996.

McMahon, Lucia. *Mere Equals: The Paradox of Educated Women in the Early American Republic*. Ithaca: Cornell University Press, 2012.

McMahon, Lucia. "'The Harmony of Social Life': Gender, Education, and Society in the Early Republic." PhD Diss., Rutgers, The State University of New Jersey, 2004.

McNeil, W.K. "The Autograph Album Custom: A Tradition and Its Scholarly Treatment." *Keystone Folklore Quarterly*, Spring 1968, 29–40.

McWilliams, Wilson C. *The Idea of Fraternity in America*. Berkeley: University of California Press, 1973.

Melton, Buckner F. *Aaron Burr: Conspiracy to Treason*. New York: John Wiley & Sons, 2001.

Midgley, Clare. "British Abolition and Feminism in Transatlantic Perspective." In *Women's Rights and Transatlantic Antislavery in the Era of Emancipation*, edited by Kathryn Kish Sklar and James Brewer Stewart. New Haven: Yale University Press, 2007.

Miles, Ellen G. *George and Martha Washington: Portraits from the Presidential Years*. Washington, D.C.: Smithsonian Institution, National Portrait Gallery, 1999.

Miles, Ellen G. "'I Have Resolved to Sit No More;' Washington and Artists' Ambitions, 1776–1800." New-York Historical Society, 2009.

Monsour, Michael. *Women and Men as Friends: Relationships Across the Life Span in the 21st Century*. Mahwah, N.J.: L. Erlbaum, 2002.

Moore, Lisa. "'Something More Tender Still than Friendship': Romantic Friendship in Early-Nineteenth-Century England." *Feminist Studies* 18, no. 3 (Autumn 1992): 499–520.

Morgan, Edmund. *American Slavery, American Freedom: The Ordeal of Colonial Virginia*. New York: W. W. Norton, 1976.

Murphy, Teresa Anne. *Citizenship and the Origins of Women's History in the United States*. Philadelphia: University of Pennsylvania Press, 2013.

Murphy, Teresa Anne. *Ten Hours' Labor: Religion, Reform, and Gender in Early New England*. Ithaca: Cornell University Press, 1992.

Nelson, Dana D. *National Manhood: Capitalist Citizenship and the Imagined Fraternity of White Men*. Durham: Duke University Press, 1998.

Nelson, Iris A. "Eliza Caldwell Browning: Lincoln's Loyal Confidante." *Journal of Illinois History* 9, no. 1 (March 2006): 23–42.

Nelson, Robert Kent. "Society of Souls: Spirit, Friendship, and the Antebellum Reform Imagination." PhD Diss., The College of William and Mary, 2006.

Newton, Judith Lowder. *Women, Power, and Subversion: Social Strategies in British Fiction, 1778–1860*. New York: Methuen, 1985.

Nord, David Paul. "A Republican Literature: A Study of Magazine Reading and Readers in Late Eighteenth-Century New York." *American Quarterly* 40, no. 1 (March 1988): 42–64.

Norton, Mary Beth. *Liberty's Daughters: The Revolutionary Experience of American Women, 1750–1800*. Boston: Little, Brown, 1980.

O'Brien, Michael. *Conjectures of Order: Intellectual Life and the American South, 1810–1860*. II vols. Chapel Hill: University of North Carolina Press, 2004.

O'Meara, J. Donald. "Cross-Sex Friendship: Four Basic Challenges of an Ignored Relationship." *Sex Roles* 21, no. 7 (1989): 525–43.

Ousterhout, Anne M. *The Most Learned Woman in America: A Life of Elizabeth Graeme Fergusson*. University Park: Pennsylvania State University Press, 2004.

Packard, Chris. "Self-Fashioning in Sarah Goodridge's Self-Portraits." *Common-Place* 4, no. 1 (October 2003). http://www.common-place.org/vol-04/no-01/lessons/.

Pascoe, Judith. *Romantic Theatricality: Gender, Poetry, and Spectatorship*. Ithaca: Cornell University Press, 1997.

Pateman, Carole. *The Sexual Contract*. Stanford: Stanford University Press, 1988.

Pearsall, Sarah M. S. *Atlantic Families: Lives and Letters in the Later Eighteenth Century*. Oxford: Oxford University Press, 2008.

Perry, Ruth. "Interrupted Friendships in Jane Austen's Emma." *Tulsa Studies in Women's Literature* 5, no. 2 (Autumn 1986): 185–202.

Pinch, Adela. *Strange Fits of Passion*. Palo Alto: Stanford University Press, 1996.

Plant, Helen. "'Subjective Testimonies': Women Quaker Ministers and Spiritual Authority in England: 1750–1825." *Gender & History* 15, no. 2 (2003): 296–318.

Pointon, Marcia R. *Hanging the Head: Portraiture and Social Formation in Eighteenth-Century England*. New Haven: Published for the Paul Mellon Centre for Studies in British Art by Yale University Press, 1993.

Pointon, Marcia R. *Strategies for Showing: Women, Possession, and Representation in English Visual Culture, 1665–1800*. Oxford: Oxford University Press, 1997.

Rader, Rosemary. *Breaking Boundaries: Male/Female Friendship in Early Christian Communities*. New York: Paulist Press, 1983.

Reddy, William M. *The Navigation of Feeling: A Framework for the History of Emotions*. Cambridge, U.K.: Cambridge University Press, 2001.

Redford, Bruce. *The Converse of the Pen: Acts of Intimacy in the Eighteenth-Century Familiar Letter*. Chicago: University of Chicago Press, 1986.

Rezek, Joseph Paul. "Tales from Elsewhere: Fiction at a Proximate Distance in the Anglophone Atlantic, 1800–1850." PhD, Diss., University of California, Los Angeles, 2009.

Ribblett, David L. *Nelly Custis: Child of Mount Vernon*. Mount Vernon, VA: Mount Vernon Ladies Association, 1993.

Ronda, Bruce A. *Elizabeth Palmer Peabody: A Reformer on Her Own Terms*. Cambridge, MA: Harvard University Press, 1999.

Rosenzweig, Linda W. *Another Self: Middle-Class American Women and Their Friends in the Twentieth Century*. New York: New York University Press, 1999.

Rothman, Ellen K. *Hands and Hearts: A History of Courtship in America*. New York: Basic Books, Inc., 1984.

Rotundo, E. Anthony. *American Manhood: Transformations in Masculinity from the Revolution to the Modern Era*. New York: Basic Books, 1993.

Scharff, Virginia. *The Women Jefferson Loved*. New York: Harper, 2010.

Schocket, Andrew. "Thinking about Elites in the Early Republic." *Journal of the Early Republic* 25, no. 4 (Winter 2005): 547–55.

Schoenfield, Mark. "Private Souvenirs: Exchanges among Byron's Southwell Set." *Wordsworth Circle* 39, no. Winter-Spring (2008): 30–34.

Schroeder, John H. *Commodore John Rodgers: Paragon of the Early American Navy*. Gainesville University Press of Florida, 2006.

Schweitzer, Ivy. *Perfecting Friendship: Politics and Affiliation in Early American Literature*. Chapel Hill: University of North Carolina Press, 2006.

Scott, Joan W. "Gender: A Useful Category of Historical Analysis." *The American Historical Review* 91, no. 5 (December 1986): 1053–75.

Sellers, Charles Coleman. *Benjamin Franklin in Portraiture*. New Haven: Yale University Press, 1962.

Shammas, Carole. *A History of Household Government in America*. Charlottesville: University of Virginia Press, 2002.

Sheumaker, Helen. *Love Entwined: The Curious History of Hairwork in America*. Philadelphia: University of Pennsylvania Press, 2007.

Shields, David S. *Civil Tongues & Polite Letters in British America*. Chapel Hill: Published for the Institute of Early American History and Culture, Williamsburg, Virginia, by the University of North Carolina Press, 1997.

Silver, Allan. "Friendship in Commercial Society: Eighteenth-Century Social Theory and Modern Sociology." *The American Journal of Sociology* 95, no. 6 (May 1990): 1474–504.

Simmons, Christina. *Making Marriage Modern: Women's Sexuality from the Progressive Era to World War II*. Oxford; New York: Oxford University Press, 2009.

Sioussat, Annie Middleton Leakin. *Old Baltimore*. New York: The Macmillan Company, 1931.

Skemp, Sheila L. *First Lady of Letters: Judith Sargent Murray and the Struggle for Female Independence*. Philadelphia: University of Pennsylvania Press, 2009.

Smith, Adam. *An Inquiry into the Nature and Causes of the Wealth of Nations*. Edited by Edwin Cannan. 5th ed. London: Methuen & Co., Ltd., 1904.

Smith-Rosenberg, Carroll. "The Female World of Love and Ritual: Relations between Women in Nineteenth-Century America." *Signs* 1, no. 1 (Autumn 1975): 1–29.

Stabile, Susan. "Salons and Power in the Era of the Revolution: From Literary Coteries to Epistolary Enlightenment." In *Benjamin Franklin and Women*, edited by Larry E. Tise, 129–48. University Park: Pennsylvania State University Press, 2000.

Stabile, Susan M. *Memory's Daughters: The Material Culture of Remembrance in Eighteenth-Century America*. Ithaca: Cornell University Press, 2004.

Stansell, Christine. *City of Women: Sex and Class in New York, 1789–1860*. New York: Knopf, 1986.

Staves, Susan. "Money for Honor: Damages for Criminal Conversation." *Studies in Eighteenth-Century Culture* 11 (1982): 279–97.

Steele, Brian. "Thomas Jefferson's Gender Frontier." *Journal of American History* 95, no. 1 (June 2008): 17–42.

Stone, Lawrence. *Road to Divorce: England 1530–1987*. Oxford: Oxford University Press, 1990.

Stone, Lawrence. *The Family, Sex and Marriage in England 1500–1800*. Abridged ed. New York: Harper & Row, 1979.

Swartz, David. *Culture & Power: The Sociology of Pierre Bourdieu*. Chicago: University of Chicago Press, 1997.

Tadmor, Naomi. *Family and Friends in Eighteenth-Century England: Household, Kinship, and Patronage*. Cambridge, U.K.: Cambridge University Press, 2001.

Taylor, Alan. "From Fathers to Friends of the People: Political Personas in the Early Republic." *Journal of the Early Republic* 11, no. 4 (Winter 1991): 465–91.

Tennenhouse, Leonard. "The Americanization of Clarissa." *The Yale Journal of Criticism* 11, no. 1 (Spring 1998): 177–96.

Teute, Fredrika. "A 'Republic of Intellect': Conversation and Criticism among the Sexes in 1790s New York." In *Revising Charles Brockden Brown: Culture, Politics, and Sexuality in the Early Republic*, edited by Philip Barnard, Mark Kamrath, and Stephen Shapiro, 149–81. Knoxville: University of Tennessee Press, 2004.

Teute, Fredrika. "Roman Matron on the Banks of Tiber Creek: Margaret Bayard Smith and the Politicization of Spheres in the Nation's Capital." In *A Republic for the Ages: The United States Capitol and the Political Culture of the Early Republic*, edited by Kenneth Bowling. Charlottesville: Published for the United States Capitol Historical Society by the University of Virginia Press, 1999.

Thomas, Evan. *John Paul Jones: Sailor, Hero, Father of the American Navy*. New York: Simon & Schuster, 2003.

Tompkins, Jane P. *Sensational Designs: The Cultural Work of American Fiction, 1790–1860*. New York: Oxford University Press, 1985.

Tuite, Clara. "Tainted Love and Romantic Literary Celebrity." *ELH* 74, no. 1 (2007): 59–88.

Tuite, Clara, and Claire Russell, eds. *Romantic Sociability: Social Networks and Literary Culture in Britain, 1770–1840*. Cambridge, U.K.: Cambridge University Press, 2002.

Turkle, Sherry. *Alone Together: Why We Expect More from Technology and Less from Each Other*. New York: Basic Books, 2012.

Verplanck, Anne Ayer. "Facing Philadelphia: The Social Functions of Silhouettes, Miniatures, and Daguerreotypes, 1760–1860." PhD Diss., The College of William and Mary, 1996.

Vickery, Amanda. *The Gentleman's Daughter: Women's Lives in Georgian England*. New Haven: Yale University Press, 1998.

Walker, Lewis Burd, B. Arnold, Edward Burd, E. Tilghman, and H. Arnold. "Life of Margaret Shippen, Wife of Benedict Arnold (continued)." *The Pennsylvania Magazine of History and Biography* 25, no. 1 (1901): 20–46.

Wallis, Lauren. "'To Form a New World, New Systems Create': Margaret Lowther Page's Poetic Revisions of Women's Roles in the Early Republic." MA Thesis, University of North Carolina at Greensboro, 2010.

Ward, Adrian F. "Men and Women Can't Be 'Just Friends.'" *Scientfic American*, October 23, 2012. http://www.scientificamerican.com/article.cfm?id=men-and-women-cant-be-just-friends.

Waterman, Bryan. "Coquetry and Correspondence in Revolutionary-Era Connecticut: Reading Elizabeth Whitman's Letters." *Early American Literature* 46, no. 3 (2011): 541–63.

Waterman, Bryan. "Elizabeth Whitman's Disappearance and Her 'Disappointment.'" *William and Mary Quarterly* LXVI, no. 2 (April 2009): 325–64.

Waterman, Bryan. *Republic of Intellect: The Friendly Club of New York City and the Making of American Literature.* Baltimore: Johns Hopkins University Press, 2007.

Welter, Barbara. "The Cult of True Womanhood: 1820–1860." *American Quarterly* 18, no. 2, part 1 (Summer 1966): 151–74.

West, Shearer. *Portraiture.* Oxford: Oxford University Press, 2004.

White, Leonard. *The Jeffersonians: A Story in Administrative History, 1801–1829.* New York: The Macmillan Company, 1951.

Williams, Raymond. *Marxism and Literature.* Oxford: Oxford University Press, 1977.

Wills, Garry. *Inventing America: Jefferson's Declaration of Independence.* New York: Houghton Mifflin Harcourt, 2002.

Wilson, Lisa. *Life after Death: Widows in Pennsylvania, 1750–1850.* Philadelphia: Temple University Press, 1992.

Wineapple, Brenda. *White Heat: The Friendship of Emily Dickinson and Thomas Wentworth Higginson.* New York: Knopf, 2008.

Wood, Gordon S. *The Creation of the American Republic, 1776–1787.* First Norton Edition. New York: W. W. Norton & Company, 1972.

Wood, Gordon S. *The Radicalism of the American Revolution.* New York: Random House, 1992.

Wood, Kirsten E. *Masterful Women: Slaveholding Widows from the American Revolution through the Civil War.* Chapel Hill: University of North Carolina Press, 2004.

Wulf, Karin A. *Not All Wives: Women of Colonial Philadelphia.* Ithaca: Cornell University Press, 2000.

Yacovone, Donald. "Abolitionists and the 'Language of Fraternal Love.'" In *Meanings for Manhood: Constructions of Masculinity in Victorian America,* edited by Mark C. Carnes and Clyde Griffen. Chicago: University of Chicago Press, 1990.

Young, James Sterling. *The Washington Community, 1800–1828.* New York: Columbia University Press, 1966.

Zaczek, Barbara Maria. *Censored Sentiments: Letters and Censorship in Epistolary Novels and Conduct Material.* Newark: University of Delaware Press, 1997.

Zagarri, Rosemarie. *A Woman's Dilemma: Mercy Otis Warren and the American Revolution.* Wheeling, IL: Harlan Davidson, 1995.

Zagarri, Rosemarie. "Morals, Manners, and the Republican Mother." *American Quarterly* 44, no. 2 (June 1, 1992): 192–215.

Zagarri, Rosemarie. *Revolutionary Backlash: Women and Politics in the Early American Republic.* Philadelphia: University of Pennsylvania Press, 2007.

Zagarri, Rosemarie. "The Family Factor: Congressmen, Turnover, and the Burden of Public Service in the Early American Republic." *Journal of the Early Republic* 33, no. 2 (n.d.): 283–316.

Ziesche, Philipp. *Cosmopolitan Patriots: Americans in Paris in the Age of Revolution.* Jeffersonian America. Charlottesville: University of Virginia Press, 2010.

Index

influence, female
  as corrupting, 8, 27, 45–46, 167–168, 171, 183, 185
  political, 1, 164, 171–173, 175, 177, 189
  as positive, 19, 26, 38, 42, 43, 45, 111, 171, 185
  See also politics; women

Jackson, Andrew, 10, 81, 176, 184, 185
Jackson, Henry, 102, 138–139
Jackson, John P., 160–161
Jefferson, Thomas, 6, 8, 36, 168, 173, 176, 235n19
  and Abigail Adams, 12, 13, 15–18, 65, 87, 168
  and Angelica Schuyler Church, 15, 16, 131–132, 134, 188
  and Deborah Norris Logan, 179, 183–184
  "Dialogue Between My Head and My Heart," 65
  and Elizabeth House Trist, 169–171, 174, 177
  in France, 13–18, 65, 168
  and John Adams, 15–18, 87
  and Margaret Bayard Smith, 11, 14
  and Maria Cosway, 15, 65, 123–124, 131–132, 135
  on women in politics, 13, 16, 168, 243n28
jewelry, 48, 127, 146–148, 149, 150
Jonathan and David (biblical story), 40, 88
Jones, John Paul, 58, 140–141
Jones, Rebecca, 89
Jones, Sarah, 92

Kames, Lord. *See* Home, Henry
Knox, Henry, 102, 105, 138–139

La Roche, Elzina de, 19–20
La Rochefoucauld, François de, 60

Lafayette, George Washington, 81, 94, 96, 147
Lafayette, Marie-Joseph Paul Yves Roch Gilbert du Motier de (Marquis de), 95–96, 146–147, 151, 155, 179
Lamb, Lady Caroline (neé Ponsonby), 49, 98–99
  Glenarvon, 48
language
  and emotion, 59–60, 63, 156, 190, 213n9
  erotic, 111–112
  for male/female friendship, 2, 74, 192–193, 213n11, 221n8
  of romance, 2, 74, 112–113, 157, 182, 213n11, 221n8
Law, Eliza Parke Custis. *See* Custis, Eliza Parke
letterwriting, 2, 8, 89, 104, 127, 141–142, 151, 152–153
  challenges of, 107
  complimentary closings in, 27, 30, 35, 94, 96, 112–116, 118, 119, 233n51
  conventions of, 9, 21, 88–89, 107–126
  in courtship, 110, 112–113, 115
  guides to, 4, 107, 109–110, 115–116, 122, 127
  and materiality, 108–109, 122, 124
  need for caution in, 22, 94, 107, 109, 116
  openings in, 21, 30, 89, 103, 112–116, 118, 142–143
  public nature of, 107, 108–109, 112, 117, 179
  and romantic language, 92, 94, 109, 115, 141
LeVert, Octavia Walton, 158–159
Lewis, Eleanor Parke Custis, 80–81, 94, 95–96, 132, 147, 176
Litchfield, 30, 85, 159–162, 205n62